Britain
A Christian
Country

A Nation Defined by Christianity and the Bible, and
the Social Changes that Challenge this Biblical Heritage

Paul Backholer

Britain, A Christian Country
A Nation Defined by Christianity and the Bible, and
the Social Changes that Challenge this Biblical Heritage

Copyright © Paul Backholer 2015, 2017 – ByFaith Media
All Rights Reserved. www.ByFaith.org.

Scripture quotations are taken from:
- NIV – The New International Version®. NIV®. Copyright © 1973, 1978, 1984 by International Bible Society. Used by permission of Zondervan. All rights reserved.
- NKJV – The New King James Version. Published by Thomas Nelson, Inc. Copyright © 1982 by Thomas Nelson, Inc. Used by permission. All rights reserved.
- AV – Authorised Version / King James Version.

All rights reserved. No part of this publication may be reproduced, stored in a retrieval system, or transmitted in any form or by any unauthorised means, electronically, mechanically, photocopying, recording, or any other (except for brief quotations in printed or official website reviews with full accreditation) without the prior permission of the Publisher, ByFaith Media, Paul Backholer, **www.ByFaith.org**. Uploading or downloading of this work from the internet, or any other device (in whole or in part) is illegal, as is unauthorised translations. For requests for Translation Rights, please contact ByFaith Media.

ISBN 978-1-907066-45-0
British Library Cataloguing In Publication Data.
A Record of this Publication is available
from the British Library.

First published in 2015 by ByFaith Media.
Second edition © 2017.
This book is also available as an ebook.

- Jesus Christ is Lord -

Chapter	Contents	Page
	Foreword	5.

Introduction: Christianity in Britain

1.	How Britain Became a Christian Nation	9.
2.	A Nation Covenanted to God	12.

Part One: The Making of a Christian Country

3.	Celtic Christianity	25.
4.	Darkness and Light	29.
5.	The Celtic Golden Age	38.
6.	Power and Pain	46.
7.	Celtic or Catholic	52.
8.	Alfred the Great	60.
9.	The Three Hundred Year Prophecy	67.
10.	Medieval Life	70.
11.	New Testament Christianity	76.
12.	Empowering Parliament	84.
13.	The Glorious Revolution	90.
14.	Liberty, Justice and Education	95.
15.	Christianity, Commerce and Civilisation	99.
16.	The Faith of Queen Victoria	106.
17.	Fighting for Liberty	111.
18.	Divine Intervention	116.
19.	The Battle of Britain	121.
20.	Turning the Tide	126.
21.	Democracy and Social Justice	136.
22.	Christianity, Devotion and Dedication	140.

Part Two: Social Changes

23.	The Great Storm of Change	151.
24.	A Bitter Price to Pay	158.
25.	An Outcry Heard in Heaven	165.
26.	Spiritual, but Not Religious	174.
27.	Tearing Down the Altar to One God	185.
28.	Society and Shared Values	199.
29.	Limitations on Liberty	208.
30.	Rejecting God's Protection	213.
31.	Christianity and Safeguarding Liberty	223.
32.	Apostasy and Conversion	237.
33.	Christian Heritage in Peril	248.
34.	We want it Now!	253.
35.	Crisis, what Crisis?	260.
36.	Being Honest about our Need	267.
37.	Hope for a Christian Awakening	272.

Foreword

Britain was once a patchwork of pagan warring kingdoms and Christian belief and mission enabled its transformation into one United Kingdom based upon Christianity. Faith in Jesus Christ equipped a land once stuttering in darkness to become a light to the nations, and created a country which sought after justice, religious freedom, the rule of law and liberty.

The first Christian monarchs in Britain set the country on the bedrock of biblical faith and laid the foundation for a nation of Christians to emerge. At the peak of the Christian fervour in Britain, during the Victorian era, their bright vision of faith shone to millions and shifted the global balance of belief in favour of Christianity. Today hundreds of millions of people are Christians worldwide because the Victorians believed that sharing their faith was essential to the global good.

This chronicle of the defining influence of the Bible upon Britain is not presented from a bleached, dull academic viewpoint, but from a position of faith and hope. In the last census 33.2 million people identified themselves as Christians in Britain. Also church plays a role in the lives of millions as they attend services, youth clubs, children's meetings, elderly groups, mother and toddlers, weddings, baptisms, christenings, and as people attend funerals or remember in national memorials.

After analysing the impact of Christianity in forming and shaping Britain from its earliest days, defining its Constitution and global mission, the second half of this book considers the decline in the national observance of faith, secularisation, the impact of multiculturalism, and the polemical issues for the future.

There are many challenges to the future strength of Christianity in the United Kingdom, and we will also examine how Christians can respond in prayer and faith to these, believing for another great Christian awakening in this land.

Introduction
The Impact and Legacy of Christianity in Britain

Chapter One

How Britain Became a Christian Nation

Christianity first arrived in Britain as believers in Jesus Christ shared their good news with native Britons during the Roman occupation. These believers followed the example of the first disciples of Jesus and met in their homes to worship, pray and share the teaching of the apostles (Romans 16:5).

The first British Christians left little for us to study their faith, but the tiny evidence we have suggests the Christian faith may have began to make inroads into Roman Britain within a generation of the last apostles who saw Jesus. Many myths were invented in the Middle Ages concerning who may have been the first missionary to Britain, to get pilgrims to visit monasteries, but the nameless people who came so soon after the apostles, brought the pure untainted faith of the New Testament with them.[1]

Archaeologists have found the potential traces of the first wooden churches in England and the oldest known church in Britain is a room, set aside in a Roman villa for worship.[2] These Roman citizens joined with the newly converted native Celtic Christians, sharing in an unadulterated translation of New Testament Christianity. What is certain from the chronicles we have received is that Celtic Christianity was to thrive in England, Wales and Scotland, and because the faith established itself without any official mission being sent from any religious authority, the first believers adopted their understanding of Christianity, without additional manmade traditions.

When Roman rule ended in Britain, the nation eventually divided into a network of kingdoms and yet in time, they were all to have one common denominator – Christianity – which facilitated the beginnings of peaceful communication, friendship, alliances and trade. Nevertheless, just as England was set to be converted to Christ, a wave of Germanic tribes invaded and decapitated the leadership of southern England, leading to a new dark age and the fleeing of Celtic Christians to the west, especially to Ireland. However, from the west Celtic believers would reintroduce Christianity into these overrun kingdoms.

The first great known prophetic voice in England was the Venerable Bede (672-735), known today as England's first historian. Bede believed "a Christian England was part of God's master plan," said the historian Professor Diarmaid MacCulloch, "it was Providence that meant it was the destiny of the Anglo-Saxons to become Christians, united in a single Christian nation. But how would this come about?"[3]

Bede lived in an age of chaotic warring kingdoms but with the eye of faith, he saw just one kingdom emerging from them all, based upon Christianity, and his narrative of "one nation, chosen by God for His purposes" was to be an inspiration to future kings in the land.[4]

Bede tells us that once Pope Gregory (540-604) saw some fair-haired and fair-skinned slaves in a slave market in Italy, and he made an inquiry about them. He was told they were Angles and to this we are told he responded, "Not Angles but angels." By 597 Gregory sent a team of forty monks and what followed was a mass baptism on Christmas Day in the same year.[5]

When this first official mission was sent to England from Rome to convert the nation, its leader Augustine of Canterbury (545-605), found a nation divided in two. In the south Germanic tribes had taken the land backwards into pagan darkness, whilst in west England, Wales, parts of Scotland and Ireland, Celtic Christianity was powerful, literate and missionary minded. These Celtic believers had already commenced the reintroduction of Christianity into pagan areas of Britain, beginning with Columba's (521-597) mission to convert Scotland's Pictland, and after success in Britain, Celtic missionaries spread their message to France, Germany and even Italy.[6]

The first known great king to accept Christianity in Britain was the Anglo-Saxon King Ethelbert of Kent (560-616), and because he ruled an extensive kingdom in Britain, he was known by the title of Bretwalda, or Britain-ruler. Ethelbert was the nominal overlord of the Kingdoms of Essex and East Anglia, and thus for the first time, three kingdoms came under the powerful influence of Christianity. His conversion led to England being established by law, as a Christian nation.

King Ethelbert made a vow and covenant with God, dedicating England to God, asking Him to bless and guide the Kingdom. To prove his sincerity the king decided to embrace biblical principles and enshrine them in law. King Ethelbert's law book, *The Textus Roffensis* is the earliest English law code, written in the English language, which established his Kingdom in Britain as inherently Christian. The king took laws from the Bible and made them apply to his land. For the first time since the Roman withdrawal from Britain, the rule of law was again embraced, from principles of protecting the day of rest, to the rights of people and property.

Ethelbert was the first Christian king in England, but he was not the first King of all England.

King Ethelbert's covenant with God dedicated his Kingdom to God, once and for all time, believing that like King David, if he kept his side of the covenant, God would bless the land. 'For God is with the generation of the righteous' (Psalm 14:5). By the 700s the Christianisation of most of Britain was achieved, until pagan Viking invaders brought chaos from the north. Every Christian kingdom in England fell to the pagans and the King of Wessex, Alfred the Great (849-899) fled for his life and remained in hiding. At stake was the loss of all Christianity in Britain.

In response, King Alfred renewed the nation's covenant with God, as he drew upon ancient convictions laid down in writing by Bede that the bitterly divided kingdoms of England were in fact, one nation, chosen by God to serve His purposes in the world. Encouraged with a renewed faith in God, King Alfred led his defeated soldiers to rearm and fight the Vikings, leading to a great victory that saved Christianity in the nation. Former British politician and broadcaster Ann Widdecombe said, "Alfred didn't just save his Kingdom, he founded the English nation. But to secure his rule he needed to establish law and order. So where did the first king of the English look for his inspiration? To the Bible of course! He used Moses as his role model, to found one of the first and certainly the most influential codes of English law…as a Christian and a law maker, it's exciting to discover that English law began with the Ten Commandments."[7]

King Alfred embraced the Bible as the fount of law in England and his guiding vision was this, "There is only one way by which to build any kingdom, and that is on the sure and certain foundation of faith in Jesus Christ, and in Jesus Christ crucified, and it is on that foundation that I intend to build my Kingdom."[8]

From these humble beginning of victory in the midst of defeat, England emerged as a nation dedicated to the God of the Bible, and its kings and rulers continued to make covenants with God, to serve Him as a Christian nation. This sentiment, beginning with King Ethelbert and solidified by King Alfred, is enshrined into English and British law and the Constitution, and is echoed when the British Head of State, the king or queen, commits, "To uphold to the utmost of my power, the laws of God within this realm and the true profession of the Christian faith."[9]

Chapter Two

A Nation Covenanted to God

The change which Christianity brought to the British nations and kingdoms was profound. Julius Caesar (100-44 BC), who led the first Roman landings in Britain in 55 BC, said the native Celts, "Believe that the gods delight in the slaughter of prisoners and criminals, and when the supply of captives runs short, they sacrifice even the innocent."[1] The historian Pliny the Elder (AD 23-79), explains that the Celts practiced ritual cannibalism, eating their enemy's flesh as a source of spiritual and physical strength. Archaeological evidence seems to confirm this and the remains of Lindow Man may be England's most prominent known victim of human sacrifice.[2]

When the new Christian leaders and kings in Britain read the Scriptures, they took all the warnings seriously. As they learnt of the sins of ancient Israel, they found a mirror into their own history. 'It came to pass, through her casual harlotry, that she defiled the land and committed adultery with stones and trees' (Jeremiah 3:9). The ancient people of Israel had to repent, confess and seek God's aid for the cleansing of the land, and so did the peoples of Britain. Confession was made for shedding innocent blood and the defiled land was cleansed. "Thus they shall cleanse the land" (Ezekiel 39:16).

England was now to be set apart as a holy nation, dedicated to the Lord God and free from the idolatry and paganism of its past. God declared, "They have defiled My land; they have filled My inheritance with the carcasses of their detestable and abominable idols" (Jeremiah 16:18). Preachers taught that the Scriptures reveal that to worship any other God, other than the Lord, is to worship another spirit. Moses said, "They sacrificed to demons, not to God, to gods they did not know, to new gods, new arrivals that your fathers did not fear" (Deuteronomy 32:17).

This seemed to be the testimony of Britain. At first it had forsaken its gods, then pagan warriors brought them back and more; but now the foreign gods of the Angles, Saxons, Jutes and Vikings were to be completely forsaken: "When you brought in foreigners, uncircumcised in heart and uncircumcised in flesh, to be in My sanctuary to defile it – My house…then they broke My covenant because of all your abominations" (Ezekiel 44:7).

King Alfred believed the Kingdoms of England fell to the pagan Vikings because having covenanted itself to God under King Ethelbert, it became half-hearted and lukewarm, sharing in old traditions, worshipping ancient gods and spirits, as well as the Lord. But under King Alfred's rule, if England was to be faithful to its covenant with God, all false altars to demons had to freely fall, and the people chose voluntarily to serve the Lord. God said, "They shall no more offer their sacrifices to demons" (Leviticus 17:7). The ancient customs of human sacrifice, long forgotten, also had to be confessed: "They even sacrificed their sons and their daughters to demons, and shed innocent blood, the blood of their sons and daughters, whom they sacrificed to the idols... and the land was polluted with blood. Thus they were defiled by their own works and played the harlot by their own deeds" (Psalm 106:37-39).

Christianity finally swept into all the nations of Britain and Winston Churchill describes the results: 'There was no kingdom in the realm in which heathen religions and practices now prevailed. The whole island was now Christian,' and, 'England became finally and for all time one coherent Kingdom based on Christianity.'[3] To be a Christian people, the British believed, was to be completely dedicated to God and to follow His law wholeheartedly, as Jesus Christ taught (Mark 12:30).

Consequently, instead of altars of idolatry being at the heart of the nation, beginning from the age of Bede, the British people found new heroes – men of faith and courage in Christ. England began its first steps to recognising St George as its patron saint, because this common Middle Eastern man was a soldier saint, who was martyred for resisting tyranny. Thus the image of St George fighting a dragon – symbolic of Satan in the book of Revelation – was self-evident to those who knew the Bible. Satan, the dragon, was to be defeated in England and wherever the English went. In the year 1415, the long connection between St George and England was ossified, as St George became the patron saint of England, after victory at the Battle of Agincourt, when Henry V (1386-1422) crippled France and its great army.

The English needed a symbol which they could all identify with, and a Christian cross became popular, identified with St George. The white flag with a red cross began appearing from the time of Edward I in the 1270s.[4] With the union of Great Britain in 1707, a flag containing Scotland's cross of St Andrew, counterchanged with Ireland's cross of St Patrick, over England's cross emerged. The Union Flag, or Union Jack was originally a royal flag, and the present design was made official in 1801.

Through this process over the centuries, Christianity emerged from a minor faith to become the faith of Britain for over a thousand years and in each century, men and women arose, kings and queens, who embraced the covenant that England's first Christian king made with God and committed themselves to renewing it. Consequently, Britain's Constitution, which has never been expressed in one single document, was codified over generations as a tacit, benign, residual Christian theocracy, limited by law and now guaranteeing the rights of all. From Magna Carta of 1215, the Provisions of Oxford and Westminster of 1258-9, the English Bill of Rights of 1689, to the Act of Settlement 1701 and the Accession Declaration Act 1910, etc., the Christian sentiment in the British Constitution is explicit. Many of Britain's laws still enshrine Christian privilege, with an acceptance of God being the source from which all authority derives. The position of the Established Church of England, with the monarch as its Supreme Governor, remains central to this Christian Constitutional monarchy.

The last time Britain's Head of State reconfirmed Britain's covenant with the God of the Bible was during the Coronation ceremony on 2 June 1953, as Queen Elizabeth II was asked by the Archbishop of Canterbury, "Will you to the utmost of your power maintain the laws of God and the true profession of the Gospel? Will you to the utmost of your power maintain in the United Kingdom the Protestant Reformed Religion established by law? Will you maintain and preserve inviolably the settlement of the Church of England, and the doctrine, worship, discipline and government thereof, as by law established in England? And will you preserve unto the bishops and clergy of England, and to the Churches there committed to their charge, all such rights and privileges, as by law do or shall appertain to them or any of them?" Queen Elizabeth II replied, "All this I promise to do."[5]

That covenant may have been infracted by Parliament and yet the seed promise of a Christian nation remains, and many prime ministers have, even recently, celebrated Britain's religious heritage as a Christian country.[6] Dr John Sentamu said, "The place of Christianity in the constitutional framework of our country, governed as it is by the Queen, in Parliament, under God, is not in question...the Christian faith has weaved the very fabric of our society just as the oceans around this island have shaped the contours of our geographical identity."[7]

Britain is Constitutionally Christian, "this is not, however, in a narrow sense, as [opponents] claim," explains one enthusiast. "The Coronation service and the Coronation Oath are shot through with Christian beliefs and values, without which they would make no sense. So is that other great pillar of our liberties: the Magna Carta. Parliament convenes with prayer and bishops of the Church of England sit in the House of Lords. National and civic occasions are marked by Christian ceremonies, and the calendar remains unabashedly Christian. The prime minister is right to say that we need a moral and spiritual framework for our national life. He is also right to say that Christianity provides a surer basis for accommodating people of other faiths than secularism. This is why people of other faiths prefer Britain being a Christian rather than a secular country."[8] Columnist Gerald Warner declared: 'Our Head of State is inaugurated by being anointed by an Archbishop: this is a Constitutionally Christian country. The Act of Settlement is the nearest thing we possess to a written Constitution.'[9]

Following her Coronation Oath in 1953, Queen Elizabeth II made a broadcast in the evening to Britain and to millions in the British Empire, saying, "When I spoke to you last at Christmas, I asked you all…to pray that God would give me wisdom and strength to carry out the promises that I should then be making…the ceremonies you have seen today are ancient, and some of their origins are veiled in the mists of the past. But their spirit and their meaning shine through the ages, never perhaps, more brightly than now. I have in sincerity pledged myself to your service, as so many of you are pledged to mine. Throughout all my life and with all my heart I shall strive to be worthy of your trust…Therefore I am sure that this, my Coronation, is not the symbol of a power and a splendour that are gone but a declaration of our hopes for the future, and for the years I may, by God's grace and mercy, be given to reign and serve you."[10]

The modern world may not think much of Divine covenants, oaths and noble promises made to God on a national or personal level, but this view is not Scriptural. In the Bible King Solomon made a covenant with God, on behalf of his nation and this covenant was accepted by God (2 Chronicles chapters 5-7). Taking this as an example, the people of Britain, as a Gentile nation, have also covenanted with God, as reflected in our ceremonies and at times of historic troubles. Britain, nor any other nation, is not, nor ever has been, nor can ever be, Israel; but if God hears and answers prayer, it seems we have the evidence to indicate that for over a thousand years, Britain was grafted into God's will, in Christ (Romans 11:17-26).

In ancient Israel, Zadok the priest and Nathan the prophet anointed Solomon King of Israel, as the nation covenanted itself to God (1 Kings 1:38-40), and the people sang, 'God save the king, long live the king, may the king live for ever! Amen, Hallelujah!' Almost three thousand years later, this scene is still mirrored during British coronations. 'Zadok the Priest' composed by George Friedrich Handel (1685-1759), has been sung at every British coronation service, beginning in 1727 with King George II (1683-1760).

Just as King Solomon committed his nation to God, so too British monarchs have covenanted, "To uphold to the utmost of my power, the laws of God within this realm and the true profession of the Christian faith."[11] When Solomon committed the nation of Israel to God, the Prophet Nathan anointed him in God's name, and in Britain, the monarch is also anointed by the most prominent religious leader in the nation. In Israel, after the king was crowned, the people would cry out, "God save the king" (1 Samuel 10:24), and after covenanting with God, the British do the same, as the British National Anthem, 'God save the Queen' parallels.

The modern world may believe that words are cheap and have little value, but the view of Scripture is that covenants are sacred to God. Making a covenant with God is akin to a legal binding spiritual agreement, made on earth by man and witnessed by God in heaven, which must never be broken.[12] God spoke to King David and revealed, "He who rules over men must be just, ruling in the fear of God" (2 Samuel 23:3). Consequently, British monarchs in the past have covenanted to be a Christian nation of justice, righteousness and holiness in the fear of God; and the Lord said, "And I will establish My covenant with you. Then you shall know that I am the Lord" (Ezekiel 16:62).

The British Constitution stresses that government is subject to a higher authority, to God, as well as the electorate, for its actions. The Constitution recognises, "The Queen (or King) in Parliament under God,"[13] and this conviction has ancient unwritten sources. We can trace the use of the phrase, 'The Queen under God' to the age of Queen Elizabeth I (1533-1603), who said, "God hath made me to be a Queen...under God...I trust by the Almighty power of God that I shall be His instrument."[14]

Britain's potent Constitution acknowledges God as the highest possible authority and this has spared the nation from oppressive rulers and government, leading to the people seeking a just and fair society. In 1701, the Act of Settlement established in the Constitution that the monarch in Britain rules 'under God.' In practice, bills passed in the Houses of Parliament are sent to the sovereign, or to his or her representative for Royal Assent, where it is formally agreed upon to make the bill into an Act of Parliament, using the authority invested in the monarch by God. However, in the modern era the monarch is obliged to given accent to, 'The will of her ministers,' even if the monarch does not believe the bill is consistent with the Christian Coronation oath; otherwise a Constitutional crisis would follow.[15]

Nevertheless, in history one of the very important roles of the monarch in Britain is to defend the nation's centuries old commitment to biblical Christianity. Queen Elizabeth I in her Act of Supremacy in 1558 safeguarded England as a Protestant nation, which for many citizens meant a return to the New Testament Christianity of the apostles; and a re-embracing of those ancient Celtic convictions of faith. This act also conferred the defence of this Constitutional position to all following British monarchs – as the Supreme Governor of the Church of England, under Christ Jesus, the Head. This is the Constitutional position of Britain to the present day.

Professor Diarmaid MacCulloch explains how the coronation ceremony in Britain echoes the history of Christianity in this nation, from its early days, to the Reformation and beyond. He said, "The millions who saw," the coronation of Queen Elizabeth II, "were witnessing the culmination of over a thousand years of English history. The service had first been designed back in the tenth century and what's fascinating is that this isn't just the handover of earthly power; it's a ritual which charts the key moments in the evolution of an idea. Bede's notion of a nation committed to God is there, alongside Alfred's that the law was the means to win Divine favour. There's the Reformation and the recasting of the chosen nation in a Protestant mould, and at the heart of the ceremony, the anointing of the monarch is the unmistakable comparison of England to God's original chosen people, Israel. It was a moment so sacred it wasn't even allowed to be televised. London in 1953 melted into Jerusalem three thousand years before, and just as Hebrew prophets and priests had anointed a Hebrew king, so now God gave His 'Anglican' seal of approval on this new reign. It reminds us that even now the sovereign rules as God's anointed."[16]

The Archbishop of Canterbury Justin Welby explains the lasting impact of Christianity upon the nation: 'It is a historical fact (perhaps unwelcome to some, but true) that our main systems of ethics, the way we do law and justice, the values of society, how we decide what is fair, the protection of the poor, and most of the way we look at society...all have been shaped by and founded on Christianity. Add to that the foundation of many hospitals, the system of universal schooling, the presence of chaplains in prisons, and one could go on a long time. Then there is the literature, visual art, music and culture that have formed our understandings of beauty and worth since Anglo-Saxon days."[17]

In 2014, the British Government's most senior law officer, the Attorney General Dominic Grieve declared that British society is "underpinned by Christian values."[18] This was said in response to more than fifty British writers, scientists, broadcasters and academics who signed an open letter dismissing Britain's claim to be a Christian nation. The Attorney General said these people were "deluding themselves," adding, "the evidence in this country is overwhelming, that most people in this country by a very substantial margin have religious belief in the supernatural or a deity…to that extent atheism doesn't appear to have made much progress in this country at all, which is probably why the people that wrote this letter are so exercised about it."[19]

In the 2011 British census, six in ten of the population, which is 33.2 million people, chose to identify themselves as Christian, which highlights the cultural and nominal nature of the faith of many in Britain. Yet, practicing Christians are not the minority some suggest. One comprehensive Tearfund report found one in seven British adults attend church at least once a month, and one in four once a year. Potentially 9 percent of the population are practicing Christians, whilst in London, 22 percent of the population attend church at least once each month.[20] Research is unable to attest to the numbers who worship in unregistered churches, or who practice their Christian faith at home in the age of Christian media. The secular media often quotes the falling numbers of worshipers in the Church of England, but the Established Church has been for years, simply one Church out of many churches and denominations in Britain. Even in the 1851 religious census, it was found that over half of all who attended Church went to churches outside of the Anglican Communion.

Britain's Attorney General said, "Our state, its ethics and our society are underpinned by Christian values," and added, "many of the underlying ethics of society are Christian based and the result of 1,500 years of Christian input into our national life."[21] Britain's Work and Pensions Secretary, Iain Duncan Smith declared that those who deny Britain is a Christian country do so by "ignoring both historical and Constitutional reality."[22]

Britain's national anthem is uncompromisingly Christian, with a dependence on God and the Lord evidently conveyed. 'God Save the Queen' or King, has many historic and extant versions, and may have originated from 1619. It was officially performed in

London in 1745 and adopted in the nineteenth century. There is no authorised version, as the words are a matter of tradition and on official occasions, only the first verse is usually sung.[23]

The first word in Britain's national anthem is 'God,' the second is 'Save.' How many nations have an anthem which commences with a theme of God's redemption at the very beginning? The third and fifth verses go like this: 'God bless our native land, may heaven's protective hand, still guard our shore; may peace her power extend, foe be transformed to friend, and Britain's power depend, on war no more…and not this land alone, but be Thy mercies known, from shore to shore. Lord, make the nations see that men should brothers be…'[24]

In Britain, the monarch's title includes the 'Defender of the Faith.' This means Her Majesty has a specific role in both the Church of England and the Church of Scotland. As Established Churches, they are recognised by law as the official Churches of England and Scotland, respectively.[25]

Some secularists have argued that Britain can no longer be a Christian nation because people of other faiths reside in the land; by contrast, the leaders of these faiths have voiced their opinion that a nation which is confident about its Christian heritage will be more accommodating to citizens of other beliefs or none, than if it adopted a secularist whitewash. One expressed his "great concern" about atheists trying to hijack the concept of 'representing minorities' to force through an intolerant, unrepresentative secularist plan.[26] Nevertheless, without doubt there has been decline in Christian observance and in the number and quality of churches in Britain, with substantial losses in traditional denominations. But between 2008 and 2013, the number of churches in Britain actually increased from 49,727 to 50,660. If this trend continues by 2020, it is estimated there will be 51,275 churches in Britain.[27]

Throughout Britain, churches remain at the heart and centre of communities, meeting numerous needs from providing food banks to facilitating meetings for all ages, making church a hub for millions. In 2011, there were 139,751 baptisms, 51,880 weddings and 162,526 funerals conducted by Church of England clergy alone, without taking into account all the activity at the heart of the community for the other large denominations and independent churches.[28] In the same year, ninety-eight percent of England's twenty thousand plus state funded faith schools were Christian and most have an extremely good reputation.[29]

In the media Britain may be portrayed as an absolute secular country, but behind the mask of consumerism, most people hold a belief in something more than the natural realm, even if they're afraid to say so publicly. The historian Diarmaid MacCulloch said, "Today in private most people still claim to believe in God, but in public He's barely mentioned." However, due to the long legacy of Christianity, "There's still a sense that this country should set a moral standard for the rest of the world, as we have done throughout history."[30]

Some have suggested that large scale Christian observance in Britain is a thing of the past and can never be repeated, but they have said that before. As Winston Churchill said, "Men remembered that Britain had been Christian once and might be Christian again." Since the 1980s, membership of Pentecostal churches in the U.K. has grown by some 200 percent.[31] This presents the case that it is not Christianity which is in decline, but instead certain traditional expressions of the faith.

Part One
The Making of a Christian Country

Chapter Three

Celtic Christianity

Now that the introduction has established the Christian heritage of Britain, we must go back in time and evaluate in detail the impact and spread of the faith throughout England, Wales and Scotland, and later throughout Ireland.

In the first century 'Britain had its own set of religious icons: pagan gods of the earth and Roman gods of the sky. Into this superstitious and violent world came a modern, fashionable faith from the east: Christianity. We tend to associate the arrival of Christianity in Britain with the mission of Augustine in AD 597. But in fact Christianity arrived long before then, and in the first century, there wasn't an organised attempt to convert the British. It began as Roman artisans and traders arrived spreading the story of Jesus Christ in Britain. Unlike the faiths of Rome, Christianity demanded exclusive allegiance from its followers. It was this pure devotion to one God, which rattled the Roman authorities and led to repeated persecutions of Christians. Christians were forced to meet and worship in secret.'[1]

Dr Robert Bedford explains, "History tells us that Christianity first arrived in Britain from the Mediterranean during the Roman occupation. It was an import, like the roads, army, drainage and everything else, and ts focus was in the cities," like Verulamium, at St Albans, in Hertfordshire, "which was once the third largest city in Roman Britain."[2]

The native Christians of this age were cut-off from Rome and there was no official attempt to impose a religious system upon them; instead Roman citizens brought their Christian faith with them, and native Celts listened to the message and responded, to join Roman citizens in their new faith in Jesus Christ.

Christianity spread in Britain and the Church Father Tertullian (160-225) of Carthage, Tunisia, states that Christianity greatly impacted Britain, and some areas inaccessible to the Romans accepted Christianity 'The haunts of the Britons, inaccessible to the Romans, but subjugated to Christ,' he declared.[3] Thus, according to Tertullian, Christianity spread further than the Roman occupation in Britain ever did, perhaps far into Scotland.

The Bishop of Caesarea and historian Eusebius (AD 260-340) believed some of the first generation of Christians, the converts of the first disciples, came to preach in Britain: 'To preach to all the name of Jesus, to teach about His marvellous deeds...and some have crossed the Ocean and reached the Isles of Britain.'[4]

The first Christians in Britain met in their homes to worship, as did the disciples of Jesus Christ, until toleration enabled wealthy Romans to set aside large rooms in their homes, to be dedicated for a permanent place of worship. In the British Museum resides one part of a Christian wall painting, showing men praying from Lullingstone, Kent, which was removed from a Roman villa. English heritage states: 'The evidence of the Christian house-church is a unique discovery for Roman Britain and the wall-paintings are of international importance...they provide some of the earliest evidence for Christianity in Britain.'[5]

Archaeological evidence also provides us with examples of Christian communities developing in the third and fourth centuries, with possible small timber churches at Lincoln and Silchester, and baptismal fonts have been discovered at Saxon Shore Fort in Richborough. By this time, ten percent of the Roman Empire had accepted Christianity, and even though we have no statistical data available for the province of Britannia, there is no reason to believe it had not achieved such importance in this land.[6]

Archaeological finds point to clear signs of the strength of Christianity among some of the middle and upper classes, who have left physical objects to study. In the British Museum, a lead tank from Icklingham provides us with firsthand data from a Christian community. The British Museum states: 'This lead tank is one of three found at Icklingham, where an early church and cemetery have been excavated. On the side of the tank in two places is the common Christian device of a Chi-Rho symbol, the first two letters of Christ's name in Greek. This is flanked by an alpha and omega, the first and last letters of the Greek alphabet, another symbol of Christ – 'I am Alpha and Omega, the first and the last' (Revelation 1:8).'[7]

The fact that Christianity was flourishing in Britain is further attested by the Christian silver plaque and gold disc from the Water Newton treasure, which the British Museum explains is: 'The earliest Christian silver yet found in the Roman Empire'[8] and it was found, having been used by Christians in Britain. In the find is a chalice, similar to ones later used in communion services. The British Museum states: 'Many of the objects in the hoard bear the monogram formed by the Greek letters chi (X) and rho (P), the first two letters of Christ's name, a symbol commonly used by early Christians. Two bowls and one plaque have longer inscriptions in Latin. One of these, on a bowl, can be translated as 'I, Publianus, honour your sacred shrine, trusting in you, O Lord.' Other inscriptions give the names of three female dedicators: Amcilla, Innocentia and Viventia, who must also have belonged to the congregation.'[9]

Throughout Britain, other ancient places of Christian worship have been found, including in Colchester and Poundbury. But we must remember that poorer Christians could not afford to leave any open legacy, so the true extent of the Church in Britain remains unknown. The fact that these Christians tended to meet in their homes makes it impossible to measure the size or scope of Christianity in Britain. Yet, when Christian leaders met in France, at the Council of Arles in 314, British Celtic Christianity was strong enough to send three bishops – Eborius of York, Restitutus of London and Adelphius, possibly a bishop of Lincoln. As we have already explained, Christians made up about ten percent of the Roman Empire by this time, so the numbers of believers in Britain could have been substantial.[10]

Theological disputes were common in this age and Britain was engaging with and being rebuked by other believers. In an open letter to many nations defending the faith, Hilary, the Bishop of Poitiers (300-368) says, 'To the bishops of the provinces of Britain...the whole faith is summed up and secured in this, the Trinity must always be preserved, as we read in the gospel, "Go ye and baptise all nations in the name of the Father, and of the Son, and of the Holy Ghost." '[11]

"The British Isles, which are beyond the sea and which lie in the ocean, have received the virtue of the Word," exclaimed John Chrysostom (347-407), the Bishop of Constantinople in 402. 'Churches are there founded and altars erected. Though you should go to the ocean, to the British Isles, there you will hear all men everywhere discoursing matters out of the Scriptures, with a different voice indeed, but not another faith, with a different tongue but the same judgment."[12]

Before Christianity was legalised in the Roman Empire, the majority of believers still clung to New Testament Christianity and many were martyred for their faith in Christ, including in Britain. Their commitment to Christ, unto death, seems to have inspired many of the pagans to convert.

Sometime during the third or fourth century, a Christian called Alban became venerated as the first official English martyr, with many others following. In the ancient book *On the Ruin and Conquest of Britain* by Gildas the Wise (500-570), he writes how the Church in Britain survived the Diocletian persecution: 'God, therefore, who wishes all men to be saved and who calls sinners no less than those who think themselves righteous, magnified His mercy towards us, and as we know, during the above named persecution, that Britain might not totally be enveloped in the dark shades of night, He, of His own free gift, kindled up among us bright luminaries of holy martyrs...such were Saint Alban of Verulamium, Aaron and Julius, citizens of the City of the Legions, and the rest, of both sexes, who in different places stood their ground in the Christian contest.'[13] This book is one of the most significant sources of history of ancient Britain, as it is the only one written by a near contemporary of the age.

To the Romans, Britain and Ireland symbolised the end of the known world, because to the west of Cornwall, Scotland or Ireland lay an impassable sea, where the sun set. All who reached Britain touched the mysterious lands of the north west, and many came. There are several myths and legends of biblical characters crossing the English Channel, such as the visit of Joseph of Arimathea in AD 37, which unsubstantiated, cannot provide us with any factual basis to claim historical reliability. In none of the earliest references to Christianity's arrival in Britain is Joseph of Arimathea mentioned,[14] and these legends were most probably invented by monks in the Middle Ages seeking pilgrims.

Before there was any organised attempt to bring Christianity to the nation, God in His sovereignty orchestrated the spread of the gospel, and by the fourth and fifth centuries, Christianity thrived. Enough evidence exists to prove that a strong Christian Church was unmistakably evident in Britain, amidst a cloud of paganism. These first believers in Britain provide us with a close link to Jesus and the apostles.

The father of English history, the Venerable Bede (673-735), in his chronicles of the *Ecclesiastical History of the English People* provides us with further details of Christianity in Britain, from its earliest days, but with the collapse of Roman rule in Britain between AD 407-410, the future became uncertain.

Chapter Four

Darkness and Light

A terrible period for Celtic Christianity emerged with the arrival of a few ships of heavily armed warriors, who landed on England's east coast, beginning in the mid-fifth century. These pagan warrior tribes were the Angles, Saxons, Jutes and Frisians. These Germanic tribes overran England and decapitated the government, filling the power-vacuum left in the province of Britannia after the Roman Empire withdrew between AD 407-410, and they also brought their horrendous pagan gods.

In a dramatic turn of events, the Roman life of villas, towns, international trade, luxury, law and order collapsed. The only part of life under Roman occupation which survived was Christianity. These Celtic Christians no longer had any form of protection and the leadership of the indigenous people of Britain fled west out of the way of the pagan invaders. As these Germanic invaders slashed and burned villages, so the great Celtic exodus began. Many Celtic Christians withdrew into the west of southern Scotland, northern England, west Cornwall, Wales and some to Ireland. Others fled into Europe, taking their faith with them as they sought a peaceful society, free from the pagan invaders.

As the Germanic pagans ravished town after town in England, literacy, technology, towns and Christianity itself disappeared, to be replaced with pagan warlike gods, chaos and illiteracy. The Brittonic languages which were once spoken in the land, withdrew into the Celtic strongholds of west Britain, especially Wales. Of these original languages spoken by Britons when the Romans ruled, Welsh is a direct descendant. As a Bible College student I studied in Wales on a campus called 'Derwen Fawr' which has Brittonic origins, as does, albeit indirectly, London, Aberdeen, York, Dorchester, Dover, Colchester and the rivers Avon, Chew and Frome.

One myth of the Germanic invasions is that they flooded the nation in such large numbers, that they overwhelmed the native inhabitants and forced them all to flee. "The Anglo-Saxon chronicle tells us that they were coming over in really quite small numbers of people – two or three long boats," explains the archaeologist Dr Neil Faulkner. "You can get about thirty, forty fifty people into a long boat. That means it's actually quite a small number of warriors who are coming in."[1]

An exodus of Celtic leaders and Christians pioneers certainly took place into the west of England, Wales, Cornwall, Ireland and Scotland, but the Anglo-Saxon invaders simply became the foreign rulers of the British inhabitants who could not flee. Those who remained chose to adopt Anglo-Saxon culture and beliefs to be accepted by their new rulers. They became culturally Anglo-Saxon and the nationality we now identify as 'English,' is a derivative of 'Anglo.' Nevertheless, the main body of people in England were still natives, Celts if you like, and this has been proved by DNA analysis of the descendants of the traditional inhabitants of Britain.

Dr Stephen Oppenheimer, an expert in genetic science analysis, has methodically examined the extensive studies of the DNA of the British and concludes, "The Anglo-Saxon contribution, in my analysis, is only five percent for the whole of England. The English are much closer to the Welsh, the Irish, the Cornish and the Scottish than they are to any continental population. This idea of the English coming in as a race – or the Anglo-Saxons coming in as a race – really just doesn't hold up in the genetic view."[2]

Therefore, the majority of the traditional inhabitants of Britain continue to be the descendants of the Britons who were living in the land when Rome invaded. Future intermarriages between the descendants of these Britons and Anglo-Saxons, Vikings, Normans and other invaders, though culturally significant, still remain relatively minor in the DNA analysis. Dr Neil Faulkner concludes, "So most of the people that we think of as Anglo-Saxon are actually British people who've been integrated into Anglo-Saxon society."[3]

Nevertheless, the pagans took over England and reversed all the progress which had been made by the Roman Empire.[4] The great Roman cities and centres with a vibrant Christian witness died a sudden death and Christianity was killed-off wherever the pagans arrived. "Only in the West and in Ireland did Christianity remain a real force," explains Dr Robert Bedford. "Ireland had never been part of the Roman Empire, but just as the Empire was collapsing, Christian missionaries arrived under the leadership of Saint Patrick and here Christianity took a radically different form. It was devoted to austerity and mysticism."[5]

It's not entirely clear what reasons the Celtic Christians gave for why God allowed the collapse of Roman rule in the province of Britannica, and the subsequent invasion of the pagans, leading to the decimation of Christianity. In the case of the city of Rome and its Empire, St Augustine of Hippo (354-430) argues in his book *The City of God Against the Pagans* that followers of Jesus Christ are strangers and pilgrims on earth, as Scripture states. As this is the case, Christians must seek the heavenly city of God, instead of putting their trust in earthly powers, like Rome (Hebrews 11:13). But what did the Celtic Christians in Britain think about their situation? Perhaps there is a case to be made that Celtic Christians in Britain believed the legalisation of Christianity in the Roman Empire had made becoming a follower of Jesus too comfortable and worldly?

Gold and silver objects used in worship, now safe in museums, may have served posterity well by surviving as a testimony to their faith, but what about Jesus' teaching about riches and James' warning against them in James 5:1-6? Jesus said, "Do not lay up for yourselves treasures on earth, where moth and rust destroy and where thieves break in and steal; but lay up for yourselves treasures in heaven, where neither moth nor rust destroys and where thieves do not break in and steal. For where your treasure is, there your heart will be also" (Matthew 6:19-21).

Jesus Christ never gave a command to build churches like palaces, nor did He ask for gold and silver objects to be made for use in worship. This is legacy of the Roman Empire and its first Christian Emperor, Constantine the Great (272-337), beginning with his churches in Rome. The Roman Empire loved gold and silver, but many of the prophets of the Old Testament shunned the world and its wealth. John the Baptist, Jesus Christ and His apostles spent time in the deserts seeking God, and they were often poor or homeless (1 Corinthians 4:11). Jesus said, "Foxes have holes and birds of the air have nests, but the Son of Man has nowhere to lay His head" (Luke 9:58). The example of Jesus Christ was one of sacrifice, austerity, death to self and helping those in need (Matthew 6:3-4).

So did Christianity in Britain become worldly when it was legalised under Roman rule, or was the Germanic invasions just one of those terrible things which happen? According to the Old Testament, God allowed the Kingdoms of Israel and Judah to fall into the hands of ungodly foreign powers, because they had not been faithful to God's will and this teaching may have made an impact on the Celtic Christians. The word 'because' is found 1,138 in the King James Bible from the year 1611, and in the biblical books of Kings, Chronicles, Jeremiah and other prophetic books, God tells His people they were to be exiled, 'Because…'

What is certain is that Celtic Christianity in Ireland and western Britain was to be vastly different from the faith of many Popes, who embraced the legacy of the golden churches of Constantine's Rome. The Celtic believers were committed to austerity and the supernatural manifestation of God's power. They spent time outside in nature, following the example of John the Baptist and Jesus, seeking God in prayer, and bringing their physical bodies into subjection to their spirit. 'Of whom the world was not worthy. They wandered in deserts and mountains, in dens and caves of the earth' (Hebrews 11:38).

As we have identified, Christianity remained strong in Cornwall, Wales, west England and the west of southern Scotland, but England's first historian, the Venerable Bede, was deeply troubled that these Celtic Christians never gained the courage to return east into the newly pagan regions of England to share the gospel with the invaders, their subjects and their descendants. Instead Christianity was first sent into Ireland, before it could flourish and bounce back into Britain, via Scotland and south into England.

The most important figure in the development of this age of Celtic Christianity was the missionary Patrick, a fifth century Romano-British man, the son of a follower of Jesus Christ. Born somewhere in England, young Patrick was at best, a nominal Christian when he was captured by pirates around AD 400 and was taken to Ireland to be sold as a slave. Whilst tending sheep in his enslavement, he re-committed himself to Jesus Christ and spent hours in prayer in the hills.

Patrick believed there was a reason and meaning for all the events which happened to him and he tells us in his own words, the reasons for his captivity: 'I was then about sixteen years of age. I did not know the true God. I was taken into captivity to Ireland with many thousands of people, and deservedly so, because we turned away from God, and did not keep His commandments, and did not obey our ministers, who used to remind us of our salvation. And the Lord brought over us the wrath of His anger and scattered us among many nations, even unto the utmost part of the earth, where now my littleness is placed among strangers. And there the Lord opened the sense of my unbelief that I might at last remember my sins and be converted with all my heart to the Lord my God, who had regard for my abjection, and mercy on my youth and ignorance, and watched over me before I knew Him, and before I was able to distinguish between good and evil, and guarded me and comforted me as would a father his son.'[6]

Patrick spent six years as a slave and he tells us, 'I prayed a hundred times in the day and almost as many at night,' and one night as he sought God, he heard God's voice saying, "It is well that you fast. Soon you will go to your own country," and after a short while, "See, your ship is ready." Patrick escaped slavery and made it across the Irish Sea to England.

It's important to separate the real human being Patrick, from the legends, myths and perceptions that have been built around him. He was not trained and sent out due to the legacy of Emperor Constantine's Church and he declared: 'I have not studied like the others.' Instead Patrick had a personal relationship with God, based upon Divine revelation from the Holy Spirit and complete submission to the authority and doctrines of Scripture. In his writings, Patrick shows a thorough knowledge of the doctrines of the apostles in the New Testament. He wrote Jesus 'was made Man, and, having defeated death, was received into heaven by the Father; and He hath given Him all power over all names in heaven, on earth, and under the earth, and every tongue shall confess to Him that Jesus Christ is Lord.'[7]

After settling back into life as a freeman in England, Patrick received a dream from God which asked of him, the very thing he never wanted to do – return to Ireland. 'There I saw in the night the vision of a man, whose name was Victoricus, coming as it were from Ireland with countless letters. And he gave me one of them, and I read the opening words of the letter, which were, "The voice of the Irish." I read the beginning of the letter, I thought that at the same moment I heard their voice...and thus did they cry out as with one mouth, "We ask thee, boy, come and walk among us once more." And I was quite broken in heart and could read no further, and so I woke up. Thanks be to God, after many years the Lord gave to them according to their cry. And another night...they called me...except that at the end of the prayer He spoke thus, "He that has laid down His life for thee, it is He that speaketh in thee," and so I awoke full of joy.'[8]

Patrick's faith was wholeheartedly committed to New Testament Christianity, which included a belief in dreams and visions from God, grounded in the veracity of Scripture (Acts 2:17, 10:9-16, 16:19). Patrick heard the voice of Jesus and he also learnt to become sensitive to the Holy Spirit, just like the apostles: 'As they ministered to the Lord and fasted, the Holy Spirit said, "Now separate to Me Barnabas and Saul for the work to which I have called them" ' (Acts 13:2). Patrick testifies: 'I saw Him praying in me and I was as it were within my body, and I heard Him above me, that is, over the inward man and there He prayed mightily with groanings. And all the time I was astonished, and wondered and thought with myself who it could be that prayed in me. But at the end of the prayer He spoke, saying that He was the Spirit; and so I woke up, and remembered the Apostle saying: 'The Spirit helpeth the infirmities of our prayer. For we know not what we should pray for as we ought; but the Spirit Himself asketh for us with unspeakable groanings, which cannot be expressed in words' (Romans 8:26-27); and again: 'The Lord our advocate asketh for us' '[9] (1 John 2).

Patrick followed the command of God and began his mission to take the Christian faith to the ends of the known earth, as far west as Christianity had ever gone. He added, 'I, however ignorant as I was, in the last days dared to undertake such a holy and wonderful work, thus imitating somehow those who, as the Lord once foretold, would preach His gospel for a testimony to all nations before the end of the world.'[10]

"When he made landfall in the north of Ireland, he brought with him the promise of a new civilisation, rooted in Christianity," explains the historian Dan Snow. "But he was entering a land where paganism ran deep. Ireland was a place of sacred trees, woods and lakes, presided over by druids, combining the roles of priest, wise man and ritual executioner. There's was a religion of animal and human sacrifice, of blood on altars and entrails that were used to tell the future. The druid religion had once extended right across Western Europe. The Romans were so disturbed by it they made it illegal on pain of death, but Rome's authority had never extended into Ireland and here it had continued to flourish."[11]

Monsignor Raymond Murray, parish priest of Cookstown in Northern Ireland explains, "Part of the pagan worship of fall to spring, from the beginning of the summer, was that a fire was lit, and first of all, the fire on the hill of Tara and no other lights at all in Ireland. This monastery on the hill of Slane is where Patrick – in direct defiance of the high King of Tara – lit a forbidden fire."[12]

Patrick plunged a spiritual dagger into the heart of paganism in Ireland and he was dragged before the king, with the expectation of being executed. Being asked to explain himself, Patrick was able to convince the king that the Christian God was more powerful than any of the gods the king was serving, and Christianity was adopted and flourished.

In 432, Patrick built the first church in Ireland, on the site of the present day St. Patrick's Memorial Church, in Saul. Thousands were baptised and hundreds of churches were planted across Ireland. Patrick, having been led by the Holy Spirit to Ireland, to glorify Jesus Christ, decided to follow a completely different direction from the bishops of Rome, and when the rich offered him gifts, he refused them. He was worried by this, confessing, 'I offended the donors...but, guided by God...I came to the people of Ireland to preach the gospel...For I am very much God's debtor.' He was not always welcome and had to 'suffer insult from the unbelievers.'[13]

Monasteries like the one at Labbamolaga "began to appear across Ireland soon after Patrick's missions of 432," explains the historian Dr Janina Ramirez, "because they were disconnected from mainland Christian Europe, in particular Rome and the Papacy, the monasteries that developed across Celtic lands were rather different to those on the Continent. Monasticism on the Continent evolved as part of the existing Roman Church hierarchy, but the Romans hadn't come to Ireland."[14]

Patrick's Celtic Christianity emphasised personal sacrifice, love for God, openness to the Holy Spirit and the apostles' conviction that believers should live as slaves of Jesus Christ. Patrick saw his life's mission was to do all to fulfil the command of Christ. He wrote: 'To Thee the Gentiles shall come from the ends of the earth and shall say, "How false are the idols that our fathers got for themselves and there is no profit in them;" and again, "I have set Thee as a light among the Gentiles, that Thou mayest be for salvation unto the utmost part of the earth." And there I wish to wait for His promise who surely never deceives, as He promises in the gospel.'

Patrick was consumed with Christ's Great Commission, that every creature must be reached with the gospel (Mark 16:15-18), and he copied out all the Scriptures concerning Jesus' command to take His gospel to the ends of the earth. He wrote: 'Go therefore now, teach all nations, baptising them in the name of the Father and the Son, and the Holy Spirit, teaching them to observe all things... I will pour out of My Spirit upon all flesh; and your sons and your daughters shall prophesy, and your young men shall see visions, and your old men shall dream dreams.' Thus, 'it came to pass in Ireland that those who never had a knowledge of God, but until now always worshipped idols and things impure, have now been made a people of the Lord, and are called sons of God.'[15]

Patrick's was a pure ministry, motivated by God's Spirit and he was bold to challenge anyone to give evidence that he abused his authority. 'When I baptised so many thousands of people, did I perhaps expect from any of them as much as half a scruple? Tell me and I will restore it to you. Or when the Lord ordained clerics everywhere through my unworthy person and I conferred the ministry upon them free, if I asked any of them as much as the price of my shoes, speak against me and I will return it to you.'[16]

His faith was a stark contrast to the example which had been set in Rome. Former British Cabinet Minister and broadcaster Michael Portillo describes the influence of Constantine on the Church in Rome, "For centuries Christians had been persecuted, they'd been fed to lions, they'd been living underground in catacombs, they'd been worshipping in churches no bigger than a house, and then along comes Constantine and showers them with riches. Well, you're not going to say no, are you? You're not going to look a gift-horse in the mouth. But if since the time of Christ you've been preaching blessed are the meek and blessed are the poor, and you inherit all this (the newly constructed golden churches of Rome), its bound to change you, isn't it?"[17]

Michael Portillo added, "The emperor showered Christians with wealth and built wondrous churches in Rome and Constantinople. Christianity moved overnight from being a minority movement of underdogs to being enthroned. Some commentators regard the change as disastrous, because Christ's revolutionary message that the meek would inherit the earth sits uncomfortably with the Church's wealth and power. On the other hand, had Christianity not become established throughout the Empire, would there have been so many converts across the centuries, each one representing, for believers, a soul saved?"[18]

Patrick, like the apostle Paul was bold enough to ask his converts if he had exploited any and invited them to come to him for recompense (2 Corinthians 7:2). By the end of his life he could testify: 'For Christ the Lord, too, was poor for our sakes; and I, unhappy wretch that I am, have no wealth even if I wished for it.'[19] Paul wrote: 'Nor did we eat anyone's bread free of charge, but worked with labour and toil night and day, that we might not be a burden to any of you, not because we do not have authority, but to make ourselves an example of how you should follow us' (2 Thessalonians 3:8-9).

Celtic Christianity, as Patrick's life proves, initially remained true to New Testament Christianity and it was also alive in the west of Britain. However, it was to be the followers of Patrick's example, who would bring Christianity back to the pagan areas of England and stretch far into uncharted areas of Scotland.

As for Patrick, he wanted to return to Britain, but he felt no liberty in the Holy Spirit: 'Wherefore, then, even if I wished to leave them and go to Britain, and how I would have loved to go to my country and my parents...God knows it, I much desired it; but I am bound by the Spirit, who gives evidence against me if I do this, telling me that I shall be guilty. I am afraid of losing the labour which I have begun, nay, not I, but Christ the Lord who bade me come here and stay with them for the rest of my life.'[20]

Patrick was an independent missionary to Ireland, resisted by men, but sent by a direct revelation of the Lord Jesus Christ, by the leading of the Holy Spirit, to risk his life so pagans could receive eternal life. His own writings testify that he walked closely with God and like the apostles of Jesus, developed a deep sensitivity to the guidance of God's Holy Spirit. In subsequent generations his writings would be ignored, as he was recast into a new religious image, to fit with the ever changing times; but when we return to his testimony, what we find is New Testament Christianity.

Chapter Five

The Celtic Golden Age

Patrick, as a young man born and raised in Britain, accepted the seeds of New Testament Christianity from his family, which they received from believers who travelled along the Roman roads. After taking his faith seriously, he was sent by God as a missionary to Ireland and the revolution which he sparked there, changed Ireland from a pagan backwater to the beating heart of a spiritual, technological and missionary minded nation. It was a spiritual revolution, just as influential as the Industrial Revolution.

Patrick preached in a nation which had never been occupied by the Romans, and when he arrived it had no roads, no towns, no stone buildings and no Christianity; but with his message of faith a transformation took place. Within fifty years of his first sermon, Ireland became a centre of civilisation, with economic dynamism, modernity, language, literacy and education, centred on the monasteries which were quickly erected.

"Nowadays books and libraries are so much part of our culture that it's impossible to imagine a time without them," said the historian Dan Snow. "But the sixth century was just such a time. Of course there would have been books under the Romans, in fact there were dozens of public libraries throughout the Empire, but after Rome fell, one chronicler wrote: 'That libraries, like tombs, were shut up forever.' If it hadn't been for the Irish monasteries and the monks in them, the culture, learning and writing could have been eradicated in Western Europe. Central to that transmission of learning were manuscripts. Soon every monastery had its own scriptorium, where newly trained scribes copied and copied everything from the Old and New Testaments, to Latin and Greek classics."[1]

Ireland thrived because of Celtic Christianity and the faith remained alive in parts of Britain, but most of Britannica was still lost in the darkness of the newly introduced paganism, brought by the Germanic tribes who seized most of England. For Patrick, his writings explain how he was consumed with fulfilling Jesus' Great Commission, to take the gospel to the ends of the earth, and Ireland was to him the very end of the world; and his converts wanted to follow his example.

Patrick reached further west than the Roman Empire and now

his spiritual descendants took New Testament Christianity further north than the Romans, deep into Scotland, to the Kingdom of the unconquered Picts. As a first step, in AD 563 twelve chosen Celtic missionaries sailed from Ireland, to the Irish territories in Scotland in the Kingdom of Dál Riata, to set up a base for reaching the furthest extent of the known world.

Columba (521-597) was a descendant of the high kings of Ireland and as an aristocrat he could have lived the high life, but instead he chose to risk his life and serve Christ as a missionary. He was the head of the twelve missionaries to reach Scotland and when they landed, it was he who spoke to the King of Dál Riata and gained permission to be in his Kingdom. As an aristocrat, he could speak on equal terms with the king and gained liberty to travel, and he was also given some land, right on the edge of the Kingdom.

When I traversed the Island of Iona, I was struck by two things; first that a Christian witness has been present for over 1,400 years and second, there seemed to be many New Age tourists and possibly priests, who had forgotten the New Testament principles instilled by the missionaries that established this base.

In this harsh windswept region on the edge of the known world, Celtic Christianity thrived, combining a love of Scripture, education and living in the supernatural realm of God. Many myths have grown about the life of Columba, yet the stories which form the basis for the books on his prophetic revelations, his miraculous powers and his visions of angels, written down a century after his life, contain a seed truth of New Testament Christianity. Signs and wonders were certainly witnessed, but having been compiled long after his death, we cannot be sure exactly what took place. Yet without doubt these events provide us with shadows of the real servant of God, who experienced things similar to the apostles, as recorded in the book of Acts.

Like the apostle Paul, Peter and Jesus, Columba exercised the gifts of the Holy Spirit, and just as the first Church thrived and spread through the miraculous power of the Holy Spirit, so too did the Church in Britain (1 Corinthians 12:4-11). Peter received visions from God which led to conversions (Acts 10:1-16), Paul saw a vision of a Macedonian calling for help (Acts 16:9), and Jesus foresaw Nathanael before he met him (John 1:47-51). Columba and the Celtic believers were the same and they always returned to the Scriptures, not visions, for doctrine.

The Irish Gaels had been colonising parts of Scotland for some time and whilst under the protection of the Kingdom of Dál Riata or on Iona, these missionaries and their new followers had a sense of safety. This gave them time to sow a biblical foundation, to establish Christianity in all of Scotland. "It was nothing less than one of the most dynamic engines of Christianity in the world," said Dan Snow of the mission base of Iona, and the monks brought with them, "the seed of a new civilisation."[2]

After setting up the community on Iona which thrived and became a centre of civilisation, by the late 560s, Columba risked his life again by crossing into pagan Pictland. Piercing through the darkness and dangers of entering a savage Kingdom, which dominated the east and north of Scotland, Columba believed his message could transform the Kingdom.

The land of the Picts, like Ireland before Patrick, was still in the Iron Age, with stone carvings instead of literature, brutish pagan rituals and the warlike tribes were so fierce that the Roman Emperor Hadrian (AD 76-138) ordered the construction of Hadrian's Wall to keep these barbarians out. The Picts refused to fight a conventional war with the Roman Empire, adopting guerrilla tactics that enabled them to inflict a defeat and disappear, and for this reason the Romans could never achieve supremacy. It was this land that Columba and his missionary band chose to enter, without protection, knowing that any angry warrior or tribe within, could capture, torture and kill them. It certainly was a dangerous mission into the pagan unknown ends of the earth.

As a miracle in and of itself, the team of missionaries crossed the land safely and stood before the gates of the pagan King Bridei, King of Fortriu, at his base in Inverness. The King of the Picts refused to hear their message, but through a series of miracles, the king changed his mind. Legend states Columba was barred from the city and by the miraculous intervention of God, the city gates opened, and the people within realised this new Divinity was the one and only true God. If something like this did happen, it mirrors the miracles which enabled Peter to keep on preaching (Acts 5:19).

"He established that the power of the King of kings (Jesus Christ) is greater than the King of the Picts," explains Dr James Fraser. "Columba and the Christian God has established their power...the greater of the two kings, the King of kings is brought to bare against the King of the Picts and there's only going to be one winner in that kind of confrontation. The King of the Picts is presented with this much more powerful force outside of his gates and he has no real opportunity to do anything, but to submit...There's an obvious power here that the Picts must recognise. This Divinity has got real power...this is a powerful religion, this is a powerful God."³

Nevertheless, the pagan druids or wizards, as some called them, realised they were the losers in this confrontation and refused to accept Columba's authority. As a Christian, Columba ordered the chief druid to free all slaves and he refused. Exactly what happened is lost in elaborate chronicles of a later age, but the result is self-evident – paganism was defeated and the Christian God was accepted as greater than all the other gods or spirits. From this encounter the message spread to the Picts that Christianity was a potent and muscular religion, with a great God, who cared about freeing the poorest person in the land and could break the power of the druids.

With Columba and his team now accepted into the heart of the Kingdom, modernity, prosperity and civilisation flourished. With Christianity thriving and uniting the peoples, the foundations were laid for the formation of the Kingdom of Scotland.

As a man of faith and education, Columba was able to help the King of the Picts build peaceful relationships with the wider world, and as a renowned man of letters, he is credited with writing several hymns and transcribing hundreds of books. "Celtic Christianity took off in a spectacular way all over the western British isles," explains Dr Robert Bedford, "creating a network of monasteries, which stretched from Iona in the north to the Bay of Biscay... against a background of traditionally Celtic culture, learning and literature flourished. What's more, these Celtic monasteries sent out missionaries."⁴

Germanic invaders had spiritually bankrupted England with their pagan darkness, but now the Celtic roots which survived the collapse re-emerged to reconnect England with its old faith. From these centres, Celtic missionaries marched throughout Scotland and into England to preach Jesus Christ. Meanwhile, Augustine landed in England seeking converts and won many.

Out of all the Anglo-Saxon territories, the Kingdom of Northumbria, in north east England and south east Scotland was to become powerful. King Edwin (586-633), ruled this Kingdom and converted to Christianity having been baptised in 627. His reign became far more peaceful, but he was killed in battle with pagans just six years later. The Kingdom was divided and King Oswald of Northumbria (604-642) desired to see it united.

Young Oswald was a man of deep faith. He spent years as an exile living in the Christian communities in Ireland and Iona, and there he converted to Christianity. He fled as a twelve year old boy and when he reached thirty, he was ready to return and was determined that the Kingdom of Northumbria was to be Christian in nature. He sent for missionaries and the first was too harsh and the people could not accept him, so a second was sent.

The Celtic missionary Aidan (590-651) believed the first mission expected too much, too soon from the pagans, and instead followed the example of Isaiah, seeking little by little, precept upon precept (Isaiah 28:10). Aidan was hugely successful as a preacher and history calls him Aidan of Lindisfarne, because he established a church on the island of Lindisfarne in 635 and it became a centre of civilisation, trade and learning, based upon Christianity.

King Oswald of Northumbria embraced the Christian faith to the full and he translated Aidan's sermons to share them with the rich and powerful in his Kingdom. Also, King Oswald prayed for a united Kingdom and he believed only God could give him the victory against the aggressors who had divided Northumbria.

Whilst deep in prayer, King Oswald received a vision of Columba, who had died over three decades previously, giving him a word from God, saying something similar to the words given to Joshua by the Lord, "Be strong and act manfully. Behold, I will be with thee. This coming night go out from your camp into battle, for the Lord has granted me that at this time, your foes shall be put to flight and Cadwallon your enemy shall be delivered into your hands, and you shall return victorious after battle and reign happily" (Joshua 1:9).

King Oswald shared his vision with his council and all agreed that if God gave them the victory, as the supernatural revelation explained, they would all convert to Christianity. Before the battle commenced, King Oswald knelt before a wooden cross he planted in front of all, and then he prayed to the Lord, asking for His aid, and King Oswald asked all his army to join in. He cried out, "Let us all kneel and jointly beseech the true and living God Almighty, in His mercy, to defend us from the haughty and fierce enemy; for He knows that we have undertaken a just war for the safety of our nation."[5]

The subsequent victory secured the future of Christianity in the north of England and southern Scotland, and from the new centres of faith, Celtic missionaries brought the gospel message to the British people. They taught confidence in the Scriptures, faith in Christ and they experienced the supernatural power of God in dreams, visions and revelations (Acts 2:17-18).

"Christianity had an enormous impact on all people in Anglo-Saxon society, at all levels," explains Professor Sarah Foot, "but I suppose one of the appeals about Christianity was it does offer an answer to that eternal question – why are we here, is this all there is, will there be anything afterwards? It offers a promise of eternal life and salvation beyond the life in this world, and perhaps an eternal life that is a little more egalitarian than the life they are living now in the world. And also of course, a heavenly existence that gets rid of social class distinctions in a way that pagan views of the after-world – which tend to perpetuate the idea that the warrior elite will have a particular enjoyable time in the afterlife – Christianity alters that view."[6]

"It's an absolutely fundamental change," says Professor Sarah Foot, "you could argue that there is really no aspect of life, at any social level in Anglo-Saxon England that isn't affected by the change to Christianity. People's worship patterns change! If they're going to follow the teaching of the Church, then they're going to start living their lives in different ways... it infiltrates every single aspect of daily life... The Church brings technologies unknown in England... everything about life in England is fundamentally changed. You could argue it was one of the most important things in the British Isles, in the first millennium – the conversion to Christianity."[7]

Wilfred of York (633-709), originally trained at Lindisfarne also reintroduced written law in England. "He's one of those people who are transforming the legal culture of Anglo-Saxon England," said Dr Martin Ryan, "the use of written documents like charters to prove possession of land. We see it at the same time, law codes coming into existence; the first law code at the start of the seventh century with the conversion to Christianity. We find charters surviving from Anglo-Saxon England from the 670s and 680s. So he's transforming the culture and its becoming a culture based upon the written word. Law is written now, so you need legal documents."[8]

Celtic Christianity, grounded in Scripture flourished in Ireland, Scotland, England and Wales, and the home-grown missionary endeavours enabled the pure gospel, which had been first brought to England along the Roman roads, to be transmitted all over Britain, to the various kingdoms and territories.

A nation which became filled with pagan darkness soon began producing the most outstanding works of art and literature, based upon the Bible. Art historian Dr Janina Ramirez said that the *Lindisfarne Gospels* are, "The finest piece of art from the Dark Ages and a national treasure... this one manuscript is the culmination of centuries of Anglo-Saxon endeavour." It shows elements of native Celtic and Roman Christianity. "Today the *Lindisfarne Gospels* are considered one of the world's greatest art works."[9]

Whilst in parts of Europe, the darkness of the legacy of the Germanic pagan expansion was still stifling progress, soon, a series of missions from Ireland and Britain would change the course of European history. Celtic Christianity was to spread from Ireland and Britain into Europe!

"One of the great things about Ireland in this period, is the relationship that it enjoyed with the European mainland," said Dr John Moreland, "and many, many scholars coming from the European mainland to attend and study in Irish monasteries; but of course, the other process going on – of Irish monasteries going out on a great wave of monastic foundations in Europe, in the early medieval period." It led to "the re-introduction of Christianity into many parts of continental Europe"[10] after the pagan invasions.

Celtic Christian monks, spearheading the pinnacle of European education, were called for and sent into Europe. They opened up monasteries and their books flourished in Europe. In France, their monastery at Luxeuil became the Oxford of its time and Bobbio in Italy became Cambridge, with a huge library. In St Gallen, Switzerland, an architectural blueprint for an Irish Celtic monastery was found – it's the only one known to survive since the fall of Rome. This was the foundation of a new civilisation in Europe, based upon Celtic Christian faith, education and design.

In Britain, the Celtic Golden Age created the greatest light of this period.[11] Whilst the Dark Age was deep in much of Europe, in Britain and Ireland, Celtic Christianity produced a civilisation far ahead of its time. At its peak the monks on Iona produced the *Book of Kells*, a masterpiece containing the four Gospels, which was the combination of the zenith of known science, literature and art coalesced. In this age, the *Book of Kells* was just as important and pioneering as the Moon Landing, the works of Shakespeare and the Mona Lisa combined. With light bursting forth all over Britain, people from Europe wanted to learn and train under the leadership of Celtic Christians.

"The English Golden Age shone and became a beacon which shone, not just in these islands, but across Europe too," said Dr Robert Bedford. "English missionaries masterminded Christianity's expansion into what was then pagan Austria and Germany." Alcuin of York (735-804), from the Kingdom of Northumbria, at the invitation of the King of the Franks Charlemagne (742-814) of Germany, became the leading scholar and teacher at the Carolingian Court of this new and vast European empire. He began to lead them in Christianity and law, and Charlemagne spread the faith around his empire. "The Holy

Roman Empire was the result," said Dr Robert Bedford, "a new Christian empire that would rule on the continent of Europe for a thousand years...English Christians had achieved so much and wielded so much influence over European affairs."[12]

However and this is a great however, Celtic Christianity did not survive to become the dominant Christian influence in Britain or Europe; in fact, it didn't survive at all. Two factors caused its downfall – the rise of a centralised religious authority in Rome, bringing all churches in Western Europe under its influence and the invasion of the Vikings into Britain from the north. To understand the former, we must evaluate the legacy of the first Christian emperor in Rome.

Chapter Six

Power and Pain

In AD 306, far off on the edge of the known world, in the Province of Britannia, one young Roman ruler was set to change the world. He bravely fought the Picts far into unknown Scotland and it was in York, England, where Constantine the Great (272-337) was proclaimed Augustus. A statue of him resides by York Minster Cathedral stating: 'Near this place, Constantine the Great was proclaimed Roman Emperor in 306. His recognition of the civil liberties of his Christian subjects and his own conversion to the faith established the religious foundations of Western Christendom.' However, he was not the only man who claimed the right to rule the entire Roman Empire. Michael Portillo, broadcaster and former Cabinet Minister explains, "Because of the enormity of the Empire, it had four co-rulers. Constantine governed Britain, Gaul and Spain,"[1] and now he wanted absolute rule over all the Roman Empire.

In 312, Constantine crossed his own Rubicon towards death or victory, and was on the outskirts of Rome, seeking to take control of the whole Empire from his surviving rival Maxentius (278-312). The historian James Gerrard tells us what happened next: 'The story that has survived centuries describes how Constantine, worried by the size of his enemy's army, sought aid from the gods and was rewarded by the appearance in the sky of a flaming cross. Later that night God came to the pagan Constantine in a dream and told him, "By this sign conquer." The next day when Constantine went into battle with Maxentius, his troops bore crosses on their shields and carried a Christian standard before them. They were victorious and Constantine, after another murderous bout of civil war, emerged as the sole and first Christian ruler of the Roman World.'[2]

The conversion of Constantine to Christianity was either the greatest triumph of Christianity over the Roman Empire, or its bleakest disaster. Critics tell us that having failed to persecute the Christian faith to death, Rome was able to give it all that was needed to corrupt it – money, power and political influence. Those who look to the good, tell us that Constantine stopped the violent and bitter persecution of Christians, enabled the slow transition of Europe from paganism towards Christianity, built churches, and brought the bishops together in peace to safeguard orthodoxy and enable the duplication of the validated Scriptures. By AD 313, the Edict of Milan legalised Christianity across the whole Empire and safeguarded toleration for all.

"The conversion of Constantine was the single most important political event in the history of the Church," argues Michael Portillo. According to his admirers, Constantine enabled the Christianisation of Europe. He brought Christian leaders together to identify the valid letters and books of the apostles, and he had fifty copies made to safeguard them; thus securing them for posterity. Additionally, the doctrines found in Scripture were debated and confirmed, "But what was Constantine's true intention?" asks Portillo.[3]

When I stood by Milvian Bridge, in Italy, the site of the great battle which led to the conversion of Constantine, it seemed peculiar that this one battle in Rome would eventually lead to the sinking of Celtic Christianity in Britain, and the demise of all the independent Christian witnesses in Western Europe. On the Triumphal Arch of Constantine, next to the Coliseum, which was dedicated in AD 315 to his victory, I saw no Christian symbols or mention of Jesus. Instead, there is a vague reference to the 'divine.' The vague wording of Constantine's inscription may be understood as his attempt to please all possible readers, being deliberately ambiguous, and acceptable to both the majority pagans and the minority Christian population. Still visible in Latin is: 'To the Emperor Caesar Flavius Constantinus, the greatest, pious and blessed Augustus: because he, inspired by the divine, and by the greatness of his mind, has delivered the state from the tyrant and all of his followers at the same time, with his army and just force of arms, the Senate and People of Rome have dedicated this arch, decorated with triumphs.'

Author and religious commentator Jonathan Bartley said, "This is one of the most tragic periods for Christianity. It completely changes the meaning of Christianity. For example, Christians go from loving their enemies, as Jesus told them to, to killing them on the battlefield and then praying for them. They go from setting slaves free to endorsing a system of slavery. They go from being opposed to torture, to actually being part of those who do the imprisoning. This is a complete one hundred and eighty degree turn. Under Constantine Christianity goes from being something which opposes the Empire, to being part of the Empire and then indeed, you have to be a Christian in order to be part of the Empire at all."[4]

Michael Portillo concluded about this historic transmutation

"Rather than Constantine converting the Empire to Christianity, it might be more accurate to say he converted Christianity to his needs as an emperor."[5]

At this point, Christians in the Roman Empire began to split into two groups; those who felt happy to be in power with Rome and the few, who felt the faith was being corrupted. Dr Caroline Humfress said, "Some Christians looked back to the early days of Christianity and they looked back to the time of the martyrs, and they believed the Empire should be separate from Christianity, and not everyone was delighted being in the centre of power."[6]

Like some of the leaders of Celtic Christianity in Britain, some followers of Jesus in the Roman Empire began to withdraw into the wilderness, rejecting its corrupt charm and sought purity. They decided it was better to become living martyrs, rejecting all power and wealth, to get to know God in the deserts and hills, and maybe return to preach, just as John the Baptist had. The monastic movement thus began, in protest.

For three hundred years Christians from Israel to Rome had worshipped in their homes, or underground, in simple sacrificial faith, but now the Emperor Constantine began building great churches in Rome. The largest monolithic church, called St John the Lateran, was built like a palace fit for Caesar, combining the opulence of Roman design with its aureate wealth. The historian Elizabeth Lev said, "Not only did he construct the enormous building, but he also gave beautiful marble columns, he gave forty golden and silver chandeliers for the nave, he gave silver plate, gold plate candle sticks. So he filled the church with beautiful objects."[7] It was all lavishly flamboyant, but what had happened to Jesus of Nazareth, a carpenter's son?

Beginning with the Church of St John the Lateran, the wealth of the Christian world, usually drawn from the poor, was soon being spent on church and cathedral building projects. A new age had dawned and it looked wonderful to the human eye, but did any of it sit comfortably with Scripture?

The apostles James warned that it is very easy for Christians to begin to deny the basic principles of their faith, to be 'in' with the rich and powerful. 'My brethren, do not hold the faith of our Lord Jesus Christ, the Lord of glory, with partiality. For if there should come into your assembly a man with gold rings, in fine apparel, and there should also come in a poor man in filthy clothes, and you pay attention to the one wearing the fine clothes and say to him, "You sit here in a good place," and say to the poor man, "You stand there," or, "Sit here at my footstool," have you not shown partiality among yourselves, and become judges with evil thoughts? Listen, my beloved brethren: Has God not chosen the poor of this world to be rich in faith and heirs of the Kingdom which He promised to those who love Him? But you have dishonoured the poor man. Do not the rich oppress you and drag you into the courts? Do they not blaspheme that noble name by which you are called?' (James 2:1-7).

In Celtic Britain and Ireland, Christians followed the path of self-denial and had spread this faith all across Britain, and exported it back into pagan areas of Europe. But now in Rome, a new kind of faith emerged from the emperor. After Constantine the Great, most of the emperors were Christians of a sort; only Julian (330-363) mounted a concerted action to re-instate paganism as the dominant religion. He failed to de-establish Christianity and by 392 Emperor Theodosius I (347-395) decreed that Christianity was to be the only legal religion of the Roman Empire. He banned pagan practices saying, "It is our will that all the peoples who are ruled by the administration of our clemency shall practice that religion which the divine Peter the Apostle transmitted to the Romans."[8]

But what about Celtic Christianity and all other free believers in Jesus Christ? Theodosius I introduces two ideas, first, Peter was the founder of the Church in Rome and second, all Christians have to follow Rome's centralised interpretation of Christianity, or be deemed 'insane' and 'heretical.' "The rest," Theodosius declared, "whom we adjudge demented and insane, shall sustain the infamy of heretical dogmas, their meeting places shall not receive the name of churches, and they shall be smitten first by divine vengeance and secondly by the retribution of our own initiative."[9]

Theodosius I helped invent the idea of Peter as the first Pope, as he ignored the fact that the Bible chronicles Paul was the first apostle in Rome. Paul ministered in the city for at least two years, laying the foundations for the Church (Acts 28:17-31). Theodosius also overlooked that Paul is the author of the Epistle to the Roman Christians. Meanwhile, Peter's letters were addressed to believers in modern day Turkey and Greece (1 Peter 1:1). Why did Theodosius invent the concept of a Pope? Centralised Christianity adopted by an absolute emperor, also needed an absolute Christian leader. If Roman emperors were going to harness Christianity for their own ends, they needed a centralised system which they could control.

When Rome was sacked in AD 410 by barbarians, a political and spiritual void was created by the weakened Roman leadership. Michael Portillo said, "Whilst in the East Church and state remained as one, in the West, Rome fell to the Barbarians and into that imperial vacuum stepped a new power that is still with us today, the Papacy."[10] From Theodosius' aided invention of a centralised faith, to the day Rome fell and the Bishop of Rome stepped into that void, the apostolic style of the New Testament was diminished in favour of following the Roman emperor's top down style of leadership.

Just as the Roman Republic gave way to an absolute emperor, so too, apostolic New Testament Christianity gave way to an absolute spiritual leader. "It enabled the Christian Church to develop a hierarchy very rapidly," explains Dr Caroline Humfress, "the Pope in Rome assumes a certain position, which is almost comparable to the one which the emperor has in the Roman world."[11]

The apostles were renegades in the Roman Empire, yet now future Popes ruled what was left of it. "In the Western Empire Constantine's legacy is the Roman Catholic Church," concluded Michael Portillo. "Having enjoyed the protection of Constantine, the Church was now strong enough to prosper in Rome, long after its protectors passed into history. In 476, the puppet Emperor Romulus Augustus was disposed. There were to be no more Roman emperors in the West, until Charlemagne in the year 800. It was the Christian Church that benefited. Into the void, left by the collapse of the Empire in the West, stepped the Pope...by the seventh century, the Papacy is the largest land owner on the Italian peninsula and its armies were fully prepared to defend, and advance those territories."[12]

The Roman Emperor was now lost to history and the office of Pope was created in its likeness. In the chaos that followed, the bishops of Rome forgot what the Bible declared – that Peter was given the charge to give the gospel to the Jews and Paul to the Gentiles, and one leader took charge of all the Church. 'When they saw that the gospel for the uncircumcised had been committed to me, as the gospel for the circumcised was to Peter (for He who worked effectively in Peter for the apostleship to the circumcised also worked effectively in me toward the Gentiles)' (Galatians 2:7-8).

The word Pope is a derivative of the Greek word father. In the first three centuries, this title was common for all bishops; by the sixth century it was commonly applied to the Bishop of Rome, and by the late eleventh century Pope Gregory VII (1015-1085) issued a declaration which claimed the title for Rome alone. The earliest record in English of the title Pope dates to the mid-tenth century.

The metamorphism of Christianity was undertaken by Emperor Constantine and Rome became the centre of Christianity, and Jerusalem, where the first council of the apostles was held was ignored (Acts 15). Pope's now ruled the Church, but investing power into one symbol of all spiritual authority, eventually led to the abuses of indulgences, the introduction of doctrines contradictory to the teaching of the apostles, the crusades, inquisitions and many Popes used the power of ex-communication to control governments all over Europe. If Rome was to rule, what was going to happen to Celtic Christianity?

Chapter Seven

Celtic or Catholic

In the modern world, Catholic and Protestant are words loaded with history, but in the days of the apostles both were not known. At first, the disciples of Jesus were called followers of 'The Way' (Acts 9:2), and at Antioch, they found a new name: 'The disciples were first called Christians in Antioch' (Acts 11:26). By the second century a Greek word, Katholikos, originally meaning universal, was adopted as a way of describing the entire Church, and by the time of Constantine the Great, this word evolved into Catholic, or 'the universal' Church of Christ. For the bishops of Rome by the time of Constantine, claiming the word Catholic meant claiming authority over all Christians, regardless of how they became followers of Jesus. Thus to be Catholic no longer meant to be part of the universal Church of Christ, but to be under the authority of Rome.

Meanwhile in Britain, a series of independent Celtic Christians centres were flourishing. By retreating into Cornwall, Wales, western England, Scotland and Ireland, the Celtic Christians survived the pagan Germanic invasions and re-evangelised Britain. Centres like Iona and Lindisfarne became instrumental for training local missionaries to reach the people of Britain, and yet each centre remained largely independent. For hundreds of years this form of Christianity thrived in Britain and Ireland, but the centralisation of Christianity towards Rome was to have a far reaching effect for Celtic Christianity.

"The Empire had gone," said the historian Dan Snow, "but the adopted religion of Christianity had survived with the Pope as its head in Rome. Where the Irish monasteries were self-governing, the Papacy was all for centralised control. It had inherited not only Rome's bureaucracy, but also its imperial ambitions. It was steadily expanding its authority in Europe, but its influence stopped short of Britain and Ireland. A new Pope, the ambitious Gregory the Great (540-604) was determined to change all that and to make it happen, he dispatched a Papal mission to Britain."[1]

At the time of this mission, Britain was a patchwork network of kingdoms, some pagans in the far south, others Christian in north east England, Wales, Scotland and Ireland. Columba had led the mission that brought Celtic Christianity back and restored it into Britain, but just as he died in 597, Augustine of Canterbury (545-605) arrived in southern England with a Roman centralised version of Christianity, with the Pope as its head.

Augustine of Canterbury, not to be confused with Augustine of Hippo (354-430), managed to secure a meeting with Ethelbert King of Kent (560-616). The king's wife was already a Christian, so Augustine's teaching was not new and he converted. The mission headed north into the Kingdom of Essex and St Paul's Church was built in London, but the mission struggled to convince people and St Paul's was later burnt down in a pagan backlash. After initial success, the mission came to a standstill, and almost all the advances made were quickly reversed. The greatest success was King Ethelbert's conversion and his new Christian law code, but his son and successor wavered between paganism and Christianity.

Augustine's greatest achievement was the mass baptism of ten thousand Anglo-Saxons, but their conversion shows all the signs of a political synthesis, rather than a hand-on-heart conversion. In the British Museum, the silver and gold buckle, originally from Crundale Down, Kent, tells another story.[2] Art historian Dr Janina Ramirez said, "In the British Museum is one of the best examples that shows how readily the Anglo-Saxons were prepared to follow both Christ and Wôdan...The silver and guilt belt buckle from Crundale Kent, is a serious piece of double-edged art." fusing pagan and Christian symbols. "This piece clearly shows it was made at a time when the Anglo-Saxons were hedging their bets; embracing Christianity and keeping hold of their pagan heritage...you can imagine the man who commissioned it – one week he is fasting for Easter, the next he is feasting for the goddess Ēostre."[3]

Augustine's mission came close to utter failure when he met with Celtic Christian leaders in Britain. Augustine knew of these native believers because Pope Gregory had proudly 'given him' authority over all the Celtic Christians, but he was surprised by their size and strength. He expected them all to quickly recognise the authority of the Pope, "but the Celtic Christians in the West rejected Augustine's Roman authority," explains Dr Robert Bedford.[4]

For Augustine this was tantamount to heresy and the exchange became bitter. "He really tried to bully them," explains Professor Nicholas Higham, "persuasion is not a strong enough word I think." In a reversal of his intention, the harsher and harder Augustine's claims were made, the more the Celtic Christians believed this man and all he stood for was not Christ-like, but imperial. "In this particular case they eventually say, 'No! You are not sufficiently a humble man for us to accept as our leader,' " said Professor Nicholas Higham. "They rejected him. The mission came extremely close to total failure."[5]

Celtic Christianity had more than half a millennia of living heritage in Britain, as it drew from almost six centuries of history. What they had received hundreds of years before was an independent witness of Christ, free from any tainted influence of the Roman Emperor Constantine, or any legacy from the Roman Empire. The heritage they embraced seemed quite different from the new concepts of a Pope, with centralised authority and a claim that Rome was still the centre of the world. "The problem with Augustine's Roman Christianity was that it was an alien force imposed on the people of Britain," said Dr Robert Bedford. "It was rejected by the people he came to convert and even by the Celtic Christians."[6]

Nevertheless, King Ethelbert's conversion was Augustine's great legacy, because at least one southern Kingdom in England would survive the Viking terror of the future, and the convictions sown into these hearts would live on. But in the present hour, a spiritual battle commenced for supremacy in Britain. Would the independent Celtic communities remain or would Roman Christianity, the legacy of the Roman Empire take charge?

In the north of England and southern Scotland, King Oswald of Northumbria (604-642) established his Kingdom as Christian and encouraged the Celtic missionary Aidan to send out missionaries to re-evangelise Britain. However, thirteen years after Aidan's death and twenty-two years after King Oswald's death, leaders from Rome met with Celtic Christian leaders at the Synod of Whitby, in Yorkshire, on the east coast of England to decide the future of Christianity in Britain.

The Synod of Whitby was not an obscure theological debate, which had no other meaning; it was as substantial European conference. It was the G7 of its day, and the questions being asked were as important as, "Should Britain join the European Union and the Euro?" If the answer was "Yes," British Christians would become part of a worldwide universal or Catholic Church, and like the European Union of today, there would be many benefits, and drawbacks. If accepted, British bishops could travel to Rome and sit as equals with Roman Catholic bishops, but to do this, they would have to give up their authority and the legacy of Celtic Christianity. Just like the European Union, any nation which wants to join has to give up their absolute claim on sovereignty to be in the club.

The Synod was held in the Kingdom of Northumbria, the most powerful Kingdom in Britain. King Oswiu (612-670) was now residing and he listened to the arguments put before him. Wilfrid (633-709) was born in Northumbria and studied at Lindisfarne, but he later studied in Rome, and he argued the case that Britain had to submit to the authority of Rome. Colmán of Lindisfarne (605-675) believed God had birthed Celtic Christianity and it must remain independent to Him.

Christianity was established in Britain by missionary minded prophets and apostles like Patrick and Columba, with signs following to confirm the Word, and now a politician was going to decide the future of the British Church!

The historian Bede tells us what happened. Wilfrid argued the Celtic Church was, "In obstinacy, I mean the Picts and the Britons, who foolishly, in these two remote islands of the world, and only in part even of them, oppose all the rest of the universe."[7] Colmán thought it was odd that a fellow believer would mock what God achieved in Britain, saying, "It is strange that you will call our labours foolish."[8] Wilfrid argued that the date of Easter, kept by the Celtic Church was out of sync with the testimony of Scripture.

For Colmán, he believed the signs and wonders given by God were the proof that God blessed them. "Is it to be believed that our most reverend Father Columba and his successors, men beloved by God, who kept Easter after the same manner, thought or acted contrary to the Divine writings?" he asked. "Whereas there were many among them, whose sanctity is testified by heavenly signs and the working of miracles, whose life, customs, and discipline I never cease to follow, not questioning their being saints in heaven."[9]

Colmán points to the central problem of Roman Christianity – it was for the Celtic believers, too worldly, lusting for power and undisciplined. It was the son of the Roman Empire; Christianity in Britain was the child of God, birthed by men and women led by the Holy Sprit to preach. But Wilfred for Rome warned all the Christians that they could find themselves outside the fold of Christ. "But as for you and your companions, you certainly sin, if, having heard the decrees of the Apostolic See, and of the universal Church, and that the same is confirmed by holy writ, you refuse to follow them. For, though your fathers were holy, do you think that their small number, in a corner of the remotest island, is to be preferred before the universal Church of Christ throughout the world?"[10]

"This is one of the most violent synods recorded in the Anglo-Saxon Church and it certainly sounds as if tempers did get quite hot," said Professor Sarah Foot. "There's a phenomenal amount at stake here. Making a decision about when you should celebrate the central festival of the Christian religion, there's nothing bigger…it's making a decision if you want to side with Iona and the Church in Ireland, or whether you want to join the European cultural mainstream."[11]

'Conflict between the Roman and Celtic Churches in Britain was inevitable,' explains the historian and expert on Anglo-Saxon England, Peter Hunter Blair. 'During its long period of isolation the Celtic Church had developed in complete independence and had diverged considerably from the paths followed by Rome, not merely in the matters of form and ritual, but more fundamentally in its whole organisation. Rome could not readily brook the continued existence of what it regarded as schismatic ways and still less could it contemplate so large a Christian community which showed remarkable missionary zeal should not recognise the Pope as its spiritual head. But on the other side, the Celtic Church, as some of its members realized, could not afford to ignore the benefits which Rome, representing by far the greater part of Christendom, had to offer.'[12]

For half a millennia Celtic Christians were free, some having been led by their spiritual leaders of austere, sacrificial faith. These servants of God proved the power of God was working through them in miracles. The prophets of the Bible and the apostles taught that spiritual leadership could not be inherited, like a title, but had to be proved by God's power working through you. Paul's case that he was not an "inferior" apostle, as some had taught (because he had not met Jesus in the flesh), because the signs and wonders God had sent through him were his evidence. 'Truly the signs of an apostle were accomplished among you with all perseverance, in signs and wonders and mighty deeds' (2 Corinthians 12:12-13). Paul argued that clever people can win debates, yet God confirms His Word by sending signs and miracles. 'My speech and my preaching were not with persuasive words of human wisdom, but in demonstration of the Spirit and of power, that your faith should not be in the wisdom of men but in the power of God' (1 Corinthians 2:4-5).

However, the future of Christianity in Britain was in the hands of a king and he had more than theology to concern himself with. King Oswiu ruled in favour of Rome, when he became convinced of the doctrine that Peter was the first Pope and the Rock of the Church (Matthew 16:18-19). "He's clearly trying to ingratiate himself with the Pope in Rome," said Professor Sarah Foot, "there's a correspondence with the Pope and his decision means he is siding permanently on behalf of the Roman Church...it makes the date of Easter the same all the way across Western Europe. It's like making a decision to join a central European currency; it's a currency of faith."[13]

A king decided the fate of Christianity in Britain and the leaders of the Celtic Church retreated into obscurity. Celtic Christianity, originally founded on New Testament principles, was dying and it would soon be dead. Perhaps they had strayed from the founding principles of the faith, or it was a time of falling away in the Church. Nevertheless, the Celtic legacy in art, literature and faith would hang on for at least two centuries, but it suffered a two-fold death – foreign spiritual supremacy from the south and pagan invasions from the north.

With Celtic Christianity giving way to Roman Christianity, a new form of Church building spread across Britain. Dr Janina Ramirez said, "A century after St Augustine landed, stone symbols of the Christian faith began to dominate the landscape. In the wooden world of the Anglo-Saxons, stone crosses made a big impact. This proved to be an effective advertising campaign, one that definitely said paganism was fading away and Christianity was here to stay. New churches and Abbey's sprung up throughout the Anglo-Saxon lands."[14]

St Martin's Church in Canterbury is the oldest stone church in Britain and is still in use, with a history of worship stretching back at least fourteen hundred years. The building resides where an ancient church once stood and it was renovated in stone by 580 As the building pre-dated Augustine's mission, he chose it as his base camp. Nearly sixty years later, Augustine's work resulted in the second stone church in Britain, called the Chapel of St Peter-on-the-Wall, in Bradwell-on-Sea, Essex, which was mentioned by Bede.[15] This was the beginning of the new architectural appearance of Britain, with stone church buildings dotted all over the land.

After the initial wave of missionaries from Rome, others followed and the grip of Roman faith on the nation began to take hold. The Celtic believers had lost out to an internationally recognised faith, and as each year passed, people gave up a little of their history, to embrace the new European way of doing things. As Roman traditions were introduced the apostolic legacy was lost further in rituals, relics, ceremonies and hierarchies.

Wilfred was the great winner in this battle between Celtic faith and Roman faith, and to the winner went the spoils! "Along with their rules, relics and architecture came the Roman Church's pomp and hierarchy," said Dr Janina Ramirez. "Wilfrid's lavish ostentation was in stark contrast to the Spartan lives of the Celtic monks of Skellig. Wilfrid was a foretaste of what monasteries and the monks who ran them would become. Hexham Abbey was his palace. He would have dressed like a king, wearing the brightest vestments made of the finest fabrics and silk brought in from the Continent. He even had his throne made, modelled on the sorts of thrones he'd seen from abbots and bishops in France. I don't think it's a coincidence that he had it made of reclaimed Roman stone. The Roman Empire has now become the Christian Roman Empire. Romulus and Remus have been replaced by Peter and Paul, and a bishop is now a spiritual king."[16]

Celtic Christianity had long suffered from the exchange with the Roman brand of faith, and its biblical heritage was watered-down as each generation tried to adopt the ways of their sophisticated European neighbours. But now the whole of Christianity in Britain was obliged to be inside Europe and to submit to the European way of doing things, and the heritage of the faith of the disciples from Israel and the Middle East began to fade. Nevertheless the centralised order of the Roman brand of the faith enabled new scholarship to thrive.

The Venerable Bede was convinced of the good the Roman faith could bring and in his book *The Ecclesiastical History of the English*, which was completed in 731, the Celtic Christians were regarded with suspicion. Bede served in the Christian Kingdom of Northumbria as a monk and due to his historical writings he gained the title of The Father of English History.

In his book Bede presented a prophetic vision that the various kingdoms of England were destined by God to be one united nation, defined by Christianity. The historian Professor Diarmaid MacCulloch said, "It was a monk who first applied this concept of a nation chosen by God to the English, before the English as a people even existed." In Jarrow, Sunderland, "in what was the Anglo-Saxon Kingdom of Northumbria, the idea of England as God's chosen nation really began with the work of a monk who was the greatest historian of his age," he said. "His name was Bede and in the course of his life as a monk he wrote books that more than anything else shaped the soul of the English...what Bede wrote here did nothing less than invent the English...what's intriguing about this history, is that Bede was describing something that doesn't actually exist...the Anglo-Saxon world wasn't a single nation, England, but a collection of kingdoms ruled by warlords, repeatedly at each others throats. Until Bede wrote this history there was no such thing as the English. Even less a people united by God."[17]

When Bede read the Bible's description of Solomon's Temple he "saw meaning for his own land," explains Professor Diarmaid MacCulloch, "it had been built after once warring tribes were united into one holy nation, chosen by God, Israel, and from that unity followed wealth and God's protection. Now all that resonated with Bede and now he applied it to his own people. So Bede gave the Angles, the English, the idea that they would be a chosen people. It was a vision rich with possibilities. But a vision was all it was. It just needed someone to take it out of the dusty library and make it real and one of England's greatest mediaeval leaders did just that. Alfred the Great."[18]

Celtic Christianity had seeded Christianity back into Britain and Europe, "but then, at the very height of their success, disaster struck," said Dr Robert Bedford.[19] Roman Christianity was now the accepted brand and from the north fierce Viking warriors began landing in Britain, attacking all. The monasteries, as centres of civilisation were targeted and Iona was sacked several times. The Vikings showed no mercy to the Lord's servants and on one raid they took sixty-eight monks to the beach at Iona and brutally murdered them. Within fifty years of the first Viking attack on Iona in 794, its light was snuffed out. "Even Lindisfarne was sacked," explains Dr Robert Bedford, "by the 870s, only the Kingdom of Wessex survived. It was ruled by a man who would become a national hero. His name was Alfred. There seems for Alfred, there was no doubt this was not your usual Dark Age squabble. It was an apocalyptic battle between the forces of good and the forces of evil. A battle for the very survival of Christian England."[20]

Chapter Eight

Alfred the Great

Throughout the centuries many kings in the divided kingdoms in Britain converted to Christianity, beginning with King Ethelbert in 597. There were several pagan lapses and by the 870s, the entire legacy of Christianity in the nation was about to be completely eradicated. Only one king was standing and he was hiding in the marshes of southern England. The pagan Viking attacks beginning in the north of Britain were catastrophic for Celtic and Roman Christianity, and for all the Anglo-Saxons and Celts. One by one, all the great kingdoms of the nation fell.

Alfred, King of Wessex was the last king standing in England and he was in retreat, running for his life. Whilst he hid in the marshes in Somerset, he gave himself to prayer and pondered why the Christian kingdoms of Britain had fallen to the pagans. His conclusion was that God Almighty had no use for a backslidden, half-hearted compromise between Christianity, worldliness and the remnants of paganism. In his view, Christians and their kings had not served the God of the Bible and for this reason His protection was removed from them. What God needs a people who claim to serve Him, but in practice rebel? How can a Christian Kingdom truly represent its God, whilst they remain ignorant or scornful of His will? "Alfred was convinced there could be no victory without God," explains Professor Diarmaid MacCulloch.[1]

One ancient thousand year old account tells us what happened when Alfred prayed about the collapse of the Christian kingdoms of Britain. Whilst he was on the run King Alfred showed kindness to a strange visitor who was in need, and he later believed that this needy 'man' was sent from heaven because Alfred was shaken by what he said (Hebrews 13:2).

The chronicler relays this account: 'Alfred alone lay awake in his bed, thinking with a sad heart of his sufferings and exile, and wondering much about the stranger and the unexpected draught of fishes. With a sudden a light from heaven, brighter than the beams of the sun, shone upon his bed. Struck with terror, he forgot all his former anxieties and looked in amazement on the brightness of the light. In the midst of which there appeared an elderly man, bearing the clerical fillet on his black locks, but having a most benignant look, and bearing in his right hand a copy of the Holy Gospels, adorned most marvellously with gold and jewels. He advanced and calmed the fears of the astonished king with these words, "Let not the brilliancy of my coming disturb you, beloved King Alfred, nor the fear of barbarian cruelty any longer harass you. For God, who does not despise the groans of His poor servants, will soon put an end to your troubles, and I, from henceforth, will be your constant helper."

'The king was comforted by these words and asked him earnestly who he was, and why he had come. Then the elderly man, smiling, said, "I am he to whom you this day ordered bread to be given; but I took not so much pleasure in the bread and wine, as in the devotion of your soul. But, whereas you ask me my name, know that I am Cuthbert, the servant of God, and am sent to explain to you, in familiar terms, how you may be relieved from the persecution, which has so long afflicted you." '[2]

When Alfred was in trouble and all the kingdoms of Britain were almost lost, he received a vision of the former Bishop of Lindisfarne, who served during the Celtic Golden Age in Britain. Cuthbert (634-687) was born in southern Scotland and served in the Church in the Northumbrian Kingdom, in the austere Celtic tradition. Cuthbert moved in signs and wonders, and like many in the Celtic Church balanced a belief in Divine inspiration from God in dreams and visions for his personal revelation, with a solid commitment to Scripture for orthodoxy.

King Alfred shared the same outlook – a commitment to the Scriptures for all doctrine and a belief in personal revelation from God. In the vision Alfred received, Cuthbert told him that God would eventually unify the whole of Britain because of his legacy. He said, "I advise you to cherish mercy and justice, and to teach them to your sons above everything else, seeing that at your prayer God has granted to you the disposal of the whole of Britain... Now put off your fears and inactivity, and as soon as tomorrow's light shall dawn, cross over to the nearest shore, and blow loudly with your horn three times. And as wax melts before the heat of the fire, so by your blasts shall the pride of your enemies, with God's will, be dissolved, and the courage of your friends be aroused."[3]

King Alfred followed the leading he received and like the Old Testament heroes, prepared his men to fight (Joshua 6:4). He spoke these words to the soldiers before the great battle to save England from complete Viking domination, "Let us be faithful to God, eschew evil, love the practice of virtue and so shall we everywhere experience the benefit of His protection."[4]

After a period of preparation, King Alfred, with deep repentance in prayer, led his new army out to battle, in the name of saving Christianity in the nation, to honour God. It was May 878 and in the Battle of Edington, an army of the Anglo-Saxon Kingdom of Wessex, under its newly committed Christian king, defeated the heathen army led by Guthrum. Alfred, in the name of God, not only saved Wessex, he saved England and Christianity in Britain.

The Vikings came as close as anyone ever had, to destroying Christianity in Britain. But God answered King Alfred's prayers and from now on, England was to be a true Christian nation, with the Bible at the heart of its law, culture, religion and identity.

After his victory over the Vikings, King Alfred could have continued in the pagan traditions and killed his enemies, but as a Christian, he followed the teaching of Christ, to love his enemies and do good to those that hurt you (Matthew 5:44).

King Alfred invited Guthrum, his defeated pagan foe and many of his dishevelled enemies to a twelve day celebration, where they were honoured. When it was all over, Guthrum and his men left the celebration as baptised Christians! Guthrum's pagan tribe renounced their god Wôdan and worshipped Jesus Christ from then on, laying the bedrock for a Christian England to emerge.

Under the terms of the Treaty of Wedmore in 878, the Viking Guthrum returned to his Kingdom in East Anglia, as a believer in Jesus Christ, and his new faith in God helped the two Kingdoms live in peace. England now had one common belief which united the two great Kingdoms – Christianity, and this faith laid the foundations for the future unification of the two Kingdoms into one, called England.

Winston Churchill (1874-1965) explains the significance of King Alfred's victory: 'The Christians, before they endured any such distress, by the inspiration of heaven judged it to be better either to suffer death or to gain the victory...if the West Saxons had been beaten, all England would have sunk into heathen anarchy. Since they were victorious the hope still burned for a civilised Christian existence in this Island.'[5]

To be a civilised people Alfred introduced the rule of law and sought to develop his Kingdom along biblical lines, and this had a significant impact on the pagan converts: 'The Christian culture of his Court sharply contrasted with the feckless barbarism of Viking life,' explains Winston Churchill. 'The older race was to tame the warriors and teach them the arts of peace, and show them the value of a settled common existence. We are watching the birth of a nation. The result of Alfred's work was the future mingling of Saxon and Dane in a common Christian England.'[6]

King Alfred built forts all around his Kingdom in England and began the process of developing the foundations of a coherent, peaceful land, based on the rule of law, sourced from the Bible. Professor Diarmaid MacCulloch explains Alfred believed God "would look with much favour on the nation if it knew His laws and obeyed them. Alfred's solution was to draw up a law code based on the Old Testament." His conviction was, "Keep God's laws and God will defend you against His enemies. In this cold northern island a new biblical identity was beginning to set firm."[7]

One fifth of King Alfred's law code, entitled the *Doom Book* – the Anglo-Saxon for law or judgment, contains King Alfred's introduction concerning his reasons for establishing a Kingdom based on Christianity. He directly copied Scripture, transcribing it into his law. He includes as foundational, the English translation of the Ten Commandments, plus several chapters from the book of Exodus. Alfred enabled England to embrace in law, the principle of justice for all and codified rules for justice which are still unavailable for most in the world today.

"You shall not circulate a false report. Do not put your hand with the wicked to be an unrighteous witness. You shall not follow a crowd to do evil; nor shall you testify in a dispute so as to turn aside after many to pervert justice. You shall not show partiality to a poor man in his dispute…and you shall take no bribe, for a bribe blinds the discerning and perverts the words of the righteous" (Exodus 23:1-3, 8).

England's law was defined by the Bible and impartial justice was at its heart. King Alfred also noted that his Kingdom was not to be Jewish in nature, but Christian, as he cites the letter written by the apostles to the Gentile believers in Jesus Christ from Acts 15:23-29. This explains that Christians are not expected to follow Jewish tradition. King Alfred divided his codes into precisely 120 chapters, a number with symbolic medieval biblical significance – being the age of Moses' death.

King Alfred embraced the principle of the Lord Jesus, "Do unto others as you would that they should do unto you" (Luke 6:31), and tried to simplify the concept for his uneducated people and make it law. This is how Alfred taught it to his people, "What ye will that other men should not do to you, that do ye not to other men." Alfred told them, "By bearing this precept in mind a judge can do justice to all men; he needs no other law books. Let him think of himself as the plaintiff and consider what judgment would satisfy him."

On my visit to Winchester, I found an idealised city with an ancient heart. Near the river stands the substantial statue of King

Alfred the Great, with his sword held high in the air, to remember his victory and the sword of justice which he brought to England. In Winchester Cathedral, it is still possible to find the oldest parts of this place of worship in the crypt, dating back over a thousand years, and in the Old Minster, King Alfred the Great was buried. Jane Austin and Mary Tudor were also buried in the Cathedral.

"Winchester was his capital city," said Dr Janina Ramirez, "under Alfred, Winchester became the very model of Anglo-Saxon civilisation; a place where art and culture would flourish. During his reign King Alfred introduced many new concepts we take for granted today," laying the solid foundations for a vibrant and civilised state. "During his twenty-eight years on the throne, Alfred made the building of new churches and monasteries a priority," explains Dr Janina Ramirez. "The Church and his faith was very important to Alfred, he believed the reason the Vikings had come to rape and pillage his land was simple; his people were not pious enough."[8]

King Alfred dreamed of the Celtic Golden Age in Britain and held a romantic view of how great the kingdoms of the nation had been. Britain, due to its biblical faith was once at the forefront of technology, science, learning, literature and art when Christianity flourished in the Celtic Age, and people had come from all over Europe to learn in Ireland and Britain. Now Alfred wanted the dark cloud of paganism over England to lift in the name of Jesus Christ, to set the nation on the path towards being once again, a Christian civilisation.

King Alfred wrote the following: 'Let it be known to thee that it has very often come into my mind, what wise men there formerly were throughout England, both of sacred and secular orders. And what happy times there were then throughout England; and how the kings who had power of the nation in those days obeyed God and His ministers. They preserved peace, morality and order at home, and at the same time enlarged their territory abroad. How they prospered both with war and with wisdom. And also the sacred orders, how zealous they were both in teaching and learning, and in all the services they owed to God. And how foreigners came to this land in search of wisdom and instruction, and how we should now have to get from abroad if we would have them.'[9]

Alfred was saddened that England was forced to look towards Europe for education and instruction, but he was grateful for the help received. 'So general was its decay in England that there were very few on this side of the Humber who could understand their rituals in English, or translate a letter from Latin into

English,' lamented Alfred, 'there were so few that I cannot remember a single one south of the Thames when I came to the throne. Thanks be to God Almighty that we have teachers among us now. And therefore I command thee to do as I believe thou art willing, to disengage thyself from worldly matters as often as thou canst, that thou mayst apply the wisdom which God has given thee wherever thou canst. Consider what punishments would come upon us on account of this world, if we neither loved it ourselves nor suffered other men to obtain it. We should love the name only of Christian.'[10]

We remember King Alfred as the monarch who saved England and laid the foundations for a civilised Christian Britain, but during his reign, he lived through a true dark age, as the nation recovered from the pagan invasions. He dreamt of that lost Celtic Golden Age, writing: 'When I considered all this I remembered also how I saw, before it had been all ravaged and burnt, how the churches throughout the whole of England stood filled with books, and there was also a great multitude of God's servants.' But sin led to the downfall of England. Alfred wrote: 'They had said, "Our forefathers, who formerly held these places, loved wisdom, and through it they obtained wealth and bequeathed it to us. In this we can still see their tracks, but we cannot follow them, and therefore have we lost all the wealth and the wisdom, because we would not incline our hearts after their example."'[11]

Alfred was convinced the laws of God had to be translated into English, so all people could hear and understand the will of God. He concluded: 'Then I remember how the law was first known in Hebrew and again, when the Greeks had learnt it, they translated the whole of it into their own language, and all other books besides. And again, the Romans, when they had learnt it, they translated the whole of it through learned translators into their own language. And also all other Christian nations translated a part of them into their own language. Therefore it seems better to me, if ye think so, for us also to translate some books which are most needful for all men to know, into the language which we can all understand.'[12]

King Alfred is the only monarch in British history with the epitaph, 'The Great,' because his victory over the pagan armies saved the nation, and made sure that England was to be a Christian nation. "The battle achieved something else too," said Dr Robert Bedford, "it started the political unification of England. The Christian unity of the English people…was now a political reality. What was a religious and cultural community now became one nation, with one religion at its heart…These are the ideas that created not just England, but the nation [of Britain] which we know today. Our links to Alfred's Kingdom are deep. We owe to it – not just the monarchy and the Church, but the jury system, common law, even the counties we live in today. As a political entity, Hampshire is older than France...Those Dark Ages gave us a sense of national identity – one state, one language and up until recently, one religion. You don't find that in many countries, but you do in Britain because of what happened all those years ago. When out of the chaos and violence which followed the collapse of the Roman Empire, the peoples of Britain created a new idea of themselves, a Christian identity, which has made us what we are today. That's why I believe the Dark Ages are the most important in our history."[13]

King Alfred embraced a grand vision for the future of all the British kingdoms, working together as one, fused by Christianity. Professor Diarmaid MacCulloch said, "Alfred defeated the Vikings and he began to see himself, not as the king of one petty region, amidst a confusion of peoples, but as leading a whole chosen nation, bound by God's laws and only a quarter century after Alfred's death, it fell to his grandson, Athelstan, finally to make Bede proud. He transformed Bede's vision of a united English people from fantasy into reality. Athelstan was crowned with a new title – King of England. So it was an idea which created England, a biblical idea."[14]

Chapter Nine

The Three Hundred Year Prophecy

King Alfred was the first great Christian King of England and his heirs expanded their power base with victories and defeats, until Alfred's great grandson King Edgar the Peaceful (943-975), consolidated the political unity achieved by his predecessors. England was now one peaceful nation, committed to Christianity.

Edgar's son, still only a child, was on the throne when more Danish invasions commenced. By 1013, a full invasion force led to him fleeing the nation and England came under Scandinavian rule or influence for almost three decades. Deliverance came when the exiled Edward the Confessor (1003-1066) peacefully took the throne. Much of his reign was benign and prosperous, leading to two decades of peace, keeping hostile foreign enemies at bay. He is remembered for being unworldly and pious, and desired to go on Christian pilgrimage. When he was unable to go, he gave the money for the relief of the poor and for the building of Westminster Abbey.

Edward the Confessor was a praying man who never forgot His devotion and vows to God whilst he was in exile. Shakespeare called him, "The most pious Edward,"[1] and the king was concerned that England was still not faithful to Christianity. He wanted to lead England, like King Josiah of Judah had led his people, to renew their covenants with God, and turn away from sin and idolatry. 'The king stood by the pillar and renewed the covenant in the presence of the Lord – to follow the Lord and keep His commands, statutes and decrees with all his heart and all his soul...then all the people pledged themselves to the covenant' (2 Kings 23:3).

There was no sign of repentance in England and whilst confined to his deathbed in January 1066, Edward the Confessor prayed earnestly about England, and a servant of God testified to seeing him in spiritual ecstasy.[2] Then, in a vision, he saw two pious monks he recalled from his youth, who told him what was to happen to England in future centuries. They said, "The extreme corruption and wickedness of the English nation has provoked the just anger of God. When malice shall have reached the fullness of its measure, God will, in His wrath, send to the English people wicked spirits, who will punish and afflict them with great severity, by separating the green tree from its parent stem, the length of three furlongs. But at last this same tree, through the compassionate mercy of God, and without any national assistance, shall return to its original root, reflourish and bear abundant fruit."[3]

The vision awakened him and he told it to the Archbishop of Canterbury and to Harold II (1022-1066), his heir-apparent, who was praying beside his bed. The Green Tree Prophecy contained a warning that England had not shown true repentance, and was taking it for granted that God delivered them from foreign dominion, and soon they would once again be conquered by foreigners.

King Edward the Confessor died on 5 January 1066 and a year and a day later, the Norman King William the Conqueror (1028-1087) was crowned King of England. After invading the nation, he defeated Harold II, who was the last Anglo-Saxon King of England. Tradition states he died after an arrow struck him in the eye and the Anglo-Saxon legacy of a few electing their leader ceased. The House of Wessex, which had covenanted with God, but was no longer faithful to that covenant, was overthrown. Like King Saul, the Divine sword fell and cut-off the heritage.

William the Conqueror eliminated the English aristocracy and churches were brought dramatically in line with Rome. At the Council of Winchester in 1070, the Archbishop of Canterbury was deposed, most probably for refusing to crown William, which would make William's reign legitimate and legal.

The famous *Domesday* book explains how English landowners were evicted and within twenty years, ninety-five percent of English land was owned by foreign invaders. In 1120, William of Malmesbury wrote: 'We have experienced the truth of this prophecy, for England has become the habitation of outsiders and the dominion of foreigners. Today, no Englishman is earl, bishop, or abbot, and newcomers gnaw away at the riches and the very innards of England; nor is there any hope for an end of the misery.'[4]

The Anglo-Saxon shires, with subdivisions were abolished and this relatively sophisticated system gave way to European top-down rule, as land was divided into manageable administrative units. French, which the Normans had adopted, became the official language and the common people, who spoke Middle English, were unable to understand the language of the state or Church.

Another legacy of William was to introduce serfdom and the feudalistic system. The widespread mosaic patchwork of English landowners was replaced with feudal lords, who were given land of up to eighteen hundred acres, including a village, manor house and church. Most common people became peasants and serfs under their feudal lord's control. Serfdom was practically slavery, as the peasants struggled in abject poverty to provide for their feudal lords and corrupt bishops who lived in luxury. Serfdom began to lose influence after three hundred years, beginning in 1347, with the Black Death.

Thus the Green Tree Prophecy was fulfilled as English land and religion became dominated by foreigners, committed to turning England into a carbon-copy of Europe, eliminating the last vestiges of Celtic and New Testament Christianity. For three hundred years the prophecy stated England was to be in this predicament: 'By separating the green tree from its parent stem, the length of three furlongs.'

As the prophecy predicted, it took three centuries for kings in England to become English in nature and for the English language to re-emerge at court. The nation was also dragged into expensive contests in parts of France for lands and titles, and the crusades commanded by the Pope, which targeted Christians in Byzantine, Jews, as well as Muslims. Meanwhile, the Norman rulers brutalised the people of England, Wales and Scotland, sowing the seeds of future discord.

Three centuries after the death of Edward the Confessor a distinct English culture and its language began to emerge. King Edward III (1312-1377) outlived the Green Tree Prophecy to transform England into one of the most formidable military powers in Europe. By the reign of King Henry IV (1399–1413), English replaced French as the mother tongue of the monarch and he was the first king since Henry II in 1066, to take his oath in the English language.

In the field of religion in 1382, a law was passed which made it illegal for the Pope to give foreigners clerical positions and in the same year, John Wycliffe (1330-1384) finished the first complete English translation of the Bible from the Latin Vulgate. Now people could read the Bible and test the teaching they received, and the Lollards inspired by Wycliffe, embraced God in a fresh way, preaching liberty in Christ to all who would heed them. The slow return to New Testament Christianity thus began.

Chapter Ten

Medieval Life

The Normans who invaded England in 1066 were originally Vikings from Scandinavia, who had been given French lands in 911 in a bid to stop Viking attacks. The land of the 'north men' became Normandy. William's ancestors had burned and looted churches, but now he invaded England with a Papal Banner giving him authority to conquer the nation, and kill Anglo-Saxon England, in a 'holy crusade' blessed by the Pope.

During the three hundred year period of Norman domination in England, many kings enforced a heavy tax burden upon rich and poor alike, to fund expensive wars and campaigns in France. One of these tyrannical kings was the despotical King John (1166-1216), who lost England's French possession in the Angevin Empire, and due to his oppressive regime, he was forced to accept a binding charter of Christian liberty.

Magna Carta, accepted in 1215, is the first document in the British Constitution and it commences with a legal right for Christian liberty – that churches should be free from government interference. 'First, that we have granted to God, and by this present charter have confirmed for us and our heirs in perpetuity, that the English Church shall be free, and shall have its rights undiminished, and its liberties unimpaired.'[1]

This law established that with freedom to worship, there was to be other liberties enshrined in the clauses including – the right to life, protection from false imprisonment and abusive taxation, and property rights etc. Dr David Starkey said that some of the clauses of Magna Carta "may seem remote now, but they established what half the world from Russia to China still lacks – that the state can't help itself to private property at will...there is something here that really matters. The sense that Magna Carta protects and defines those three key fundamental freedoms of the Anglo-Saxon world: life, liberty and property."[2]

Magna Carta also laid the foundations which later enabled a Parliament to form and democracy to emerge. Dr David Starkey said, "The demands of the Great Charter led to an assembly of bishops and barons, who met to approve taxation and sanction its collection. This assembly was the embryo of the modern Parliament, with its two houses of Lords and Commons...

monarchs also found themselves grappling with a new idea, of a legal system whose first home was Westminster Hall. Magna Carta called for professional judges and a fixed place for the law courts; before, kings administered justice themselves and the courts moved the king. Magna Carta changed that. The king's law was becoming the common law of England."[3]

The second magnificent legacy of the Christian Constitution of Britain was established by the principles laid out in the Provisions of Oxford and Westminster of 1258-9. Simon de Montfort (1208-1265) challenged the corrupt King Henry III (1207-1272), to act justly and love God wholeheartedly. Simon wanted England to remain covenanted to God and said to the king, "Who could ever believe that you are a Christian? Have you never been to confession?" The king replied, "I have indeed," and Simon rebutted him, "What good is confession without repentance and atonement?"[4]

Under pressure, the king accepted a new way of governing England, as outlined in the Provisions of Oxford, which made the king share power and provided greater accountability. "This is one of the most important documents in British history," said the historian Dan Jones, "everybody thinks of Magna Carta as the great bill which limited king's power, but the Provisions of Oxford are actually more extreme." Twenty-four leaders were chosen to manage the affairs of England with the king, and "Parliament will meet three times a year, whether or not the king summons it."[5]

Simon believed England's new Constitution could only be safeguarded if the king and the leaders of the nation made a solemn covenant with God, which they made in Blackfriars Church in Oxford. "The barons demand that everyone swears an oath before God to abide by the provisions," said Dan Jones, "the problem is Henry's and Simon's attitudes to the oath are polls apart. Everyone knows that Plantagenet kings and their barons have a long history of breaking their oaths, but for Simon, once he's made a sacred oath with God, he's really boxed himself into a corner."[6] A chronicler tells us: 'Each one swore on the holy Gospels that he, for the glory of God and in loyalty to the king, and for the benefit of the Kingdom' made the oath.[7]

Just as the kings of Israel made covenants with God for the future of their nation, so too Simon committed England to God in a solemn covenant, which he could never allow to be broken. However the king quickly broke his oath and war was the result. Simon's men "truly believe that God is on their side," said Dan Jones, embracing "a dream of a different kind of England where the king no longer calls the shots. Henry is fighting for the absolute supremacy of the king. Simon may have God on his side, but the king has far more men," but Simon's men won and "for the first time in England, a political movement succeeded in crushing a tyrannical king."[8]

The result was the first elected Parliament in England, as they met at the Palace of Westminster in 1265. By 1295, the Model Parliament embedded the concept of elected representatives further. The English Parliament followed the example of Moses, who encouraged representatives from the people to be heard. Moses said, "I spoke to you at that time, saying: 'How can I alone bear your problems and your burdens and your complaints? Choose [yes, choose], wise, understanding, and knowledgeable men from among your tribes, and I will make them heads over you' " (Deuteronomy 1:11-13).

Tyrannical monarchs in the future would ignore some of these principles, but as the gradual transition from absolute monarch to democracy commenced, all would in time, look back to Magna Carta of 1215 and the Provisions of Oxford of 1258.

Nevertheless, life in the Middle Ages for the common people could be short and painful. Loss of life was all around them and with no access to modern medication, an insignificant problem could lead to another life lost. With death ever-present, people were very aware of the claims of eternity upon them, and even though most could not read the Bible for themselves, the murals on church walls and story telling, enabled them to get a grasp of the life of Christ and their need to respond to Him in faith.

Eternity was very close to all people and they were able to comprehend that this world is not our final home. Most saw their lives as just one short step away from eternal torment in hell, or peace with Christ in heaven. With such serious consequences, there was no time to be silly with religion and pretend that heaven or hell is not a choice. 'It is appointed for men to die once, but after this the judgment' (Hebrews 9:27). In one sense these people were closer to the 'big picture' of eternity, but many were stuck in a religious institution, whether they liked it or not.

'The Church was the single most dominant institution in medieval life, its influence pervading almost every aspect of people's lives. Its religious observances gave shape to the calendar; its sacramental rituals marked important moments in an individual's life (including baptism, confirmation, marriage, the eucharist, penance, holy orders and the last rites); and its teachings underpinned mainstream beliefs about ethics, the meaning of life and the afterlife...The success of the Church as a dominant force can be attributed in no small measure to its highly developed organisation, which over the course of the Middle Ages developed a sophisticated system of governance, law and economy.'[9]

Life could be terrible during the Middle Ages, yet it would be wrong to paint all as misery. Even though there were no such things as free time or holidays as we know them, many did look forward to Christian festivals, where they would get a break from the normal routines, to celebrate Christ's birth, or His death and resurrection. These were not necessarily sombre religious observances, but just like the Old Testament feasts, the people would have access to food not normally available to them, which was made in a symbolic way, to remind all of Christ. These feasts were true celebrations and in such a way, life revolved around Christianity and observance. "I was glad when they said to me, 'Let us go into the house of the Lord' " (Psalm 122:1).

Expert on the Middle Ages, Paul B. Newman explains: 'For example the twelve days of Christmas, from 25 December to the 6 January, were a time for feasting and were celebrated in some areas with festivals led by 'Lord of Misrule,' a common person selected as part of a symbolic and comic reversal of social order. The days of carnival immediately before Ash Wednesday (the start of Lent the forty day period of fasting before Easter) and the week after Easter were also times of indulgence and celebration. Easter was also often a time for religious plays depicting the Passion of Christ.'[10] These traditions continue in Germany, as people embrace such celebrations.

"For hundreds of years life was built around the parish church," said Professor Diarmaid MacCulloch, "you came here each week for Sunday services, you marked the passing seasons. The church provided the christening ritual that marked your entry into the world. This is where you'd come to get married and after it all, this would be your final resting place."[11]

Just as Christianity came to be at the centre of life for people in Britain, so too each nation of the British Isles honoured famous Christian heroes of the past, and set them up as symbols for the nation. In Ireland, Patrick, the young missionary who was led by the Holy Spirit to preach Christ to the nation was adopted as their patron saint. In England, its people began to look back several hundred years before Patrick, to a Middle Eastern martyr, who was born in Israel's biblical town called Lod/Lydda (The city is mentioned in Ezra 2:33, Acts 9:32). Professor Diarmaid MacCulloch said, "The story of George is that he was a soldier in the Roman army, but when the Emperor Diocletian began persecuting Christians George objected. He was imprisoned for his defiance and eventually killed...St George – the soldier Saint – and that's what appealed to Kings of England from the thirteenth century."[12]

In Wales, a Celtic Welsh bishop named David or Dewi Sant in Welsh, famed for struggling for doctrinal purity and resistant to Rome, became the nation's symbol. In Scotland, the people harked back to the disciples of Jesus and chose Andrew, Peter's brother and a disciple of Christ, as the person to represent their nation (John 6:8). All of the patron saints of Britain were committed to sacrificial faith and to New Testament Christianity, and they were adopted by the nations because the peoples within wanted to follow their example, as they followed Christ.

To understand life in Britain in the Middle Ages, you have to imagine a large network of monasteries across the nation, at the heart of each city or town. The art historian Dr Janina Ramirez said, "By 1300 there were more than five hundred, and over ten thousand people in monastic orders across the British Isles. It had become a land of monasteries...Monasteries redrew the map as new towns clustered around their great abbeys. They transformed the skyline, as their churches soared higher and higher."[13]

These monasteries became the centre of life and combined a religious order, university, school, hospital, farm and business centre together with a tourist hub. St Bartholomew's hospital in London is the direct descendant of one of these monasteries which was founded in 1123. As centres of education, "monks didn't just preserve ancient knowledge they were making new discoveries too," explains Dr Janina Ramirez. "Many of the most intellectually ambitious and passionately curious people of the age were monks. The great philosopher Thomas Aquinas was a Dominican, the pioneer of the scientific method – the Englishman Roger Bacon was a Franciscan."[14]

The only problem was that success tended to draw the wrong kind of people to monasteries; men who sought money or influence and corruption undermined their validity. To combat corruption, new splinter groups formed, trying to get back to the message of Jesus and with success, the cycle would commence again. "By the fifteenth century the medieval monastery had been transformed," said Dr Janina Ramirez, "it had turned itself, inside out, becoming active in the world, while neglecting its own spiritual core. As they became increasingly entangled with the world outside the cloister, many monks fell victim to its temptations."[15]

Meanwhile in Rome, vile men infiltrated the Church structures and the Papacy and bishops engaged in an age of corruption. In a series of struggles for power various Popes tried to extend their authority over England. In 1208, the Pope enforced an interdict which in practice meant a complete shutdown of all churches in England. For five years there were no marriages or burials, etc. By 18 November 1302, Pope Boniface VIII issued the Papal Bull, or law of Unam Sanctam which declared the Pope had authority, not only over every church and all Christians, but also over all kings and rulers. It ended with this: 'We declare, we proclaim, we define that it is absolutely necessary for salvation that every human creature be subject to the Roman Pontiff.' In other words, if you don't obey the Pope and his bishops, you are going to hell.

The problem was that the common person had no access to the Bible and could not check what they were being taught with Scripture. Imagine living in an age where people had no access to the Bible and priests taught in a foreign language – Latin. Consider knowing that corrupt men had designed oppressive religious rules, which impoverished the people, but had to be followed, or else damnation would follow. In such a culture, there were many faithful priests and others struggling for the pure sacrificial faith to be expressed, and some of these men came to the fore in a battle against corruption, as they sought a return to the faith of Jesus Christ and the apostles.

John Wycliffe (1330-1384) followed in the spirit of John the Baptist, for he was an English preacher who promoted a return to biblical Christianity. Famously he is called The Morning Star of the Reformation. Deeply disturbed by the rottenness and false teaching coming out of a corrupted Rome, he was a forerunner of the Protestant Reformation which began in 1517, as he called the Church and believers back to the Bible, and set an example from which many others would learn and follow.

Chapter Eleven

New Testament Christianity

In 1517, Martin Luther (1483-1546), a German priest, outlined his concerns with his Ninety-Five Theses, stating that the Church had departed from the faith of the apostles to embrace traditions which have no biblical precedent. Luther, like many faithful priests, wanted the Church to reform and return to the teaching of the New Testament; what they did not expect was that bitter persecution would be directed against them, to compel them to be silent and renounce their newly discovered biblical truths.

As the Catholic hierarchy arrested and murdered many leading lights, instead of reforming, the Church in Europe was split. The Reformation divided Christians. Those who wanted a return to New Testament Christianity were labelled as Protestants, as they protested about unbiblical beliefs and actions within the Church. John Wycliffe had enabled this process, as he produced the first English translation of the Bible from the Latin Vulgate, allowing people to read how the Church departed from the teaching of the apostles, and the Lollards preached reform.

What also followed was the tragic persecution and martyrdom of many Christians, whose desire was to follow the Lord Jesus whole-heartedly, and to read a Bible of their own in English. William Tyndale (1494-1536) was burnt at the stake for translating the New Testament into English and Protestants were harassed and killed all over Europe, leading to the European Wars of Religion (1524 to 1648), as Catholics and Protestants struggled against each other.

In Britain, the release of the Bible in English, although illegal, enabled public opinion to swing in favour of reform and return to New Testament Christianity. The various motives of Henry VIII in establishing England as a Protestant nation in 1534, independent from Rome, have been tested and found wanting, and yet many in the nation embraced the change as a chance to return to biblical Christianity.

When King Edward VI (1537-1553) came to power in 1547, he became the first King of England to be born and raised as a Protestant. When he died, Queen Mary I (1553-1558) attempted to restore England to Catholicism, through a series of bloody persecutions of Protestants and hundreds were burnt at the stake at her request; she was nicknamed Bloody Mary.

Former British politician Ann Widdecombe explained that in 1553, "The king died and his sister Mary became Queen. Unlike Protestant Edward, she was a devout Catholic. After twenty years of religious change, Mary ordered the people to convert – yet again. For the last time in history, England became an officially Catholic country. Protestants faced five dark years of persecution…in the Market Town of Lewes, seventeen men and women were tried for heresy. They treasured their English Bibles and were committed to Protestantism. So each was dragged through the town's high street and burned alive. The Protestant martyrs are remembered every bonfire night."[1]

This kind of persecution for Catholics and Protestants was widespread in Europe. In France, Protestants lost their battle for religious freedom and in 1572, 10,000 Protestants were killed in the St. Bartholomew's Day Massacre. This went on for five days, as the French authorities stood back and allowed Catholics to murder their Protestant neighbours. It began when the Catholic leaders of France sent soldiers to kill fifty influential French Protestants in the night. Professor Mark Greengrass said, "Things seemed to be going more or less to plan through the night, until day-break. By five o'clock it seems, the bodies were beginning to stack up of the leading Protestant nobles."[2]

When it was discovered that the government had sent men to kill Protestants, Catholics turned on their neighbours and killed them, believing they had a free pass from the government to do so. Professor Mark Greengrass said, "If you've been told from the pulpit, as Parisians in this city were, that their city was going to be under God's judgment if they allowed Protestant heretic pollution to survive within its walls, then it's not surprising, is it, that people take it into their own hands, believing their not just doing the king's will, but that their doing God's will."[3] Ann Widdecombe, a Catholic, was horrified by this massacre of 10,000 Protestants in France and the other abuses of Papal authority, saying, "When the Pope heard of the slaughter, he had a medal struck to celebrate, 'A glorious Catholic victory.' "[4]

In England, many Christians felt bewildered by the tyrannical rule of Queen Mary. They prayed that God would send a godly monarch to return the nation to New Testament Christianity, which had first arrived in the land with Roman travellers and flourished during the Celtic Golden Age. When Queen Mary died, the hopes of many were pinned on her half-sister Elizabeth (1533-1603), believing that she was to be the monarch sent by God to restore biblical Christianity to the nation. She was passionately committed to Protestantism and England was to be returned to a Protestant Christian footing, seeking to re-embrace the New Testament foundations for Christianity. This conviction was ossified by Queen Elizabeth I in her Act of Supremacy in 1558, which made England's separation from Rome permanently enshrined in the Constitution.

When Elizabeth I embraced her title of the Supreme Governor of the Church of England, she did not take it lightly. The Queen said, "Since I first had consideration of myself to be born a servitor of Almighty God, I happily chose this kind of life in which I yet live...I trust God, who hath hitherto therein preserved and led me by the hand, will not now of His goodness suffer me."[5]

The Queen was deeply disturbed that there were still too many corrupt allegiances to the Pope in the nation, and when she was urged by some Parliamentarians to return England to submission to Rome, she rebuked them. The Queen reminded them that Christianity was corrupted by Rome and said, "Our realm and subjects have been long wanderers, walking astray, whilst they were under the tuition of Romish pastors, who advised them to own a wolf for their head (in lieu of a careful shepherd) whose inventions, heresies and schisms be so numerous, that the flock of Christ have fed on poisonous shrubs for want of wholesome pastures."[6]

The Queen reminded all in Parliament that Christianity had independently made a great impact in England, hundreds of years before the Pope sent any mission to England: "And whereas you hit us and our subjects in the teeth that the Romish Church first planted the Catholic within our realm, *the records and chronicles of our realm testify the contrary*...when Austin [St Augustine] came from Rome, this our realm had bishops and priests therein, as is well known to the learned of our realm by woeful experience. How your church entered therein by blood; they being martyrs for Christ and put to death because they denied Rome's usurped authority."[7]

Queen Elizabeth's commitment to New Testament Christianity put her at odds with one of the world's great superpowers of the age, Spain. By returning to the Bible as the sole source of doctrine and practice, many in England believed they had 'now sided with God,' and this would lead to God blessing England – in accordance with the historic covenants Christian monarchs of England had made with the Almighty. But this was not the view in Rome and the Pope gave his blessing to any nation to invade England and force it to return to Catholicism.

England was still a weak, divided nation, on the edges of

Europe, surrounded by a sea of great powers. Thus, when the world's most powerful superpower, Catholic Spain, decided to invade and force the weakened England to return to Catholicism – a test case was made. If God wanted England to be subject to Rome and its teaching, the Catholic superpower would invade the land; but if God was pleased with England's return to biblical Christianity, David would see Goliath defeated.

A year before Spain tried to invade England, Sir Francis Drake (1540-1595), before the Battle of Cadiz, sought God's aid, praying, "O Lord God, when Thou givest to Thy servants to endeavour any great matter, grant us also to know that it is not the beginning, but the continuing of the same, until it be thoroughly finished, which yieldeth the true glory; through Him that for the finishing of Thy work, laid down His life, our Redeemer, Jesus Christ."

When Drake destroyed many enemy ships as they harboured, which delayed Spain's invasion plans by a year, many saw this as a sign that prayer had indeed been answered. Nevertheless, the real battle for England's survival as a nation committed to New Testament Christianity was ahead, when Spain sent a fleet of one hundred and thirty ships to overwhelm England and return it to Catholicism.

The fleet of ships heading towards England was called the 'Invincible Fleet,' and all strategists knew that if the conditions were favourable, the Spanish fleet could be blown into shore, and overwhelm the nation with foreign troops.

On 8 August 1588, Queen Elizabeth spoke to her forces at Tilbury saying, "I am come amongst you as you see at this time, not for my recreation and disport, but being resolved, in the midst and heat of battle, to live or die amongst you all – to lay down for my God, and for my Kingdoms, and for my people, my honour and my blood even in the dust. I know I have the body of a weak and feeble woman; but I have the heart and stomach of a king – and of a King of England too, and think foul scorn that Parma or Spain, or any prince of Europe, should dare to invade the borders of my realm…we shall shortly have a famous victory over those enemies of my God, of my Kingdom, and of my people."

On 20 August 1588, a thanksgiving service was held at St Paul's in London, to praise God for His victory. The Spanish fleet had been obliterated and Queen Elizabeth gave the credit to God, for the 'Protestant wind' had blown the world's largest invasion force onto the rocks and sunk them. She ordered a special medal to be made, which was inscribed with these words:

'God blew and they were scattered.' Other comical medals were also made, mocking Philip of Spain saying, 'He came, he saw, he fled.'

English losses stood at below one hundred killed and none of the Queen's ships had been sunk, whilst a third of Spain's fleet never returned home. To further break the morale of the Catholic vision of Spain, the remainder of Philip's ships had to sail all around Britain to get home, and many ships were smashed onto the Scottish and Irish rocky coasts.

This victory helped raise a new paradigm shift in the minds of many English people. Could it be possible that their tiny nation could be used by God overseas, with a navy, to defeat tyrants, spread Christianity and establish liberty?

The defeat of the Catholic Spanish Armada was a miracle beyond anything that had happened in England, since King Alfred's turnaround from almost total annihilation to victory against the Vikings seven hundred and ten years before. This was England's Red Sea moment of deliverance, as it escaped a far stronger and vehement enemy, and it was God's direct intervention which saved the nation. Winston Churchill said, "The Armada had completed the process which persecution under Mary had begun, that of making England a Protestant Christian country."

Now that the Queen believed she was on God's side, she was passionate about making sure that England made a full return to New Testament Christianity. The Thirty-Nine Articles of the independent Church of England, established in 1563, were to be embraced in full. Article XXII, on purgatory states: 'The Romish Doctrine concerning Purgatory, Pardons, Worshipping and Adoration, as well of Images as of Relics, and also Invocation of Saints, is a fond thing, vainly invented, and grounded upon no warranty of Scripture, but rather repugnant to the Word of God.' It may be of interest to know that the Thirty-Nine Articles continue to be invoked today in the Anglican Church, to remind progressive activists that the Church of England should be committed to New Testament Christianity and nothing else.[8]

The Queen saw herself as a servant of Christ and a pilgrim on earth, just as the New Testament describes (Hebrews 11:13). Speaking in Parliament she said, "One matter touches me so near as I may not overskip; religion is the ground on which all other matters ought to take root and being corrupted may mar all the tree...seeing so great wickedness and griefs in the world in which we live, but as wayfaring pilgrims, we must suppose that God would never have made us but for a better place [heaven] and of more comfort than we find here...Yet mind I not hereby to animate Romanists (which what adversaries they be to mine estate is sufficiently well known) nor tolerate newfangledness. I mean to guide them both by God's holy true rule."[9]

The Queen committed herself to returning England to New Testament Christianity, but trying to establish exactly what that would mean, caused divisions between 'Romanists' who wanted a return to the Pope, and 'newfangledness' – people who were far ahead of the Queen in their desire for reform. By committing herself to Protestantism, the Queen also became the victim of many assassination plots. The historian Diarmaid MacCulloch said, "In 1570, the Pope excommunicated Queen Elizabeth I, absolving English Catholics from any loyalty to her and her laws. It was a moment which cast Catholics as potential traitors."[10] The Queen survived all the many plots and safeguarded England's Christian heritage.

Speaking to Parliament on 30 November 1601, the sixty-eight year old Queen Elizabeth I, spoke of her mission to defend England from enemies and to safeguard "His Kingdom," as she prepared her own heart for eternity, and the Day of Judgment. The Queen said, "I do not so much rejoice that God hath made me to be a Queen, as to be a Queen over so thankful a people...I trust by the Almighty power of God that I shall be His instrument to preserve you from every peril, dishonour, shame, tyranny and oppression...I have ever used to set the Last Judgment Day before mine eyes and so to rule, as I shall be judged to answer before a Higher Judge...I know the title of a king is a glorious title, but assure yourself that the shining glory of princely authority hath not so dazzled the eyes of our understanding, but that we well know and remember that we also are to yield an account of our actions before the great Judge...For myself was...delighted that God hath made me His instrument to maintain His truth and glory, and to defend His Kingdom."[11]

The reforms under Queen Elizabeth I, though tested severely later, transformed England and confirmed its status as a nation committed to New Testament Christianity. However, many were frustrated at the Queen's balancing act, trying to keep all factions content, and they sought a faster and more substantial rejection of all unbiblical tradition, in a return to the Bible.

In Scotland, John Knox had secured the nation's future as a Protestant Bible believing country, and when Queen Elizabeth I died, Scotland's King James VI (1566-1625) inherited the throne and became James I of England, Scotland, Wales and Ireland.

King James I sponsored the translation of the Bible into English and gave us the King James Version. Also, in 1604, at the Treaty of London Spain sued for peace and renounced its plans to force England's return to Catholicism.

King James I was committed to Protestantism and his heirs guaranteed that the British nations would remain Protestant. This caused great misery for Catholics in England and in 1605, a few radicals drew a plan to force a return to Catholicism. We tend to think of the Gunpowder Plot as a pantomime, as each year for four centuries in Britain, people light bonfires and now setoff fireworks to remember the failed plot. However, the Gunpowder Plot was the most daring terrorist attack ever planned in Britain, as they came close to blowing up Parliament.

If the plot had succeeded, "It could have been a turning point," said Dr Clare Jackson. "I don't think one should underestimate what those thirty-six barrels of gunpowder would have done."[12] "The whole intention of the Gunpowder Plot is to do something on a grander scale than has ever been see before," said Dr Mark Nicholls, "to erase the entire political nation. They're literally looking at a clean slate...the plot is to erase the entire political nation, to destroy the buildings and monuments that symbolise the power of the state."[13]

One of the conspirators said, "We will blow up Parliament with gunpowder...perhaps God prepared that place for their punishment."[14] If they succeeded they planned to raise an army, with weapons they had prepared, to turn England back to the Catholic faith by force. Another of the conspirators, Tom Winter, warned that if it failed, "The scandal to the Catholic faith would be so great that our friends, as well as our enemies would, with good reason, condemn us."[15]

When the plot was exposed, Guy Fawkes was arrested and the others fled to Holbeche House. Whilst there, some of their own gunpowder exploded. "It is a supremely ironic moment when the gunpowder explosion occurs at Holbeche House," said Dr Clare Jackson. "There is a sense that this is the moment when some of them begin to think, 'Is this a sign of Divine displeasure?' Some are badly injured, one is blinded...it focuses their minds that God may not be on their side and this is now, where they are all going to die together."[16]

As the sheriff's men besieged the house where the conspirators hid, one of them confessed, "I fear we have offended God by this bloody act. I have prayed to our Lady for forgiveness."[17] It was a Catholic who warned Parliament of the danger, and when the men were caught and the plot was known, English Catholics were spared violent persecution. But for two centuries, it stained all Catholics with the tar of being dangerous and friends of foreign enemies. If the plot had succeeded, the future of the land as a Protestant nation would have been in peril and the prospect of the great missionary movement, and the evangelisation of Africa, Asia and the Pacific, with millions of converts, would have been put into jeopardy.

In the first seating of Parliament since the plot, the 5 November Act 1605 was passed, making services and sermons commemorating the event an annual feature. The 1662 book of *Common Prayer* includes a prayer of thanksgiving for 5 November for: 'The happy deliverance of King James...and England...from the most traitorous and bloody, intended massacre by gunpowder...for the deliverance of our Church and nation.' Many were deeply grieved that an act of terrorism of such a scale was organised, and the custom of burning effigies of the Pope, or the devil, may have begun in the reign of Charles I (1625-49), and became more popular during the crisis over the succession of James II in 1678-81. Over the decades, effigies of Guy Fawkes replaced the Pope, as the plot lost its efficacy.

The plot was the last serious attempt to restore Catholicism to Britain by force and the result was the opposite of its intention. England hardened its Protestant position and Britons down the ages have sung, in jest, the variations of: 'Remember, remember the fifth of November. Gunpowder, treason and plot...by God's mercy he was catch'd...God save the king."

The Reformation and dissolution of the monasteries changed Britain forever. In 1530, there were more than 800 monasteries with over 7,000 people living in these religious communities. Just over a decade later, not a single monastery remained.[18] England was now Protestant and Bible believing, and at liberty.

Chapter Twelve

Empowering Parliament

During the sixteenth and seventeenth centuries many Christians in England began to believe Scripture warranted them liberty to worship as they chose, and to be clearly compelled to one type of worship or church was unbiblical. Their spiritual freedom also informed their belief in political liberty, leading to the evolution of a Theology of Liberty.

Queen Elizabeth I guaranteed England was to be a Protestant nation, but her Elizabethan Religious Settlement, responsible for forming Anglicanism into a distinctive tradition, limited religious freedom and many believers felt the return to New Testament Christianity was far from complete. The 1588 Act of Uniformity demanded the population to attend Sunday service in an Anglican church, at which a new version of the *Book of Common Prayer* was to be used. Consequently, Protestant exiles, unhappy with the religious establishment were drawn together and become known as Puritans, because they wanted 'pure' New Testament Christianity, with no hint of Rome.

These Puritans wanted to witness a reform of the practices, but not the central doctrines of Anglicanism. They wished to abolish the Catholic ranking systems above parish priests, and Popish prayers and rituals, to return to apostolic Christianity. But the Puritans were blocked from changing the Established Church from within, and were severely restricted in their religious liberty, by laws controlling the practice of religion. Nevertheless, as the decades past, they grew in confidence and in numbers.

Christian dissenters, seeking New Testament Christianity were fined, like Catholics, for not attending Anglican meetings, under the Recusancy Acts. Discontent flourished as the Puritans further felt their liberties were fundamentally undermined by corrupt kings, and by the 1630s, the Puritans grew in power to become a major political force in England. They were not alone on the British mainland in their strong religious convictions and by joining forces with Scottish Presbyterians, with whom they shared core biblical beliefs, they brought about huge change in the land. Eventually, the conflict between another corrupt king and the Puritans led to the English Civil War of 1642-1652, which would empower Parliament in a way never seen before in the modern world.

King Charles I (1600-1649) of England, Scotland and Ireland, was a firm believer that the monarch was God's representative on earth and could not be made subject to man-made laws. During his reign, Archbishop William Laud (1573-1645) began to renew persecution of the Puritans and without Parliament sitting none could keep the king accountable.

The dispute between Parliament and the monarch finally came to conflict when the English Civil War broke out in 1642. On 4 January Charles I entered the English Commons with a group of soldiers to arrest five members of Parliament, and ever since that day, no monarch has been allowed to enter the Commons whilst in session to interfere. The war lasted for three years; with the king fighting for his belief in his 'Divine Right' to rule absolutely, whilst the Puritans stood with Oliver Cromwell (1599-1658), who fought for religious and political liberty. For Cromwell, individual freedom and his Christian faith were one and the same; he called the people to fight for, "The maintenance of our civil liberties as men and our religious liberties as Christians." For the Puritans, the behaviour of the king was in strict defiance of Deuteronomy 17:16-20, which is a code of conduct calling leaders to financial integrity, personal morality and confirms that all leaders, including the king, must be in total subjection to the law.

Oliver Cromwell believed that this corrupt king had lost his legitimacy and as such, he and all the Puritans with him, were serving the will of God by seeking a new order of justice, law and liberty. "What is all our histories," he asked, "but God showing Himself, shaking and trampling on everything that He has not planted?" In the view of many Puritans, just as the kings of Israel and Judah had rebelled and lost their legitimacy, so had Charles I. The cause was righteous and liberty was its aim. After a decisive battle, where the professional army of the king was defeated, he said, "Then I saw the enemy draw up and march in gallant order towards us, and we a company of poor ignorant men, to seek how to order our battle...I could not, but smile out to God in praises, in assurance of victory, because God would, by things that are not, bring to naught things that are."

Lord Melvyn Bragg believes the translation of the King James Bible, published in 1611, was instrumental in providing the intellectual and spiritual case for England to move away from the corrupt absolute rule of King Charles I, to begin to lay the foundations for democracy. "The King James Version not only influenced the English language and its literature more than any other book," said Lord Melvyn Bragg, "it was also the seedbed of

Western democracy."¹

When King Charles I was captured and put on trial, the case brought against him rested on the new Protestant concept that the king must also be an absolute subject of the law, and to the higher eternal law of God. "In his final summing up," of the case against the king, explained Lord Melvyn Bragg, "Lord President Bradshaw rested what he clearly thought was a fragile case on thunder rolls of biblical quotations. Charles I had been called 'the man of blood,' responsible for all the blood shed in the wars. Bradshaw pointed out that we know what God Himself had said concerning the shedding of man's blood – that 'thou shalt do no murder.' That extends to kings, he said, as well peasants. For the first time, a king was fighting for his life because of a completely legal challenge based on the authority of the Bible. Three days later, Charles was executed and so the Bible was empowered to be the chief instrument in reshaping the English-speaking world."²

The Puritans, based on their belief in the biblical case for justice, with Oliver Cromwell as their leader, delivered England from the tyranny of an absolute monarch, but they were not able to evolve a new suitable system to replace it. Together they dissolved the past, but in the complexity of the conflict, they were unable to embrace the future, and Cromwell was honest about his own inabilities, "Shall we seek for the root of our comforts within us?" asked Cromwell. "What God hath done, what He is to us in Christ, is the root of our comfort. In this is stability; in us is weakness. Acts of obedience are not perfect and therefore yield not perfect peace. Faith, as an act, yields it not, but as it carries us into Him, who is our perfect rest and peace; in whom we are accounted of, and received by, the Father, even as Christ Himself. This is our high calling. Rest we here and here only."³

With Charles I dethroned, Cromwell expected England would be reformed, to renew its covenant with God, but when the Rump Parliament of England failed, Cromwell lost confidence in all on 20 April 1653, saying, "You have sat too long for any good you have been doing lately…in the name of God, go!"

A new government was formed and whilst Cromwell was at a prayer meeting on 12 December 1653, General John Lambert, gathered men together to vote to dissolve Parliament and bring in a formal Constitution for the nation. The new Constitution, accepted on 16 December 1653, called the Commonwealth Instrument of Government placed all authority in Cromwell, as Lord Protector of the realm.

This Constitution of 1653, was the first sovereign codified and written Constitution in the English speaking world, and arguably was used to help guide the creation of the U.S. Constitution. The new Constitution re-confirmed England's covenant with God and established all nations in Britain as committed to New Testament Christianity. The following articles exemplify this:

'XVII. That the persons who shall be elected to serve in Parliament, shall be such (and no other than such) as are persons of known integrity, fearing God, and of good conversation, and being of the age of twenty-one years.'

'XXXV. That the Christian Religion, as contained in the Scriptures, be held forth and recommended as the public profession of these Nations.'

'XXXVI. That to the public profession held forth none shall be compelled by penalties or otherwise: but that endeavours be used to win them by sound Doctrine, and the example of a good conversation.'

'XXXVII. That such as profess faith in God by Jesus Christ, (though differing in Judgment from the Doctrine, Worship or discipline publicly held forth) shall not be restrained from, but shall be protected in, the profession of the faith, and exercise of their Religion; so as they abuse not this liberty to the civil injury of others, and to the actual disturbance of the public peace on their parts: Provided this liberty be not extended to Popery nor prelacy, nor to such as, under the Profession of Christ, hold forth and practise licentiousness.'

This Constitution only lasted for just over three years and a second attempt was made on 23 February 1657, in The Humble Petition and Advice On. In this second Constitution, Cromwell was offered the Crown, and he refused it on 8 May 1657.

Article XI of the Constitution is more of a statement of faith, which articulates the doctrines of New Testament Christianity. A part of it, is as follows: 'That the true Protestant Christian religion, as it is contained in the Holy Scriptures of the Old and New Testament, and no other, be held forth and asserted for the public profession of these nations; and that a confession of faith, to be agreed by your Highness and the Parliament, according to the rule and warrant of the Scriptures, be asserted, held forth, and recommended to the people of these nations...and such who profess faith in God the Father, and in Jesus Christ His eternal Son, the true God, and in the Holy Spirit, God co-equal with the Father and the Son, one God blessed for ever, and do acknowledge the Holy Scriptures of the Old and New Testament to be the revealed Will and Word of God..."

On 3 September 1658, Oliver Cromwell on his deathbed

prayed, "Lord, though I am a miserable and wretched creature, I am in covenant with Thee through grace. And I may, I will come to Thee for Thy people. Thou hast made me, though very unworthy, a mean instrument to do them some good...pardon Thy foolish people. Forgive their sins and do not forsake them, but love and bless them. Give them consistency of judgment, one heart, and mutual love; and go on to deliver them, and with the work of reformation; and make the name of Christ glorious in the world. Teach those who look too much on Thy instruments, to depend more upon Thyself...and give me rest for Jesus Christ's sake, to whom, with Thee and Thy Holy Spirit, be all honour and glory, now and for ever! Amen."

Thomas Hobbes (1588-1679), writing during the English Civil War argued that England must now further disentangle itself from the Pope's unbiblical 'ghosts of the Roman Empire.' In his book *Leviathan*, which is derived from the Bible, he wrote: 'For, from the time that the Bishop of Rome had gotten to be acknowledged for bishop universal, by pretence of succession to St. Peter, their whole hierarchy, or kingdom of darkness, may be compared not unfitly to the kingdom of fairies; that is, to the old wives' fables ...if a man consider the original of this great ecclesiastical dominion, he will easily perceive that the Papacy is no other than the ghost of the deceased Roman Empire, sitting crowned upon the grave thereof: for so did the Papacy start up on a sudden out of the ruins of that heathen power. The language also which they use, both in the churches and in their public acts, being Latin, which is not commonly used by any nation now in the world, what is it but the ghost of the old Roman language?'[4]

During the English Civil War another concept was presented, which if embraced, could have birthed a full democracy in England. Unfortunately, with the war unsettled at the time, the future Constitution of England was set to one side, until the war was completed, and thus, the moment was lost.

"With Oliver Cromwell in the chair, the general council of the New Model Army came together at Putney church, in October 1647, to argue the case for a transparent, democratic state, free from the taint of Parliamentary or courtly corruption," explained the historian Tristram Hunt. "It proved to be one of the greatest intellectual encounters in Western political thought...on the second day of the debates, after a good five-hour prayer session, the soldiers focused on the question of franchise. Who had the right to vote? For the Levellers, the answer was clear, all those who placed themselves under government should have the right to elect it. The vote was a natural right, irrespective of property or position. 'I think that the poorest he that is in England hath a life to live, as the greatest he,' in the celebrated words of Colonel Rainsborough, 'and therefore...every man that is to live under a government ought first, by his own consent, to put himself under that government; and I do think that the poorest man in England is not at all bound in a strict sense to that government that he hath not had a voice to put himself under.' "[5]

Who were the men presenting these modern democratic ideals for a new Christian Constitution for England? Were these men inspired by Athenian democracy, or were they men of faith, reading the Bible and seeking to create a new Constitution which embodied the Christian idea of equality? Tristram Hunt gives the answer, "The Levellers were not simply secular democrats in prototype: the Putney debates were more a mass prayer meeting than Constitutional symposium. Every day the soldiers sought God's guidance in their search for a political solution to the civil war and a post-monarchical settlement. While the likes of Christopher Hitchens and Richard Dawkins might find it uncomfortable, the story of British democracy is intimately bound up with the theology of Protestant Christianity."[6]

Prime Minister David Cameron said, "The Putney debates in the Church of St Mary the Virgin in 1647 saw the first call for One Man, One vote and the demand that authority be invested in the House of Commons rather than the king. Reading the Bible in English gave people equality with each other through God and this led them to seek equality with each other through government."[7]

Chapter Thirteen

The Glorious Revolution

In the modern world, the difference between a Catholic or Protestant leader may seem to be insignificant, but during this age, it was the most important question, akin to the Middle East nations of today being forced to live under the blinded tyranny of Islamic extremists, instead of pragmatics. The Catholic Counter Reformation, beginning in 1545 and continuing to 1648, was at first a means of addressing all the faults, failures and corruption within the Catholic Church, but soon it led to grave persecutions of Protestants, in order to force their return to the Catholic faith. What transpired was the European Wars of Religion with all sides committing atrocities; most remembered is the Thirty Years' War in Europe (1618-1648), and also in the British Isles, the Wars of the Three Kingdoms (1639-1651), affecting England, Scotland and Ireland. Though there was always more to these conflicts than the question of religion, the importance of Bible believing faith leading to liberty was entrenched.

None had forgotten that Queen Mary I (1553-1558) had earned the name Bloody Mary, as she plunged England into a bitter bloodbath. She had married the Catholic, Philip II of Spain (1527-1598) and sought to enforce England's return to Catholicism. During this period it was documented that she had almost three hundred religious dissenters burned at the stake in the Marian Persecutions, and the bishops Latimer, Ridley and Archbishop Cranmer were among those burnt at the stake. This Catholic monarch had been a disaster for England, but after her death, Queen Elizabeth I (1558-1603) re-committed the nation to Protestantism and England entered its first modern Golden Age.

When God intervened and many of the one hundred and thirty invasion ships of the Spanish Armada were wrecked before they could invade England, the service on 20 August 1588 in St Paul's credited God with saving the nation, enabling it to stand firm, committed to New Testament Christianity. These lessons from history were transparent to Protestants in England. Based upon their experiences Catholic kings and queens led to tyranny at home, submission to a foreign Pope, and allegiances with the often enemies of England – France and Spain. But Protestant kings or queens meant liberty at home and victory over enemies abroad.

Now, in England and Scotland Protestants did not want a return to the past and James, Duke of York (1633-1701), the Catholic heir apparent could never, in their opinion, become king after Charles II. Therefore, the great Exclusion Crisis ran from 1679-1681. Sir Henry Capel summarised the general feeling of the people, when he said in a Parliamentary debate in the House of Commons, on 27 April 1679, "From Popery came the notion of a standing army and arbitrary power...formerly the crown of Spain and now France, supports this root of Popery amongst us; but lay Popery flat, and there's an end of arbitrary government and power."

As the battle for the future of England raged on, those who wanted to deprive the Catholic James, Duke of York, of the throne after Charles II were disappointed. On 6 February 1685, the second surviving son of Charles I, (the king who was executed in the English Civil War), came to power. From the onset it was suspected that his allegiances were pro-Catholic and with the enemies of England. In other words, he wanted a return to absolute monarchy, and when he produced a Catholic heir, the tension exploded and the leading nobles called on his Protestant son-in-law and nephew, William III of Orange (1650-1702), to come from the Netherlands to save England's liberty.

William III of Orange was invited to be the new king on the condition that he defended England's Christian faith and all the nation's new freedoms. William was King James II's son-in-law and James' daughter, Mary II was to rule with the new king. The historian Dan Snow said, "On the top mast of William's flagship, he flew a banner with his family motto on – 'I will maintain.' But he added, in letters three-feet-high, "The liberties of the English and the Protestant religion." His testimony was straightforward and when William landed on the south coast of England, he was greeted with cheers. Over the next few weeks, it became obvious the English weren't going to fight for James II. He fled the country and was replaced as king by William."[2]

As King James II fled England for France, a peaceful transition was secured. The British National Archives state: 'After the short-lived Constitutional experiments that followed the Civil War, the supremacy of Parliament was finally enshrined in the Bill of Rights passed in December 1689. The Bill of Rights firmly established the principles of frequent Parliaments, free elections, and freedom of speech within Parliament.'[3]

During the Coronation of William III of Orange and his wife Mary II were required to commit the realm to God, and vowed to rule in a way, which would maintain the laws of God and the true profession of the gospel of Jesus Christ. The Archbishop asked them, "Will you to your power cause law and justice in mercy to be executed in all your judgments?" The king and queen replied, "I will." They were asked, "Will you to the utmost of your power maintaine [Sic] the laws of God the true profession of the Gospell and the Protestant Reformed Religion established by law? And will you preserve unto the bishops and clergy of this realme and to the churches committed to their charge all such rights and priviledges as by law doe or shall appertaine unto them or any of them?" The king and queen replied, "All this I promise to doe." Afterwards, they both laid their hands upon the Bible and said, "The things which I have here before promised I will performe and keepe. Soe help me God," and they kissed the Bible.[4]

The Library of the House of Commons in Britain explains: 'The basis for the Coronation Oath, which forms part of the coronation ceremony, is enshrined in statute in the Coronation Oath Act 1689. This Act required King William and Queen Mary, as joint monarchs, to swear an Oath during the coronation ceremony. The Act of Settlement 1701 and the Accession Declaration Act 1910 make a statutory requirement on the monarch to take the Coronation Oath. The text of the Oath as set down in the 1689 Act is appended to this note. The text includes the promise that they would to the utmost of their power to – maintain the Laws of God the true profession of the Gospell and the Protestant Reformed Religion established by law...'[5]

With these new additions to law, England and later Britain confirmed itself to be, for now and forever, Constitutionally a Protestant Christian nation. To be Protestant at this point meant returning to New Testament Christianity, and to the teaching of Jesus Christ and His apostles.

The Act of Settlement of 1701, confirmed once again that all monarchs in the realm rule under God, and England's ancient covenant with God was renewed: 'Your Majesty to whom (under God)' and the Constitution continues: '...Crown and Government shall from time to time descend to and be enjoyed by such Person or Persons being Protestants...Rights and Liberties by the Providence of God...the Reformed Religion and the Liberties...in the said recited Act contained doe constantly implore the Divine Mercy for those Blessings.'

Commencing from 1689, the line of succession of power in Britain, Constitutionally, derives from God, to the monarch and then to Parliament. For over three hundred years, without swearing an Oath to God to maintain the laws of God and the true profession of the gospel, British monarchs would be unable to be crowned, Parliament could not sit and the government could not operate. As Dr John Sentamu explained, "The place of Christianity in the Constitutional framework of our country, governed as it is by the Queen, in Parliament, under God, is not in question."[6]

In a way no-one ever expected, the unity created amongst Protestants in England in the Glorious Revolution enabled an extension of toleration and religious freedom for all. The historian Diarmaid MacCulloch said, "This is a moment of unity for all Protestants, Anglican and dissenters alike. The dissenters demanded a reward and what they got from the new King William and the new Queen Mary was a law, finally legalising all Protestant denominations. It was known as the Act of Toleration...what this act is saying is that dissenting bodies like Quakers or Baptists were no longer in any danger of going to prison for their beliefs, and better than that, if they signed up to certain specified Christian beliefs then they could worship freely in their own buildings."[7]

England had now overthrown, in peace, a Catholic monarch who desired absolute rule, to welcome a Protestant in his place, who was subject to the law and Parliament, to protect their religious and political freedoms. Once again, a test was ahead of them. Would God in heaven judge England for overthrowing a Catholic king, by making them lose a war with a Catholic nation, or would God honour England for returning to the faith of the Bible? For many in England, great and small, they all had their individual choices to make – back to Catholicism, or to the faith of the apostles.

A certain John Churchill (1650-1722) had previously watched in horror as King James II embraced Catholicism, and he knew several Protestant nobles who denied their faith to maintain their position in court.[8] This was not an option for Churchill, a devout Protestant. Risking being arrested for treason in late 1688, he wrote a letter supporting bringing William of Orange to England, to restore the faith: 'I think it is what I owe to God and my country...being resolved to die in that religion that it has pleased God to give you both the will and the power to protect.'[9] Churchill put everything he had into securing the future of a Protestant Bible believing England, and William of Orange took the throne, with barely a shot being fired, in this almost bloodless revolution.

John Churchill went on to be a part of and to lead some of the most successful military campaigns of the era. France was a military superpower and England, with all its troubles at home, had rarely seen military success in land battles with Europeans. Nevertheless, by 1702, Churchill, known to us as the First Duke of Marlborough, reached the zenith of his power. On 13 August 1704 at the Battle of Blenheim, he led the successful defeat of the French army, who were devastated with over 30,000 killed, wounded and missing. Moreover, the myth of French invincibility was destroyed and France's King Louis' dream was shattered. The English squirrel had become a lion.

The historian Sir Edward Shepherd Creasy called this one of the fifteen most decisive battles in world history, saying, "Had it not been for Blenheim, all Europe might at this day suffer under the effect of French conquests resembling those of Alexander in extent and those of the Romans in durability."[10]

John Churchill's victories continued, as he became the de facto leader of the Allied forces during the 1701-1714 War of the Spanish Succession, winning more victories at Ramillies in 1706, Oudenarde in 1708 and Malplaquet in 1709. The man who risked treason to protect his faith became one of Europe's greatest generals. Blenheim Palace was Churchill's reward for rebalancing power in Europe and on that grand estate in 1874, was born the future Prime Minister Winston Churchill, who said of him, "He commanded the armies of Europe against France for ten campaigns. He fought four great battles and many important actions...he never fought a battle that he did not win, nor besieged a fortress that he did not take."[11]

If England needed a sign they were on God's side, they had it.

Chapter Fourteen

Liberty, Justice and Education

England and Scotland were by now, completely committed to New Testament Christianity and the two countries, still separate, had shared a monarch since 1603, when King James VI of Scotland inherited the English Crown from Queen Elizabeth I, and became known as James I of England as well. In 1606, 1667 and 1689 attempts were made to merge the nations into a union, but it always failed: until finally, Scotland lost twenty-five percent of its entire wealth in a disastrous trading colony in Panama. With an English bailout package, the leaders of Scotland agreed to the 1707 Act of Union, which merged the Parliaments of both nations to create the Parliament of Great Britain. Both nations had already overthrown a monarch in the name of their religious and political liberties, and both believed that God is the author of all authority and all, including monarchs must be subject to Him.

What began as a shared crown through a Scottish economic disaster, led to the most successful union of nations in world history. Whilst other nations that shared borders tore each other apart and defied the possibility of common prosperity, the British pulled their strengths together and laid the foundations for a global empire. The union led to hundreds of years of peace between the inhabitants of the British mainland, and allowed them to create the world's largest empire, exporting their values to the world. (The last battle to be fought on British soil was the Battle of Culloden of 1746). Britain was now formed into one nation from several.

Beginning in 1542, Welsh constituencies started sending members of Parliament to Westminster, just six years after Wales was Constitutionally united with England in 1536. In that act, the seeds of a United Kingdom Parliament was sown, which met at irregular intervals, until 1689, when they started to meet every year in sessions. These people may have thought they were creating something new, but in fact, the people of Britain were re-discovering the unity of the past, when Celtic Christianity brought together the various kingdoms of Britain into one shared faith. There were no borders which the Celtic Christians did not cross and according to guidance from Scripture, God must have destined the nation to be one United Kingdom (Acts 17:26).

One of the great changes which shaped Britain after the Reformation was the idea that an individual can choose his or her religion and church. By finding religious liberty and fighting for it, the people of Britain began to get used to the idea that free will and choice is something God gives to us. Journalist Cristina Odone explains, "Non-conformists Christians introduced the idea of competition to the people. If your church was stale and had nothing to offer, it would close. But those who had a genuine experience of Christ to share, thrived. Citizens became used to the idea of choice and this competition and choice soon found itself way into business and politics. Leaders and entrepreneurs learn to offer something better than their rivals and the results were lower prices and better products."[1]

This concept, of being free to choose one's church and beliefs, would later flow into politics, and this was brought to its greatest height during the British Great Awakening of 1739-1791. John Wesley (1703-1791) and George Whitefield (1714-1770) travelled the length and breath of Britain during this age, and preached the gospel of Jesus Christ. As people responded on mass, this return to Christianity changed people's attitudes and beliefs in a profound way. My brother, Mathew Backholer states in his book *Revival Fires and Awakenings*: 'During this time a quarter of the population, approximately 1.25 million people were converted to the Lord Jesus Christ. Over a period of time many places, villages and towns were completely transformed, so much so that the whole character of the nation was changed. Many historians believe that it was because of this move of God that Britain did not have a revolution, a bloodbath, like the French Revolution of 1789.'

Whilst the people of Britain rediscovered Christianity, the anger of the people of France was brewing due to oppression, which ultimately led to the chaos of the French Revolution. What began in France in 1789 with declarations of liberty, soon led to a state of terror and the first modern police state, where no life was safe. The French philosopher and historian Élie Halévy in his book *History of the English People* considered why France had a terrible bloodbath of a revolution and why England was saved the massacre. He presented his famous thesis concluding that the influence of Christianity in Methodism saved the nation. Élie Halévy summarised that the evangelical revival produced: 'The extraordinary stability which English society was destined to enjoy throughout a period of revolution and crises; what we may truly term the miracle of modern England.'

Whilst the French felt powerless to influence any area of their lives, the people of Britain actively took hold of their Christian faith and expressed it as they desired. By doing so, Christian charities began to appear all over Britain and they met many of the urgent needs which, still undone in France, would lead to its revolution. In France, subsequent kings oppressed the people because of belief in their Divine Right to rule, whilst in Britain, people looked to the Bible for a vision for justice. Jesus spoke of those who served Him unknowingly, " 'Lord, when did we see You hungry and feed You, or thirsty and give You drink? When did we see You a stranger and take You in, or naked and clothe You? Or when did we see You sick, or in prison, and come to You?' The King will answer, 'Assuredly, I say to you, inasmuch as you did it to one of the least of these My brethren, you did it to Me' " (Matthew 25:37-40).

The lasting legacy of the British Great Awakening of 1739-1791 was that generations of people became devout Christians, who inspired by the teaching of Jesus, sought to make the world better – starting with those in need around them. They did not look to government to provide the way, because they believed the world was changed one life at a time, by direct action.

In Britain, people's lives were being improved by Christian charity and a new sense of duty grabbed Christian politicians, and legislation soon followed, leading to substantial progress. For the people of Britain, when Christianity became real to them, the exhortations of God in the Bible took on far greater meaning and action had to be taken. Christianity was not something to be embraced on Sunday; it had to shape every area of their lives. Passages from the Bible on helping the poor were no longer abstract concepts, now they provided a mission statement and a new vision for England to embrace: 'Pure and undefiled religion before God and the Father is this: to visit orphans and widows in their trouble, and to keep oneself unspotted from the world (James 1:27). It was this reawakening of Christianity in Britain which led in the following century to leaders such as William Wilberforce and the Clapham Sect, who campaigned to abolish the slave trade, slavery, and improve the lives of the poor in Britain and abroad.

The historian Sir C Grant Robertson in his 1911 book, *England under the Hanoverians* explains: 'Methodism and the French Revolution are the two most tremendous phenomena of the [eighteenth] century. John Wesley swept the dead air with an irresistible cleansing ozone. To thousands of men and women his preaching and gospel revealed a new heaven and a new earth; it brought religion into soulless lives and reconstituted it as a comforter, an inspiration and a judge. No one was too poor, too humble, too degraded, to be born again and share in the privilege of Divine grace, to serve the one Master, Christ, and to attain the blessed fruition of God's peace. Aloof alike from politics and the speculations of the schools, Wesley wrestled with the evil of his day and proclaimed the infinite power of a Christian faith, based on personal conviction, eternally renewed from within, to battle sin, misery and vice in all its forms. The social service that he accomplished was not the least of his triumphs. It is certain that into the moral fibre of the English people, even in the classes most anxious to repudiate the debt, were woven new strands' by Christian teaching.

Prime Minister David Lloyd George (1863-1945) acknowledged this transformational power. On 20 June 1922 he said, "I come from a country that owes more to the Methodism Movement, of which Wesley was the inspirer and prophet and leader, than to any other movement in the whole of its history...John Wesley inaugurated a movement that gripped the soul of England, that deepened its spiritual instincts, trained them and uplifted them. That movement which improved the conditions of the working classes, in wages, in hours of labour, and otherwise, found most of its best officers and non-commissioned officers in men trained in Christian institutions, which were the result of Wesley's Methodism."[2]

Due to the spiritual awakening in Britain, Christians felt compelled to address the social injustices of the day, which gradually improved the lot of the common people. For the first time in history, there was a large push to give education to all, and churches became the centre of this new movement. If these new Christians were to improve their lives, they had to be able to read the Bible, and to read they needed an education.

Author Albert D. Belden traced how the freedoms of Christianity led to political aspirations: 'The free churches were one of the pure sources from which free democracy came. It was by the dynamic of free religion that masses were inspired by escape from the quagmire of misery and injustice. The Christian faith persevered the masses from being soulless things, obedient to the convenience and advantage of economic forces.'[3]

Chapter Fifteen

Christianity, Commerce and Civilisation

The Evangelical Revival (1739-1791) in Britain wrought grand social revolutions and improved the lives of millions of people, also it provided them with a vision of another home in heaven. Injustice was still being fought against in their daily lives and the British Christian vision was to go global. There were many Christians who believed God Almighty gave Britain an Empire, and power was placed under the guardianship of Britain by God, for them to fulfil His purposes in the world. 'For the Kingdom is the Lord's and He rules over the nations' (Psalm 22:28), and, 'blessed is the nation whose God is the Lord' (Psalm 33:12).

During her lifetime, many believed Queen Victoria (1819-1901) presided over a Golden Age of rapid progress in the world. At home industry ushered in the modern age, global trade networks were established abroad and Christianity brought reform. Many believed God was blessing Britain's efforts at bringing moral reform to the world, and His approval was found by the Empire doubling in size during her rule, during an age which was almost free from global war, known as the British Peace from 1815-1914.[1]

Queen Victoria gave her name to an age of Christian belief, missionary endeavour and global moral advance. The British believed God had given them the Empire for the good of the world, but how His mission was to be completed was open to debate. When pioneer missionary David Livingstone (1813-1873) witnessed the slave trade continuing in Africa, he came to believe that the work of William Wilberforce, who had worked to outlaw the slave trade, was only half complete. The law was made and now the law had to be enforced.

In Britain, people began to preach how the British Empire could be used to transform the lawlessness and chaos abroad in some lands, to become ordered, legal, moral societies. From their Victorian viewpoint, the immoral chiefs and leaders in Africa, Asia and the Pacific needed civilisation. Now the illegal trade of slaves had to be replaced with modern commerce and trade, and the vacuum of religious values was to be filled by Christ. If the world was to be changed, it had to begin in the hearts of men and women. The same civilising power which transformed Britain from a pagan land to a world power was to be exported. Thus the threefold vision unfolded of the British Empire exporting Christianity, commerce and civilisation.

David Livingstone wanted missionaries and sacrificial business leaders to go to Africa, putting themselves last, to help Africans create a bright future. This sentiment was echoed by Queen Victoria's four time Prime Minister W. E. Gladstone, who believed the British Empire had no right to command the world, and should lead by example. He is one of Britain's most devout Christian prime ministers who wore his religious and social conscience on his sleeves. His substantial political opponent, Benjamin Disraeli, was the most cunning politician, who cared more about the prestige and advancement of British rule.

David Livingstone's vision was embraced by many hearers of his Cambridge University speech of 1857, where he said, "My object in going into the country south of the desert was to instruct the natives in a knowledge of Christianity...I might have gone on instructing the natives in religion, but as civilisation and Christianity must go on together...My desire is to open a path to this district, that civilisation, commerce and Christianity might find their way there...A prospect is now before us of opening Africa for commerce and the gospel. Providence has been preparing the way.

"The natives of Central Africa are very desirous of trading, but their only traffic is at present in slaves, of which the poorer people have an unmitigated horror. It is therefore most desirable to encourage the former principle, and thus open a way for the consumption of free productions, and the introduction of Christianity and commerce...to the first teachers of Christian truth in regions which may never have before been blest with the name and gospel of Jesus Christ."[2]

The British response to Livingstone's appeal was phenomenal. Almost thirty years later, British zeal for spreading Christianity to the world was undiminished. In 1885, seven intelligent and prominent students at Cambridge University committed themselves to be missionaries in China. The Cambridge Seven became international celebrities for their sacrificial choices and all joined Hudson Taylor's China Inland Mission. Before they left, they toured university campuses of Britain, holding meetings for the students and encouraging people to take up the vision. Queen Victoria was thrilled when she received a booklet of the testimonies of the Cambridge Seven's experiences. The book *The Evangelisation of the World: A Missionary Band* became a bestseller and this inspired The Student Volunteer Movement in the U.S., with the same missionary zeal.

Queen Victoria believed such endeavour was part of Britain's role serving its destiny. The Victorians believed God gave Britain power in the world to serve His eternal purposes – to right wrongs, abolish the slave trade and slavery, to bring tyrants to justice, and export law and order to lands in chaos. The first speech the Queen's husband, Prince Albert (1819-1861) gave in English was his acceptance of the presidency of the Society for the Extinction of the slave trade and for the Civilisation of Africa, in which he proclaimed that slavery was, "Repugnant to the spirit of Christianity."

In 1839 to Parliament, Queen Victoria said, "I shall continue to pursue with perseverance the negotiations, in which I am engaged, to persuade all the powers of Christendom to unite in a general league for the entire extinction of the slave trade, and I trust that, with the blessing of Providence, my efforts in so righteous a cause will be rewarded with success."[3]

In 1841, she once again committed Britain and the Empire to the advancement of the Christian religion and morality, saying to Parliament, "It is always with entire confidence that I recur to the advice and assistance of my Parliament. I place my reliance upon your wisdom, loyalty, and patriotism; and I humbly implore of Divine Providence that all your councils may be so directed as to advance the great interests of morality and religion, to preserve peace, and to promote by enlightened legislation the welfare and happiness[4]...in the adoption of such measures as are necessary to maintain that high station among the nations of the world which it has pleased Divine Providence to assign to this country."[5]

In her speeches to Parliament throughout the years, the Queen spoke of the importance of religion – which meant Christianity, and the need for Divine Providence, at home and abroad. In 1843, as she worked to help persecuted Christians abroad, she said, "In concert with her allies, Her Majesty has succeeded in obtaining for the Christian population of Syria, the establishment of a system of administration which they were entitled to expect from the engagements of the Sultan, and from the good faith of this country."[6] In 1849, "It is my earnest hope that by cultivating respect to the law and obedience to the precepts of religion, the liberties of this nation may, by the blessing of Almighty God, be perpetuated."[7] In 1850, "The favour of Divine Providence has hitherto preserved this Kingdom from the wars and convulsions which during the last two years have shaken so many of the states of the continent of Europe."[8] In 1872, "I shall continue to rely, under Divine Providence..."[9]

In 1834, the Palace of Westminster was destroyed by fire and a new building for Parliament was needed, which was completed in 1870. Interwoven into the design of the modern Palace was the Christian heart of the British people. The building at the centre of British power was to be filled with Christian images, quotations and biblical aspirations. Engraved on the floor in the Central Lobby, at the very centre of Parliament is: 'Except the Lord build the House, they labour in vain that build it' (Psalm 127:1). The Victorians made faith in the God of the Bible the substance of Parliament. The Chapel of St. Stephen continued to retain its role and the Moses Room, containing a large fresco of Moses and another of Daniel, is persistent in its cry for biblical justice. The Queen's Robing Room is dominated by paintings of Christian knights and in the House of Lords there is a fresco of the baptism of King Ethelbert, the first known Christian King of England.

In her confidential journals, the Queen also kept her personal accounts of the missionaries she and Albert met, who told them of the spread of Christianity throughout the British Empire:

Tuesday, 14 October 1851.

'Bunsen gave us some interesting accounts of the African Missionaries & of Mr Crowder, a black one, who is over here with his wife.'[10]

Tuesday, 18 November 1851.

'On coming home I saw, in Albert's room an African Missionary Mr Crowther, who was brought by Ld Wriothesley Russell. Mr Crowther was ordained a few years ago by the Bishop of London. He...comes from Abekuta, speaks English extremely well & is very intelligent & pleasing with quiet unaffected manners. He was liberated from slavery 29 years ago, when he was 13, & he has the marks of his tribe on his face. He gave us very interesting accounts of the decimation of the slave trade, the progress of Christianity & the great fortitude & courage displayed by the Christians, even when tortured by the native Priests.'[11]

Thursday, 13 July 1854.

'We went again to see the Maharajah sitting for his picture. He had brought with him the Pandit Nehemiah Gori, a young Brahmin Christian, converted since 6 years, the son of a Brahmin Priest! He belongs to the Church Missionary Society & is singularly modest & retiring. His manner, dress, & everything, were very striking. Albert talked with him for an hour.'[12]

Friday, 4 August 1854.

'Sir George praised the Fingoes very much, who were very like the Zulus...they have made great progress in civilisation & the

Missionaries have been successful amongst them.'[13]

Queen Victoria gave her name to the age and missionary to Africa David Livingstone became the pioneering face of the age. On 13 February 1858, the two met at Buckingham Palace. Victoria was delighted by his accounts of missionary activity throughout the unknown and unmapped parts of Africa, but was shocked to find how the Scotsman had adopted a strong foreign accent, after spending years not speaking any English. In her private diary she chronicles: 'In the afternoon saw...the wonderful traveller & explorer in Africa, Dr Livingstone, who is going there again. He is unassuming, pleasing & very interesting, I should say about 43 or 4. He speaks a rather singular English, much like a foreigner.'[14]

Fourteen years later, whilst Livingstone's adventures in Africa became a worldwide sensation, because Henry Stanley (1841-1904) sought and found him, the Queen read with excitement of his mission in Africa. 'The Dss of Roxburghe read me an interesting account of Dr Livingstone who is safe & well.'[15] Just a little more than a month later, the Queen met with Stanley to hear his firsthand account of searching for and finding David Livingstone.[16] A year and a half later, the Queen notes: 'Poor good & distinguished Livingstone's funeral took place at Westminster Abbey today. His death which we heard of about 2 months ago, must have occurred nearly a year ago & the poor faithful Blacks carried his remains, which they managed to embalm after a fashion, — through all that wild unknown country, at considerable risk.'[17]

The Queen was interested in the spread of Christianity around the world.

Tuesday, 2 July 1861.

'The Maharajah Duleep Singh...found his nephew much improved – asking for a Bible – wishing to learn, & not believing any longer in his own religion. He has brought his mother back with him; she is free from prejudice, not minding going about & being seen & frequently wears European dress. She even will go to Church!'[18]

For Christians who lived during Queen Victoria's reign, it was important for them to perceive the events which unfolded in the nation's faith, as a return to and continuation of Britain's covenant with God, and the doubling of the British Empire was to them, God's reply. 'He makes nations great and destroys them; He enlarges nations and guides them' (Job 12:23).

Commencing with King Ethelbert in the sixth century and King Alfred in the ninth, England had made a covenant with God, and

Queen Victoria, as Head of State and Supreme Governor of the Church of England, was personally committing herself, Britain and the British Empire to be used by God, for His eternal purposes. 'For God is with the generation of the righteous' (Psalm 14:5).

It was the faith of the British people which enabled the British Empire to overcome evil within and help it to attempt to do something to improve the lives of people around the world. Professor Diarmaid MacCulloch said, "The Church created the sense that the English are somehow destined to play a big role on the world stage,"[19] and that sense of mission to help the spread and safeguarding of liberty worldwide has never truly subsided.

The British vision to end injustice overseas was underpinned by the Christian campaigners in Holy Trinity Church, Clapham, London, who succeeded in outlawing the slave trade in 1807 and the institution of slavery by 1833. Professor Niall Ferguson said, "You could say the moral transformation of the British Empire began right here in this church...The Clapham sect as they were known excelled in generating a new wave of grass roots activism...so widespread was the popular revulsions, the government simply caved in and abolished the slave trade."[20]

Now that the British had, in the name of Christianity, outlawed the slave trade, it had to enforce the rule of law. This led to the British tax payer funding the first global 'Police Force' to enforce British convictions, based on the Bible, that the slave trade and slavery are illegal. This was the first case of what we might now call the belief in and the enforcement of international law. The Royal Navy declares: 'Between 1807 and 1866, the Royal Navy captured well over 500 slave ships and prevented many more from loading their slave cargo. The abolition was also very demanding for the sailors enforcing the act; the Royal Navy committed up to 13% of its total manpower to its West Africa squadron, which in one year lost 25% of those serving on the station mainly to disease. Overall, the nineteenth century costs of suppression were bigger than the eighteenth century profits.'[21]

Professor of History, David Eltis explains the cost of such an endeavour: 'The Royal Navy's early success in suppressing the British slave trade was quick and dramatic, but the slave trade was hydra-headed. As British ships withdrew from the trade, others were quick to take their place – first the French, and then the Spanish and the Portuguese. As one slave depot on the coast of Africa was driven out of business, another would spring up a little further away. Britain did indeed pay heavily in 'subsidies' to other European countries to induce them to give up or at least curtail their trade in slaves; somewhat less to numerous chiefs on the African coast for the same purpose; vast sums to its own slave-owners in the West Indies to purchase the freedom of their slaves in 1833; more again to meet the costs of maintaining a squadron on the coast of Africa. It has been estimated that great as was the wealth generated by the slave trade in the half century before 1807, the costs of suppressing it added up to a similar sum.'[22]

The concept that Christian missionaries made the world a better place was adopted by most Britons and continued long into the twentieth century. In 1931, Winston Churchill gave a speech on 'Our Duty in India,' seven decades after the Indian Mutiny. Having travelled to India, he still believed Christianity could do a great deal more to help the Indian people.

In the Royal Albert Hall, he proclaimed, "Let me just direct your attention once more upon these untouchables, fifty or sixty million of them, that is to say more than the whole population of the British Isles; all living their lives in acceptance of the validity of the awful curse pronounced upon them by the Brahmins. A multitude as big as a nation, men, women and children deprived of hope and of the status of humanity. Their plight is worse than that of slaves, because they have been taught to consent not only to a physical, but to a psychic servitude and prostration.

"I have asked myself whether if Christ came again into this world, it would not be to the untouchables of India that He would first go, to give them the tidings that not only are all men equal in the sight of God, but that for the weak and poor and downtrodden a double blessing is reserved.

"Certainly the success of Christianity and missionary enterprise has been greater among the untouchables than among any other class of the Indian population. The very act of accepting Christianity by one of these poor creatures, involves a spiritual liberation from this obsession of being unclean; and the curse falls from their minds as by a miracle. They stand erect, captains of their fate in the broad sunlight of the world. There are also nearly five million Indian Christians in India, a large proportion of whom can read and write, and some of whom have shown themselves exceptionally gifted."[23]

Chapter Sixteen

The Faith of Queen Victoria

Queen Victoria's journal provides us with an illustration of her faith and values, and they serve to exemplify the Christian beliefs of millions of her subjects in Britain. In these private writings Queen Victoria provides us with a fascinating insight into her real Christian faith, her personal prayers, and the supplications she makes for the nation and Empire. She often records insights into the inspirational sermons which have touched her and aided her understanding of what it means to be a believer in Jesus Christ. She notes some of the Christian books she is reading and records the progress of missionaries.

When the Queen visited the British Museum, she records how archaeology corroborates Scripture. In her journals there are 1,974 entries about God, 862 of prayer, 78 of Christ, 66 of faith, 39 of preaching, 37 of Bible, 27 of Scripture, 40 of missionary or missionaries, 21 of Jesus and 9 of Christianity. The following are some examples:

Sunday, 14 September 1834.

'At 11 we went to church. Mr. Pope preached an excellent sermon. It was taken from the 3rd chapter of St. Paul's Epistle to the Colossians, 23rd and 24th verse. "And whatsoever ye do, do it heartily, as to the Lord and not unto men; knowing that of the Lord ye shall receive the reward of the inheritance: for ye serve the Lord Christ."[1]

Sunday, 11 January 1835.

'Dr. Shuttleworth preached a very fine sermon. The text was taken from the 16th chapter of Acts, 29th verse: "Then he called for a light, and sprang in and came trembling, and fell down before Paul and Silas, and brought them out, and said, 'Sirs, what must I do to be saved?' And they said, 'Believe on the Lord Jesus Christ, and thou shalt be saved, and thy house.' "[2]

Sunday, 6 December 1835.

'We went down to prayers with Lady Flora, dear Lehzen, and Sir J.C. The service was performed by the Dean of Chester, who likewise gave us a very good sermon. The text was from Matthew chapter 6th, 9th and 10th verses: "Our Father which art in heaven, Hallowed be Thy name, Thy Kingdom come, Thy will be done on earth as it is in heaven."[3]

Sunday, 9 October 1836.

'We went to the Church at Ramsgate with Ly Catherine & Lehzen. Mr Harvey preached. The text was from the 5th chap: of 2d Epistle to Cor: 10th verse: "For we must all appear before the judgment seat of Christ; that every man may receive the things done in his body according to that he hath done, whether it be good or bad."[4]

Tuesday, 15 December 1840.

'I am sure I have reason to be sleepy thankful to that Almighty Providence, for having so wonderfully preserved me throughout & I humbly pray, fervently trust that Our Heavenly Father will protect & bless both my beloved Albert & myself, as well as our precious Child. I also pray that I may be strengthened in all my good resolutions & in conquering my faults & bad habits.'[5]

Sunday, 31 December 1843.

'I must also & indeed do feel unbounded gratitude to Him who has ever been so merciful to us. I pray to Him, through His blessed Son, for the long continuation of our happiness.'[6]

Tuesday, 31 December 1844.

'This year has however brought us our 2nd little Boy, & many very interesting & delightful events, for which we must be grateful. I humbly & fervently pray God to preserve us two, safe & well, with our dear Children, & those near & dear to us, for many years!'[7]

Thursday, 1 January 1846.

'The clock struck 12 before we fell asleep & we wished one another warmly & tenderly joy. I feel such confidence in God's mercy & goodness, that I look with security to the beginning of another year & trust in His protection of us together. May He equally protect & bless our dear children, dear mother & relatives. Then I also pray for my Country, & for its safety.'[8]

Friday, 25 December 1846.

'Service at 11...read out of the Bible, the accounts of our Saviour's birth.'[9]

Saturday, 6 February 1847.

'We talked of France & the danger of war, which I can't hear to think of, & which I pray day & night, may long be averted.'[10]

Wednesday, 23 February 1851.

'We both slept well, but our thoughts were naturally entirely engrossed with the very important events of the last days, & only pray for wisdom & strength to do what is best & safest for the Country in these troubled times.'[11]

Sunday, 8 October 1854.

'To the Kirk at 12. Mr McLead of Glasgow, son of the old Dr

McLead, performed the service & preached. I never heard anything finer, than the sermon, entirely extempore, so beautifully argued out & put, yet so simple & eloquent. The text was the story of Nicodemus coming to Our Lord to ask what he should do to obtain eternal life & Dr McLead showed why Jesus told him to sell all he had, though he was a good & moral man, seeing where the weak point was & that there the cure must be made. Dr McLead pointed out how we all tried to please self & live for that, thereby finding no rest. Christ had come, not only to die for us, but to show us how we were to live. — Everyone came back edified & delighted.'[12]

After one service at St Paul's Cathedral in London, Queen Victoria asked her chaplain, "Can one be absolutely sure in this life of eternal safety?" The Queen did not receive a satisfactory reply and the news of her question was published, and came to the attention of an evangelist by the name of John Townsend, who sent the following letter to the Queen.

'To her Gracious Majesty, our beloved Queen Victoria, from one of her most humble subjects: With trembling hands, but heartfelt love, and because I know that we can be absolutely sure now of our eternal life in the Home that Jesus went to prepare, may I ask your Most Gracious Majesty to read the following passages of Scripture: John 3:16; Romans 10:9,10? These passages prove that there is full assurance of salvation by faith in our Lord Jesus Christ for those who believe and accept His finished work. I sign myself, your servant for Jesus' sake, John Townsend.'

Two weeks later an unexpected reply was received. "To John Townsend: Your letter of recent date I received and in reply would state that I have carefully and prayerfully read the portions of Scripture referred to. I believe in the finished work of Christ for me, and trust by God's grace to meet you in that Home of which He said, "I go to prepare a place for you." Signed personally by Queen Victoria.[13]

Years later, an elderly lady said nervously to the Queen, "Your Majesty, will I see you in heaven one day?" With a smile of faith, the Queen said, "By the all-availing blood of Jesus, you most certainly shall, my dear! I have His Word on it!"

Saturday, 23 June 1855.

'We went at 5, with Jane C., &c. – to the British Museum, where Col: Rawlinson, just returned from Baghdad met us. Visited new rooms for the Antiquities, which really are most interesting &, upstairs, saw some of the curiosities from Nineveh & drawings of the stones, which are shortly expected. There is a small alabaster vase, containing the actual sweetmeats of the time of

Nebuchadnezzar!...most curious of all, a cylinder in terra cotta, upon which are engraved histories of the greatest importance, which Col: Rawlinson says was placed in the very spot where he found it, by Nebuchadnezzar. This inscription gives an account of his madness. All that has been found tends to corroborate Scripture & to clear up, in a very satisfactory way doubts on many subjects.'[14]

Wednesday, 9 November 1859.

'Dear Bertie seemed so happy, & I pray God to bless him & keep him in the right path.'[15]

Thursday, 5 June 1862.

'Every evening I go to the sacred Blue Room & pray there.'[16]

Saturday, 29 August 1863.

'How dreadful it is to have no-one on whose judgment I can safely & ent rely rely & feel no anxiety, or question of a doubt. Now I turn from one to the other & know not what to do. I pray daily for God to guide me aright.'[17]

Monday, 28 September 1868.

'Thank God! He is very well, & one can but commit him to God's protection, & pray that he may return safely to us.'[18]

Saturday, 23 December 1871.

"Oh! God, the father of all mercies, Thou that liftest us up from the gates of death, we yield Thee hearty thanks that, though it seemed good to Thee, that we should have at this season sorrow upon sorrow. Thou didst yet turn Thee again at the last and in the greatness of Thy power, hast preserved one who was at the point to die...now hast Thou given back to us, as yet, a brother and a son. Continue we beseech Thee, Thy Fatherly care over him. Watch over him in the turn of weakness and day by day increase his strength. And if it please Thee that he recover his bodily health, grant that having Thy great goodness always in remembrance, he may walk before Thee in newness of life, so that following in the steps of Thy servant his father, by serving Thee in his generation, he may, after this life be partaker with him of Thy Heavenly Kingdom. Through Jesus Christ our Lord – Amen."[19]

Monday, 1 January 1872.

'I pray God to help me on & preserve all dear to me.'[20]

Friday 1 January 1875.

'I pray for God's blessing on all my dear ones, & for guidance & strength during this year.'[21]

Wednesday, 20 December 1876.

'Finished reading Dr Farrar's *Life of Christ*, which is certainly very fine, but the ending...is very painful.'[22]

Sunday, 1 April 1877.

'Dr Farrar, who preached a fine sermon on Immortality, comparing the dreadful scepticism of many in the present day, with the blessings of Christianity & the blessed hopes it holds out to us. The text was from 1rst Corinthians, XV. v. 13, "But if there be no resurrection of the dead, then is Christ not risen." ' [23]

Sunday, 9 June 1878.

'Service at 10:30 in the house, performed by Principal Tulloch, who preached beautifully. The text from Col: III. v 1 & 2. "Ye then being risen with Christ, seek those things, which are above, where Christ sitteth on the right hand of God." v. 2. "Set your affections on things above, not on things on the earth." The sermon was so true, so charitable.'[24]

Saturday, 1 January 1881.

'God spare all I most love, for many a year, & help me on! I feel how sadly deficient I am, & how over sensitive & irritable, & how uncontrollable my temper is, when annoyed & hurt. But I am so overdone, so vexed, & in such distress about my country, that that must be my excuse. I will daily pray for God's help to improve.'[25]

Wednesday, 1 January 1890.

'Another year begun! I will not say much, but thank God for His goodness, mercy & protection in the past, & pray Him to continue to protect & help me in my arduous task. May I yet be allowed to labour for the good of my Country, children, & children's children.'[26]

Sunday, 20 June 1897.

'This eventful day, 1897, has opened & I pray God to help & protect me as He has hitherto done during these 60 long eventful years!...God will surely help me on!'[27]

Tuesday, 31 July 1900.

'I pray God to help me to be patient & have trust in Him, who has never failed me!'[28]

Chapter Seventeen

Fighting for Liberty

Britain's Victorian Golden Age came rudely to an end with the death of Queen Victoria in 1901. With a gasp, those in the know began to lose confidence, as the new industrial powers like Germany, the U.S.A, and Japan began to expand, Britain's position in the world was shrinking. Nevertheless, Britain still had the world's biggest navy and the largest empire in earth's history. But in the secret halls of power, men with dark suits began to analyse the situation of a tiny nation, dominating the oceans and seas of the world, whilst ruling much of Africa, Asia, the Caribbean and parts of the Pacific. They began to call it, "The world's largest confidence trick." In 1901, India had a population of almost 240 million, whilst Britain had about 38 million, and yet the coming war would leave Britain with more territories and peoples overseas, especially in the Middle East.

Much had been achieved for the peace and prosperity of the world during Britain's Golden Age, as the pre-eminent global superpower throughout the years 1815 to 1914. But now Britain's hundred year preservation of world peace ended, with the outbreak of the First World War.

On 28 June 1914, the assassination of Archduke Franz Ferdinand (1863-1914), heir to the throne of Austria-Hungary became a catalyst to terror. The complex series of European alliances meant that the shooting of this one man, to what was a minor throne in Europe, led to more than seventy million military personal being mobilised, and more than nine million combatants and seven million civilians died as a result. Nevertheless, there was one aggressive nation who perceived the war as a means to expand.

During the nineteenth century, the many principalities and states of the German people were being united into one federalised nation, which officially occurred on 18 January 1871, after French capitulation in the Franco-Prussian war of 1870-1871. A unified and militarised Germany upset the balance of European power which the British established after 1815, and now Germany felt like a caged tiger, in a world of European Empires.

When the war broke out, the leaders of Germany felt this was the time for the German influence to be felt abroad, and the invasion of Belgium commenced in 1914. What followed is what historians call, 'The Rape of Belgium.' Many German soldiers, encouraged by their superiors made no distinction between military personal and civilians, and a campaign of murder, pillage and rape commenced. Over five thousand civilians were killed within three months and twenty thousand buildings were burnt down. The city of Louvain was incinerated and looted for five days. History Professor John Horne said it created, "1.5 million Belgian and 500,000 French refugees...the roads were absolutely crammed."[1] In 2001, Germany's Secretary of State, Walter Kolbow, apologised to Belgium for the brutal campaign which, "Indulged in murder, desecrated churches and torched your residential areas."

The rape of Belgium provided many in Britain with a conviction that the war against Germany was just, with tyranny on one side, and liberation on the other. Many British people entered the war with a false hope that the war would be over by Christmas, and as the troops became ensnared in the trenches, many Christian organisations did everything to help.

Scripture Gift Mission printed and distributed over forty-seven million items of Scripture, including the Gospel of John and the New Testament, which were, 'designed to fit in the top pocket of a uniform, with rounded edges to prevent creasing. They had hymns at the back so that chaplains could use them to lead church services in the field, and a 'decision form' that soldiers could sign as a declaration of faith.[2] Each one contained the message of Field Marshal Lord Roberts (1832-1914), one of the most successful commanders of the 19th century, and the last Commander-in-Chief of the Forces. His message to the troops on 25 August 1914 was, "I ask you to put your trust in God. He will watch over you and strengthen you. You will find in this little Book guidance when you are in health, comfort when you are in sickness and strength when you are in adversity. Roberts.'

Not all the soldiers wanted to receive the Scriptures and yet, many sceptical people and nominal Christians became believers. One said this, "When your small Testaments were distributed on the Common at Southampton, I, among others, accepted one in a more derisive than a complimentary manner...I little dreamed that I should use it and find in it great consolation in lonely hours...I have learned to realise the great personality of the Saviour. When at night I have been on duty alone with Him by my side and the Germans but thirty yards away, I realised that I needed more than my own courage to stand the strain. When the shells of the enemy have burst periodically at my feet I have marvelled at the fact of still being alive."³

Another letter in response to the gift said, "Just a few lines to let you know that I have filled in the decision form, at the end of the Gospel of John that was given to me at the station. I accept Christ as my Saviour. I wish you would pray for me in the hour of trial." Many more responded. "Twenty men signed the decision cards today," said one man visiting a camp in Hampshire, "that makes the number of men signed 163."⁴

As trench warfare brought the immediate question of eternity into the hearts of many young men, one evangelist wrote: 'Never have workers witnessed such hunger for pocket testaments and Gospels as during the past few days. The decision for Christ has been most real...one day's work alone has witnessed seventy men definitely yielding to Christ.'⁵

When the young men on both sides of the conflict realised they had been led into a terrible war, it was their shared Christian traditions which enabled them to perceive their common humanity in such cruelty. On Christmas Eve in 1914, both German and British soldiers joined in singing Christian hymns together, which gave them the confidence to meet and agree an unofficial truce, which lasted for five days in some places. Words from the Bible took on new meaning, "Glory to God in the highest and on earth peace good will toward men" (Luke 2:14).

Nevertheless, the German leadership had to be defeated and when Winston Churchill took charge of Britain's Royal Navy, he too needed guidance. As he explained in his memoirs: 'That night when I went to bed, I saw a large Bible lying on a table in my bedroom. I thought of the peril of Britain, peace loving, unthinking, little prepared....I thought of mighty Germany...I opened the Book at random and in the 9th Chapter of Deuteronomy I read: "Thou art to...possess nations greater and mightier than thyself...understand therefore this day, that the Lord thy God is He which goes over before thee; as a consuming fire...not for thy righteousness, or for the uprightness of thy heart...but for the wickedness of these nations the Lord thy God doth drive them out from before thee, and that He may perform the word which the Lord sware unto thy fathers." It seemed a message full of reassurance.'⁶

The tragedy of the First World War has overshadowed one of the most costly and great victories of the war. Emeritus Professor of Military and Security Studies, Richard Holmes said, "It's somehow characteristic of the British that glorious defeats can overshadow hard-fought victories. Between the Battle of Amiens, which began on August 8, and the Armistice of November 11, 1918, the British Army (including substantial contingents from Australia, Canada, India, New Zealand and South Africa) pushed the Germans right back across northern France, to reach Mons, where they'd fired their first shots in 1914. In the process they captured 188,700 prisoners, while the Belgians, French and Americans between them took some 197,000. The British showed mastery of techniques learnt earlier at such shocking cost, and many commanders demonstrated a real flair for mobile offensive warfare. The German rearguards fought doggedly, and the toll of British casualties (180,000 in the first 50 days) shows that this was no walkover. Yet by early November the Germans had been defeated in the field, and they knew it.'[7]

An international coalition fought for freedom and defeated the tyranny of Germany; and the First World War also changed history in the Middle East. During the 'Great Game' of Britain's struggle with Russia in the nineteenth century, Britain propped up the Middle Eastern Muslim Ottoman Empire, as a buffer to keep Russia out of the region. When the Ottoman's joined with Germany, Britain had no reason to support it any longer. During the Battle of Megiddo from 19 September to 31 October 1918, in present day Israel, Jordan and Syria, Britain led the allies into a shocking advance taking Damascus and Aleppo, before the Turks sued for peace in October 1918.

The world's last Muslim empire, which was responsible for the Armenian Genocide of 1,500,000 mostly Christian deaths, and which had allowed its own Muslim and Christian populations, particularly in Syria and Lebanon to starve in their hundreds of thousands, as they fought in the First World War[8] was crumbling. Thus Britain was soon to be used by God, to help enable His end time biblical purposes to be fulfilled. Ezekiel's vision of a dead nation, rising to life again, over 1,800 years later, was about to come to pass (Ezekiel 37:10-14).

'The people of Britain made a unique contribution to the establishment of the State of Israel,' explained Derek Prince, Bible teacher and former fellow of Cambridge University. 'For more than three centuries, Christians in Britain had nourished a vision, based on the Bible, that God desired to make of the Jewish people a sovereign nation once again in their own land. Politically, this vision found expression through such men as Lord Shaftesbury and Lord Balfour. In 1917, it was the Balfour Declaration made on behalf of the British government that set in motion the political processes that issued, thirty-one years later, in the establishment of the State of Israel. It was the British government too, that took the decisive step of placing before the United Nations the future of Palestine.'⁹

"The Church is rightly criticised for centuries of Christian anti-Semitism," said Rabbi Jamie Cowen, "but what is overlooked is the pivotal role British Christian Zionists played in the establishment of modern day Israel...the theology of British Puritans with regard to God's plan for the Jewish people, so influenced British public opinion that governmental leaders in the nineteenth century began manoeuvring international events towards the reestablishment of a Jewish Israel."[10]

In this Middle Eastern war, devout Christian General Allenby (1861-1936) wrought victory after victory against the Turks on his way to liberate Jerusalem. Allenby was a God fearing man who did not want to shed blood in the holy city of His Lord, and when the Turks heard the British were coming, the people who had fought so viciously before, trembled in fear and fled, crying out that God was against them. When General Allenby reached Jerusalem, he dismounted from his horse, entering the city which was liberated without a shot being fired, saying, "No one but the Messiah should enter this city mounted."

A month before Jerusalem's liberation, Lord Balfour (1848-1930), with the full backing of the British government, issued the Balfour Declaration which prepared the way for a Jewish state. The Balfour Declaration set an international precedent, as the great powers of the world began to accept the concept of a restored Jewish state in the holy land, and it was soon legally accepted by the forerunner to the United Nations.

The First World War changed the global balance of power and the Middle East forever. It was also very costly for Britain in the tragic loss of lives and economically. The world's banker became a debtor and for every £1 Britain earned in 1919, it owed someone £1.27.[11] Unfortunately, things did not get any easier; with the costs of new colonies in the Middle East and unrest, plus a financial crisis, debts grew by 1933, as Britain owed £1.79, for every £1 it had.[12] Interest on this debt fluctuated between nine and ten percent, which meant Britain entered the Second World War with huge debts weighing it down.

Chapter Eighteen

Divine Intervention

The early twentieth century fundamentally weakened Britain and its strength, and by the end of 1939, Britain found itself dragged into another war; this time to stop Adolf Hitler and the Nazi regime from taking over Europe and the world. Throughout this bleak period in history, many of the leading politicians and generals spoke openly and honestly, about their faith in God to save Britain and the West from the Nazis. There were many times when sincere prayer and faith rose in the darkest of months to believe that the 'invincible' Nazis could be defeated.

In May 1940, Britain faced losing its entire army to a terrible defeat in Dunkirk, when her soldiers were trapped in France as the Nazis encircled them, and the nation turned to prayer. During this trial His Majesty King George VI called for a National Day of Prayer on Sunday, 26 May 1940, saying, "In this fateful hour we turn, as our fathers before us have turned in all times of trial, to God Most High...I have asked that Sunday next be observed as a national day of prayer...let us with heart and soul humbly but confidently commit our cause to God and ask His aid that we may valiantly defend the right, as it is given us to see it."[1]

The king and members of the cabinet, alongside the public attended Westminster Abbey to seek God's aid, whilst millions of others flocked to churches to pray. That Sunday the whole nation was at prayer. The following day, newspapers printed pictures of the long queues of people anxious to get in and pray. One reporter said, "Nothing like it has ever happened before."[2]

After this day of seeking God, the most remarkable turnaround of events transpired. The top-brass in Britain expected only thirty thousand men could be saved from France; by contrast hundreds of thousands escaped the pincer movement of the German army and were delivered to England, to later go on and defeat the Nazis in North Africa, Italy and in Europe. Even the most cynical saw the nature of the miracle and one national newspaper declared, "The prayers of the nation were answered...the God of hosts Himself supported the valiant men of the British Expeditionary Force...two great wonders stand forth, on them have turned the fortune of our troops. I have talked to officers and men who have got safely back and all of them tell of these two phenomena. The first was the great storm which broke over Flanders on Tuesday, 28 May. The second was the great calm which settled on the English Channel during the days following. Officers of high rank do not hesitate to put down the deliverance of the British Expeditionary Force to the fact of the nation being at prayer on Sunday, 26 May, two days before that great storm in Flanders and the calm that came over the Channel."[3]

Winston Churchill believed only 30,000 soldiers could be saved, consequently, when he spoke in the House of Commons, he said, "335,000 men have been carried out of the jaws of death and shame to their native land," and he called it, "A miracle of deliverance."[4] The *Oxford Dictionary* defines the word miracle as: 'An extraordinary and welcome event that is not explicable by natural or scientific laws and is therefore attributed to a divine agency.'

The 9 June 1940 was set aside in Britain as a Day of National Thanksgiving to God, for His mighty deliverance and all over the nation, people sang Psalm 124, which seemed to sum up the miracle of deliverance: "If the Lord Himself had not been on our side, now may [Britain] say, if the Lord Himself had not been on our side, when men rose up against us; they would have swallowed us up quick, when they were so wrathfully displeased at us. Yea, the waters had drowned us...but praised be the Lord, who has not given us over for a prey unto their teeth. Our soul is escaped even as a bird out of the snare of the fowler: the snare is broken and we are delivered. Our help standeth in the name of the Lord, who hath made heaven and earth."

For all his life Winston Churchill was overshadowed with a sense of destiny residing on him, that in his lifetime Britain and the British Empire would be in trouble, and some how, he would be called to help and save them. Churchill is often called, 'A man of destiny.' It is an often neglected point that destiny, which is 'an event (or a course of events) that will inevitably happen in the future,' is impossible without an all-knowing, sovereign and unstoppable Power being able to foresee events and intervene in history to change them. The *Oxford Dictionary* states destiny is: 'The hidden power believed to control future events,' which for Christians can only be God. There can be no destiny, without One who destines. As Paul says: 'For we are His workmanship, created in Christ Jesus unto good works, which God hath before ordained that we should walk in them' (Ephesians 2:10). For the non-Christian, Britain was extremely fortunate to have the right man, in the right place at the right time to save Britain from cutting a false deal with Adolf Hitler. For believers, Winston Churchill was like Esther, sent for such a time as this (Esther 4:14), or Cyrus, God's anointed as the Scriptures state, who did not initially know he was an instrument in the hands of the Almighty (Isaiah 45:1).

Winston Churchill became prime minister on 10 May 1940 and needed to confront the failed appeasement policies of his predecessor, which had put Britain in an impossible military predicament. That evening he wrote in his diary: 'As I went to bed about 3am, I was conscious of a profound sense of relief. At last I had the authority to give directions over the whole scene. I felt as I was walking with destiny, and that all my past life had been but a preparation for this hour and for this trial.'[5]

On 13 May 1940, Churchill recalled Parliament and made his first speech as prime minister, setting out his government's new policy, that there would be no negotiations with Hitler, no appeasement, and no surrender. He declared, "I have nothing to offer but blood, toil, tears and sweat. You ask, 'What is our policy?' It is to wage war by sea, land and air, with all our might and with all the strength that God can give us: to wage war against a monstrous tyranny, never surpassed in the dark, lamentable catalogue of human crime. That is our policy. You ask, 'What is our aim?' I call answer in one word: Victory – victory at all costs, victory ill spite of all terror: victory however long and hard the road may be." An almost defeated nation was soon energised!

Hitler was shocked that a weak Britain no longer wanted to listen to his overtures, so on 16 July 1940, he issued Directive No. 16, which stated, "As England, in spite of the hopelessness of her military position, has so far shown herself unwilling to come to any compromise, I have decided to begin to prepare for, and if necessary to carry out, an invasion of England...and if necessary the island will be occupied." He said, "I will succeed where Napoléon failed. I will land on the shores of Britain."[6]

The initial invasion plan called for landings on a 200 mile front from Lyme Regis to Ramsgate, and German troops and boats began amassing in France waiting for the perfect conditions for the attack. Due to the huge logistics, and the need to control the air and sea, this was to take until September 1940. Up to 2,400 barges mounted on French shores, as the battle for the command of the skies commenced. If the Germans could cross the English Channel, the British defences were known to be weak, because the bulk of the British army's weapons had been lost in Dunkirk. It was expected that 60,000 German tanks were to be involved in the first overwhelming wave assault.[7]

Prayer was most certainly answered during the war and what was unknown to many at the time, was that at the Bible College of Wales, in Swansea, U.K., over one hundred committed believers were engaged in ceaseless intercession, with up to five prayer meetings a day, crying out to God for deliverance in all of the major battles of the war. These were not ordinary Christians, but men and women who had followed the command of Christ to sell all. They lived by faith and all served together, unpaid, at the school of the Bible College. This enabled them to meet together in many daily prayer meetings, seeking the will of God, and 'praying through' each situation, as the Holy Spirit led. Their lives exemplified total commitment to Christ, in full sacrifice, which enabled their prayers to be more than empty hopes, but truly led by the Holy Spirit (Romans 8:26, 1 John 5:14).

Rees Howells (1879-1950) was their leader, a man who had learnt that to truly engage intercession, one needs to surrender all to Christ and invite the Holy Spirit to fill every area of one's life. Rees Howells made an unconditional surrender to the Lord Jesus Christ and learnt to become sensitive to the Holy Spirit. This led to him discovering he was to pray only the prayers the Holy Spirit gave. The Lord taught him "prayer means answer," and because of this, he had confidence that when he prayed according to God's will – "Thy will be done, Thy Kingdom come," in each circumstance, the Spirit of God would reveal specific burdens.

When I spoke with many who were present in these meetings during the war years, I heard many remarkable testimonies. One woman who worked for the government was visiting the College, and she feared she would be arrested, because Rees Howells shared something which God had showed him to pray, and this lady had just seen the exact same thing in a private confidential secret government report the day before! She was never able to tell Rees Howells, because of the Official Secrets Act, but after six decades she felt at liberty to testify. Another person explained how the Lord showed Rees Howells that Russia had to enter the war, because it would be key to the defeat of the Nazis. At the time, the Soviet Union and the Nazis had a mutual pact, so it seemed very unlikely. But as they prayed for God to pull the Soviet Union into the war, Adolf Hitler made one of the gravest mistakes of the war – attacking this huge nation, with endless supplies of land and people.

When Winston Churchill summarised Britain's fight to survive and eventually defeat the Nazi system, he viewed it as nothing less than a total war "for the survival of Christian civilisation." Liberty, democracy, the rule of law, good government, and Christian moral values were all being fought for. Churchill declared, "The Battle of Britain is about to begin. Upon this battle depends the survival of Christian civilisation! Upon it depends our own British life, and the long continuity of our institutions and our Empire. The whole fury and might of the enemy must very soon be turned upon us. Hitler knows he will have to break us in this island or lose the war. If we can stand up to him, all of Europe may be free and the life of the world may move forward into broad, sunlit uplands."

For Rees Howells and his team, the intercessions for the defeat of the Nazis and the liberty of the world, was nothing less than a cry to God, for the conditions to be right for the fulfilment of the Jesus' Every Creature Commission of Mark 16:15-18. If the world was to hear the Gospel of Jesus Christ, the doors of the nations had to be opened and people needed to be free. This is why his concern shifted to international events. Rees Howells said, "The world became our parish and we were led to be responsible to intercede for countries and nations."

Rees believed the Nazi system was the greatest hindrance to missionary endeavour, by shutting the doors of the nations, and by cutting off the finances. In addition, Hitler's anti-Semitism was directly inspired by evil spirits, trying to resist God's end time plan for the Jews. Rees reached out to save young Jews from the massacre taking place by the Nazi machine, and brought some to Britain. Rees Howells declared, "The Lord has made known to us that He is going to destroy Hitler and the Nazi regime, that the world may know that it was God and God alone who has scattered the dictators. Three and a half years ago, the College prayed this prayer for weeks and months, and we firmly believe He will now answer it. He has isolated Germany so that He may get at this evil system, which is antichrist, and release Germany, the land of the Reformation. He will deal with the Nazis as He dealt with the Egyptian army in the time of Moses."

Chapter Nineteen

The Battle of Britain

If Adolf Hitler was to successfully invade Britain, he had to gain mastery of the skies and this is what led to the fiercest battles in the air ever witnessed. Rees Howells and his team prayed everyday at their base in Wales for years and they witnessed God answering prayer in unbelievable ways.

On 12 September 1940 Rees Howells said, "We prayed last night that London would be defended and that the enemy would fail to break through, and God answered prayer. Unless God can get hold of this devil and bind him, no man is safe. If we have protection for our properties, why not get protection for the country?"[1]

15 September 1940 was the fiercest day in the Battle for Britain, and Winston Churchill was present in the Royal Air Force (RAF) Operations Room, where he was able to learn how the Nazi squadrons flooded into the South of England. Churchill watched as British planes were sent up to battle and understood that the Royal Air Force was at breaking point. He asked the Air Marshal, "What other reserves have we?" "There are none," was the reply, and Churchill's face drained of colour. Then, within a few minutes, the German squadrons turned and fled! Just as Britain was at the edge of total defeat in the air, the Nazis fled and never came again n such numbers.

The German retreat on this day signalled the end of Hitler's plans to invade Britain and when Air Chief Marshall Sir Hugh Dowding (1882-1970), recounted the victory of the RAF, he said, "I say with absolute conviction that I can trace the Intervention of God…and if it had not been for this Intervention, the battle would have been joined in conditions which humanly speaking, would have rendered victory impossible."

When the German strategy to gain air superiority failed, Hitler tried to break the morale of the British, by ceaselessly bombing civilians. The devastation of the Blitz astounded the free world and many began to appreciate what kind of enemy the Nazi regime was. Many people in Britain began praying for protection, with the very real fear that they could be burnt or buried alive in their own homes. What followed in response to prayer was a miraculous series of angelic sightings, which confirmed for many that God was hearing and would turn the tide of the war.

One national newspaper reported that a white light had been spotted in the sky on the Sussex downs, which: 'Took the shape of Christ crucified on the cross. Then six angels took form... villagers working on the land said they had also seen it.' One eyewitness said, "We could see the nail in the crossed feet of Christ and one of the angels with arms up-stretched, appearing to be praying." The reporter said, "Similar statements have been made by other villagers."[2] Another report of a vision of a white cross was seen in the sky, which brought masses into the church of Rev. Harold Green, of St Nicholas' Church, Ipswich, and the events were widely reported.[3]

In South London, during the height of German air raids an angel was seen in the sky by residents. It was reported as: 'Angel seen in Peckham During Air Raid,' in the newspaper. One resident said, "The figure was perfect; there was no mistaking it," and he believed the angel was sent to shield the inhabitants from the bombs. At least eight others witnessed the vision.[4] Dr Victor Pearce was able to document numerous cases of angelic visions and revelations during both world conflicts, as a testimony to future generations, of the Divine nature of the intervention during these wars.[5]

The suffering of Britain during the Blitz enabled great sympathy to emerge in the United States for Britain's struggle. On 10 August 1941, Winston Churchill and U.S. President Roosevelt signed the Atlantic Charter, which proposed a new world order – Hitler would have to be defeated, and a new age of free nations was to emerge. When Churchill and Roosevelt met on the high seas, aboard HMS *Prince of Wales*, Winston Churchill personally chose several Christian hymns which incorporated the shared values and mission of the two nations. He later recorded: 'I chose the hymns myself: 'For Those in Peril on the Sea' and, 'Onward, Christian Soldiers.' We ended with, 'O God, Our Help in Ages Past'...every word seemed to stir the heart. It was a great hour to live. Nearly half those who sang were soon to die.'[6]

The reports of these world leaders singing 'Onward, Christian Soldiers' was an inspiration, and the hymn incorporated Churchill's understanding that the war against Nazism was a battle for 'Christian civilisation.' Winston Churchill broadcast this message to the British Empire: "We sang 'Onward, Christian Soldiers' indeed, and I felt that this was no vain presumption, but that we had the right to feel that we serving a Cause for the sake of which a trumpet has sounded from on high. When I looked upon that densely packed congregation of fighting men of the same language, of the same faith, of the same fundamental laws, of the same ideals...it swept across me that here was the only hope, but also the sure hope, of saving the world from measureless degradation. And so we came back across the ocean waves uplifted in spirit, fortified in resolve."[7]

Imagine how these words took on deep, purposeful meaning to the Prime Minister of Great Britain and the President of the United States, as they sang, whilst planning the defeat of Nazism: 'Onward, Christian soldiers, marching as to war, with the cross of Jesus going on before. Christ, the royal Master, leads against the foe; forward into battle see His banners go!' Second verse: 'At the sign of triumph Satan's host doth flee; on then, Christian soldiers, on to victory! Hell's foundations quiver at the shout of praise; brothers, lift your voices, loud your anthems raise...' Fourth verse: 'Crowns and thrones may perish, kingdoms rise and wane, but the Church of Jesus constant will remain. Gates of hell can never 'gainst that Church prevail; we have Christ's own promise, and that cannot fail.'[8]

Britain was fighting on a global scale to defeat Nazism and then the Empire of Japan. To its critics the British Empire was built on the oppression, plunder and exploitation of people with lesser technology, and certainly there are many examples of this being true. The high ideals of the Empire were not always manifested by greedy people in far away colonies. Nevertheless, the last stand of the British Empire was against Nazi Germany and the Japanese Empire, and if might ever found itself on the side of right, it was against these evil powers. Both these nations showed what could happen when power and technology found a place in nations which lost their moral compass.

The British Empire had survived for centuries because it was based on commerce, rather than conquest and plunder. It paid for its bills by trading, instead of plundering like Napoléon. It was able to defend democracy and liberty against Nazi Germany and Japan because it was a leader in technology. The plundering nations thought there is a limited amount of wealth in the world which has to be taken from others, but the British showed that wealth can be created through business, innovation, technology and trade.

According to the Bible, a nation which obeys and serves God will be the head of the nations, and not the tail. It will be blessed with an economy which can pay its bills and defend itself. 'The Lord will open to you His good treasure, the heavens, to give the rain to your land in its season and to bless all the work of your hand. You shall lend to many nations, but you shall not borrow.

And the Lord will make you the head and not the tail; you shall be above only, and not be beneath, if you heed the commandments of the Lord your God, which I command you today and are careful to observe them' (Deuteronomy 28:13-14).

One of the reasons Britain was able to defend liberty around the world was because God blessed the nation with numerous technological breakthroughs and the money to pay for their development, plus the wisdom to use them for good. On 15 September 1916, in the First World War, Britain revealed its top secret technology – the world's first tank. The design emerged from the tank Little Willie which ran in September 1915 and developed into the D1, the first tank ever to engage in battle. In the war, Britain produced 2,600 tanks of various types.

God has blessed Britain with pioneering technology throughout its history, from inventing the incandescent light bulb to the first train network and underground, to the fastest and most effective sail boats. HMS *Victory* was launched in 1765 and prepared the way for the great victory of 1805 at Trafalgar, and by 1860 HMS *Warrior* became the first armour-plated, iron-hulled warship. In 1906, HMS *Dreadnought* revolutionised naval power and made all other ships obsolete. By 1918, HMS *Argus* became the world's first carrier capable of launching and recovering naval aircraft.

In the air, Britain's Spitfire was developed just in time to play a critical role in maintaining air supremacy over England during World War Two, and it helped keep Hitler on the other side of the English Channel. Just as this plane was being produced, Frank Whittle (1907-1996), who had single-handedly invented the jet engine in England in 1928, had his first turbojet engine running by April 1937. Four years later, the Gloster Meteor was born and the Allies had their first operational jet aircraft.

By the outbreak of World War Two, Britain also engineered the world's first installation of aircraft detection and tracking stations, known today as Radar; enabling the Royal Air Force to see Nazi planes crossing the English Channel and to be ready for them. Meanwhile at Bletchley Park, code-breakers penetrated the secret communications of the Axis Powers, including the German Enigma and Lorenz ciphers. With the Allies being able to know the plans of the enemy, this put the Axis Powers of Germany and Japan in a similar situation to the Bible's King of Syria. 'Therefore the heart of the King of Syria was greatly troubled by this thing; and he called his servants and said to them, "Will you not show me which of us is for the King of Israel?" And one of his servants said, "None, my lord, O king; but Elisha, the prophet who is in

Israel, tells the King of Israel the words that you speak in your bedroom" (2 Kings 6:11-12).

Nevertheless, technology and economic strength have never been enough to win wars. Historians engage in profound self-delusion when they present their cases that, 'It was inevitable.' for one side to win in various wars. The variables in most wars can change events beyond prediction and things only become 'obvious' after the events have occurred. Many times in history, small weaker nations have defeated the strong, and certain battles have with hindsight become decisive to the victory. Due to this, the hand of God is always the deciding factor. 'The horse is prepared for the day of battle, but deliverance is of the Lord' (Proverbs 21:31). The Fall of Singapore in 1942 is an example of one of Britain's most disastrous military defeats, which shows what happens when miracles do not occur, and this loss gave Japan supremacy in Asia, leading to millions of war crimes.

The historian Chalmers Johnson said, "It may be pointless to try to establish which World War Two Axis aggressor, Germany or Japan, was the more brutal to the peoples it victimised. The Germans killed six million Jews and twenty million Russians; the Japanese slaughtered as many as thirty million Filipinos, Malays, Vietnamese, Cambodians, Indonesians and Burmese, at least twenty-three million of them ethnic Chinese. Both nations looted the countries they conquered on a monumental scale, though Japan plundered more, over a longer period than the Nazis. Both conquerors enslaved millions and exploited them as forced labourers – and, in the case of the Japanese, as prostitutes for front-line troops. If you were a Nazi prisoner of war from Britain, America, Australia, New Zealand or Canada you faced a 4% chance of not surviving the war; [by comparison] the death rate for Allied POWs held by the Japanese was nearly 30%."[9]

Chapter Twenty

Turning the Tide

In Britain's North African campaign against the Italians, who had occupied Libya, Britain fought a see-saw series of battles, with Italian and then German forces, in the war for control of Libya, Tunisia and Egypt. For Churchill, Britain's position in Egypt and its defence was indispensable. If the Axis Powers could take Egypt, Nazi forces would sweep the Middle East, take its oil fields, and occupy the Holy Land, sending all the Jews in the Middle East to concentration camps. If Hitler could overrun the region, he would cut-off Britain's oil supplies, sever the link to Britain's Empire in the Far East, handing Asia to Japan, and the Russian southern flank would be exposed.

Field Marshal Montgomery (1887-1976) was a deeply religious man, who was bold about his Christian convictions. He also believed that Christian civilisation was at stake and with such a conviction, could not stomach any thoughts of retreat or defeat, which had defined Britain's North African Campaign so far. He believed England, fighting for liberty and peace, was on God's side, and in a war where the Lord's will was self-evident, victory was the only option. As the new commander, he met with his officers who had often retreated and provided them with a new vision, of total victory or death. He declared, "I have cancelled the plan for withdrawal. If we are attacked, then there will be no retreat. If we cannot stay here alive, then we will stay here dead."

The Second Battle of El-Alamein was the turning point in the war in North Africa. The troops were inspired by Montgomery's no retreat rhetoric and they now thought they could win. 'Monty,' believed that God answered prayer and is sovereign in history; yet mankind has its part to play and must align itself with the will of God, so that, in the words of Jesus, "Your Kingdom come, Your will be done, on earth as it is in heaven." Montgomery was outspoken about his faith, to the point of annoyance to some senior staff in London, but for him, if the battle was the Lord's, then British soldiers had to fight as if losing was impossible.

On 23 October 1942, Montgomery sent a notice to all in the British Eighth Army outlining the vision, stating: 'When I assumed command of the Eighth Army, I said that the mandate was to destroy Rommel and his Army, and that it would be done as soon as we were ready...we are ready NOW. The battle which is now about to begin will be one of the decisive battles of history. It will be the turning point of the war. The eyes of the whole world will be on us, watching anxiously which way the battle will swing. We can give them their answer at once, 'It will swing our way.'...AND LET NO MAN SURRENDER SO LONG AS HE IS UNWOUNDED AND CAN FIGHT. Let us all pray that 'the Lord mighty in battle' will give us the victory.'

Montgomery believed the spiritual preparedness and the moral strength of the soldiers was as important as military readiness. In his notice, Montgomery quoted from Psalm 24, which outlines the power of God to grant victory, to those fighting in righteousness, for a just cause: 'The earth is the Lord's and the fullness thereof; the world, and they that dwell therein...who is this King of glory? The Lord strong and mighty, the Lord mighty in battle' (Psalm 24:1-8).

On the first day of the new battle, by Divine intervention, Hitler's foremost military commander Rommel (1891-1944) was stuck in Germany and his replacement, General Stumme died of a heart attack in the early hours of the battle. If any two people had the knowledge of how to outwit Montgomery, it was them. Prayer was answered and in the adage of Scripture, 'Smite the shepherd and the sheep shall be scattered' (Zechariah 13:7).

The battle commenced with Montgomery declaring that his men, "Must have faith in God," and they went to war with a new spirit and heart. With victories being reported several days into the bitter war, Winston Churchill went to speak to miners in Wales, about the sense that God was working through and for Britain, "I sometimes have a feeling of interference. I want to stress that. I have a feeling sometimes that some Guiding Hand has intervened," changing the course of events. "I have a feeling that we have a Guardian, because we have a great Cause, and we shall have that Guardian so long as we serve that Cause faithfully and what a Cause it is!"[1]

After years of defeats, the following twelve days were decisive, as British and Commonwealth forces overwhelmed German and Italian forces, and the Axis powers began their long retreat. For the first time in the war, it was proved conclusively that the Nazis were not invincible, and they could be defeated. The psychological blow to Germany and the transformation in the Allies' belief in Nazi defeat became concrete.

This was a victory for Christian civilisation and in Montgomery's view, God's victory, handed to the Commonwealth forces. Winston Churchill gave the order that church bells in Britain, which had been silent since 1939, should be rung aloud to celebrate the victory. One journalist summed up the thoughts of a nation in a national newspaper, when he announced his own amazement at the turn around from defeat to victory: 'Only the thoughtless can fail to realised how great a part Providence has played in the swift and successful transformation of the war situation...it is not the only feature of a great undertaking that will suggest to others the need for expressing their gratitude to God, when the victory bells begin their cheering chimes.'[2]

On 13 May 1943 one continent was redeemed. Winston Churchill later declared, "Before Alamein we never had a victory. After Alamein we never had a defeat." This great campaign commenced with Montgomery declaring that his men, "Must have faith in God," and after prayer for victory had been answered, he gave glory to God saying, "He has done so and I know that you will agree with me, when I say that we must not forget to thank Him for His great mercies."

The faith of Montgomery was not unusual at this time, as many of the great commanders of the war were also men of deep devotion to their Christian faith. Field Marshal Alan Francis Brooke (1883-1963) was a senior commander in the British Army and the foremost military advisor to Winston Churchill during the darkest days of World War Two. When he was appointed the role, he later noted: 'I remember the night Winston offered me the job...I was so overcome that my natural impulse was, when left alone, to kneel and pray God for His assistance in my new task. I have often looked back during the last three and a half years to that prayer."[4]

The struggle during World War II was a battle for religious freedom, democracy, the rule of law, peace, liberty and for all the hallmarks of Christian civilisation. Britain was a religious nation at the time and this was exemplified by the National Days of Prayer, and in the speeches and exhortations of its leaders. When war broke out in 1939, King George VI, the father of Queen Elizabeth II, as Defender of the Faith and Supreme Governor of the Church of England, both official Constitutional titles, told all in Britain and the British Empire to, "Reverently commit our cause to God."

The king insisted that the following message be inscribed in copies of the New Testament, which were given to every British fighting man in the war: 'To all serving in my forces by sea or land, or in the air and indeed, to all my people engaged in the defence of the Realm, I commend the reading of this Book. For centuries the Bible has been a wholesome and strengthening influence in our national life, and it behoves us in these momentous days to turn with renewed faith to this Divine source of comfort and inspiration.'[5]

During those years of intense trial and struggle, the King of Britain, followed the precedent set by King Jehoshaphat of Judah, to call for National Days of Prayer, seeking God's aid in time of need. For a believing people, these days were not empty ritual, but sincere days of pious supplication. Facing the threat of invasion and defeat King Jehoshaphat of Judah prayed for his people, "Lord, the God of our ancestors, are you not the God who is in heaven? You rule over all the kingdoms of the nations. Power and might are in your hand and no one can withstand you...our God, will you not judge them? For we have no power to face this vast army that is attacking us. We do not know what to do, but our eyes are on you." In response, a prophetic word was given to the nation, "Do not be afraid or discouraged because of this vast army. For the battle is not yours, but God" (2 Chronicles 20:5-16).

Britain cried out to God when an invasion was imminent, and God intervened, and the nation sought God's aid many times, asking for Divine intervention. These National Days of Prayer were not called for by the Church, but by the state. Advice would have been sought from Lambeth Palace, but it was the monarch and the cabinet who drove the plea forward. In total, King George V and King George VI called Britain to prayer on fifteen separate occasions during the two world wars, and that same confidence in the Christian faith is evident in the witness of Queen Elizabeth II.

By 1944, the task ahead was no longer survival, now it was a struggle for total victory. The Allies were to fight, not only to liberate France, but also to deliver Germany from the Nazis. To achieve this aim, the Allies had to send the largest armada in history, across the English Channel to land on the French coast, which had been fortified by the Nazis over several years.

People in Britain and America had been praying for Divine aid for the successful future invasion of France for years, because they knew that one unexpected change in the weather could sink the entire invasion force, due to the low base of the landing craft. These crafts, when full, were easy to submerge in the sea and were prone to sink in stormy seas. The disaster at Slapton Sands in England proved this, when 749 Americans were killed under fire and a third of all vessels were struck, with two sunk, in an unexpected German attack. This proved how vulnerable the D-Day craft would be and none took victory for granted.[6]

On 4 June 1944, General Dempsey (1896-1969), Commander

of the British and Canadian forces on D-Day, responsible for taking Gold, Juno and Sword beaches in France, worshipped at Christchurch, Portsdown, in Portsmouth. Over four hundred officers joined him, "To dedicate to Almighty God the task which lay before them," and he called it, "one of the most moving experiences of my life." Two days later, prayers of thanks were said and each year, the church still meets to recall, saying, "We remember today God's help given you on the threshold of the greatest adventure in your history."[7]

The American General Dwight Eisenhower (1890-1969) had the final responsibility of choosing the day to invade Europe and fulfil Operation Overlord. On 5 June he decided to cancel the invasion because of a terrible weather report, which threatened to sink all the landing vessels. There was much prayer and on the following day, he made the decision to proceed, knowing that regardless of the report he received, the weather was in God's hands.

General Eisenhower explained later the burden upon him, "This day eight years ago, I made the most agonising decision of my life. I had to decide to postpone by at least twenty-four hours, the most formidable array of fighting ships and of fighting men that was ever launched across the sea, against a hostile shore. The consequences of that decision at that moment could not have been foreseen by anyone. If there were nothing else in my life to prove the existence of an Almighty and merciful God, the events of the next twenty-four hours did.

"The greatest break in a terrible outlay of weather occurred the next day and allowed that great invasion to proceed, with losses far below those we anticipated...You may say to me, 'The nation prayed on this last National Day of Prayer but what did the Army do about it?' All officers were called to church services and all ranks came to pledge themselves."[8]

Suddenly during this speech, Eisenhower's mind drew back to what the Allies were fighting for, as he recalled his boyhood, "I want to call attention to the virtues of the times," he said, "to at least as my brothers and I devoutly believe, the extraordinary virtues of our parents. First of all, they believed the admonition, 'The fear of God is the beginning of all wisdom' (Psalm 111:10). Their Bibles were a live and lusty influence in their lives. There was nothing sad about their religion. They believed in it with happiness and contentment; that all would be well if a man would take the cards that he had been dealt in this world, and play them to the best of his ability...and yet, in spite of the difficulties of the problems we have, I ask you this one question: If each of us in his own mind would dwell more upon those simple virtues –

integrity, courage, self-confidence and unshakable belief in his Bible – would not some of these problems tend to simplify themselves?"[9]

General Eisenhower was the Supreme Allied Commander and second was Field Marshal Montgomery. On the eve of D-Day Montgomery sent this message to all the troops: 'The time has come to deal the enemy a terrific blow in Western Europe. The blow will be struck by the combined sea, land and air forces of the Allies together...we have a great and a righteous cause. Let us pray that, 'The Lord Mighty in Battle,' will go forth with our armies and that His special Providence will aid us in the struggle. I want every soldier to know that I have complete confidence in the successful outcome...let us go forward to victory.'[10]

The Archdeacon of the Forces, the most senior Church of England chaplain, Canon Llewellyn Hughes (1894-1967), who was appointed Chaplain General to the Forces in 1944, preached in the service of dedication on the eve of D-Day, "It is not enough for an army or a nation to have a vague faith in God. It is not enough for us to rest content that our commanders are godly and that God's flag is publicly flown. Faith in God is useless until it governs action. What does God want done? We believe in God – as what? As a nonentity, content to be recognised and then ignored? As a vague power, meaningless, purposeless, inarticulate and therefore unfit to command a platoon, let alone a world? No. We believe in God who wants and means to have done, all that Christ embodied, taught, lived out. Let an army and a people learn what God stands for, and then they will know when they are for or against His purpose, and support or oppose with confidence, as His commissioned servants. That is where the solid toil of consecration comes in. The character of Christ must be known; His goodness perceived and loved; Himself accepted as Master. No special effort thrown off in an emergency will accomplish that; and there is no short-cut. So the chaplains are going forward with the forces preaching the simple gospel of Christ, the Author and Finisher of all the fine qualities of men. There is no ideal of character better than the one God sent to us again in Jesus Christ our Lord. Read the New Testament."[11]

On 6 June 1944, D-Day, King George VI sent this message to the nation, "Four years ago our nation and Empire stood alone against an overwhelming enemy, with our backs to the wall. Tested as never before in our history, in God's Providence we survived the test...now once more a supreme test has to be faced. This time the challenge is not to fight to survive, but to fight to win the final victory. We shall ask not that God may do our will, but that we may be enabled to do the will of God. And we dare to believe that God has used our nation and Empire as an instrument to fulfil His high purpose. I hope that throughout the present crisis of the liberation of Europe there may be offered up earnest, continuous, and widespread prayer...

"The Queen joins with me in sending you this message. She well understands the anxieties and cares of our womenfolk at this time. She knows that many of them will find, as she does herself, fresh strength and comfort in such waiting upon God... surely not one of us is too busy, too young, or too old to play a part in a nationwide, a worldwide vigil of prayer as the great Crusade sets forth. If from every place of worship, from home and factory, from men and women of all ages and many races and occupations, our intercessions rise, then, please God, both now and in the future not remote, the predictions of an ancient song may be fulfilled: 'The Lord will give strength unto His people, the Lord will give His people the blessing of peace.' "[12]

General Eisenhower sent this message to the troops: 'You are about to embark upon the Great Crusade...you will bring about the destruction of the German war machine. The free men of the world are marching together to victory! Let us beseech the blessing of Almighty God upon this great and noble undertaking.'[13]

Throughout the day, over 75,000 British, Canadian and Commonwealth troops, with 57,000 American troops, in 7,000 crafts landed in France.[14] The fighting was bitter and many miracles transpired, including better weather conditions, which enabled the ships and landing crafts to arrive safely. Within an hour of fighting, British troops secured parts of Gold beach and Sword beach was also taken, in some places, without resistance. The Canadians at Juno beach and the Americans at Utah fought long and hard, and overcame victoriously. Tragedy struck at Omaha beach and U.S. Lieutenant General Omar Bradley considered retreating, with over 2,000 dead and only two of twenty-nine amphibious tanks launched. Their most heroic attack continued and by nightfall, a tenuous toehold was secured.[15]

But why had God allowed the terrible storm on 5 June and the postponement? Records later revealed that on 6 June, General Rommel was not at his post, believing the treacherous weather had made the 'worst kept secret in Europe' – the forthcoming invasion of France, utterly impossible. One reporter summarised: 'The German commanders were advised by their meteorological service that there could be no invasion in the period including

June 6 because of continuous stormy weather. That is why D-Day forces landing during a brief break in the windiest month in Normandy for at least twenty years, found so many German troops without officers, and why other enemy coastal units were having exercises at the time of the landing.'[16]

It transpired that potentially, tens of thousands of lives were saved as God used the bad weather on 5 June to encourage the Nazis to let their guard down, enabling a safe crossing for the Allies the following day.

With the beachhead secured, the Allies sent wave after wave of men and supplies to win the battle in Europe. As the Nazis began a speedy retreat towards Germany, by 19 August 1944, the battle for Paris began and was liberated on the 25. The speed of the advance was astounding and Montgomery praised God for the victories, "Such an historic march of events can seldom have taken place in such a short space of time...this is the Lord's doing and it is marvellous in our eyes."[17]

When victory came on 8 May 1945, called Victory in Europe Day, Winston Churchill spoke in the House of Commons, saying, "We have all of us made our mistakes, but the strength of the Parliamentary institution has been shown to enable it at the same moment to preserve all the title-deeds of democracy, while waging war in the most stern and protracted form...I recollect well at the end of the last war, more than a quarter of a century ago, that the House...did not feel inclined for debate or business, but desired to offer thanks to Almighty God, to the Great Power which seems to shape and design the fortunes of nations and the destiny of man; and I therefore beg, Sir, with your permission to move: That this House do now attend at the Church of St. Margaret, Westminster, to give humble and reverent thanks to Almighty God for our deliverance from the threat of German domination."[18]

As members of Parliament thanked God at St. Margaret's, at Westminster Abbey services were held every hour, from 9am in the morning till 10pm at night with more than 25,000 attending.[19] On Sunday 13 May 1945, the BBC broadcast an hour-long Thanksgiving and Dedication service to Almighty God at 9.30am, and the main service of thanksgiving from St Paul's Cathedral in the afternoon, followed by services from Wales and Scotland.

Germany fell to Nazism because it rejected its Christian heritage, and now they wanted to embrace it again. Officials in defeated Germany asked for one million Bibles to be sent to help re-set the nation's moral compass and several other formally occupied nations made similar requests. The work of world evangelism commenced again!

After the war, when the British government was planning memorials to the fallen, Winston Churchill never forgot that the battle against Nazi Germany was to save Christian civilisation and he declared, "I am very anxious indeed...to do everything that is possible to emphasise the distinctively Christian and religious character of these memorials."[20]

General Sir Frederick E. Morgan (1894-1967) was the Chief of Staff to the Supreme Allied Commander and the original planner of D-Day's Operation Overlord. Two years after the defeat of the Nazi regime, he publicly acknowledged the miraculous nature of the Allied victory. He declared, "As the old adage had it, 'Man proposes but God disposes.' There comes a point in so many of our affairs at which we hope so often for a miracle, and miracles happen still. How many of them have we not seen enacted before our eyes in these past few years? There was Dunkirk and its flat, calm sea. Who planned that? During those fateful hours I was riding up to battle...our main army was hemmed in on those northern beaches. There were many others who, like us, saw no way out barring a miracle. There came a miracle!

"Then, two years later, a U-boat caught sight of the tail ship of one convoy. The German observer, apparently, thought what he saw merely worthy of a routine report [and North Africa was invaded due to his ignorance]. Then, but a day before General Patton was due to land on the Casablanca beaches, open to the full Atlantic swell, just as it seemed inevitable that his whole affair must be called off, the wind changed from on-shore to off-shore and let the small craft in...I doubt if any will be such as to compare with the miracle of D-Day in 1944!"[21]

In Britain, many of the chief leaders involved in planning and administering the battles gave glory to God, for helping them in their most desperate need. With the war in Europe at a close, they now sensed they had to serve God's continuing purposes in the world. Sir Archibald Sinclair (1890-1970), the Secretary of State for Air said, "God has delivered us and brought us to our present position for some great purpose, and now we must seek humbly to discover what that purpose is and then to be faithful to it." The theme of being saved for a purpose remained strong in Britain for years to come, and many interpreted this purpose as continuing to send Christianity to the world, with a mass missionary movement, fighting for liberty and the oppressed abroad and maintaining the Christian religion at home.

Many began to pay heed to the words of three times British Prime Minister Stanley Baldwin (1867-1947) who said, "That aspect of the responsibilities which I should like to consider is the aspect of spiritual leadership, for in my view, the British Empire has a solemn duty to the world at this time, a duty which I have described in those words, 'Spiritual leadership.' " [22] Author James Mcwhirter wrote: 'When we consider how Britain is helping the world to find Christ through the distribution of the Scriptures! ...Britain has translated the Bible, in whole or in part, into close on a thousand languages. The Anglo-Saxon race is the greatest missionary people of all time. The advance of the Empire was equally phenomenal and the object of colonial expansion was stated to be the propagation of the gospel.'[23]

Contrary to popular myth, Christianity did not collapse in Britain after the First or Second World Wars. The Christian faith was still a hot topic in the nation and remained so for over a decade. In the 1945 election, Churchill's approval rating was eighty-three percent, but the people voted for a new Britain of welfare and justice, saying, "Cheer Churchill – vote Labour."[24]

After being defeated, as Winston Churchill sought re-election which he gained in 1951, he embraced themes which were still important to the Christian people of Britain. His first commitment to the electorate, was that his future government was going to uphold the Christian religion and resist all attacks upon it. He said, "Our main objectives are: To uphold the Christian religion and resist all attacks upon it..."[25]

Chapter Twenty-One

Democracy and Social Justice

In the twentieth century, Britain fought and won two world wars, struggling for liberty and democracy, and these left the nation bankrupted, thrust into a decade of harsh austerity.

Britain was the world's first industrial nation in the eighteenth and nineteenth centuries, and pioneered the Agricultural Revolution, laying the foundations of the modern world. Due to these two transformations, for the first time in world history millions left the fields to converge in cities, to work in hostile steam-powered factories, billowing out smoke. In revulsion to the abuses of the industrial age, the poet William Blake (1757-1827) penned a short poem in his *Prophetic Books*. 'And Did Those Feet In Ancient Time' dates to 1804 and it was incorporated into the unofficial English national anthem – 'Jerusalem,' with music written by Sir Hubert Parry in 1916. The poem was inspired by the mythical journey of Jesus Christ and Joseph of Arimathea to visit Glastonbury in England. As a man who loved the Bible, the author drew from the New Testament touching on Christ's second return to earth, to build a New Jerusalem (Revelation 3:12, 21:2).

William Blake, pondering the mythical nature of Christ's visit to England, contrasts what Jesus would have seen – the green mountains and clouded hills – to the new dark satanic mills. The modern world of satanic billowing factories, low pay, abusive employers and limited rights, were not the vision God had for the nation. Blake called to mind Elijah and God's chariot of fire from 2 Kings 2:11. He perceived the need for Divine aid, for Britain to be able to build anything like a nation of justice or 'Jerusalem,' which God desired. The nation had so far failed.

Beneath the poem he inscribed an excerpt from Numbers 11:29: Would to God that all the Lord's people were Prophets: 'And did those feet in ancient time, walk upon England's mountains green: And was the Holy Lamb of God, on England's pleasant pastures seen!...I will not cease from mental fight, nor shall my sword sleep in my hand: Till we have built Jerusalem, in England's green and pleasant land!'

In 1945, Clement Attlee became prime minister after declaring his party would build 'a new Jerusalem' in Britain, using the themes of the poem, as their campaign slogan. For the Archbishop of Canterbury William Temple, it was contradictory to call Britain a Christian nation, whilst it ignored the injustices of homelessness, poverty and illness. How could a nation claim to be Christian whilst ignoring the teaching of the prophets, the apostles and the Lord Jesus on helping those in need? Were Britons loving their neighbours as themselves (Mark 12:31), being good Samaritans to all (Luke 10:25-37), and did justice run like rivers in Britain (Amos 5:1-24) – whilst abject poverty was still vivid? Did the nation heed John or Ezekiel? 'If anyone has material possessions and sees a brother or sister in need but has no pity on them, how can the love of God be in that person?' (1 John 3:17). "Now this was the sin of your sister Sodom: she and her daughters were arrogant, overfed and unconcerned; they did not help the poor and needy" (Ezekiel 16:49).

Dr John Sentamu explained the response, "In our time, this socialising and transforming power of corporate-discipleship is illustrated further by three Christian men at the University of Oxford: Richard Tawney, William Beveridge and William Temple, who were challenged to go to the East End of London to 'find friends among the poor, as well as finding out what poverty is and what can be done about it.' In the East End their consciences were pricked by poverty: visible, audible, smellable. After university, Tawney worked at Toynbee Hall, creating a fraternal community. William Beveridge paved the way for the welfare state, in his report, which for the first time set out to embody the whole spirit of the Christian ethic in an Act of Parliament. William Temple, as Archbishop of York and then Canterbury, mobilised the Church support for a more just, equal and fraternal Britain. His book *Christianity and Social Order* is one of the foundation pillars of the welfare state as we know it today."[1]

The original intention of the welfare state in Britain was to ensure that the historic injustices of the past would never again plague the nation. The Christian leaders spearheading its creation believed it could be possible, to attempt to reflect just a little of the mercy of God to all, in imperfect human institutions, through respect, welfare and healthcare. The nation itself was to be the collective good Samaritan; it was to love its neighbour as itself, and, "Inasmuch as you did it to one of the least of these My brethren, you did it to Me" (Matthew 25:40).

In the Parable of the Good Samaritan Jesus said, "When he departed, he took out two denarii, gave them to the innkeeper, and said to him, 'Take care of him; and whatever more you spend, when I come again, I will repay you.' So which of these three do you think was neighbour to him who fell among the thieves?" (Luke 10:35-36). This is why British Minister for Health, Nye Bevan, who was at the heart of the creation of the welfare safety-net, said of the National Health Service, "The NHS is a little piece of Christianity." However, the welfare state recognised there are responsibilities as well as rights, to receiving a hand-up out of poverty (2 Thessalonians 3:10).

The modern welfare state can be abused, but Christians in Britain asked themselves one difficult question, "What would Jesus do?" In Britain, Christians who despised communism and embrace ethical capitalism and democracy believed that government – which is the reflection of the will of the people – has a responsibility to help the poor based upon the teachings on national justice unveiled in the Bible (Acts 4:32-35).

Attempting to raise the standard of living for all, the Beveridge Report of 1942 identified five 'Giant Evils,' which plagued Britain: squalor, ignorance, want, idleness and disease. Its plan was to help the poor of Britain – millions who still lived in slums, to give them a hand-up out of poverty. In response to the report, which sought to address many injustices, William Temple said, "This is the first time anybody had set out to embody the whole spirit of the Christian ethic in an Act of Parliament." This was to be a nation seeking the principles of charity and concern found in Exodus 30, Leviticus 19, Psalm 74:21, 112:19, Isaiah 10:2, 14:30, 25:4, Amos 5:12, Zechariah 7:10, Matthew 19:21, Luke 12:33, 14:13, 2 Corinthians 9:9 and James 2:2-6, etc.

At last, the nation was beginning to confront its historic and lasting injustices: ' "What do you mean by crushing My people and grinding the faces of the poor?" declares the Lord, the Lord Almighty' (Isaiah 3:15). Now there was a new vision for Britain: 'Defend the weak and the fatherless; uphold the cause of the poor and the oppressed' (Psalm 82:3). For, 'I know that the Lord secures justice for the poor and upholds the cause of the needy' (Psalm 140:12). 'The poor will eat and be satisfied; those who seek the Lord will praise Him' (Psalm 22:26).

The concept was that in a Christian nation, there should never again be a poor underclass, which is denied a roof over their heads, medical care, food, warmth, and a decent education, because of generations of poverty and injustice. Appalling abject poverty, which had always plagued Britain, was finally to end, and by 2010, the definition of poverty was changed to address the improvements in living conditions: now British poverty is measured as household income below sixty percent of median income. Consequently, in 1945 the government adopted the Beveridge proposals and implemented many social policies. These included the Family Allowances Act 1945, National Insurance Act 1946, National Health Service Act 1946, Pensions Increase Act 1947, Landlord and Tenant Act 1949, National Insurance and Industrial Injuries Acts of 1948/9.

Finally the injustices of poverty, aristocratic wealth gained unjustly and the abuses of those who impoverished the masses to gain riches were to be addressed. For, 'Whoever oppresses the poor shows contempt for their Maker, but whoever is kind to the needy honours God' (Proverbs 14:31). But could Britain afford such a venture after World War II? The answer was that God would bless those who cared for the poor. 'Whoever is kind to the poor lends to the Lord and He will reward them for what they have done' (Proverbs 19:17). ' "He defended the cause of the poor and needy and so all went well. Is that not what it means to know me?" declares the Lord' (Jeremiah 22:16).

One of the reasons the government was able to accept the new proposals was because General William Booth (1829-1912) and the Salvation Army, inspired by the teaching of Jesus Christ had already been proving since 1878, that the problems of poverty in Britain could be addressed. The poor uneducated underclass, they found, had been manufactured by injustice and direct Christian justice, with individual responsibilities to respond in the affirmative, changed countless lives. Yet, in a nation of millions there would always be a limit to what charity could do, and there had to be a strategy implemented on a national scale. In 1890, William Booth's book *In Darkest England And The Way Out* provided a practical demonstration of the means to address the evident manifestations of poverty. By 1899, the Salvation Army had lodged 11 million homeless people, served 27 million meals, found work for 9,000 people and traced 18,000 missing people. With such a record, these ideas provided a successful blueprint which was incorporated into Britain's welfare state.

Chapter Twenty-Two

Christianity, Devotion and Dedication

In the twentieth century in Britain, Christian belief went through a period of profound change, especially as the British Empire vanished and its citizens lost the vision it gave. At home, as the decades progressed, traditional, formulaic and cultural Christianity diminished, leaving in its place the rapid growth in personal Bible believing faith in Jesus Christ. A separation began between nominal and personal faith, and in each decade, especially after the 1960s, the tradition of cultural Christianity began to die a steady death, whilst there was resurgence in the conviction of a need to return to the faith of the apostles.

In Wales in 1904-1905, up to 150,000 people made a profession of faith in Jesus Christ, as Evan Roberts led in the great Welsh Revival. During World War Two, Oxford academic C.S. Lewis became a national celebrity as his broadcasts talks on BBC radio, led to hundreds of thousands of people tuning in to re-engage with Christianity.[1] Lewis' books, all with a strong Christian influence, have sold over two hundred million copies. In northern Scotland, the Lewis Awakening of 1949-52 led to the transformation of parts of the Hebrides, and still today the region has been called the Bible-belt of Britain. By 1954, during a period of intense austerity, a young American evangelist called Billy Graham preached at the Harringay Crusade. The four week campaign was extended to three months, as Britain came as close as it ever came in the twentieth century, to a mass revival. Up to two million people came to listen to Billy Graham and it led to a resurgence in biblical Christianity in the country. Many of the next generation of Christian leaders trace their faith back to their conversion in this crusade.

In the U.S., following the overflow of the Welsh Revival, on 9 April 1906, the Azusa Street Revival began, leading to the birth of what we now recognise as Pentecostalism. In Wales, the preaching of the Jeffreys' brothers began the influential spread of the personalised Christianity of Pentecostalism in Britain, and according to the BBC, 'Pentecostals are the fastest-growing group of Christians in the U.K.,' as there are now up to one million Pentecostals in Britain.[2]

Up until the 1960s, Pentecostals in Britain, with their belief in the outpouring and power of the Holy Spirit were separate from most believers. Then, the Charismatic Movement shook many fellowships, as dry traditional churches accepted Jesus' teaching that, "These signs will follow those who believe: In My name they will cast out demons; they will speak with new tongues...they will lay hands on the sick and they will recover" (Mark 16:17-18).

As Christians followed Jesus' teaching to wait for power from on high, the subsequent outpouring of the Holy Spirit led to the reviving of parts of the Church in Britain, but not the nation as a whole. It has been argued that the Charismatic Movement and the House Church Movement played an important role in saving the Church in Britain from the kind of collapse of faith, which was seen in mainland Europe.

Today, up to half a million people attend churches in Britain which began as house churches, and are identified as the British New Church Movement. Allan Anderson explains, "The fastest growing churches in Britain today are the 'new churches,' mostly independent charismatic churches, sometimes led by former Anglican ministers and forming loose associations. These have probably outstripped the classical Pentecostal churches in influence and extent."[3]

The shift away from nominal religious tradition in Britain, to a return to Bible believing Christianity is attested by the large numbers of evangelical and Charismatic Christians in the U.K. Journalist Ed West explains his experience at such a church: 'Evangelical Christianity is rapidly spreading in the U.K. The median age of this church was about 20; in most Catholic parishes in London you're considered an energetic young go-getter if you're under 75.' Ed West then explained the problems of traditional churches denying their core beliefs and stated: 'In contrast the Evangelicals, whether anyone likes it or not, believe, and it shows. Doubt and scepticism are fine things but a religious community that does not believe in its own message will wither and die, and be replaced by others. I'm not remotely surprised Evangelical Christianity is on the march in England.'[4]

In the twenty-first century, 33.2 million people in Britain identified themselves as Christian in the last census,[5] highlighting the nominal aspect of faith. Meanwhile, 9.48 million British adults attended church at least once a month, with 16.4 million attending at least once in a year.[6] Another new religious phenomenon in Britain is the explosion of Christian media, with faith-based TV channels, radio stations and internet sites.

Christians have always been aware of believers who are either no longer able to attend a church, or have struggled with church politics, and continue with their religious convictions and devotions, without appearing on an official religious register. In the new age of Christian media, it has now become possible for Christians to engage with other believers on a daily basis, without utilising traditional means. The number of practicing Christians in Britain may be larger than statistics indicate, because they do not include the believers who worship in non-registered churches, house churches, or who engage with the wider Christian community through multimedia, and in person for Christian festivals and special events.

Christianity is therefore not extinguished as a faith in Britain; nevertheless, the future status of Britain being a Christian nation is unclear in an age of secularism and plurality; but this was certainly not the expectation of Britain in 1953, when Queen Elizabeth II was enthroned.

Journalist Damian Thompson asked: 'Is Queen Elizabeth II the true Christian leader of our country? An odd question for a Catholic to ask, you might think, but consider the feebleness of senior bishops – Anglican and Catholic – during the 60 years of her reign. She has been served by great prime ministers, but no great Archbishop of Canterbury. The Queen's last few Christmas broadcasts demonstrate the intensity of her faith. She reminds Christians that the feast marks "the birth of our Saviour" the "Prince of Peace" who is "our source of light and life in both good times and bad." In old age she has underlined this message more heavily than she once did – not in an obtrusive way that would cause offence to non-Christians, but boldly enough to make some of us sit up from our post-lunch slumber and think: "She really believes what she says."... The anxiety for Christians is that this effect depends on the personal convictions of Elizabeth II, who is not only more pious than her children but has also taken her religious duties more seriously than many of her predecessors. If the British monarch of the future recasts itself as a mere guarantor of religious liberty – as Prince Charles seems to envisage – then the secularisation of public life will be complete. That's a miserable prospect, in my opinion, but not one we should dwell on today. For sixty years, the Queen has defended not 'faith' in the abstract but the revelations of Christianity. That she has done so in such an unassuming and gentle manner makes her witness no less powerful.'[7]

In 2012, in tribute to the sixtieth anniversary of Queen Elizabeth II's accession to the throne, Damian Thompson commented: 'I often think that the Queen is the most impressive religious leader in Britain. She says little in public about her Christianity, but what she does say – usually at the end of her Christmas Day broadcast – is powerful in its directness.'[8] Author and columnist Francis Phillips added: 'Her Majesty, intuitively and skilfully, manages to remain the still centre of the ever-turning Anglican world simply by affirming her faith in Jesus Christ. In her Christmas message last year, she stated, "God sent into the world a unique Person – neither a philosopher nor a general, important though they are, but a Saviour, with the power to forgive. Forgiveness lies at the heart of the Christian faith. It can heal broken families. It can restore friendships and it can reconcile divided communities. It is in forgiveness that we feel the power of God's love." The Queen has met plenty of philosophers and even more generals in her time. With her unique place at the summit of the Establishment, she has had innumerable opportunities to encounter the masters of this world in every walk of life. She knows their place and she knows her own. More than other modern monarchs, I think, she understands the spiritual significance of her coronation oath: a lifelong dedication to her people and her public duties; something to be undertaken with utmost seriousness. This dedication is deeply admirable.' In 1953, at Queen Elizabeth II's coronation, Cecil Beaton observed 'that after she had taken the Oath and had been anointed with the holy oil, there was an aura, a definite radiance about her. This was nothing to do with vanity, ambition or ego (things that constantly drive politicians); it was the instinctive response to the most solemn moment of a strange and solemn destiny.'[9]

On 2 June 1953, Queen Elizabeth II, a year after her ascension to the throne, in her official coronation, dedicated herself before God to be the monarch of the United Kingdom, Canada, Australia, New Zealand, South Africa and other nations. Entering Westminster Abbey in London, where kings and queens of England have been crowned since 1066, the choir sang, "I was glad," from Psalm 122:1. As the twenty-seven year old Queen prayed, she sat on the Coronation Chair dating from 1296, to the south of the altar, as the bishops carried in the Bible, paten, and chalice. Those invited to attend were addressed: "Sirs, I here present unto you Queen Elizabeth, your undoubted Queen: wherefore all you who are come this day to do your homage and service, are you willing to do the same?" They replied, "God save Queen Elizabeth," each time asked.

The Archbishop of Canterbury led the Queen in the Coronation Oath to uphold Christianity in the United Kingdom and protect the Church of England, saying, "Will you to the utmost of your power maintain the laws of God and the true profession of the Gospel? Will you to the utmost of your power maintain in the United Kingdom the Protestant Reformed Religion established by law? Will you maintain and preserve inviolably the settlement of the Church of England, and the doctrine, worship, discipline, and government thereof, as by law established in England? And will you preserve unto the bishops and clergy of England, and to the Churches there committed to their charge, all such rights and privileges, as by law do or shall appertain to them or any of them?" Queen Elizabeth responded, "All this I promise to do." The Queen proceeded to the altar where she affirmed, "The things which I have here promised, I will perform and keep. So help me God," before kissing the Bible and putting the royal sign-manual to the oath, as the Bible was returned.

Then the Moderator of the General Assembly of the Church of Scotland took the Bible and presented it to the Queen, saying, "Our gracious Queen: to keep your Majesty ever mindful of the law and the Gospel of God as the rule for the whole life and government of Christian Princes, we present you with this Book, the most valuable thing that this world affords. Here is Wisdom; this is the royal Law; these are the lively oracles of God."

The communion service was conducted, involving prayers by both the clergy and Queen, with the prayer, "O God...grant unto this Thy servant Elizabeth, our Queen, the spirit of wisdom and government, that being devoted unto Thee with her whole heart, she may so wisely govern, that in her time Thy Church may be in safety, and Christian devotion may continue in peace." Readings were taken from Peter's first letter, the Psalms and Matthew's Gospel, and the Queen was anointed, in the tradition of Israel's King David and his son King Solomon (1 Kings 1:38-40), as the assembly sang of Israel's 'Zadok the Priest.'

As the anointing was considered sacrosanct, it was concealed from view by a silk canopy, and then the sign of the cross was made on the Queen's forehead. The Sword of State was then handed to the Queen, who, after a prayer, placed it on the altar. The Queen was then invested with the Stole Royal, Robe Royal, and the Sovereign's Orb, followed by the Queen's Ring, the Sceptre with the Cross, and the Sceptre with the Dove.

The Sovereign's Orb is a Christian symbol which represents the monarch's role as Defender of the Faith and Supreme Governor of the Church of England. 'The Orb is a representation of the sovereign's power, symbolising the Christian world, with its cross mounted on a globe.'[10] During the coronation, the Queen held the Sceptre with the Cross in her right hand and the Sceptre with the Dove in the left, while the Archbishop placed St Edward's Crown on the Queen's head. All from 1661, the Sceptre with the Cross symbolises the temporal authority of the monarch under the Cross, a symbol of Christianity. The Sceptre with the Dove 'represents the sovereign's spiritual role, with the Dove representing the Holy Ghost.'[11]

As Queen Elizabeth II was crowned by the Archbishop of Canterbury, the crowd shouted, "God save the Queen!" at the exact moment St. Edward's ancient Crown touched her head, and a twenty-one gun salute was fired from the Tower of London, as the people cried out, "God save Queen Elizabeth. Long live Queen Elizabeth. May the Queen live for ever." The Queen then removed her royal regalia, knelt and partook of the communion, remembering Christ's death and resurrection. She confessed and with the congregation recited the Lord's Prayer. Then, wearing the Imperial State Crown and holding the Sceptre with the Cross and the Sceptre with the Orb, the guests sang, "God Save the Queen," as the Queen left Westminster Abbey and was transported back to Buckingham Palace.

In September 2015, Queen Elizabeth II will become the longest-reigning monarch in British history, indicating that God has answered the proclamations of a nation who seek Divine favour for a godly monarch to "long to reign over us." Since the Norman Conquest, Queen Elizabeth II is arguably the most respected of all the forty-one monarchs of England; because of her selfless commitment to public duty in Christian service, embracing the claims of others before herself and due to her unstinting devotion to the covenant she made with God in 1953. Great leaders of history, such as her first Prime Minister Winston Churchill or U.S President John F. Kennedy have all met her as Queen, and yet at age eighty-nine she continues on in service, as a coherent and godly bridge between our past and future.

Britain became a free nation, with justice and a belief in human rights, precisely because of the Christian heritage and tradition which was expressed at the Queen's Coronation. The reason democracy and liberty developed and congealed in the U.K. was because the Christian tradition laid the foundations for it. The challenges of democracy, free speech, the rule of law and religious liberty trying to establish themselves in the Middle East and other regions of the world, prove how the core values of a religion or culture tend to make people either embrace or reject these Western ideals. Due to the teaching of the Bible, Christians believe all are created equal in God's sight and deserve to be treated freely and fairly under one law for all, and must have a say in their governance. But not all books which are regarded as holy by the adherents of other religions present the same case.

For Britain, freedom began with spiritual liberation and thus Christianity paved the way for our cherished values to flourish. Jesus taught all people need two births – the first is physical, the second is spiritual. Jesus said, "Most assuredly, I say to you, unless one is born again, he cannot see the Kingdom of God... I say to you, unless one is born of water and the Spirit, he cannot enter the Kingdom of God. That which is born of the flesh is flesh and that which is born of the Spirit is spirit. Do not marvel that I said to you, 'You must be born again' " (John 3:3, 5-7).

In the Queen's 2011 Christmas message to Britain and to the fifty-three nations of the Commonwealth, the Queen echoed this exhortation, "...Jesus was born into a world full of fear. The angels came to frightened shepherds with hope in their voices: 'Fear not,' they urged, 'we bring you tidings of great joy, which shall be to all people. For unto you is born this day in the City of David a Saviour who is Christ the Lord.' Although we are capable of great acts of kindness, history teaches us that we sometimes need saving from ourselves – from our recklessness or our greed. God sent into the world a unique Person – neither a philosopher nor a general, important though they are, but a Saviour...In the last verse of this beautiful carol, O Little Town Of Bethlehem, there's a prayer:

'O Holy Child of Bethlehem,
Descend to us we pray.
Cast out our sin
And enter in.
Be born in us today.'

"It is my prayer that on this Christmas day we might all find room in our lives for the message of the angels and for the love of God through Christ our Lord. I wish you all a very happy Christmas."[12]

Part Two
Social Changes – the Revolution of the 1960s, Secularisation, Islam and Multiculturalism

Chapter Twenty-Three

The Great Storm of Change

The 1960s led to a storm of change in Britain, as the old order of a Christian culture and society gave way to an identity of secular consumers in a multicultural nation. The transformation of Britain was twofold: First there was the secularisation of the native population and second, mass immigration changed the spiritual makeup of the nation. In the second half of this book, we examine the impact of both on Britain, with the potential future explored and the response by Christians. As secularisation and Islam are the two prominent factors in Britain's evolving identity, we will examine their impact in-depth.

Evan Roberts, the prominent revivalist used during the Welsh Revival of 1904-5, spent most of his years after this revival, deeply burdened that Wales and Britain were turning away from God. The flag of St David was designed to be a sign and symbol of the Christian heritage of Wales and yet, Evan Roberts was concerned about the rising prominence of the other flag of Wales, with a large dragon at its heart (Revelation 12:9). Evan declared: 'As I was burdened for Wales and prayed for the success of the Kingdom of God, and battled against the forces of darkness, I was burdened by the necessity of removing the dragon from being the emblem of our country. As the religion of Wales is based on the Holy Scriptures and because the red dragon in the Scriptures is a symbol of the devil, is it not scriptural to remove it? When the devil sees his symbol on the flag of a Christian country that professes to hate him, it is a source of joy to him. Is there not a cry in the hearts of thousands of followers of the Lamb in Wales against this inconsistency between their profession and their emblem?' Eight years after Evan Roberts' promotion to glory the Red Dragon was officially recognised as the Welsh national flag.

The Rev. Duncan Campbell was the last great British preacher to be swept up in a genuine 'no hype' heaven-sent awakening in the years 1949-1952, that helped transform some parts of the Hebrides. In 1954, he gave this stark warning to the nation, "There is without question, a growing conviction that unless revival comes, that is a God sent revival, other forces that are out to defy every known Christian principle will take the field. Indeed the observant eye can already see shadows that we are ripening and ripening fast for repentance or judgment...unless revival comes, other forces will take the field that will sink us still deeper into the mire of humanism and materialism..."[1]

In Britain, the bitter austerity which followed victory in World War II lasted long into the 1950s, leading to a sense of abiding poverty, grey and bleakness. But suddenly with a burst of prosperity the 1950s was disappearing into history, as the 1960s emerged flourishing with colour and ideas, and a youth oriented phenomenon captured the hearts of the new generation. London became swinging London, as youth culture, fashion and sexual hedonism began to flourish. Young people now wanted to forget the austerity and rationing of their childhood, and embrace all things new, in a spirit of optimism – it was a cultural revolution, just as influential as China's. Standing back in horror, the older generation criticised the young for not counting the cost, and a counterculture movement was the result, with anti-establishment sentiments flourishing, seeking to reject all things old and embrace anything new.

The Christian heroes of another age, like the missionary explorer David Livingstone or the medical pioneer Florence Nightingale were soon to be forgotten by most, and in their place came cultural idols, breathtaking bands, books and films free from strict censorship, leading to the rise of alternative lifestyles. A dynamic subculture unfolded, celebrating experimentation, creativity and these ideas became popular through controversial media outlets.

The transformation of Western culture is often highlighted by the music of two young men who met in a church on 6 July 1957. St Peter's Church Hall in Woolton village, Liverpool, is where John Lennon met Paul McCartney. John's Aunt Mimi, with whom he lived, was a regular member of the congregation and in the graveyard stands a memorial to Eleanor Rigby, featured in the 1966 Beatles' song.

The religious differences between Aunt Mimi's generation and John's were to have a lasting impact. The spiritual glue which held Britain together for a thousand years was rejected, as the 1960s spearheaded a titanic struggle between the established and the young untried. Fashion, pleasure and image, quickly replaced character, determination and innate value. The opinions which mattered were no longer based on facts, evidence or achievement, but on celebrity and spin. Fashion became the great bluff of the few, over the many. High art transformed into low art, and a flick of paint on a canvas was deemed as equally valuable as a masterpiece from history. The changes in art became an object lesson of how Western culture transformed from seeking the transcendent to the trashy. The ideal of seeking the highest standards of excellence and quality were dropped for anything will do, all expression is equal.

The fantastic dream of the 1960s was to extinguish all that was past, as myths of perpetual and wise youth, painted the older generation as obsolete. Great slogans of peace were heralded, as long as you didn't want anything from me, or get in my way. To be deemed wise you had to be against something, and instead of waiting and planning for a happy life, you had to have pleasure now – and forget about the future cost. "People were fooled and have been persistently fooled that by taking part in the 1960s rebellion against the old culture, they were freeing themselves," said journalist and author Peter Hitchens, "but in fact what they were doing was chaining themselves up in a whole new conformism, but one which still refuses to recognise that it is conformist."[2]

In the 1950s Britons served a God who wanted their hearts; by contrast by the 60s, their children began serving capitalists who wanted their money. Instead of worshipping in churches, they began to live for and worship in new cathedrals of consumerism. Writer and critic Terry Eagleton explains how cynical business leaders manipulated these young people and transformed their attitudes, "In trying to make people to consume, it had to turn them into hedonistic free floating characters."[3]

The 1960s commenced a seismic shift in Western worldviews, from which we have yet to awake. Sir Peregrine Worsthorne said, "The novelty ay in the hedonism, which had not been a characteristic of Britain until the 1960s. If you see hedonism as the peak of progress then, of course, it was fine. But if you see hedonism as the mark of decay, then it was less fine."[4]

The term hedonism derives from the Greek word hedone, for pleasure. Hedonism is a school of thought that argues that pleasure is the central and most important experience for any individual. In its simplest understanding, a hedonist culture exists only to maximise pleasure, without any particular regard for its own future well-being or for the well-being of others. In hedonist thought, the measure of any experience is not determined by something being 'right or wrong' or 'good or bad' for self or others, but does the experience feel good? There may be a cost, but that must be ignored because the net pleasure, after the pain is subtracted, will be worth it. Consequently, from this time onwards unacknowledged hedonism became popular, as the feelings and experiences of today became elevated above the best interests of oneself and others, in pursuit of another 'shopping fix,' 'love fix,' 'food fix,' etc. The instant pleasure of 'the now' became of greater net value than one's long-term peace and joy, and eternity – let's pretend it doesn't exist.

In the hedonistic worldview if anything gets in the way of people having a feeling of pleasure, such as a Christian moral worldview, then it must be rejected. Thus in the 1960s, the 'old stuffy' restrictions of Christian moral values had to be expelled, because the momentary thrill of experimental 'free love,' pornography or consumerism became regarded as more valuable than objective truth, eternity or sacrificial real love.

The Bible predicted that hedonism would become the defining characteristic of the last days (2 Timothy 3:1-4), and on the subject, Jesus taught about the kind of man who lives for pleasure only, saying to himself, " 'You have many goods laid up for many years; take your ease; eat, drink and be merry.' But God said to him, 'Fool! This night your soul will be required of you; then whose will those things be which you have provided?' So is he who lays up treasure for himself and is not rich toward God" (Luke 12:19-21). Therefore, the hedonist exchanges his or her eternal soul for unsatisfactory moments of fleeting pleasure.

To turn Britain into a nation of consumers, big business had to change people's core beliefs, transforming the way they thought about what was valuable, and made them embrace a new false economy. Advertisers had to convince people that their reliable products, which could last decades, had to be replaced with anything new – those cheap and nasty products – sold through illusion. The Christian conviction of delayed self-gratification in all things, also had to be replaced with have it all now, pay later, and maybe someone else will pay. The vast advertising industry thus sought to convince Britons that perpetually acquiring more new things will make them happy, regardless of experience.

Major multinational companies found the best way to get people to buy was to exploit their vulnerabilities, lack of self-esteem, or sense of identity, experienced by many because of the loss of the Christian worldview. Their underlining message, clothed in luxurious advertising, is that you are not enough on your own, and you need this product to make you acceptable to others. We are encouraged, persuaded, or manipulated to ask ourselves if we are 'good enough' to spend ten times the products true value on their special brand. Are you part of the elite? What does your car say about you? Are your clothes so last year? They told consumers that all are rich enough, regardless of income, to buy into the lifestyle of that group of young, beautiful models dancing around in those perfect dream-like TV adverts.

As perfect images and air-brushed bodies were presented to people through advertising, in an idealised make-believe world of the media, the number of cosmetic surgeries, eating disorders, self-harm and suchlike increased – as young people questioned why their lives and looks did not correspond with those glossy ads.

Advertisers began to treat the young in particular, not as human beings, but as units in the economy to be squeezed dry, as they cleverly manipulated their hopes, fears and self-image, for profit. Dr Susie Orbach said, "On a daily basis women are bombarded with impossibly perfect images created by artifice, which they will always aspire towards, but can rarely achieve because these images depend on serious transformation by photographers."[5]

The media began to create, reinforce and then exploits the preoccupation with physical attractiveness and declared it has the answer. Today, studies have found that female models weigh almost twenty-five percent less than the average woman, whilst men are fifteen percent more muscular in adverts than real life.

As advertisers inadvertently told people to think more about themselves and what they should own, the concept of the greater good or even truth were set aside. Family life and community were diminished, as selfish individualism triumphed, enabling people in their cathedrals of commerce, to be in a crowd and often alone, even amidst a group of friends. People became another lonely stranger amongst a thousand strangers that feel they don't really fit in – so they'd better buy something.

With advertisers encouraging people to feel they're not quite right without their product, low self-worth exploded, and people turned to consumerism and empty sex. In this new age, which cast off restraint, the sexual exploits of the powerful and famous fed the new appetite for the young to give promiscuity a go. Peter Hitchens said, "It allowed people to believe that the weak, undisciplined, immoral behaviour of rich irresponsible people became accepted as the standard that everybody should follow."[6] In this new world of free sex, only the ignorant believed there was no price to pay.

In the age where everything was cheaper, it wasn't just the 'new stuff' people bought that was thrown away, it was other people too. As the sexual revolution tore up the old rules, men no longer needed to respect women as someone's daughter, made in the image of God and of immense value, instead they could say in their minds, "I want the use of your body, but I don't want you."

Consequently, even the concept of 'love' was diluted from sacrificial selfish Christian commitment to everyday following our feelings to see where they lead; if they led to another's bed, so what? "I'm sorry, my feelings have changed."

Oxford don and Cambridge Professor C.S. Lewis tried to address this fallacy by saying, "We use a most unfortunate idiom when we say of a lustful man prowling the streets, that he 'wants a woman.' Strictly speaking, a woman is just what he does not want. He wants a pleasure for which a woman happens to be the necessary piece of apparatus. How much he cares about the woman as such may be gauged by his attitude to her five minutes after fruition (one does not keep the carton after one has smoked the cigarettes). Now Eros makes a man really want, not a woman, but one particular woman. In some mysterious but quite indisputable fashion the lover desires the beloved herself, not the pleasure she can give."[7]

With the 1960s revolution came a hidden epidemic of sexually transmitted infections and diseases, alongside unwanted pregnancies, which led to abortion being legalised in 1967. But this didn't trouble men, because they were now free to walk away and let another sort out the mess they made. Within fifty years, one in five children would be raised by a heroic single parent, in Britain's 1.8 million single parent households, with rapid increases each decade.[8]

Women have in general been more responsive to Christianity, and in the past have helped pass their faith onto their children, whilst benefiting from the protection of Christian morality, by bringing men to account. However, from the 1960s onwards the role of women in society changed forever. Journalist and editor Cristina Odone said, "We thought women were going to be freed by the pill, we thought it meant that they would be in control of not having twelve babies, one after the other – so they could study, work and affirm themselves. What we didn't think about, was that for many, the pill meant the freedom to have sex, lots and lots of sex, and that was no freedom at all in the end."[9]

Columnist and Critic David Aaronovitch said, "For women the concept of the progressive sixties essentially was – where they were expected to sleep with as many men, as wanted to sleep with them. That was the notion of sexual liberation."[10]

The respect of the wedding night was exchange for an awkward drunken experience in a toilet with a stranger at a party, or a string of hollow relationships, where groping and fast-tracked sex undermined emotional intimacy and the desire for life-long sacrificial commitment. The 1960s are presented in the media as glamorous, exciting and seductive, by contrast journalist and author Virginia Ironside recalls it differently, "To be honest, I mainly remember the 60s as an endless round of miserable promiscuity."[11] With so many 'blurred lines,' incidents of sexual assault and rape rapidly rose. By 2013, approximately 85,000 women are raped on average in England and Wales each year, and over 400,000 women are sexually assaulted, mostly by people they know.[12]

After the 1960s, without Christian moral values as its bedrock, the West became more abusive and corrupt. The West now has a hidden epidemic of sexual violence and abuse, and charities that help victims, crushed by the juggernaut of the sexual revolution, say that official statistics have always masked the real numbers, who are afraid to come forward and go through their ordeal with police, or any other authority. Some charities now believe that the real numbers of abuse survivors, based upon anonymous surveys is one in four women.

In the West we fail to appreciate how sexual promiscuity has become by nature, exploitative. One study found that four in ten teenage schoolgirls aged between thirteen and seventeen in England have been coerced into sex acts and one in five girls have suffered physical violence from their boyfriend.[13]

Promiscuity exploits vulnerability, ignorance, intoxication and takes what it wants, without any regard to the long-term costs to the other, or the responsibility for them to carry, often alone. The West says that consensual sex with various people is fine, but what exactly does a teenager know about all they are consenting to? How often in consensual sexual relationships, have people thought they are consenting to one type of relationship – a permanent, exclusive and honest relationship – whilst the other was consenting to something else? How many alcohol fuelled sexual experiences would have been deemed sexual abuse or rape, in the clear light of day? The Bible warns it is a significant sin to get people drunk, with the intent of breaking down their resistance, to use their bodies (Habakkuk 2:15-16).

Chapter Twenty-Four

A Bitter Price to Pay

In the eighteenth and nineteenth centuries the West celebrated people who made substantial contributions to humanity by improving human rights, advancing science, pioneering and so forth: from William Wilberforce ending the slave trade to Lord Shaftsbury establishing human rights, to Florence Nightingale transforming nursing and David Livingstone opening Africa. Most of our national celebrities were Christians, like the scientist Michael Faraday, whose work makes the modern electrical world possible. But from the 1960s onwards, the West embraced celebrities for being celebrities. Our heroes are now actors who pretend to be others in films and TV, who read lines that others have made-up; whilst film crews, editors and computer experts make it appear they are taking risks and having adventures. Or they're singers who sing about "sexy, sexy," as they make semi-pornographic music videos in their make-believe world.

Meanwhile, few young people know of the real-life Christian pioneers who fought for their liberties or the missionaries who risked their lives and changed the world, yet one in four have viewed porn at age 12 or under.[1] Instead of seeking eternal meaning in the words of the prophets, apostles and abiding in the teaching of Jesus, Western culture turned to song writers for guidance and wisdom, from those who admit to being blind themselves, and the world changed for the worse. New celebrity gurus now help people to find what to wear, how to behave and what to believe. As people worship their new idols, a few became rich and life became cheap, people expendable, and the miracle of pregnancy became for some an unwanted distraction.

In 1967 abortion was made legal, overruling sections 58 and 59 of the 1861 Offences Against The Person Act, and since then, 7.5 million abortions have taken place in Britain.[2] A study by Dr Peter Saunders found that in 2010, "In all there were 493,242 deaths in England and Wales from 'all causes'...if we add the pre-born babies who died as a result of abortion the total number of human deaths comes to 682,816. In other words, 189,574 out of 682,816 deaths, or 27.76% were due to abortion.'[3]

Writer and broadcaster Ann Atkins said, "What happened with the Abortion Act was a complete philosophical shift...it became a right to do away with the unborn child, if it was inconvenient and that has been the most monumental philosophical change. For those of us who see the unborn child as a human being, it is the most phenomenal abuse of human rights since the Holocaust. It's on the same scale as the Holocaust. Whenever big human rights abuses happen, it is always argued on the grounds that these people, because their black or Jewish, or their working class, or not yet born, are not human, in the way that the rest of us are. So we can do what we like to them."[4]

The current U.K. law allows for pregnancies to be terminated up to twenty-four weeks and one mother, who tragically saw her baby die after birth just twenty-four weeks into the pregnancy, has called for a change in abortion laws, after releasing a photo of her beloved baby. "Our picture shows Adelaide was not a foetus, she was a fully formed human being," said Emily Caines with her husband, "and to think that a baby like her could be legally terminated on grounds of a lifestyle choice is to me is horrifying."[5]

People who argue for abortion often say that 'real babies,' such as the fully formed foetus shown in an image by a protester in the street, are not being aborted; it is only a few cells, an undeveloped foetus. But even if we only measure the number of late-term abortions of recognisable human beings with eyes, feet and fingers, we find that by the fiftieth anniversary of the legalisation of abortion in Britain, the nation will have destroyed up to 120,000 late-term pregnancies.[6]

David Steel, the Member of Parliament (MP) who introduced the 1967 Abortion Bill is concerned that abortion is being used as a contraceptive, as 68,105 abortions have been given to those who already had at least one abortion. David Steel said, "It is odd that so many women present for repeat abortions, some more than twice, which does suggest they are treating abortion as contraception. This was never the purpose of the 1967 reform."[7]

Josephine Quintavalle of the Pro-Life Alliance said, "David Steel needs to face the reality of the provision of abortion in this country, that it is not just being provided for women in dramatic need but is available on demand. It was verging on the ingenuous of him to imagine when he brought forward his legislation in 1967, that abortion wouldn't end up being available on demand. The trouble is that many people think there s nothing wrong with repeat abortions. They say, 'Abortion is either right or wrong,' so if you can have one, you should be able to have as many as you can ask for."[8]

What can be said about our culture? 'They have no pity on the fruit of the womb' (Isaiah 13:18), and choose to ignore that God is at work in every womb. 'Your eyes saw my unformed body; all the days ordained for me were written in Your Book before one of them came to be' (Psalm 139:16).

The 1960s changed everything and it came at a profound cost, and still does. There was overconfidence in all areas, which made people blind to what they were doing, based upon a belief that all things new are always better. Within a few decades, a thousand years of Western heritage was sold for a superficial illusion of consumerism, 'being sexy,' and celebrity. The right to promiscuity became more important than a child's right to a home, and today's thrill became more valued than tomorrow's earned pleasure. Writer and columnist Peter Oborne said, "Everything was supposed to have got better in the sixties, but actually, almost everything got worse."[9]

It wasn't just the value of a human being or the stability of the family and society that fell in the 1960s, so too did many historic buildings. All over Britain, in the age of the 'new,' elegant and historic regal Victorian buildings were demolished. The heart of Bradford's town centre, once as beautiful and elegant as any Victorian palace, was torn-down to be replaced with a bleak concrete monstrosity because it was new. Meanwhile, modest family homes were demolished to be replaced with concrete tower blocks, which due to regulation, turned out to house fewer people on the land, than new modern homes would have. Then on 16 May 1968, a twenty-two story high-rise partially collapsed in East London, as the myth gave way to reality.[10]

In the sixties we gained a few tunes which people really love and we lost much. The sixties entranced the youth of Britain with the greatest of illusions – that consumerism could fill their inner void, that promiscuity would cost no one, that 'being spiritual, but not religious' could provide meaning, and that reform of the family would make a better and happier society.

The sixties took us to a new empty void in culture, destitute of real meaning and it flooded the West with the empty distraction we call entertainment. It was a decade of prestidigitation which gave birth to the disillusionment of the 1970s and consumerism.

Theologian and author Richard J. Foster said, "Because we lack a divine centre our need for security has led us into an insane attachment to things. We really must understand that the lust for affluence in contemporary society is psychotic. It is psychotic because it has completely lost touch with reality. We crave things we neither need nor enjoy…we are made to feel ashamed to wear clothes or drive cars until they are worn out.

The mass media have convinced us that to be out of step with fashion is to be out of step with reality. It is time we awaken to the fact that conformity to a sick society is to be sick."[11]

The 1960s had a party and we all live with the perpetual hangover. From then on, family breakdown exploded and new reasons for childhood poverty rapidly increased, until by 2014, t affected almost one in three.[12] But childhood itself almost disappeared, as media savvy young girls come close to skipping the age of innocence, to buy into capitalism's sexualisation of children, to give girls skimpy see-through clothes, so older boys can make them feel 'special,' for a second. In a media age of sexuality, children have become so worried about popularity, their looks, image and sex, that one survey suggests they lose their innocence by the age of 12, or even 10.[13]

By 1969, Britain awoke to a scorching headache. Family life was dissolving, leading to soaring benefits, more women were being sexually harassed instead of courted, the Empire was crumbling, and the former Workshop of the World and birthplace of the Industrial Revolution was being decimated. Britain was on the verge of economic and industrial collapse, which led straight into the pessimism, violence and upheaval of the 1970s.

Afterwards all those 'happy' people from the 1960s, some of whom were the victims of sexual and drug abuse, sought restoration, and most churches have stories to tell concerning how they have helped the forgotten broken people of yesterday's pleasure. "The thing which people who celebrate the sixties tend to forget is the victims," said journalist Peter Oborne. "Human beings are at their worst when they try to play God and their arrogant, and that's what happened in the sixties, they played God, and we're still living with the terrible consequences of this inordinate piece of arrogance."[14]

Perhaps the most important thing to realise about the 1960s is that the change in culture did not overcome the older generation, but instead, the young people swept up in the revolution passed on their new secular values, post-Christian beliefs and casual moral attitudes to their children. For those who knew they had made terrible mistakes, they felt they had little or no authority to challenge their children to live to a higher standard, because of fear of hypocrisy. Therefore the implications of the 1960s did not begin to sweep the nation until the late 70s and 80s. By 2000 many of the old Christian values were considered preposterous.

According to Christian thinking, a loving God has put limits on sexual behaviour to protect us from ourselves, to guard its beauty, to avoid sex being separated from an emotional and spiritual union, and to save the vulnerable from abuse etc., (Leviticus 18:1-28, 20:10-21). Sexual revolutions may be called great, as long as no-one considers the victims and the full cost.

In the 1920s, Kinshasa, in Congo, gained a reputation for the place to be, to have a really good time, where anything was possible. All the Christian moral rules from home no longer applied, and colonists, workers, traders, tourists and others, enjoyed a free sex environment. What no-one knew was that a mutated version of a chimpanzee virus, known as simian immunodeficiency virus, had just jumped species through an unknown transferral of blood from one species to the other. This was the birthplace of the Aids pandemic. Dr Andrew Freedman said, "HIV in humans arose by cross species transmission from chimpanzees in that region of Africa," and what followed was, according to experts, "the perfect storm" for spreading the virus from one, or a few infected humans to the world.[15]

Through viral archaeology, scientists have been able to trace the linage of the genetic code of HIV, to learn how it spread from one person in the 1920s to over 34,000,000 worldwide.[16] The most important factor to its spread is promiscuity, with infected needles and drug users as second, all adding to the immense human cost. The financial burden of treating it is predicted to rise to $35 billion annually by 2031.[17]

Today, the number of people worldwide infected with a sexually transmitted infection (STI) or disease has grown exponentially, because people have little or no understanding of how many people they are sharing infections with. C. Everett Koop, M.D., former U.S. Surgeon General said, "When you have sex with someone, you are having sex with everyone they had sex with for the last ten years, and everyone they and their partners have had sex with for the last ten years."[18] This means people are potentially exposed to share any sexually transmitted infection or disease, with any person they have had sex with in the last decade, and all the people they have had sex with – and all their partners, until a long chain of sexual partners builds.

If a man and a woman decide to save sex for marriage, and only have sex with each other throughout their lives, their sexual exposure will always only be to one person. But if two people cohabit, having had ten other sexual partners each, their real sexual exposure, on a minimalist scale is 2,047 people!

This is the difference between people's 'supposed exposure' to STIs and their 'real exposure.' Sexual exposure charts try to unveil the mystery of how STIs are spreading rapidly on a global scale. It's a complicated process needing a great amount of personal detail, but with a simplified example, the numbers stack up like this: 1 sexual partner in life = 1 exposure. 2=3. 3=7. 4=15. 5=31. 6=63. 7=127. 8=255. 9=511. 10=1,023. 11=2,047. 12=4,097. This calculation made by Wish Medical, assumes the sexual partners share the same number of other partners, for example, both parties had sex for the first time together.[19]

In Britain, Lloyds Pharmacy was inspired by the concept of Six Degrees of Separation to create their Sex Degrees of Separation calculator. By adding more detailed personal information to the calculator, users can move beyond hypothetical calculations to find their estimated 'real exposure' to STIs, which can be far higher than the example above.[20]

On a global scale the World Health Organisation states: 'More than 1 million people acquire a sexually transmitted infection every day. Each year, an estimated 500 million people acquire one of four sexually transmitted infections: chlamydia, gonorrhoea, syphilis and trichomoniasis. More than 530 million people are living with HSV2. More than 290 million women have an HPV infection, one of the most common STIs.'[21] Millions of innocent children are also born HIV positive and by 2015, there is an estimated twenty-five million HIV/Aids orphans.[22]

In the 1960s, the Rev. Duncan Campbell gave his conclusion to the changes in society, "We are living in desperate days but unfortunately, a pleasure crazed and morally bankrupt generation refuses to face the facts of grim reality, and I fear that that spirit has somehow entered the Christian Church."[23]

With such problems around the world, what is the government doing? Journalist Graeme Paton wrote that British 'schools are being told that children should be able to have consensual sex at the age of 13 as part of government-backed guidance. The guidelines – which can be used as part of sex education lessons – say that having sexual relationships when children reach their teens represents a "safe and healthy" part of growing up. They have been produced by a national charity as part of a plan endorsed by the Department for Education to improve standards of advice given to pupils...for 13 to 17-year-olds, normal behaviour includes taking an interest in pornography, having sexually explicit conversations, using the internet to chat online and consenting to oral or penetrative sex with the same or opposite gender... Speaking at a committee hearing, MP Graham Stuart, said critics of the guide will argue that "not to send out a message that it's wrong, that it's harmful, it's dangerous, is in fact to almost to collude with something which we know is damaging to young people." ' Sarah Carter, trustee of the Family Education

Trust, told the committee that the guidance was illegal, "The law states that young person should wait until they are 16 at least."[24]

Proponents of the sexual revolution hoped women would become free, what happened in practice was they were told to be available, and in subsequent generations, increased sexual pressure has been heaped upon girls and women to be more sexier, younger, thinner, perpetually young, and the legacy is the commoditisation of the female body. Instead of being healthy, women became encouraged to starve themselves until their bodies appear like that of a thirteen year old boy.

Thus, the West without Christianity at its heart became intoxicated with self image and people believed they too could 'feel like a celebrity,' as they bought their brands and listened to the 'wisdom' of these famous people. Consequently, as people's lives became dominated by empty consumerism, image and celebrity, they turned in their millions to antidepressants. By 2013, the British population of 64 million consumed up to 60 million prescriptions of antidepressants and became known as a nation on antidepressants.[25]

Celebrities also made taking illegal drugs popular in the West, as they played a cat and mouse game with the police.[26] Young people followed this example and supplied money to drug gangs, enabling them to expand their activities to include the slave trade of human trafficking into sexual abuse, and other areas of illegal activity. Meanwhile, drug producers destabilised poor countries, ruining life for millions, as they grow drugs with the money they receive to supply 'trendy' Westerners. Today, nearly one in three British adults has taken an illegal substance.[27] Also, petty crime waves in the West can be traced back to some people addicted to drugs and the drug culture led to a crisis in mental health.[28]

The tragedy of the revolutions of the 1960s is that the victims it creates are also the people who defend the principles it has enshrined in Western culture. They do not appreciate how these values and the consequences in their lives are conjoined.

Chapter Twenty-Five

An Outcry Heard in Heaven

If we could hear the sound of earth from heaven, would we hear a sound to please, or an outcry of violence, abuse and shame? God said, "The outcry against Sodom and Gomorrah is great and their sin is very grave" (Genesis 18:20), and, "her sins have reached to heaven" (Revelation 18:5).

It has been said that, "If you remember the sixties, you weren't there," and that's probably because no-one wants to think about what truly happened, nor the full cost of the decade and its consequences for all. The spin, the popular movies and music have remained an enticing mirage, and the aspiration that anything is possible seemed true for a time – but, oh, what a cost! Millions of children in single homes, millions of tiny lives cut short, millions of women sexually abused and hurting, millions of men ashamed of what they've done. Peace and love rules, as long as we don't think about the 7,300,000 criminal offences in Britain in 2013, or the fact that charities believe twenty-five percent of all British and American women have experienced some form of sexual violence at least once.[1]

When God sets boundaries, it is not because there is an oasis of life outside of them, which He wants to keep us from, but a series of unending dangers which will cause great harm. A loving God, who 'gives us all things richly to enjoy' (1 Timothy 6:17), has to warn us when we seek to exploit, manipulate and abuse the liberties He has given to us. The cost of the 'freedom' of the sixties is now born by all – in their homes, society and by taxation. The Relationships Foundation's annual index of the cost of family breakdown, has shown that the total cost to the British taxpayer in one year was £41.74 billion, which is £1,364 for every taxpayer.[2] Also, the direct costs of treating the results of sexual promiscuity costs the NHS one billion a year.[3]

Scripture reveals what happened in the 1960s and onwards was not a social experiment which went terribly wrong, but a spiritual battle which was lost. Jesus said, "Most assuredly, I say to you, whoever commits sin is a slave of sin. And a slave does not abide in the house forever, but a son abides forever. Therefore if the Son makes you free, you shall be free indeed" (John 8:34). Mankind is either in service of God and His will, or slaves of demonic powers and their will. 'You who were dead in trespasses and sins, in which you once walked according to the course of this world, according to the prince of the power of the air, the spirit who now works in the sons of disobedience, among whom also we all once conducted ourselves in the lusts of our flesh, fulfilling the desires of the flesh and of the mind, and were by nature children of wrath, just as the others' (Ephesians 2:1-3).

Jesus Christ witnessed a real Satan (Luke 10:18), but those who think they are too sophisticated to believe in a real Satan, are fooled because they picture the devil as a cartoon character with a pitchfork. These people have fallen into the trap which Satan laid for them. C.S. Lewis explains it like this: 'There are two equal and opposite errors into which our race can fall about devils. One is to disbelieve in their existence. The other is to believe, and to feel an excessive and unhealthy interest in them. They themselves are equally pleased by both errors and hail a materialist or magician with the same delight.'[4]

Based upon his reading of Scripture, C.S. Lewis believed that Satan is able to exercise his power to the greatest effect, when those under his spell have become incapacitated to perceive him, and think they are too sophisticated to believe in the biblical revelation of a spiritual realm of angels and demons. Paul wrote: 'The natural man does not receive the things of the Spirit of God, for they are foolishness to him; nor can he know them, because they are spiritually discerned' (1 Corinthians 2:14).

Lewis describes the hold demonic powers can have: 'The more a man was in the devil's power, the less he would be aware of it,' he wrote, 'it is the people who are fully awake and trying hard to be good who would be most aware of the devil. It is when you start arming against Hitler that you first realise your country is full of Nazi agents."[5] Only those who try to break an addiction truly acknowledge and begin to find the control it has over them. The first aim of devils "is to give you an anaesthetic – to put you off your guard. Only when that fails do you become aware of them."[6]

According to Jesus Christ and the teaching in the Bible, we are in a spiritual struggle, with an unseen realm influencing events on earth. Jesus taught Satan is the chief of all fallen angels, spirits who chose wickedness instead of servanthood to God's will (Matthew 25:41, John 8:44). Jesus called Satan, "The ruler of this world" (John 12:31), and Paul tells us his influence upon it: 'Whose minds the god of this age has blinded' (2 Corinthians 4:4). He is an unseen spiritual being 'called the devil and Satan, who deceives the whole world' (Revelation 12:9).

God is open and upfront in His call for followers and the cost of obeying Him, by contrast Satan seeks to control people, and ensnare them by spiritual fraud (John 8:34, Hebrews 2:14-15). God reveals Himself, Satan conceals himself. Back in the 1950s, a thousand years of Christian influence made it hard for Satan to spread his net over people's lives. But since the 1960s, evil spirits have been able to plant thoughts and ideas into people's minds, using the mass media that spread his infection into as many hearts as possible.

The fall in morals and rise in sexual violence amongst the young has been called by experts the 'Normalising of Sexual Violence' in culture.[7] The Unicef report *Hidden in Plain Sight...Violence Against Children* found that 120 million girls and female adolescents under twenty worldwide have endured rape or other forced sexual acts.[8] How did a culture of desired respect change to a culture of abuse? Have films and TV influenced the morals of millions, just like TV adverts influence them?

The breakthroughs of the 1960s became the new normal for the West's post-Christian 'moral' compass. In the 1960s, the first mainstream film with a female nude scene was released.[9] Also, in 1967 the first 'F' word was used in a film.[10] Today the most popular TV series in a major network's history, a global phenomenon, watched by tens of millions of young adults worldwide has been called little more than 'torture porn.' It is criticized for containing prolonged exploitative female nudity, sexual violence and torture of women, with dehumanising sex.[11] Also, one of the big movie hits of 2013, contained 569 'F' words, another 935.[12]

We are convincingly told by experts that films, TV and the internet have limited or even no impact on people's behaviour. If this is the case, why are billions spent each year on advertising and product placements?[13] In June 1999, the Asian hermit nation Bhutan allowed Western TV to be shown in the nation for the first time. Within a decade, Western brands were sought out and flooded into the nation, and family breakdown, with promiscuity increased. Bhutan's experiment provides independent verifiable data of the media's influence. The facts do not discriminate and have no political or religious agenda. Kinley Dorji, a local young person's development worker said the youth, "Want and need what they see on television – the fashion, the clothes, the whole changing lifestyle, going to bars, drinking...if you look at the items being stolen, it's directly related to what they're seeing."[14]

In the West, studies have shown that people who regularly view sexual violence and pornography become desensitised, and seek out 'more extreme' material instead. A study by the head of

Britain's police paedophile unit concluded by the millennium, the U.K. had 250,000 paedophiles including those with no conviction because there were too many to police and only five percent are caught.[15] Paedophiles have a history of beginning to view adult pornography and then seeking extreme and younger images.

In 2014, the journalist Andrew Gilligan wrote of his horror at an academic presentation delivered at one of Britain's leading universities, where one respected academic said, "Paedophilic interest is natural and normal for human males," and other presentations and books have tried to remove the 'prejudice' against child sex.[16] In 1984, the Paedophile Information Exchange (PIE) which tried to change attitudes was rightly closed. Andrew Gilligan said, "With the Pill, the legalisation of homosexuality and shrinking taboos against premarital sex, the seventies was an era of quite sudden sexual emancipation. Many liberals, of course, saw through PIE's cynical rhetoric of 'child lib.' But to others on the Left, sex by or with children was just another repressive boundary to be swept away – and some of the most important backing came from academia."[17]

Columnist and author Pamela Paul observed, "It is easier to get pornography than to avoid it. We have protected the rights of those who wish to live in a pornified culture while altogether ignoring the interests of those who do not."[18] Due to the internet, smart phones and many TVs at home, one study found that the average age of initial exposure to pornography is now just eleven.[19] We place ratings on games and films, because our culture acknowledges that children need to be protected from certain content, but these ratings have become ineffective in a multimedia age of on-demand content.

What is the result? Anything adults view will also be viewed by children. Shadow Health Minister Diane Abbott has warned that British culture is "increasingly pornified" and is damaging the young. She explained that fast-developing technology and an "increasingly pornified British culture" has led to a "strip-tease culture in British schools and society, which has been put beyond the control of British families."[20] One charity found that over a third of young people have received a sexually explicit text or email, with the majority of these coming from peers.[21]

Diane Abbott said, "For so long, it's been argued that overt, public displays of sexuality are an enlightened liberation. But I believe that for many, the pressure of conforming to hyper-sexualisation and its pitfalls is a prison. And the permanence of social media and technology can be a life sentence."[22]

One of the unpredicted phenomena of the digital age is the rise of 'sexting,' which is the voluntary act of sending sexually explicit messages or photos, primarily between mobile phones. Today children and young people are sending sexually explicit images of themselves to others, notably to boyfriends or girlfriends, voluntarily or sometimes under pressure. Jon Brown, the head of the prevent sexual abuse programme in the National Society for the Prevention of Cruelty to Children (NSPCC), said 'sexting' is taking some young girls "into an underworld of abuse where they are constantly pestered for sex or urged to pose for provocative pictures."[23]

Journalist Zoe Williams explains how the public space has been bombarded with graphic semi-pornographic images in which, "one gender is a trussed-up, passive sex toy for the other."[24] Williams pointed out that, "Magazines with naked women on the cover sit next to kids' comics in newsagents" and, "scantily clad models are draped across the nation's billboards."[25]

If TV, films, magazines and our high streets are overwhelmed with sexual imagery, what about those female models and actresses? Are they worthy of anything more than to be exploited and disregarded? One study states actresses are now sexual targets. An examination of 238 sitcoms and dramas airing during four weeks in 2011 and 2012, found a third of the episodes included content that 'rose to the level of sexual exploitation' of females. The study relied on the United Nations' definition of sexual exploitation, as involving abuse of a position of vulnerability, power, or trust for sexual purposes including profiting financially, socially or politically.[26]

A number of young actresses, models and female artists, having matured, now look back and have condemned a 'culture of demeaning women' that forces vulnerable young stars to sell themselves as sex objects.[27] One successful female artist with over ten million album sales, said she was 'pressurised' into wearing revealing outfits in videos by male executives when she was 19 or 20, adding that young female artists are routinely "coerced into sexually demonstrative behaviour in order to hold on to their careers."[28] "Whilst I can't defer all blame away from myself," she said, "I was barely out of my teenage years and the consequence of this portrayal of me is that now I'm frequently abused on social media."[29]

Two young female actresses, one a teenager, explained how they felt like "prostitutes" whilst making a well publicised film and complained that in no other industry could a boss expect employees to demean themselves in such a way. One actress said, "The thing is, the director has all the power. When you're an actor on a film...and you sign the contract...in a way you're trapped...most people don't even dare to ask [to film] the things that he [the director] did."[30]

One actress, looking back seventeen years from a movie she made as a teenager said, "I was uncomfortable with the explicit nudity. I was in denial, head in the sand about that day's work. I just nodded my head and agreed and got on with it."[31] Meanwhile, the pregnant wife of the male actor in the scene said she "trembled" when she saw this actress for months. "That is the only time I have ever felt jealous," she added.[32]

Some models have been campaigning for a union to protect young vulnerable girls saying, "Models are pressured into having sex with clients, doing nude photoshoots, even if they are underage and staying dangerously thin."[33] 'The mistreatment, exploitation and illegality they cite includes sexual harassment by clients and photographers, ranging from lewd and suggestive comments to groping and attempts to persuade models to sleep with them. They say girls are often too intimidated or embarrassed to complain and that some agencies, ignore models' concerns in order to maintain good relationships with important clients. Drug-taking is commonplace in the industry, with some models, including those under sixteen, using cocaine and amphetamines to stay as thin as possible.'[34]

Pimps exploit women's bodies for profit, without regard to their humanity or the price they will pay, by dehumanising them as objects – is the mass media – films, TV, magazines, newspapers etc., any different? A minority of women become millionaires due to the media and become powerful, whilst the ninety-nine percent are unknown, used and cast off, after they have been exploited for a quick profit. Those who succeed often complain of the practices they encountered when they were young, poor, vulnerable and desperate for a job, in an industry that turned out to be very exploitative. The apostle Paul asks would you want your female relative to be treated poorly? (1 Timothy 5:1).

After a series of child and teenage sex abuse scandals were exposed in Britain, committed by an unrepresentative minority in the Pakistani Muslim community, Ann Coffey MP, chaired an inquiry, and said that the "normalisation of quasi-pornographic images...has given rise to new social norms and changed expectations of sexual entitlement." She added that child sexual exploitation has become a "social norm" in some areas. In Greater Manchester Ann Coffey said, "It is an everyday occurrence for" many young girls in the area to be approached by older men. "That indicates they are living in an environment where it is felt to be ok to go and touch, and harass, and pester girls in [school] uniforms. That is what I mean by it being a new social norm." When she asked the girls – school children – why they did not go to the police, they replied, "Well it happens so often, so many men, what can the police do?"[35]

Sue Berelowitz, whilst giving evidence to Britain's Home Affairs Select Committee, listed shocking examples of abuse, torture and rape of teenagers and children, by adults and children, in a national abuse scandal. "What I am uncovering is that sexual exploitation of children is happening all over the country," she told the cross-party committee. "In urban, rural and metropolitan areas, I have hard evidence of children being sexually exploited. It is very sadistic, it is very violent, it is very ugly."[36] She revealed how child on child, and teenage on teenage sexual violence has spread, and how gangs of men have groomed vulnerable young teenage girls. "As one police officer who was the lead in a very big investigation, in a very lovely, leafy, rural part of the country said to me, 'There isn't a town, village or hamlet in which children are not being sexually exploited,' " she said.[37]

Paedophiles and sex offenders emerge from all ethnic, religious and social backgrounds, but journalist Melanie Phillips argued that a 'witch-hunt' against 'Islamophobia' led to a few in minority communities thinking they had a 'free pass' from the police, to abuse young girls in gangs, without prosecution, as the authorities sought to avoid any race and religious tensions.[38] She wrote: 'The question immediately arises: how on earth could a blind eye have been turned to all this by the social services departments under whose care these girls were living, as well as by the police to whom they went for help?...This is about religion and culture – an unwesternised Islamic culture which holds that non-Muslims are trash and women are worthless. And so white girls are worthless trash."[39] Nazir Afzal, the Chief Crown Prosecutor for north west England, said, 'that "imported cultural baggage" played a role in the crimes but what defined the convicted men was their attitude to women. They think that women are some lesser being. The availability of vulnerable young white girls is what has drawn the men to them.'[40]

The West has yet matured to a place where it is prepared to face up to the full consequences of the sexual revolution, in an objective way. Presently, the West is still burying its head in the sand and pretending that all the scandals, abuse and trends towards sexual exploitation – from teenagers sending sexually explicit images of themselves to 'be liked,' or models being abused, or to the pornification of high streets, as somehow unrelated to the sexual revolution.

When the media celebrates the sexual revolution, what it rarely thinks about are the millions of victims. If the West continues on this path, tragically, the innocent children in schools today will become the victims of tomorrow. Professor Anthony Esolen said, "What strikes me most powerfully about the defenders of the sexual revolution is their immovable abstraction. Always the matter is couched in terms of rights, or individual desires – what I want, what I may pursue. That this sexual laissez-faire destroys the common good, by undermining families and rotting whole neighbourhoods from within, seems not to matter. Honest sociologists can give us the numbers of children growing up without fathers or mothers, of the incidence of venereal diseases, of births out of wedlock, of delinquency and crime. I think instead of the people I have known."[41]

Statistics hide the fact that victims are real people, each with his or her own story, concerning the hurt and abuse suffered. Broadcaster and journalist Bel Mooney said, "My generation created the sexual revolution – and it has been wrecking the lives of women ever since," because it ignores the link between cause and effect. "I'm always amazed at the way the liberal Left," she said, "is eager to make excuses for any dubious results of their progressive ideas. Yet the damaging consequences of that sixties revolution are obvious in the society we now live in...the dangerous 'anything goes' attitude which challenges any idea of restraint in speech or behaviour.

"Today, those of us who express doubts about the long-term effects of such cultural changes are dismissed as prudes suffering from a permanent moral panic-attack. The denial of the liberals is ongoing: a blinkered refusal to admit the causes and effects of history. But this is what the distinguished historian Eric Hobsbawm writes about the shift in standards in his authoritative book, *Age Of Extremes*: 'The crisis of the family was linked with quite dramatic changes in public standards governing sexual behaviour, partnership and procreation...and the major change is datable and coincides with the sixties and seventies.'[42]

Looking back, Bel Mooney confessed that, "To be a 'nice girl' was to be looked on as a freak. The truth was, however, the new permissiveness gave men permission to exploit you...it may be cruel to say it, but today's young girls primping and un-dressing for Saturday night, when they will get drunk and get laid (and feel doubly bad in the morning) are the inheritors of this destiny."

The sexual revolution, she said, "has not encouraged mutual love and respect between the sexes but instead has given us the trashy 'pornogrification' of our society…in her book, *Bodies,* psychotherapist Susie Orbach writes: 'Girls as young as four have been made bodily self-conscious and are striking sexy poses in their mirrors which are more chilling than charming.' The question we must all ask ourselves is – what made them so bodily self-conscious?" The answer is the media and fashion. "The sad thing is young women today are still being conned – victims of the pervasive sex industry which uses 'liberation' as a mask for degradation."[43]

According to a survey conducted by NSPCC ChildLine, a tenth of twelve to thirteen year olds fear they are 'addicted' to pornography. Twelve percent of those surveyed said, 'They had taken part in or had made a sexually explicit video,' and the charity says that viewing porn is 'a part of everyday life' for many children who contact them.[44] Young teenage girls are also telling charities that boyfriend's who view porn go on to abuse them, copying the images they have seen.[45] In 2015, Britain's most senior judge, Lord Chief Justice Thomas warned that extreme online pornography is now being mirrored in cases brought to the courts, as ideas portrayed have fuelled examples of rape and murder.[46] He added, "What is available to download and to see is simply horrific, and it played a real part in the way in which this particular murder was carried out." Citing several cases, the parallels between abuse in pornographic material and the real-life crime is astonishing.[47]

'The Lord looks down from heaven upon the children of men, to see if there are any who understand, who seek God…they have together become corrupt' (Psalm 14:2-3).

Chapter Twenty-Six

Spiritual, but Not Religious

If the 1960s changed everything, how did the Church respond? Despite many misconceptions about the world wars sinking faith in Britain, church attendance actually rose in the 1940s and 50s, getting closer to the levels of the early 1900s. In the U.S. camp meetings and healing evangelists drew large crowds, whilst in Britain it was still popular to be considered a Christian. However, the evangelistic hopes and optimism of the 1945 report *Towards the Conversion of England* gave way to deep despondency. In the 1960s, the Christian concepts of love, peace, joy and hope seemed to be hijacked by the secular and distorted, then hollowed out – but outwardly the new mirage shone. The grand narrative of Christianity, with eternal answers and hope seemed lost in Church debates and internal politics.

Churches struggled to know how to respond to the changes of the 1960s and outwardly many seemed to lose the little vision they had. The harvest festivals of the past were hugely important to Britain, when ninety-eight percent of the people worked on the land, or during the austerity of the war, but they lost credibility in the eyes of many, when only two percent of the population farmed. Church traditions seemed stuffy, old, dull and it felt like the powerful message was lost by the messengers. Outside of churches was an image of sex, music, dance, life and new liberties; inside were the routines and rituals of the late 1800s. 'Where there is no vision, the people perish' (Proverbs 29:18).

Film, music and TV stars all seemed to be having so much fun, that no-one stopped to question why so many of them became dependant on drink and drugs, and why there is a tragic link between celebrity, depression and above average suicide. They 'enjoyed' themselves so much that they needed their real-self to be constantly suppressed by substances just to survive.

In the late eighteenth and early nineteenth centuries German scholars pioneered Higher Criticism, which is the scientific study of biblical writings to determine their origins and meaning. Their flawed work spread in Europe and undermined the faith of many, and people began entering the ministry as unbelievers. By the 1960s, churches then came under immense pressure to change their message, to conform to this new world and some of the theological leading lights in Britain, did just that. In 1963, Bishop John A.T. Robinson wrote the book *Honest to God*, stating: 'The whole scheme of a supernatural being coming down from heaven to 'save' mankind from sin...is frankly incredible to man 'come of age.' ' Leading bishops in the Anglican Communion wanted all to know how brilliant their new philosophies were becoming, and tried desperately to appear wise in the eyes of all. One bishop said the doctrine of the Trinity is "outdated, incomprehensible and nonessential."[1] Another said Christ's virgin birth was a 'primitive myth,"[2] and the Archbishop of Canterbury said, "Heaven is not a place for Christians only," concluding he expected to fellowship with atheists and even Judas.[3]

The Rev. Duncan Campbell said, "This statement gives you an idea of the appalling situation today in Great Britain...Are we not in the days spoken of by Paul in his letter to Timothy? 'For the time will come when they will not endure sound doctrine, but after their own lust they will heap to themselves teachers having itching ears. They shall turn away from the truth' (2 Timothy 4:3-4)."[4] John said, "They are of the world. Therefore they speak as of the world and the world hears them" (1 John 4:5).

In 1963, in the United States, an Episcopal theologian rejected this biblical warning: 'Beware lest anyone cheat you through philosophy and empty deceit, according to the tradition of men, according to the basic principles of the world, and not according to Christ. For in Him dwells all the fullness of the Godhead bodily' (Colossians 2:8-9). Instead he began "trying to find an utterly nontranscendent way of interpreting the gospel," and atheists were thrilled, as he became the reluctant poster-boy for the 'God is Dead' movement.[5]

All these great minds were so thrilled with their progressive philosophy that they could not understand why their 'Death of God Theology' was driving people from Church and not into it. The foundations of the Church, which were laid with solid stones of faith and sacrifice, were being replaced with sand and by 8 April 1966, the cover of *Time* magazine asked, 'Is God Dead?'

When these comments were challenged as heresy by Bible believing leaders, in 1967, the U.S. Episcopal Church responded by adopting a resolution declaring that heresy is out of date. At the Lambeth Conference in England the following year, a vote was passed no longer requiring Anglican clergy to accept the 39 articles of faith from 1563, which effectively defined Anglicanism. Therefore, instead of standing strong in their Christian faith and believing their beliefs, Sir Peregrine Worsthorne said, "The Church of England caved in, you had bishops saying they didn't believe in God, and instead of standing firm and holding the line, they all caved in."[6]

Christianity was still alive, but perceptions are important and a view was presented that doubt and revision are normal. When C.S. Lewis, who is credited with creating interest in Christianity in the 1940s, was asked about the huge success of *Honest to God* and his thoughts; he replied, "I prefer being honest, to being '*Honest to God*,'[7] and he published an article in a large national newspaper defending New Testament Christianity.[8] C.S. Lewis said we "need to believe in the One who saves us from our sins. Not only do we need to recognise that we are sinners; we need to believe in a Saviour who takes away sin...as Christians we are tempted to make unnecessary concessions to those outside the faith. We give in too much. Now, I don't mean that we should run the risk of making a nuisance of ourselves by witnessing at improper times, but there comes a time when we must show that we disagree. We must show our Christian colours, if we are to be true to Jesus Christ. We cannot remain silent or concede everything away."[9]

By 1979, Robert Runcie became the Archbishop of Canterbury and many thought he also set aside Jude's warning of 'contending for the faith,' in a bid for unity at all costs (Jude 1:3). In 1982, the United Kingdom received its first visit by a reigning Pope on a 'pastoral visit,' instead of an official state visit. Just over a month before the Pope's visit, Archbishop Robert Runcie presented his vision of all churches being reunited with Rome by the year 2000. He said, "I dream of unity with Rome, and with the great Reform tradition and with the orthodox, by the end of the century, but we will have to get a move on." He believed the Pope had much to offer all Christians as the central figure of the faith, "There is advantage in having a central focus of affection, even a central spokesman to articulate what the churches in different parts of the world are thinking. I think Anglicans recognise that there is value in that sort of concept."[10]

Many Christians were shocked. Were the sacrifices, struggles and in some cases the martyrdom of Bible believing Christians like John Wycliffe, William Tyndale, Martin Luther, Hugh Latimer, Nicolas Ridley, Thomas Cranmer and John Knox going to be swept aside as nothing? When the Pope spoke protestors brought signs stating: 'Our Faith Our Bible,' and 'Jesus What More?'[11] Many wondered what had happened to defending and following the doctrines of New Testament Christianity, which had been fought for to the death. Was Britain going to throw away the pillars of Bible faith, for the sinking sand of believing whatever we feel like believing, for a false unity? To non-Christians, it seemed obvious that a faith where you can pick and choose what you want to believe, is no faith at all.

To the average person in the street, many bishops appeared to be queuing up to coherently and unashamedly compromise God's Word, and undermine confidence in New Testament Christianity, as they denied their own faith in the Bible in a bid to appear wise (1 Corinthians 3:19). C.S. Lewis foresaw this trend coming and spoke out in 1959. He feared the Church of England did not understand it was undermining itself and devaluing its authority, by compromising on the authority of the Bible. He feared that those engaging in New Testament criticism were ignorantly, the blind leading the blind. Jesus said, "Can the blind lead the blind? Will they not both fall into the ditch?" (Luke 6:39).

C.S. Lewis said, "Scepticism is the father of ignorance," and he added, "once the layman was anxious to hide the fact that he believed so much less than the vicar; now he tends to hide the fact that he believes so much more. Missionary to the priests of one's own Church is an embarrassing role; though I have a horrid feeling that if such mission work is not soon undertaken the future history of the Church of England is likely to be short."[12]

To Church leaders who tried to re-interpret the Bible for a secular and cynical age, Lewis warned revisionist theologians were unable to see the elephant in the room, "These men ask me to believe they can read between the lines of the old texts; the evidence is their obvious inability to read (in any sense worth discussing) the lines themselves. They claim to see fern-seed and can't see an elephant ten yards away in broad daylight."

By publicly undermining Scripture these bishops were sowing the seeds for the destruction of the Church they claimed to serve. How could these men be allowed to continue in the Church whilst seeking to reinterpret theology and claiming to understand Scripture more clearly than the first generation of Christians? Lewis declared, "The idea that any man or writer should be opaque to those who lived in the same culture, spoke the same language, shared the same habitual imagery and unconscious assumptions, and yet be transparent to those who have none of these advantages, is in my opinion preposterous."[13]

Nevertheless, the Church of England and other leading denominations seemed to be rewarding those who doubted their faith and promoted them to positions of greater influence. In 1984, David E. Jenkins was confirmed to be the next Bishop of Durham, a post he held for a decade. In a groundbreaking TV interview he shared his many doubts and this is how one journalist sums up what happened. He explained 'that he doubted God would have arranged a Virgin Birth, or allowed Jesus to walk on the water. He also allowed that people who did not consider Jesus to be more than a Divinely inspired human could consider themselves Christians.'[14]

Journalists understood immediately that these comments challenged central Christian belief and the authority of the Bible, and quickly, 'arranged for every bishop in the Church of England to be asked whether or not they agreed with him...about half of them then gave credo replies, which suggested that they agreed with him. They probably did. At once, Dr Jenkins became a symbol of everything modern and liberal in the Church of England. Some 12,000 people signed a petition against his consecration. The Archbishop of York, Dr John Habgood, who had been his predecessor at Durham, grasped the symbolic importance of the battle at once, and determined that Dr Jenkins must be consecrated. On 6 July 1984, he was consecrated in York Minster. Two protesters shouting about blasphemy had to be thrown out in the course of the service. The remaining congregation of 2,000 shouted in his favour. Two nights later, the Minster, one of the most beautiful cathedrals in the world and a relic of a long-lost age of faith, was gutted by fire following a lightning strike.'[15]

On Friday, 6 July 1984, at York Minster, David Jenkins was consecrated as the new Bishop of Durham, and he became infamous for his comments on Christ's resurrection, which contained the appalling phrase "a conjuring trick with bones."[16] 1,678 years previously in the very same place, Constantine the Great was proclaimed as the new Augustus or Roman Emperor, and the Church was to be fused with politics in such a way, that it was soon gutted from within. In this one act in 1984, the Church of England and many traditional denominations summed up their loss of biblical faith, prophetic edge and spiritual authority.

Former Cabinet Member Michael Portillo suggests this was always what the government wanted of the Church: 'The wishy-washiness of the Church of England, about which many critics complain, is the very point of it.'[17] In the official friendly future of Christianity in Britain, no-one would need to stand up for their faith, because there was no faith to stand for anymore. It could all be watered-down, diluted into a multi-faith friendly society of pic 'n' mix spirituality, with spiritual 'politicians' promoted into high ranks of Church leadership to guard the unity at any cost, even if this included denying the faith straight into apostasy. Those who stood up for the Bible within were now in danger of finding themselves in the spiritual wilderness, set aside, so the spiritual politicians of this new diluted compromising faith could take charge and 'keep up with society.'

Thus, on Friday, 6 July 1984, denying the faith was honoured at York Minister, then on Sunday, 8 July, the Archbishop of Canterbury Robert Runcie, who had said, "I dream of unity with Rome," led a service and a few hours later, in the early hours of Monday, lightning struck the Minster and the great fire began.

Many Christians thought the lightning strike and destruction of the cathedral by 'an act of God,' as insurance companies say, was a sign from God,[18] that Britain which was once 'a light to the nations,' had offended the Holy Spirit, challenged the authority of Scripture and mocked Jesus Christ. 'He covers His hands with lightning and commands it to strike' (Job 36:32). Now, it seemed the Established Church had presumptuously severed the nation's religious covenant with God, founded over a millennia and a half before. 'For their heart was not steadfast with Him, nor were they faithful to His covenant. But He, being full of compassion...did not destroy them' (Psalm 78:37-38).

The cathedral was rebuilt, yet the reputation and authority of the Church of England, and many other denominations seemed devastated. The perception that all the major denominations had lost faith and were now far too busy with internal politics, division and catching up with society has never really gone away. Perhaps 1984 was the consummation of the religious changes in Britain within the twentieth century. From this point on, to be Protestant no longer meant accepting and following New Testament Christianity; instead it could mean being liberal in your approach to Scripture, or sectarian. Peter warned: 'There will be false teachers among you. They will secretly introduce destructive heresies, even denying the sovereign Lord who bought them' (2 Peter 2:1), and this seemed to be taking place. Others were bolder and pointed to Paul's warning to Timothy: 'The Spirit clearly says that in later times, some will abandon the faith and follow deceiving spirits and things taught by demons. Such teachings come through hypocritical liars, whose consciences have been seared' (1 Timothy 4:1-2).

As Church leaders began denying the fundamentals of their faith, many Bible believing Christians thought they had to separate themselves, from those who no longer regarded the Bible as the final authority in all matters of faith and conduct. Over the decades, hundreds of thousands of Christians left the traditional denominations to find religious conviction in the New Church or other movements. To separate themselves from those who challenged the authority of Scripture, these followers of Christ no longer openly called themselves Protestant, but born again Christians, or evangelical. However, the re-branding did not last too long, as some elements in the new group tried the old trick of undermining Scripture, whilst still calling themselves born again or evangelical, and so it goes on today.

In the Church of England and other denominations, the faithful witness continued and some bishops tried to address the problem with the Bishop of Durham's thoughts, but for many outside, it was too little, far too late. The fact that the bishop was allowed to remain for a decade and that there was no repentance, made it appear that most in old denominations and the Church of England were secretly in agreement. This legacy flows over to the troubling conviction of some, that a few former Archbishops' of Canterbury were unbelievers whilst in office.[19]

C.S. Lewis was once asked, "Do you feel that modern culture is being de-Christianised?" He replied, "I cannot speak to the political aspects of the question, but I have some definite views about the de-Christianising of the Church. I believe that there are many accommodating preachers, and too many practitioners in the Church, who are not believers. Jesus Christ did not say, 'Go into all the world and tell the world that it is quite right.' The Gospel is something completely different. In fact, it is directly opposed to the world...in a civilisation like ours, I feel that everyone has to come to terms with the claims of Jesus Christ upon his life, or else be guilty of inattention or of evading the question.[20]

Influential former British politician Ann Widdecombe said, "I was brought up a Protestant in the Church of England...but fifteen years ago, I went through my own personal reformation; the Church of England had abandoned its roots and its traditions, and seemed immersed instead in the liberalism and political correctness of the modern world. That wasn't the Church I'd been brought up in and I didn't feel I belonged there anymore. So I left (in 1993) and I became a Roman Catholic."[21]

After interviewing Dr Rowan Williams in 2012, whilst he was Archbishop of Canterbury, concerning the role of the Church of England in society, Professor Diarmaid MacCulloch concluded from his remarks that, "The Archbishop sees his role as a broker of all religious points of view in society, rather as the defender of one Church."[22]

Britain once knew what it stood for and so did the Church, but one by one, compromise after compromise, the values which made Britain a great nation have been quietly shelved to accommodate a broad range of views, which have proved in other nations to lead to a very different kind of civilisation.

Nevertheless, Bible believing evangelical Christianity still grew and lived on in the nation, but the high moral and spiritual ground was lost. Why go to the people who do not believe their own beliefs, to seek answers? What followed was the first 'spiritual' transformation in over a thousand years in Britain, which did not compel people to Christ. Instead they turned to wavering incoherent beliefs, half-baked extracts from Eastern religions, with all the thrills and no demands, or drugs and meditation, or consumerism and materialism. Those who stopped believing in Christianity, now believed in anything. Leo Tolstoy wrote: 'In the world today, real faith has in most cases been replaced by public opinion. People do not believe in God, but they believe in many minor things which are taught by other people.'

Soon there was an explosion in New Age spirituality, with people hoping to channel and embrace the supernatural realm, without any understanding that there are only two sources of supernatural power – God or Satan. Without knowing it people opened themselves up to demonic powers who exploit séances, palmistry, fortune telling, charms, zodiac/birth signs, spiritism, tarot cards, hypnosis, clairvoyance, incantations, 'holy' objects, crystals, reincarnation, healing stones, mantras, feng shui, positive energies, negative flows, auras, subtle energy fields, light energy, stones ceremonies and horoscopes, etc. Also, alternative medicines and martial arts, developed by Eastern religions became popular – acupuncture, reflexology, ju-jitsu, taekwondo, taoism, kung-fu, karate, yoga, t'ai chi ch'uan and so forth. 'For You have forsaken Your people, the house of Jacob, because they are filled with Eastern ways' (Isaiah 2:6)

Thus, Christianity declined and so did the culture. 'So I gave them over to their own stubborn heart, to walk in their own counsels' (Psalm 81:12), and, 'Even as they did not like to retain God in their knowledge, God gave them over to a debased mind, to do those things which are not fitting; being filled with all unrighteousness, sexual immorality, wickedness, covetousness, maliciousness; full of envy, strife, deceit' (Romans 1:28-29).

In many ways, Britain turned back its clock to the dysfunctional society before the Wesley's of the eighteenth century, or to the pagan practices of our ancient forefathers, or to the customs of the 'heathen' that the Victorians sent missionaries to redeem. It is now Britons who tattoo their bodies, pierce and cut themselves, stretch their ears to distortion and pollute their bodies with sexually transmitted infections and diseases, through promiscuity. As a direct result, it is now Britons who sacrifice innocent lives and disregard life itself. We may not build altars to the unseen spirit 'gods' of our ancestors, but the demons who fed off of their worship, still seek to feed off our idolatries. After the 1960s, Britons did not evolve into the enlightened beings of the future; they devolved into the paganism of the past. 'The things which the Gentiles sacrifice, they sacrifice to demons and not to God, and I do not want you to have fellowship with demons' (1 Corinthians 10:20).

As many in Britain tried to give God His marching orders, He withdrew much of His hand of protection and blessing – just as prophecies were being fulfilled which describe our condition: 'But know this, that in the last days perilous times will come: For men will be lovers of themselves, lovers of money, boasters, proud, blasphemers, disobedient to parents, unthankful, unholy, unloving, unforgiving, slanderers, without self-control, brutal, despisers of good, traitors, headstrong, haughty, lovers of pleasure rather than lovers of God' (2 Timothy 3:1-4).

In one of the most fraudulent exchanges in history, Westerners gave up searching for meaning in the words and life of Jesus Christ, and began putting their confidence in luck, a vague spiritual idea of destiny, crystals, the stars and the religious cosmos, and became 'spiritual' but not religious.

The famous war correspondent John Simpson has seen the worst of life, as he covered wars, tragedies and disasters around the world. After witnessing first-hand how Christianity saved South Africa from a civil war after Apartheid, he became a practicing Christian. Today, one of his observations is people in the West have rejected following Jesus Christ without knowing anything about Him. He said of his son, "I don't want him growing up not knowing about religion," thinking that Christianity, "doesn't have any relationship to me. I don't want that. He can reject it, fine, that's his business, but he must reject it from the basis of knowing about it, not of ignorance. And so many people now, it seems to me, don't understand what it's all about. It's just something they have not been exposed to, so they don't understand, what it is, that they're not interested in."[23]

C.S. Lewis, one of the intellectual giants of the twentieth century said of his faith, "I believe in Christianity as I believe that the sun has risen. Not only because I see it, but because by it I see everything else."[24] For Lewis, Christianity provided him with a rich and satisfying unifying vision of reality. He found atheism too simple, lazy and empty. In Christianity he saw a broad vision of the meaning of life, of eternal purpose, the innate value of all, and a vision of the history and future of planet earth.

Lewis thought there was nothing more important on earth than to come to terms with the Person of Jesus Christ – what He said, claimed and did. Was Christ Divine as He claimed? Is there a heaven and hell? Is there such a thing as spirit or soul? Lewis had read all ancient myths and knew how to discern myth from historical fact and in Christ He saw fact. Jesus – the Divine Man who claimed to be God, who said He could forgive sins, who healed the sick and raised the dead. A Man who spoke like no other, who claimed things no-else would dare, and who convinced His disciples that He was, who He said He was. Jesus said, "I and my Father are One" (John 10:30).

After reading the Gospels, C.S. Lewis argued that logic dictates that Christ was either a liar or a lunatic, or the only other option – what He claimed, the Lord of all. Those who knew Jesus personally rejected the first two claims that were made by the Jews about Him, and worshipped Him as their resurrected Lord (Matthew 28:9, John 20:28, Colossians 1:16, 1 Timothy 3:16).

For Lewis, the teaching of Christ and the New Testament made sense of a seemingly senseless world. Christianity brought the world into focus and gave Lewis a logical explanation for good and evil, pain and joy, love and hate. The Christian narrative of the fall of man, redemption and consummation provided him with a grand vision to understand the purpose of life.

The Emperor Napoléon, in ignorance, once mocked Christianity and distained Christ, but after his great wars of conquest and defeat, he had time to read the words of Jesus. After pondering the claims of Jesus in the Gospels, he said, "I will tell you. Alexander, Caesar, Charlemagne and myself have founded great empires. But our empires were founded on force. Jesus alone founded His empire on love and to this day millions would die for Him. I think I understand something of human nature and I tell you, all these were men, and I am a man. Jesus Christ was more than man...Christ alone across the chasm of eighteen centuries makes a demand which is beyond all others difficult to satisfy. He asks more than a father can demand of his child, or a bride of her spouse, or a man of his brother. He asks for the human heart. He will have it entirely to Himself. He demands it unconditionally and forthwith, His demand is granted. Wonderful! In defiance of time and space, the soul of man with all its powers and faculties becomes an annexation to the empire of Christ. This phenomenon is unaccountable; it is altogether beyond the scope of man's creative powers. Time, the great destroyer, is powerless to extinguish this sacred flame. This is what strikes me most. This is what proves to me quite convincingly that Jesus Christ is God."[25]

One person said Jesus was, "The meeting place of eternity and time, the blending of Deity and humanity, the junction of heaven and earth." Author Charles Edward Jefferson said, "There is something so pure and frank and noble about Him that to doubt His sincerity would be like doubting the brightness of the sun."[26]

The historian Kenneth Scott Latourette said, "As the centuries pass, the evidence is accumulating that, measured by His effect on history, Jesus is the most influential life ever lived on this planet." The author J. Sidlow Baxter wrote: 'Fundamentally, our Lord's message was Himself. He did not come merely to preach a gospel; He Himself is that gospel. He did not come merely to give bread; He said, "I am the bread." He did not come merely to shed light; He said, "I am the light." He did not come merely to show the door; He said, "I am the door." He did not come merely to name a shepherd; He said, "I am the shepherd." He did not come merely to point the way; He said, "I am the way, the truth, and the life." '[27]

'If you confess with your mouth the Lord Jesus and believe in your heart that God has raised Him from the dead, you will be saved. For with the heart one believes unto righteousness and with the mouth confession is made unto salvation' (Romans 10:9-10). "Repent and believe in the gospel" (Mark 1:15).

Chapter Twenty-Seven

Tearing Down the Altar to One God

Britain was once completely committed to Christianity, but after World War Two, the government decided to invite thousands of people of other faiths and convictions, a few with moral compasses set in other directions, to come and live in the United Kingdom. Meanwhile, the government encouraged Britons to emigrate to Australia on subsidised tickets. 'Between 1945 and 1965 more than two million migrants came to Australia.'[1]

The new arrivals brought much to Britain and made significant contributions – they came to build new lives for themselves and their children, and for their children's children. They also built new altars of worship – no longer to the Lord Jesus Christ, but to other gods. For the first time since Winston Churchill described, a thousand years previously, that, "England became finally and for all time one coherent Kingdom based on Christianity,"[2] other spirits were honoured. At the same time, Britain was also bolstered by the lively and powerful Christian convictions of many from African Caribbean heritage, and later by the hundreds of thousands of Eastern Europeans that entered Britain in recent years, who have strengthened Christianity in the land.[3]

For those who do not believe that there is a God and Britain's covenant with God, which lasted for over a thousand years does not exist, the question of establishing new centres of worship to other gods is not a problem. If however, you accept the biblical view that God hears and accepts covenants made by monarchs, governments and their peoples, and consequently blesses or removes His hand of covering from that nation, depending on how faithful they are to their covenant promises – then this has profound consequences. In the Bible, the Jewish people received special protection and blessing from God, when their leaders or kings obeyed God and kept true to their covenants with Him. They were blessed and protected "because Abraham obeyed My voice and kept My charge, My commandments, My statutes, and My laws" (Genesis 26:5).

The immigrants who arrived in Britain became a reminder to all, that as an island, to some extent all Britons are descendants of immigrants – from the first inhabitants, to the Romans, the Angles, Saxons and Jutes, the Vikings, Normans, Huguenots,

Eastern European Jews, and the famous German Saxe-Coburg royal family. In all generations, the beliefs and heart convictions of all immigrants, from which all Britons descend, has had a profound and lasting impact on the nation. What began with a tiny trickle of Christianity during Roman rule in Britain, went on to form its national religion and identity.

Winston Churchill was not in power when Britain first opened its doors to mass migration of people of other faiths and convictions. Some worked so hard that they put Anglo-Saxons to shame, others brought in beliefs which are incompatible with the British Constitution. Many of the migrants did not receive the welcome the Bible said they deserved (Exodus 23:9, Leviticus 19:33-34, Deuteronomy 10:19), but instead were treated shamefully, and it became clear to Winston Churchill that Britain had to carefully consider the future. In the U.S. 'a melting pot' policy enabled people from many nations to embrace a single national identity, based upon indispensable shared values, by contrast in Britain, a hostile welcome led to isolated and segregated communities developing, with various imported convictions thriving, independent of British values and law.

British Christians had the opportunity of reaching out to the first generation of immigrants of other faiths to share Christ's message of, "Love your neighbour as yourself" (Matthew 22:39), but in these years of harsh austerity and post-war rationing, many felt overwhelmed in their own struggles. By 1955, Winston Churchill in government sensed the urgency of addressing the problems of segregation, as a report found 13.8 percent of the immigrant community were unemployed or receiving benefits.[4] Churchill was concerned that Britain's liberties which are founded on Christianity had to be protected. After all, his government had been elected with his first manifesto promise being, "To uphold the Christian religion and resist all attacks upon it. To defend our monarchical and Parliamentary Constitution."[5]

For Winston Churchill, the liberties of Britain and Christianity were intertwined, and history has shown that no other nation has achieved one without the other.[6] But many in the Cabinet believed it was not the right time to talk about it and instead on 10 July 1952 turned their attention to the 'Sugar: for Jam Making' problem.[7] By 1955, Churchill complained that immigration and integration "is the most important subject facing this country, but I cannot get any of my ministers to take any notice."[8]

British law permitted subjects of the British Empire overseas to gain automatic residence in the country and it was not until the Commonwealth Immigrants Act of 1962, 1968 and 1971, that restrictions on unlimited immigration began. Consequently, in the twentieth century, immigration from the 1950s onwards had a profound impact. The 2001 censes showed that up to half the population increase between 1991 to 2002, which was 4.9 million people, was due to foreign born immigration.[9] Between 2005 to 2010, one study found that over 572,000 people arrived to live in the U.K. on a long-term basis, whilst 346,000 emigrated. This left Britain with 226,000 new arrivals searching for jobs, homes, schools and medical help, and after a few months, having access to benefits paid for by tax payers.[10]

Britain's 1,500 year old Christian identity was also challenged by the very fast changes in demographics. In 1925, there were an estimated 10,000 Muslims in Britain,[11] by 1961, official figures identified 46,196.[12] Today one in ten babies born in England are Muslim and according to Sharia law must always remain Muslim, or be punished.[13] Religious Affairs Editor John Bingham said, "A new analysis of the 2011 census shows the number of Muslims in England and Wales surged by 75 percent – boosted by almost 600,000 more foreign born followers of the Islamic faith...while almost half of British Muslims are under the age of 25, almost a quarter of Christians are over 65."[14]

In 1925, the Muslim population of Britain represented 0.02 percent and since that time there has been an increase of close to 35,000 percent, leading to the Muslim population growing to an estimated 5 percent of the population, or 3,300,000 people. There are now an estimated 1,750 mosques in Britain, many in hired buildings.[15] In France, the Muslim population has grown to eight percent of its citizens and in the U.S., the number of Islamic places of worship soared seventy-four percent between 2000-2012.[16]

The self-proclaimed 'old-fashioned immigrant' from Ireland and journalist Ruth D. Edwards, explained that as Britain and Europe embraced secularism, 'birth rates plummeted,' whilst the Muslim population of Europe is exploding, because of their perception of a religious duty to Allah to have big families: 'Europe is changing because Europeans are failing to reproduce. Just to keep the population steady, you need 2.1 live births per woman. However, in 2005, the European average was 1.38.' She adds: 'The sharp-suited, soft-spoken undercover agents of the Muslim Brotherhood (the banned Egyptian group whose former members include Osama Bin Laden) understand that power is best secured by stealth – by infiltrating institutions and seducing the media. Libya's Colonel Gaddafi once exemplified this policy. He said, "There are signs that Allah will grant Islam victory in

Europe – without swords, without guns, without conquests. The 50 million Muslims of Europe will turn it into a Muslim continent within a few decades."[17]

Colonel Gaddafi's case is over-stated and yet, what will Britain, America or Europe be like in one hundred years, as Westerners continue with abortion, low birth rates and the denial of our heritage? What will happen when Western nations find that forty or sixty percent of their population are Muslim? When I first heard of Gaddafi's prediction that Islam will dominate Europe and by implication, later the United States, I thought it was hyperbole. But then I studied the statistics. A combination of high birth rates, plus a desire for Muslim children born in the West to marry a foreign born Muslim, has led one study to find that the Muslim population is 'rising ten times faster than the rest of society.'[18] Between 2004 and 2008, the Muslim population in Britain grew by more than 500,000 to 2.4 million.[19] Today it is close to 3.3 million. This increase is expected to continue: data from the 2011 census shows one in twelve schoolchildren were Muslim and less than half were born in the U.K.[20]

Journalist Adrian Michaels said, "Britain and the rest of the European Union are ignoring a demographic time bomb: a recent rush into the EU by migrants, including millions of Muslims, will change the continent beyond recognition over the next two decades, and almost no policy-makers are talking about it. The numbers are startling. Only 3.2 percent of Spain's population was foreign-born in 1998. In 2007 it was 13.4 percent. Europe's Muslim population has more than doubled in the past 30 years and will have doubled again by 2015.[21]

Professor David Voas, a sociologist of religion observed that "Muslims already contribute ten percent of British births; within several decades people of Muslim heritage will form ten percent of the population, even if immigration came to an abrupt halt tomorrow." If present religious trends persist in Britain, the future religious landscape of the nation, according to Professor David Voas, will be shaped by Islam and black majority churches. The number of Anglican worshippers on parish electoral roles fell by forty-one percent between 1980 and 2012, whilst this collapse has been offset by growth in black majority churches and within charismatic and Pentecostal churches.[22]

Islam in Europe has become the watchword for the religious changes in the continent, as the spread of its new Muslim population is the most transformational religious influx in the region since Christianity, and like Christianity two thousand years ago, it will have many unpredicted consequences. The continent is living through its biggest religious transition for two millennia.

At present, the greatest threat to Christianity in the West is the indifference to faith and the hedonism and secularisation of the native Caucasian population who do not, in general convert to other faiths. However, if present trends continue, in a century or two, mass Islamic immigration and their descendants may have the power to change Britain, Europe and America for ever.

The Islamic presence in Europe is strong and growing. What will Islam in Europe be like in 2050, 2100 or 2200? Will most Muslims be moderate, or will they follow the trends of Turkey? In 1923, Mustafa Kemal Atatürk (1881-1923) established Turkey as a secular, moderate nation for Muslims and non-Muslims. But with each decade life for non-Muslims has been getting harder, as the nation becomes Islamised. In 2002, the Islamic Justice and Development Party came to power, and life for women and non-Muslims changed for the worse. The BBC reported: 'Women's rights organisations say violence against women has risen sharply.'[23] Meanwhile, attacks on Christians, who were once the ruling majority has increased.

"To be a Turk now means you have to be Muslim," said Father Iulian Pista, a Christian leader in Turkey. "In the past, being a pious Muslim was looked down upon. Now Friday prayers are encouraged Society here is becoming Islamised. Recently, I've seen youngsters defecate and urinate in my church. They shout 'Allahu akbar.' I also believe God is great but the way they say it is threatening."[24]

For close to a millennia Hagia Sophia, the most important Orthodox Christian cathedral stood at the heart of the Christian Byzantine Empire in modern day Turkey. But in 1453, an Islamic army attacked and overthrew the last bastion of this Christian empire which once ruled throughout the Middle East and North Africa. Since that time, Christians have been expelled or their lives have been made so harsh that they want to flee. In the twentieth century there was the Armenian Genocide and the Greek exchange and expulsions – all targeting Christians. From a population of two million Armenians fewer than fifty thousand remain today. "The ethnic cleansing of these non-Muslim minorities was a huge brain drain," said Turkish writer Cengiz Aktar, "Istanbul lost its entire Christian and Jewish heritage."[25]

In 1452, Christians were the majority in today's Istanbul. By 1923 they were twenty percent of the population, now they are just 0.2 percent.[26] "Most of the believers hide their cross inside their shirt," said Cengiz Aktar. "They can't open it and walk freely on the street because they could prompt a reaction. I don't want to say all the Turkish population is against Christianity but nationalism is so high that people are afraid to express themselves."[27] The BBC reported: 'New mosques are flourishing, while the world-famous Halki Orthodox theological school near Istanbul has remained closed since 1971 under Turkish nationalist pressure. One of the remaining Greeks of Turkey, Fotis Benlisoy, says the community feels squeezed, "The threatening feeling for non-Muslim minorities here is coming again."[28]

History shows that when a nation becomes Islamised, the entire structure of the nation becomes directed towards making life for the committed Muslim man desirable. But for Muslim men who are not devout or for Muslim women, non-Muslims or any minority, it can feel like the entire state exists to restrict your rights. This is why tens of thousands of moderate and modern Muslim women in Turkey have been protesting for years, which broke-out into mass resistance on 28 May 2013 in the Gezi Park protests. Many who reject any further adoption of Sharia law, and the women who feared being forced to wear veils, found their voices united in these protests. Turkish President Recep Tayyip Erdogan responded by saying, "You cannot put women and men on an equal footing, it is against nature...our religion regards motherhood very highly."[29]

Many Turkish Muslims, especially women, do not want to follow the example of Islamised nations like Saudi Arabia. They feel beleaguered as Turkey's transformation from a nation committed to secular government, to one embracing Islamic principles has been substantial.

The difference between Islam in Saudi Arabia and moderates abroad, is the same as strong coffee, to weak and watery. The ingredients are the same; it is the strength which matters. Special Correspondent for the BBC Sue Lloyd-Roberts went to the birth-nation of Islam. She said, "I met a Saudi woman studying in the U.K. who told me, 'Saudi Arabia is the biggest women's prison in the world,' and had to investigate. "Few dare criticise the country openly, though the restrictions on women are scarcely believable in the twenty-first century...a woman can't drive and she is not allowed to work or travel without the permission of her male guardian, father or husband," she continued. "Customs such as arranged marriages, under-age marriage and polygamy still prevail...women in the Kingdom are not allowed to come into contact with any man who is not a family member. Even the few women who run businesses have to employ a male manager to negotiate with other men."[30]

In the slums of Jeddah, Sue Lloyd-Roberts found the 'non-women' of Saudi Arabia. These are "women without guardians – widows or women whose husbands have left them without the formality of a divorce and who have no legal identity." What hope have these women, if they're not allowed to go outside on their own, or work, or have a bank account without a male family member being present?

Sue Lloyd-Roberts asked the local Muslim men why women were treated differently. "I asked them why their wives hadn't joined them?" and received these replies. "Just because we say that a woman stays at home doesn't mean that we are not giving her rights," one of them answered. "A woman sits at home, she can eat, drink, she's comfortable and everything comes to her...in our religion, men are responsible for women. My mum, my sister, my wife, can stay at home and I'll take care of them. In our religion, women obey their men. If she wants to work, she can work, but only with my permission. I won't be forced."[31]

History provides us with many examples of what happens when Christian civilisations are overrun by Islam. We forget the Middle East and North Africa were once the heart of the Christian world before the Islamic conquests. Also, in the twentieth century, Islam spread through immigration and high birth rates in many areas, and Lebanon is an example. Jesus once preached in Lebanon (Mark 7:24-26) and in 1920, Lebanon was established as the only Middle Eastern Christian nation, where Christians would be safe from the discrimination and persecution, which is experienced in majority Muslim nations. In 1925, 84 percent of the population was Christian, but that number more than halved to 40.5 percent by 2014.[32] Christians are now the minority in a nation established for Christians. Politically, in the Lebanese Parliament, Christians hold 64 seats in tandem with 64 Muslim seats.

Due to rising violence against Christians in the Middle East, the former President of Lebanon Amine Gemayel, said, "If present negative trends continue to intensify, we must start thinking about the unthinkable: the extinction of Christianity" from the region, which will "destabilise the region for generations." He said there is an "inexplicable" lack of attention to this issue from the international community and in particular, "The response by the United States has been a resounding non-response."[33]

Jesus Christ was born in Bethlehem and Christians have lived there since the birth of the Church. In the early 1920s, only one Muslim family lived in this Christian town, today only a third are Christian.[34] In the Palestinian territories, local Christians support peaceful negotiations with Israel and reject violent confrontation. They abhor the Islamist rhetoric of "driving Israel into the sea," in a Jihad to create an Islamic Caliphate, with Jerusalem as its capital. For this reason, they are made to feel second-class and unpatriotic, so it's easier to flee, than remain to be treated as 'the enemy' within. These Christians think the Islamist agenda has made the suffering of all people in the region worse. But this conviction finds no place in those with an Islamic extremist faith commitment towards Jihad and the total destruction of Israel.

In the places where Jesus and His disciples preached, not now under the control of Israel, the Christian population is shrinking, because radical Islam is spreading, creating a 'them and us' mentality. Meanwhile, Israel is the only Middle Eastern nation where Christians are truly free and their numbers are increasing.

Historical facts are impartial and unbiased. They tell us what took place, regardless of whether they are found to be politically correct or not. Nonetheless, the future of Islam in Western nations is uncertain. Some say most Muslims will integrate, birth rates will plummet and if governments put limits on the numbers of arranged marriages between poor uneducated foreign Muslims and Western-born Muslims, the numbers will stabilise.

Moderate Muslim experts have already warned that some arranged marriages for poor foreign-born Muslims are little more than domestic servitude and a form of slavery. Meanwhile, up to 8,000 British Muslims have been forced to marry by the age of 15 or under, in Sharia Islamic marriages, unrecognised under British law.[35] In 2005, the British government established the Forced Marriage Unit and has dealt with 1,468 cases involving children under the age of 15.[36] Addressing the issue of forced marriage, David Cameron said it "is little more than slavery."[37]

Some experts suggest there is a trend among a few Muslim men to swing from being promiscuously secular and Western to radically extremist, and this inclination is identified in the offences committed. Journalist Nigel Morris said, "Muslims represent only 4.7 percent of the population in England and Wales, according to the most recent Census (in 2011), yet one in seven prisoners (14 percent) in England and Wales is a Muslim, according to the statistics. In some jails the proportion of Islamic inmates is more than one-third, and in Whitemoor, a Category A prison in Cambridgeshire, it is as high as 43 percent. Other jails with a startlingly high proportion include Isis (34 percent) and Feltham (33 percent), both in London."[38] Prisoner officers have warned that prisons have become a breeding ground for Islamic extremism and one prison officers' union source said Category A

Prison Whitemore is "now effectively run by Muslims, many of whom are Jihadis."[39]

This phenomenon is found throughout Europe. In France, where the Muslim population is up to eight percent, the BBC reported: 'As many as sixty percent of France's 70,000 prisoners have Muslim origins and their backgrounds and criminal records make many ripe for radicalisation.'[40] It has also been reported widely in Europe that Muslims who have been sent to prison, after exploiting the liberties of aggressive secularism, become ripe for conversion to what is called 'true Islam' by the radical Muslim leaders inside. The BBC reported: 'Early signs of radicalisation in prison may be difficult to spot, because they are those of a regular religious awakening – such as swapping Western clothes for an Islamic robe, refusing to watch TV, praying frequently, or demanding halal food.'[41]

Many believe the silent majority of peaceful Muslims are integrating and any fear of the Islamification of the West is naive. Minority projections of the spread of Islam in Europe indicates that if fertility falls by 2030, Muslims will make up ten percent of its total population.[42] Philip Jenkins of Penn State University estimates that by 2100, Muslims will compose about twenty-five percent of Europe's population.[43] Some have indicated these predictions have already been proved far too limited, because of mass immigration and the increase of large Muslims families. Therefore, if current trends continue in Europe – with mass immigration from Muslim nations and a population boom amongst European-born Muslims – combined with secularisation of the native-born formerly Christian populations (and the decline of the aging Christian demographic), the future of Europe may be further integrated with Islamic ideals.

The Church of England's former Bishop of Rochester, Michael Nazir-Ali, originally from Pakistan, understands firsthand what it means to be born and raised in a nation defined by another faith – Islam. He said of Britain, "Our ideas about the sacredness of the human person at every stage of life, of equality and natural rights and, therefore, of freedom, have demonstrably arisen from the tradition rooted in the Bible. Different faiths and traditions will not necessarily produce the values and virtues which have been so prominent in the history of this country. It is quite wrong to presume that they will...some faiths may emphasise social solidarity more than personal freedom, others publicly enforce piety over a nurturing of the interior life and yet others stress honour and shame rather than humility, service and sacrifice."[44]

Nazir-Ali, ever concerned about peaceful friendships with all faiths, has also warned that Islamic extremism is flourishing in the West and has turned "already separate communities into 'no-go' areas," and stated there have been attempts to "impose an Islamic character on certain areas."[45] At the same time, Britain's then Labour government suggested something had to be done about the, "No-go areas of Muslim ghettos."[46] Bishop Michael Nazir-Ali and his family subsequently received death threats and he was escorted by Kent police for his protection.

Where does the concept of 'no-go' areas and religious segregation for non-Muslims come from? Mecca in Saudi Arabia is the only city in the world which refuses entry to anyone but Muslims. Would a similar policy be acceptable in Beijing, Delhi, New York, Paris, Johannesburg, Canterbury or Jerusalem? On the road signs to Mecca it openly and defiantly states: 'Muslims only,' while the other direction is labelled, 'Obligatory for non-Muslims.' Religious police are stationed beyond the turnoff on the main road to prevent non-Muslims from entering Mecca.[47] One guide states: 'The ban on non-Muslim visitors is mentioned in the Koran as follows: "Oh you who believe! Truly the idolaters are unclean; so let them not, after this year, approach the Sacred Mosque...." (in Mecca)' (9:28).[48]

What history reveals is that the values of devout Muslims are different from those which have been embraced in the West. The Western media proclaimed the Arab Spring, beginning in 2010, as a surge towards democracy and liberty. But Mahmoud Ahmadinejad in Iran called it an "Islamic awakening," saying, "The arrogant powers and uncultured Zionists have reached the end of their path, heading toward a dead end."[49] "Without the least doubt, the wave of Islamic Awakening is sweeping the Arab world," declared *Kayhan*, an influential newspaper closely associated with Iran's supreme leader, Ayatollah Ali Khamenei.[50] This view was mocked by Western political and media elites, and yet since 2010 the Middle East has lived through perhaps the most extensive purge of non-Muslims from the region since its conquest by the Islamists.[51] However, the expulsion of non-Muslims from the Middle East is nothing new. From 1992-1997 life for Christians in moderate Islamic nations became so unbearable that 2,000,000 fled.[52]

What is often ignored is that majority Muslim nations refused to accept the basic principles of the Universal Declaration of Human Rights. In its place they signed the Cairo Declaration of Human Rights, which is overshadowed in every matter by Sharia, imposing 'restrictions on nearly every human right based on Islamic Sharia law.'[53] The Center for Inquiry expressed grave concerns to the United Nations that this declaration by Muslim nations gives no protection: It 'undermines equality of persons and freedom of expression and religion by imposing restrictions on nearly every human right based on Islamic Sharia law.'[54]

Corruption is another problem around the world and it is rising in the West too. In 2009, it was found that democracy was being undermined in Britain by voting fraud in some immigrant communities. Baroness Warsi, the then Foreign Office Minister stated the Conservative party lost three seats at the general election because of voter fraud in the Asian community.[55]

In 2013, Britain's Attorney General warned that immigrants from nations with epidemic corruption have imported corrupt practices, and politicians need to 'wake up.' He said electoral corruption was a problem in constituencies such as Slough in Berkshire. Six men were jailed in 2009 for ousting a councillor using 'ghost' votes and, 'The audacious scam was described by the Crown Prosecution Service as part of an 'epidemic' which threatens to destroy democracy in the U.K.'[56]

The Attorney General was criticized for raising the issue and said, "The point I was making is that, as a law officer, it's my duty to ensure the rule of law is upheld, and one of the issues that I feel requires close attention is any potential for a rise in corruption to undermine civil society."[57] After being forced to apologise the following day, he confirmed again the positive contribution immigrants have made to Britain and pointed out that corruption is found in the "white Anglo-Saxon" community. But he warned that the growth of corruption was "because we have minority communities in this country which come from backgrounds where corruption is endemic. It is something we as politicians have to wake up to."[58]

Britain's first elected Muslim mayor was 'ousted in disgrace' in 2015, for voting fraud and bribery, as ballots were double-cast or cast from false addresses. In a ruling handed down by election judge Richard Mawrey, QC, he said the mayor "ran his campaign on the basis that it was the religious duty of faithful Muslims to vote for him," and he, "Let loose a mob of excitable, politically committed, young men" who "approached voters, particularly Bangladeshi voters and harangued them." The judge who sacked this Muslim mayor warned of "postal voting factories" and thousands of ballots being sold across Britain. The politically correct police dropped the election fraud allegations and the mayor's corruption was only exposed because four ordinary voters took a private case against him.[59]

Some Muslim leaders have been found to hold views which

make them feel at odds with elements in society. Britain's first Muslim Lord was jailed for sending a text message shortly before his car was involved in a fatal crash. In an interview he blamed "the Jews...who own newspapers and TV channels." The Labour Party suspended him, adding the party "deplores and does not tolerate any sort of racism or anti-Semitism."[60]

Faith offers a different view of reality and a vision for the future. It shows what it believes is wrong with the world and how it can be changed. That reality in the West was once based upon Christianity, which led to liberty, accountability and justice was the result. Other religions, such as Islam, view the world through a different lens and seek to establish another reality. The Middle East is the result of over a thousand years of Islamic influence.

The first Muslim Cabinet Minister in Britain has an excellent record, yet she resigned from the Cabinet without speaking personally to the prime minister, having felt Britain's policy in the Israel/Gaza crisis was 'morally indefensible.'[61]

It is estimated that potentially half of all Muslims in Britain are nominal or secular, whilst the others are religious, ranging from practicing amicable Islam, to a minority with extremist beliefs. Sadly in Europe radical Islam has been flourishing. On 7 January 2015, twelve people were massacred in Paris by French-born radical Muslims. Journalist John Ware said, "What happened here in Paris raises an obvious question: Why is it that some Muslims feel justified in killing their fellow citizens in the name of Islam?" He answered by interviewing "a group of British Muslims who say they believe they have an answer – that an extreme but non-violent ideology helps push Muslims into the arms of violent extremists: an interpretation of Islam which seems unable to coexist with core Western values and is growing."[62]

After speaking with many moderate Muslims, John Ware found that non-violent extremist Islamic ideologies have been allowed to spread like cancer among some Western Muslims, leading to a few embracing violent radical action. "For some time, clerics whom the government say promote an extreme but non-violent interpretation of Islam have claimed their interpretation is shared by most Muslims in the West," he said. John Ware studied clips from various Muslim conferences and TV channels available in the West. From the Peace Conference Scandinavia in Oslo, 2013, one preacher said, "How many of you agree that the punishments described in the Koran, whether it is death, whether it is stoning for adultery, whatever it is, that is the best punishment ever possible for human kind? Who agrees with that?" About ninety-eight percent of all the Muslims present raised their hands.⁶³

To achieve global Islamic dominance John Ware explained that extremists urge, "Muslims in the West to exploit the freedom of Parliamentary democracies, run by what he calls the 'kuffar' or unbelievers, so one day they can replace democracy with theocracy." One radical Muslim was filmed saying, "We as British Muslims, we became part of society, so they have to cater for us." John Ware explained that although this man "does not promote violence against the U.K., he believes that in an Islamic state, Muslims who abandon Islam should be executed." The Islamist declared, "Apostasy deserves, once the conditions are met, deserves capital punishment in an Islamic state. I can say this openly. I'm not here to hide it, OK?"⁶⁴

John Ware asked the President of the Muslim Association of Britain if he agreed with this view. He replied by saying, "When a person says apostates should be killed, but they shouldn't be killed here, they should be killed in a state, they are saying that is how I believe the country should practice law." Ware interrupted him saying, "Whether it's sanctioned by due process is surely not the point. The point is it's abhorrent in any event?" The Muslim leader disagreed saying, "But that is making the assumption that as humans, we all have the same definitions and the same arbitrary acceptances, which we don't."⁶⁵

Adam Deen, founder of Deen Institute said, "Apostasy killing is the height, pinnacle of irrationality. When you train or when you propagate, when you teach young Muslims that part of your faith is to accept irrationality – to accept heinous crimes, such as apostasy killing, then it all goes." Sara Khan, the Muslim director of Inspire said, "What non-violent extremists are very good at doing is that they take people by the hand and they take them to the front door…violent extremists open that door, ISIS (The Islamic State in Iraq/Syria) opens the door. That's why you're seeing so many young people leave this country to join IS."⁶⁶

There is also troubling reports concerning the expectations for women within Islamic communities. In the 2011 census it was found that seventy-one percent of Muslim women between the ages of 16 and 24 were not in employment, compared to approximately half the general population. ⁶⁷

John Ware asked the President of the Muslim Association of Britain questions about equality, liberty and democracy, saying, "Would you define calling democracy filthy, as non-violent extremism?" "That is a view," was the reply, "a person can have a view. If they want to have a view that it is filthy, that is up to them. It doesn't mean they are extremists."⁶⁸

It seems that some radical Muslims are urging all Muslims to use the freedoms of democracy and the rule of law against itself, and the West must ask: Does the freedom to debate and broadcast Islamic beliefs, also include the freedom for Islamists to end all debates, to seek to dissolve democracy and undermine the rule of law? What will happen in a hundred or two hundred years, if the Muslim population continues to grow to become twenty-five or fifty percent of Europe's population, and this extremist ideology spreads further amongst moderate and secular Muslims, as it has in Turkey? Can British, European and American Islam take a different path from Islam in the Middle East or will the same faith values create similar problems?

Chapter Twenty-Eight

Society and Shared Values

For a society to function and be identified as one nation there must be shared values, and a sense of common identity. In a democratic society, with a strong Christian heritage, there are certain convictions which must be unwavering – the impartial rule of law, freedom of expression and religious liberty, the respect for all life, equality among the sexes and the need for a democratically accountable government. Unfortunately, events of recent years have proved that not all, in various cultures or faiths, are able to accept these minimums for a functioning cohesive and peaceful society. It should not come as a surprise then, that those who choose not to embrace these values also reject the conviction of a shared distinct heritage, history and culture, all intertwined with the Christian faith.

Many of the first generation of Muslims and people of other faiths that immigrated to Britain from the 1950s onwards, arrived to escape Sharia law and extremism, and they respected the traditions and rights which Britain gave them. Unfortunately, due to political correctness, secular governments have chosen to be blind to the hopes of extremists, as they planned to radicalise moderate Muslims. Many governments have allowed radical imams from abroad to enter and preach hatred throughout the West. In 2014, after a British-born Muslim beheaded an American journalist in Iraq, a former Foreign Office Minister stated the blame should be laid at successive governments and imams in Britain, for allowing the radicalisation of Muslims.[1] Dr K. Howells said, "Governments have been afraid to touch it... they've allowed those communities to become isolated to look inward, instead of trying to integrate with the rest of society, and they've said, 'That's alright, that's multiculturalism.' "[2]

Muslim communities in Britain have been shocked by the many terrorist plots which have emerged and most Muslims abhor them. These moderate Muslims have expressed their dismay that politically correct governments have granted asylum, visas and citizenship to radical foreign imams, who have encouraged the radicalisation of their sons and daughters.[3]

Islamic extremist asylum seekers and radical converts have cost the British taxpayer hundreds of millions in prison costs, legal fees, benefit payments, surveillance and extra security measures etc.[4] The cost in lives lost is beyond measure and the security services tell us it can take a team of up to twenty-two people to provide full surveillance for just one dangerous Islamic extremist.

Born in Egypt, one Islamist preacher became famous in Britain for his 'hook,' and for preaching his own brand of Islamic hate. In 1997, he arrived at Finsbury Park mosque which was opened three years before in a ceremony attended by Prince Charles. Partly funded by Saudi Arabia, the mosque like many around the world, have been funded by that nation with the provision that it addresses favourably, the Wahhabi version of Islam. After being ejected from the mosque in 2003, this Islamist preacher was permitted to illegally close a street to preach his hatred, and he received police protection, as he exploited British liberties.[5] Numerous Islamic terrorists have been linked to this mosque, including the 'Shoe Bomber' who tried to blow up a plane.[6]

Moderate Muslim Dr Taj Hargey believes Britain's tradition of openness, is being ruthlessly exploited, and Muslim communities are being betrayed into the hands of extremists, by elites who choose to ignore the threats. Speaking about Saudi Arabia's exported Wahhabism version of Islam he said, "This toxic brand of fundamentalism is being propagated, throughout Muslim communities across Britain. The young are particular targets for indoctrination by the hardliners...there are more than forty such schools in Britain, inculcating more than 5,000 pupils with the warped values of Wahhabism...the same spirit of savagery is found in the way Sharia law is implemented in Saudi Arabia. The Wahhabis run a regime where women are executed for suspected adultery and the most cruel punishments are meted out against petty criminal. So why is Britain turning a blind eye to these schools and the wider sinister influence of Wahhabism?"[7]

When extremist mosques and schools have been investigated, insiders tell secretly that their leaders use the Islamic doctrine of 'Al-Takiyya,' which can be interpreted as 'allowable deception,' to calm the fears of naive investigators of 'an isolated incident.'

Dr Taj Hargey said, "The increasing fashion for young Muslim women in Britain to wear the burka (in contrast to their mothers, who do not) is one of the most sinister developments of our times...everyone in Britain, including Muslims, should oppose the insidious spread of this vile piece of clothing, which imprisons women, threatens social harmony, fuels distrust, has grave health implications and is a potent security risk...we cannot continue to accept the creeping Arabisation of Islam in the U.K.

and consequent destruction of our cherished British freedoms. A stand must be made now."[8]

In the U.S., all immigration was targeted towards the creation a 'melting pot' with the pledge of the nation's seal of – "Out of many, one." The U.S. once had a robust belief in citizenship which traditionally was confident enough to expect all immigrants to share certain core values, or to lose their right to remain, whilst in Europe, various convictions flourished in segregated communities. America may have racial tension, but it does not have deep-rooted clashes of core values.

Secretary of State for Communities and Local Government Eric Pickles, summarised in 2014, what happens when extremism is ignored. He said, "This summer, we have seen Christians being systematically persecuted and murdered in the Middle East; anti-Semitic attacks and protests soaring in response to the Israeli government's intervention in Gaza; institutionalised political correctness leading to appalling sexual abuse against children by Pakistani Muslims; and murders carried out by Isil terrorists who may have included Britons indoctrinated to preach evil at home and enact it abroad The common theme is the politics of division and hate: attitudes and mantras that seek to divide rather than unite. Aggressive secularists would advocate the suppression of religion in the public sphere. Yet this would only perpetuate the message of intolerance towards others...the best response is to champion the British values that define our country, many of which are founded in faith. At heart, we are a Christian nation – from the Established Church in England, to the language of the King James Bible, deeply woven into the fabric of our culture. But most important, we are a place of justice and tolerance towards others. Our defence of freedom, the rule of law and the evolution of our democracy have all grown from the seedbed of faith. This is why Britain has long been a safe haven for persecuted people.

"Our Christian values have helped us to identify and rectify our own prejudices and injustices: the 1689 Act of Toleration that protected nonconformists, the Catholic emancipation of the nineteenth century, or William Wilberforce's tireless campaign against slavery. For centuries, these ideals have been the salt and light of the nation, illuminating our international reputation as a just and tolerant country. Freedom of speech and freedom of religion go hand in hand – but both should operate within the law. Britain has a broad and generous vision of citizenship. It is important that we all take responsibility for defending it. The first is by standing up to the overt and noisy bullies. Second is constant vigilance against the sly pedlars of hatred whose crude prejudices masquerade as religious piety. Jesus recognised this risk when he warned us to 'watch out for false prophets. They come to you in sheep's clothing, but inwardly they are ferocious wolves.' "[9]

In the United States, a multiracial society developed in which most people share the same values, which includes a belief in democracy, one law for all, freedom of speech, religious liberty and so forth. But in Europe, politicians decided to choose a path of multiculturalism, which is the doctrine that several different cultures with differing values, can coexist, often in segregation in a nation, without diminishing each others rights. In 2011, Prime Minister David Cameron, German Chancellor Angela Merkel and the French President Nicolas Sarkozy, all gave speeches to announce that multiculturalism has failed in Europe. President Sarkozy said, "We have been too concerned about the identity of the person who was arriving and not enough about the identity of the country that was receiving him."[10] Angela Merkel said multiculturalism has "utterly failed."[11]

Concerning its failure Pakistani-born and former Bishop Michael Nazir-Ali said, "One of the governing features of multiculturalism, as it came to be, was tolerance, which is a dangerous word in England because it quite often means leaving people alone, and in fact this is exactly what happened. Some people were left alone and communities became segregated – each to their own. There was no common language in the literal sense of a lingua franca, there was no common vision of national life; there was no emphasis on integration, common citizenships – any of those things. If diversity had been accommodated in a Christian way, this would have been the values of hospitality, of engagement, of dialogue, of saying, 'Look this is how we have come to be a nation in which the Bible and the Christian faith has played a formative role. You are welcome.' "[12]

Professor Diarmaid MacCulloch said, "Even though history shows us that to be English is to be diverse, the wealth of new cultures in twenty-first century England is posing a challenge. This plural society is at a cross road. The English have become so diverse that they're confused about who they are. They're facing an identity crisis. I think part of the reason may be the English approach to multiculturalism, which has allowed separate communities to develop in isolation from one another. There's no shared identity. If you don't have one system of values for everyone to buy into, then you create a void, and into that void, rush all sorts of passionate opinions, like air into a vacuum, hot air in fact...I've watched one possible response to that threat emerging in England. You might call it secular liberalism. The idea is that you confine religion to the private sphere and you don't promote any alternative values, beyond the general notion of liberty and tolerance. In a multicultural society, you can see why this resolute rejection of public religion might seem a good thing, but there's an underlining problem for a nation which must tolerate all views. How does a liberal society resist extremism, if its only ultimate value is toleration? Is it actually entitled to resist extremism? It's a big dilemma."[13]

The threats to Christian liberty, freedom of speech, the impartial rule of law and democracy are vast, from Islamic extremism at home or abroad, to the superrich imposing secular liberal humanist values on the West, by sheer economic brute force to get the people they want into power. Meanwhile, whilst Islam is flourishing in the West because of immigration and freedom of worship, Christians in the Middle East and all non-Muslim minorities are being brutally repressed.

In the Middle Eastern lands where Christianity spread long before it reached Britain, there has been a largely unreported and systematic expulsion and exodus of Arab Christians. Since the Arab Spring began on 18 December 2010, life for Christians in the Middle East has become intolerable – with bomb attacks in Christian areas I have visited in Egypt, to Syrian Christians being targeted in their civil war; to the expulsion of Christians in parts of Iraq, or the daily abuse given to believers in Lebanon, Jordan and in the Palestinian territories.[14]

Reza Aslan, an Iranian-American writer and scholar of religions said, "At the start of World War I, the Christian population of the Middle East may have been as high as 20 percent. Today, it is roughly four percent. Although it is difficult to be exact, there are perhaps 13 million Christians left in the region, and that number has likely fallen further, given the continued destabilization of Syria and Egypt, two nations with historically large Christian populations. At the present rate of decline, there may very well be no significant Christian presence in the Middle East in another generation or two. .this would be a profoundly important loss. Christianity was born in the Middle East and had a deep, penetrating presence in the region for hundreds of years before the rise of Islam...the ascension of transnational Jihadism over the last two decades has raised the campaign against Christians to a fever pitch...but it is important to note that the removal of the region's Christians is a disaster for Muslims as well. They are the ones who will be left with the task of building decent societies in the aftermath of these atrocities. And that task will be made immeasurably harder by the removal of Christians from their midst...the only lasting guarantor of political rights is the sort of social and religious diversity that Muslims in the region are in the process of extinguishing. If nothing is done to reverse the situation, the hope for peace and prosperity in the Middle East may vanish along with the region's Christian population."[15]

If aggressive Islam is trying to extinguish two thousand years of Christianity in the Middle East, then aggressive secularism, funded by a wealthy elite is threatening the Christian heritage, expression and liberties in the West. In America, a study by the political scientists Professor Martin Gilens of Princeton and Professor Benjamin Page of Northwestern, argued that the U.S. is now dominated by a rich and powerful elite.[16] Whilst in theory, any American can become the President of the United States, in practice, one has to know the right people, be in the right clubs, and be pliable to the interests of the rich – to be able to raise the seven billion dollars spent in the 2012 election.[17]

'Multivariate analysis indicates that economic elites and organised groups representing business interests have substantial independent impacts on U.S. government policy, while average citizens and mass-based interest groups have little or no independent influence,' states the study. 'When a majority of citizens disagrees with economic elites and/or with organised interests, they generally lose. Moreover, because of the strong status quo bias built into the U.S. political system, even when fairly large majorities of Americans favour policy change, they generally do not get it...Americans do enjoy many features central to democratic governance, such as regular elections, freedom of speech and association and a widespread (if still contested) franchise. But we believe that if policymaking is dominated by powerful business organisations and a small number of affluent Americans, then America's claims to being a democratic society are seriously threatened.'[18]

Initially, the claims of the U.S. being run by an oligarchy, with an unofficial aristocracy seem ridiculous, until studies indicate how many people in power are from political dynasties – such as the Kennedy, Bush or Clinton families and how the system is funded. President George H.W. Bush (1989-1993) was succeeded by President Bill Clinton (1993-2001), followed by the son of his predecessor, President G.W. Bush (2001-2009), and the wife of his predecessor, New York Senator Hillary Rodham Clinton (2001-2009), was narrowly defeated from running for president and instead became U.S. Secretary of State (2009-2013). Now she is hoping to be president in 2016.

Is Britain different? Is it the will of the vast majority of citizens driving politics and law, or is there an elite undermining and eliminating our Christian foundations, without regard to the majority? Evidence indicates there is a political and media elite that has become intoxicated with power and have behaved for decades, with the assumption that they know what is best for all. This has led to many feeling disconnected, disenfranchised and unrepresented by the existing political elite.

Member of Parliament Zac Goldsmith said, "Lying is a staple here in Parliament. You can behave in any manner you want in Parliament. You can break every single promise you made and there's nothing your constituents can do about it. People who are pulling away from politics are doing so because they don't believe there's a link between how they vote and how things are done in government – politicians make a promise before an election, and break it after the election, whatever party they belong to."[19] Before the 2015 election, 101 broken promises by the government before the last election were highlighted.[20]

Government spin-doctors, responsible for manipulating the media to get the best image across, explain that because each political party has its own agenda, they have to give all voters the appearance that they are on their side, even if they know their policies will be harmful for one part of the electorate. They do this by, 'Lying without lying.' For example, if a hospital is marked for closure, instead of a politician saying, "If we are in power, we will axe the hospital," what they say is something vague, "If anyone comes to me and tells me the hospital must close, I will show them the door." By being vague they give the appearance of support, when in reality, they did not specifically promise that the hospital will not close, which may be their policy. Three days before the 2010 general election David Cameron indicated he had no plans to redefine marriage, which he subsequently forced through without consent whilst in power.[21]

Damian McBride, former spin-doctor to Prime Minister Gordon Brown said, "I think the majority of politicians are basically honest people, but when you get to that senior level, when you're having to make statements that will be hung around your neck, then you find this way not of openly lying, not of telling barefaced lies, but of what I describe in my books as 'Lying without lying'...I worked as a spin doctor for Gordon Brown for years and what I found over time is that I became part of that culture. I became part of that culture where you understood what you needed to do was lie without lying."[22]

Britain has strict rules concerning how party funds can be

raised and spent, which includes banning American style political TV adverts, where the richest candidate bombards voters with his or her message. However, in 2014, the three main political parties were still able to raise over forty-three million pounds. At one fund-raiser, the prime minister and government ministers hobnobbed with billionaire oligarchs, millionaire bankers and powerful executives. The guests were reported to be worth a staggering eleven billion pounds and five million pounds were raised. MP Zac Goldsmith said, "I think donations are there for a reason. People want to have access to power, access to decision-makers...it's almost irrelevant who is in office, when you have permanent relationships between big business and the civil service. And I have seen decisions that are born of that relationship. I have seen with my own eyes decisions effectively being written up, policy decisions being written up by big business, by vested interests."[23]

In any democracy, the voter must also take responsibility for giving power to people who do not share their values. In a careful study of why people vote for certain parties and candidates, it was found that many adults simply vote for the same party as their parents. In immigrant communities, voters historically have tended to stay with the party their community votes for – in Britain its Labour; in the U.S. it's the Democrats. In 2010, sixty-eight percent of voters from ethnic minorities gave support to Labour, whilst sixteen percent voted Conservative.[24]

Since America's first televised political debate on 26 September 1960, as TV viewers believed John F. Kennedy won the debate, and radio listeners thought it was Richard Nixon, voters tend to be swayed by personalities and looks, rather than policies. One analysis found candidates have a two percent advantage if they are more physically attractive than their opponent.[25] Professor Larry Sabato, a political analyst at the Center for Politics at the University of Virginia, believes everything changed with the 1960 TV debate, "When parties are considering their candidates they ask: Who would look better on TV? Who comes across better? Who can debate better?" he said.[26]

Finally, studies show voters have strong opinions on subjects they know nothing about. In one study, fifteen percent of those questioned gave support for, or withheld it, from a Parliamentary motion which was invented as a test. In the 2010 election, the British Election Study found that 5,300,000 people claimed to have participated in the election, despite not doing so.[27]

Liberty was paid for, over a thousand years, with a difficult struggle and now it seems it is being sold for nothing. "British values are fundamentally Christian values, the values brought to the British Isles 1500 or more years ago. Common law is steeped in these values," said Professor Roger Trigg. "We should be very concerned about this attack on our own values, this secular attack which tries to be neutral and involves one being not just neutral towards but often opposed to religion…we must be very careful therefore not to go along too much with the secular idea of neutrality of the state. Where does the state stand if it is neutral? The answer is by definition nowhere…it is not surprising that totalitarian states attack religious freedom. Religious freedom is a pre-requisite for all democracy and it is terribly important. Once religious freedom is restricted all freedoms are under attack…the more the state sets itself up to decide who will have what freedom, even the most basic freedoms, the more freedom is endangered."[28]

Sir Edward Leigh said, "The truth is that real British values are Christian values. It is the influence of Christianity that made us one of the most tolerant and successful nations on earth. Not this artificial nonsense dreamed up by officials."[29] Government Cabinet Member Michael Gove wrote, 'The kind of people who built our civilisation, founded our democracies, developed our modern ideas of rights and justice, ended slavery, established universal education and who are, even as I write, in the forefront of the fight against poverty, prejudice and ignorance. In a word, Christians.'[30]

Chapter Twenty-Nine

Limitations on Liberty

What has happened with democracy and liberty in the West? The British signed up to an economic pack with Europe and by stealth, governments handed over sovereignty of its borders and law, to vague and seemingly unaccountable Eurocrats. You had to be born at least in the 1950s, to be eligible to vote in the last referendum on Britain's position in Europe, which took place in 1975. There was a four decade wait for the 2017 reappraisal. The sense that the European Union is being forced upon citizens against their will is felt by most Europeans, as demonstrated by their rejection of the EU, when they are given a vote.

The one conviction which has been shared in the heritage among all nations in the E.U., for over a thousand years is Christianity. However, in the Lisbon Treaty of 2009, Christianity, God and Providence were not mentioned. Most nations were denied a vote on the Treaty, whilst those who were permitted to vote, the French and Dutch, rejected it at their polls. Therefore the treaty was changed and was no longer a new treaty, but 'an amendment' of former treaties. When the Irish voted to reject the treaty, they were told to retake the vote, and were quickly warned of the dire consequences of rejecting it a second time.

The Irish spoke for most Europeans who were denied a vote as they rejected the E.U. treaty, and they were forced to vote again under this condition: accept the iron-fist undemocratic treaty or go bust, and so they voted to accept it. One commentator said, "The real Achilles heel of the Treaty of Lisbon was its failure to acknowledge God and the Christian roots of Europe. This omission alienated a large block of voters in Ireland…as long as the E.U. fails to acknowledge its Christian roots – which are the very foundations of Europe, and without which Europe is nothing – it is doomed to failure."[1]

In the 2014 European elections, the electorate across Europe dramatically changed their voting habits, bringing to power more people than ever who are sceptical about the direction of Europe. People can only accept being dictated to for so long by obscure politicians who force their will on them.

In many Western nations, and especially in Britain and America, there is a direct link to be sourced between Christianity and our liberties. Why are they being undermined? Without widespread Christian values being protected in Britain, the freedoms that have been fought for and won over a thousand years are at threat. American legal scholar Harold Berman said, "In virtually all societies the established legal processes of allocating rights and duties, resolving conflicts, and creating channels of cooperation are inevitably connected with the community's sense of, and commitment to, ultimate values and purposes."[2]

The values which made the West strong are being undermined in the West. Even the concept of what marriage is, or the family, has been substantially transformed from the Christian concept. Professor Julian Rivers said, "As Lord Denning suggested, there can be no doubt that the law of marriage and family has historically been significantly influenced by Christian ethics. In many detailed ways one can still trace the direct impact of Christian teaching and canon law. At the same time, secular family law has departed in various ways from historic Christian teaching, not least in its acceptance of divorce. However, this is still compatible with a recognisable Christian view in which the secular law sustains a basic, 'natural' and universal framework of rights, responsive to human needs and weaknesses, while the Church is free to teach a higher ideal, to which Christians and others can aspire."[3]

In the West, promiscuity, co-habitation and the redefinition of marriage has changed society, far beyond any recognition of what it once looked like. Many men no longer know who their children are, or never visit them and millions live alone. Bigamy, which means having two spouses at the same time, is a statutory offence in England and Wales, according to the Offences Against the Person Act 1861.[4] It is also outlawed in Scotland. Christian convictions in the West banned polygamy – the practice of having more than one spouse at a time – because of the numerous examples of its flaws in the Old Testament and the teaching that a servant of God must be 'the husband of one wife' (1 Timothy 3:2). It was accepted that men cannot support and properly care for two families (Exodus 21:10). The Bible states: 'Let deacons be the husbands of one wife, ruling their children and their own houses well' (1 Timothy 3:12).

But in many ways, Britons have returned to polygamy, with the provisos that their several wives or girlfriends are separated over an entire life, and not at the same time – in theory at least. However, traditional polygamy has already made a comeback in parts of the population. It is estimated there are up to twenty thousand polygamous Muslim marriages in the U.K.[5] In these

Islamic marriages, men live several days with one wife and their children at one home, then move to the next. As polygamy is illegal in Britain, these Muslims sidestep British law, by exploiting Britain's legal apartheid, where the two incompatible systems of law – Sharia law and British law – come into conflict. Traditional Islamic marriages are unrecognised by the state, which enables these men to remain 'unmarried' and their wives to be 'single parents,' whilst they claim benefits for multiple households. Thus the principle of one law for all has already been swept away by governments afraid to act.

One unemployed polygamist Muslim from Sheffield, spoke on TV about his three 'wives' and children, with three households on benefits, provided by taxpayers. Mohammed said, "We've got three wives, one husband, eleven children: we are a family."[6]

One Muslim woman spoke on TV, explaining she is a 'married' mother of eight living on benefits, who was seeking a separation from her polygamous Muslim marriage. She said, "Men are polygamous by nature."[7] Journalist Rachel Stewart said, "The truth is that co-wives are extremely vulnerable. Muslim polygamists circumvent U.K. law using unofficial Islamic ceremonies, or Nikkah, which offer the woman no legal or financial protection in the event of marriage breakdown."[8]

The benefit system in Britain was fought for and designed to be a Christian safety-net, to guarantee that the abject poverty of Victorian era could never return. It was not contrived to support polygamous Muslim marriages or to aid work avoidance.

In Britain, Minister for Health Nye Bevan, who was at the heart of the creation of the welfare safety-net said, "The NHS is a little piece of Christianity." Richard Tawney, William Beveridge and William Temple, the Christian men who transformed Britain into a nation that cared for the poor, believed the country was embracing the teaching of Jesus. "Then the righteous will answer Him, saying, 'Lord, when did we see You hungry...' And the King will answer and say to them, 'Assuredly, I say to you, inasmuch as you did it to one of the least of these My brethren, you did it to Me' " (Matthew 25:37-40).

What these men could never have anticipated, is the ruthless exploitation of the system by polygamists, Islamic extremists or by promiscuous Western men. Meanwhile, young hard-working tax payers are becoming labelled, 'Generation Pause,' as they are forced to put-off life's big decisions, getting married, buying a home and starting a family, because the system no longer rewards their hard work.'[9] Nevertheless, the demonisation of helping people who legitimately need support is a harsh swing away from the Christian convictions of helping all in need. After all it was the actions of the superrich that created our most recent financial crisis.

The 2015 report called *Church Action on Poverty* has identified the growing inequality in Britain, as the poorest are being forced to pay the greatest cost and carry the heaviest burden in the age of austerity. It states: 'We have concluded it is very hard to justify a system which impacts most harshly on the people who most need help and support...it is incumbent on the Christian community to speak out against any system which treats people so unjustly.'

The root of the West's financial problems is greed, which makes the rich think only of profit. Those who believe their primary endeavour is to make profit, regardless of the cost to people, are causing severe harm to society. One example is house building. For two decades Britain has built half the homes its population needs, because governments have benefited as homeowners felt artificially wealthy with rising house prices, whilst developers limited supply to increase profit and environmentalists block new housing developments. Add into this mix family breakdown, leading to more homes needed, mass immigration, buy to rent profiteering and benefit subsidised homes for young rebels, and we have a toxic mix which has punished people for working hard and rewarded those who do not. In 1960, the average first time house buyer was age 23, today it is close to 40, as rents have reached an all time high.[10] Meanwhile, there are up to 6,000 council house tenants – homes designed for the low paid – being occupied by families who earn over £100,000 and up to 34,000 with incomes over £50,000![11]

Britain is right to care for the poorest and it is Christian belief in action to help all who need it, but breaking the link between the Protestant Work Ethic of hard work, sacrifice and future rewards, in favour of rewarding those who have made poor choices has caused an economic nightmare for Britain. Between 2004-2014, the cost of welfare rose from £140 billion to £167billion, and it rose by 1,250% in real terms since creation. The second most expensive part is housing benefit, costing £23.8 billion in 2013-14, which goes to private landlords, instead of investing in homes which will last for the future.[12] In total, Britain's national debt in 2014 was £1.4 trillion, and the nation still spent up to £100 billion more than it earns.[13]

One trillion is hard to picture, so let's put it like this:

1 x 1,000 = 1,000 (One thousand).

1,000 x 1,000 = 1,000,000 (One million).

1,000 x 1,000,000 = 1,000,000,000 (One billion).
1,000 x 1,000,000,000 = 1,000,000,000,000 (One trillion).

Economic experts remind us that all Western nations have a pile of 'hidden debt,' or massive off-balance sheet accumulation of unfunded obligations, which are the promises governments have made to pay for things in the future, but have yet to find funding for – for example, a bulging Baby Boomer pension pot.[14] Some experts predict Britain's 'hidden debt' or 'debt promises' may be six times the present debt, making it £8.4 trillion!

Britain should be proud of its Christian tradition of helping the poorest and we must never return to Victorian poverty. "Without the welfare state, the position would have been far worse," said Professor Julian Le Grand, "welfare services are arguably the only bulwark against increasing poverty and ill-health, social misery and perhaps social instability. The question is not whether we can afford to have a properly funded welfare state; it is whether we can afford not to."[15]

Christian morality played a central role in shaping the family, the NHS and the welfare safety-net. But what is forgotten is that the early church provided strict guidance concerning those who could claim help. People who refused to work, busybodies and those who would not give of whatever they had – their time, hospitality etc., excluded themselves from help (2 Thessalonians 3:10-12, 1 Timothy 5:9-16).

Faith has shaped Britain, but sadly the faith which enabled Britain to become strong, is itself is also under attack, because all religions and all faiths are sometimes tarred with one brush. British Christian faith schools have a remarkable achievement levels, but they are being challenged because of problems with new Muslim schools. In 2011, an undercover investigation found that 'religious apartheid' and, 'hatred' was being taught in 'moderate' Muslim schools.[16] In 2014, the 'Trojan Horse' Islamic take-over scandal of thirteen schools erupted: The leaders had 'an aggressive Islamist agenda…a coordinated, deliberate and sustained action to introduce an intolerant and aggressive Islamist ethos.'[17] Such scandals make faith itself a target and to be 'unbiased' all faith schools and faith charities, have greater restrictions and limitations placed upon them.

Chapter Thirty

Rejecting God's Protection

Will aggressive secularists continue to impose their beliefs on Britain until the last vestiges of Christianity are removed, will the convictions of Britons continue to be ignored and will Islamic beliefs take deeper root as the Muslim population rises?

Polls have found British Muslims feel loyal to the nation and its laws, and yet extremism is also on the rise. We have already allowed legal apartheid to develop, with Sharia law overriding the protection of British law in some communities. In 2008, the Archbishop of Canterbury, Rowan Williams was the first to openly acknowledge how Sharia law is already being accepted in parts of Britain, saying, "As a matter of fact certain provisions of Sharia are already recognised in our society and under our law." With the Muslim population increasing he thought the implementation of Sharia, in part at least, "seems unavoidable."[1]

In a politically correct view of Islam in the Middle East, Western nations have found the solutions they like, whilst choosing to ignore the facts they are not comfortable with. Islam and Christianity create different civilisations, with adherents clinging to different values. One faith gave birth to Saudi Arabia, Iran and Pakistan, the other to Britain, the United States and Australia.

Lord Carey, the former Archbishop of Canterbury said in 2014, Britain must "recover a confidence in our nation's values...for too long we have been self-conscious and even ashamed about British identity. By embracing multiculturalism and the idea that every culture and belief is of equal value, we have betrayed our own traditions of welcoming strangers to our shore. In Britain's hospitable establishment different beliefs were welcomed but only one was pre-eminent – Christianity. The fact is that for too long the doctrine of multiculturalism has led to immigrants establishing completely separate communities in our cities. This has led to honour killings, female genital circumcision (FGM) and the establishment of Sharia law in inner-city pockets throughout the U.K...Muslim communities need to state, more clearly than they have done so far, their denunciation of these fanatical forms of Islam. Young people who travel abroad to commit violent Jihad should know before they go that there is no way back to civilised society."[2]

According to the Bible, we are living in a world damaged by an invisible spiritual battle, between an evil power feeding off sin and rebellion, and defying the will and plans of God. C.S. Lewis said, "Enemy-occupied territory – that is what this world is. Christianity is the story of how the rightful King has landed, you might say landed in disguise, and is calling us to take part in a great campaign of sabotage."[3] In Ephesians 6:12, Paul elaborates on the structure of the demonic systems which are battling against God's will, to get people to sin and rebel, to undermine the good God has planned for them. Paul tells us an evil spirit is at work, encouraging sin and decline because it suits his purposes (Ephesians 2:2). Jesus calls this evil spirit, "Satan, the ruler of this world" (John 12:31). So, do we serve Christ in the Holy Spirit or another spirit?

On a national level we are told, 'Righteousness exalts a nation' (Proverbs 14:34), and God blesses nations which are true to their covenants and promises to Him. In the invisible spiritual realm, we learn that an obedient people enable God to raise a 'hedge of protection' and a 'wall of fire' around them. "Have You not put a hedge around him and his household and everything he has? You have blessed the work of his hands, so that his flocks and herds are spread throughout the land" (Job 1:10). ' "I myself will be a wall of fire around it," declares the Lord, "and I will be its glory within" ' (Zechariah 2:5).

One of the signs of God's blessings is that enemies are unable to penetrate our defences and instead, we possess the gates of our enemies (Genesis 22:17). All these promises originate with the Jews, and we 'are Abraham's seed and heirs according to the promise' (Galatians 3:29). Consequently, Christians in Britain and the U.S. have witnessed that this 'special Divine protection' has been with us for centuries. King Alfred from the ninth century believed his Kingdom was defeated because it was not faithful to God, and he covenanted with God and victory was achieved. Later, when Britain committed itself to New Testament Christianity, the Spanish Armada, Napoléon's invasion force and Hitler's Germany were unable to defeat Britain.

Students of British history will find that the nation tends to lose some battles and goes on to win wars. For over a thousand years no nation could invade Britain! In America, within just two centuries the U.S. emerged to project power all over the world, and many believed that mainland North America was safe from any attack, until Islamic extremists struck on 9 September 2001. On 7 July 2005 Britain suffered its worst terrorist attack as a few British Muslims murdered fellow citizens in London, and another attempted attack followed on Thursday, 21 July 2005. The events seemed to highlight a growing trend of lack of safety at home, larger threats overseas, and a shrinking influence abroad.

Now we are no longer safe at home and a conviction began to awake in many minds, especially in the U.S., that God no longer protects America or Britain, because we have tried to expel Him and His will from our nations. Much of the hedge of protection and wall of fire which once protected us was not taken down by an enemy, but by us. We punctured substantial holes in them by encouraging sin in and bit by bit, they ripped open. As the Holy Spirit began to leave, others spirits came into our nations, empowered by sin and rebellion.

In Britain our monarchs have historically made a covenant with God to honour Him and rule 'under God' as the 1701 Act of Settlement clarifies. But this is in danger. Queen Elizabeth II, the Supreme Governor of the Church of England and Head of State has already been called, 'The last Christian monarch of Britain' because the heir-presumptive Prince Charles has stated in the past that he wants to be, 'The defender of the faiths,'[4] or 'faith' instead of 'the faith.'

What exactly will future monarchs in Britain be defending? If they intend to be the defender of faith in general, or all faiths – does that include Islamic extremists that behead people? What about traditional Mormons who believe their faith compels them to take several wives, or radical Jehovah Witnesses, who deny life-saving blood transfusions to their children because of their faith commitment to their historic and now defunct teaching? In the past in the West and in parts of the world today, there are hideous examples of expressions of certain faiths or faith – is this what future monarchs of Britain are seeking to defend, or is this another concession of our historic rights, culture and liberties to a vague multiculturalism, which has not been asked for, and has not been thought through?

To be the Defender of the Faith involves standing up for and protecting the legacy and heritage of Christianity in Britain. Through the Coronation Oath the monarch promises to defend and safeguard for the future, the Christian religious convictions which inspired the values that made this civilisation emerge. Having travelled to over forty nations, I have found that different faiths produce different civilisations, because their religions place an emphasis on different values.

One senior Church of England leader, instead of defending the faith, seems to agree that there is a need for change, arguing that any future coronation service should be opened with a reading from the Koran. Lord Harries, former Bishop of Oxford, suggested the gesture would be a 'creative act of accommodation for Muslims.'[5] Journalist and author Douglas Murray debated Lord Harries and argued that if you make one concession to one faith, you must make concessions to all faiths and to those with none. This would lead to a politically correct shambles of a service, without any coherent theme and will be unsatisfactory to all. Douglas Murray said, "You must ask of course, which passages from the Koran will or will not be read. I assume that Richard Harris wouldn't want the passages from the Koran which say kill the infidel wherever you find them, or cast terror into the hearts of the unbelievers, smite them?"[6] (Koran 2:191, 2:216, 3:151. 5:33). Many faiths have polemical texts, but only in Islam are violent texts being referenced, by a plethora of Muslim preachers around the world, to encourage violence, oppression and terror today, to the horror of peaceful Muslims. During the Arab Spring in the Middle East, after Friday prayers at the mosque, violent protests became notorious, and one study counted all the Islamic inspired terror attacks worldwide in the last few years and numbered them at over 20,000.

In Britain, Douglas Murray reminded Lord Harries that tolerance and concessions must work both ways, and only the West is denying its heritage and diluting its traditions to accommodate. He said, "Christians cannot worship or be in Mecca!...and if there is going to be inclusive reciprocity, it has to be returned. Jews in this country have a prayer for the Queen in their synagogues, in their services. Whenever I mention to Muslims this should happen in mosques, they say, 'That's very provocative.' But if there are to be some readings from the Koran at the coronation, surely, as a matter of reciprocity, that all mosques in the United Kingdom have prayers for our monarch and the armed forces every week at Friday prayers. What's wrong with that?"

Douglas Murray concluded his arguments by saying that believers are dismayed at Christian leaders who deny their own beliefs, adding they, "Don't want the leadership of their faith to be so fuzzy and apparently unconfident in their own faith, that they want to include all other faiths in it. Part of faith is saying, 'This is what we believe; this we believe to be correct.' That doesn't mean you needn't be polite," and he summarised the importance of having "a Defender of the Faith, in the most important Church in the United Kingdom, affirming the Christian faith."[7]

Simon Calvert of the Christian Institute think-tank responded by saying, "Most people will be amazed at the idea that a Christian leader would consider the use of the Koran at a Christian service in a Christian abbey. People are just so disappointed when senior Church of England figures lose confidence in the claims of the Christian faith.'[8]

Why are Britons being urged by secularists and liberal Christian leaders to give up their traditions, heritage and faith convictions, in order to be accommodating to people who came to the West to benefit from the freedoms granted by our traditions, heritage and faith convictions? We could ask, is there one Islamic nation which is free and fair for all?[9] Having heard first-hand testimonies of the persecution of minorities in many majority Muslim nations in Asia and the Middle East, I was shocked at how unaware the West is of the abuse of non-Muslims in these nations.

Meanwhile, in Britain, to be a Defender of the Faith means to defend the religious conviction which gave birth to the West. We are free because we are Christian. But a 'defender of the faiths' or 'faith' is profoundly different from the convictions outlined in the 1689 Settlement, the 1701 Settlement and the 1953 Royal Titles Act – of the monarch being the Defender of the Faith, that of Protestant New Testament Christianity.

Liberty was achieved in the United Kingdom and the U.S. because Christians fought for and achieved freedom, so what happens when that link is broken? Secularisation masquerades as objective, but in fact it is subjective in what it tolerates and has a clear agenda it wants to promote.

Chipping away at the biblical bedrock of the West is leading to undoing centuries of Christian heritage and tradition. In Britain since 1521, the monarch has been known by the title Defender of the Faith and this title took on deeper symbolism after the 1534 Act of Supremacy, which set the course for Britain to be a Protestant nation, with an independent Church of England, separate from Roman authority.

An official statement from the British monarch explains: 'The Sovereign holds the title Defender of the Faith and Supreme Governor of the Church of England...the Sovereign must be in communion with the Church of England, that is, a full, confirmed member. The Preface to the 39 Articles of the Church of England describes the monarch as 'being by God's Ordinance, according to Our just Title, Defender of the Faith and...Supreme Governor of the Church of England.'[10]

Prince Charles identifies himself as a Christian and has earned respect for speaking out, often in a world of silence, to defend the rights of Christians in the Middle East, who have experienced the harshest persecution for a century, since the Arab Spring. He is a regular church goer, but as one journalist explains he cannot be pigeonholed, 'From embracing Islam to attending Catholic masses and plans for a 'multi-faith' coronation, Prince Charles' religious beliefs are wide-ranging...the Prince has form in embracing Islam. For the last two decades, he has been patron of the Oxford Centre for Islamic Studies, where he gave a speech in 1993 on 'Islam and the West' that was reprinted enthusiastically in newspapers across the Middle East.'[11]

In the future will Britain have a monarch who is the defender of the faiths, instead of the faith? Recently the tone changed again. It seems those spin-doctors who once suggested this idea could be popular in a multicultural society have found themselves in a quagmire. Such a transformation to the Constitution is based upon the assumption that all expressions of faith are benign and will enable the common good to spring forth; history proves this assumption false. Any visitor to any minority group in the Middle East will find this supposal decimated by true stories persecution.

In 2015, on a tour of the Middle East the Prince of Wales' views appeared to be evolving, potentially signalling a U-turn away from the politically correct advisors who encouraged the concept of becoming, 'The defender of the faiths,' or 'faith,' to continue to defend 'the faith.' This change of heart may have been spurred on by witnessing the profound suffering of Christians and others in the region. "There is a real worry that there could come a time when there are no Christians left in the Middle East because the numbers have gone so dramatically down," said Prince Charles. "With what has happened in Mosul in Iraq and other centres, there are very few Christians left because they were intimidated to a degree you can't believe. Everything has been taken from them. Many of them are so fearful now of ever going back...The radicalisation of people in Britain is a great worry and the extent to which this is happening is alarming, particularly in a country like ours where we hold values dear. You would think that the people who have come here, or are born here, and who go to school here, would abide by those values and outlooks."[12]

After meeting Christians who fled their homes in Syria, Prince Charles said, "The tragedy is even greater because Christians have been in the Middle East for two thousand years, before Islam came in the eighth century." Having earned respect in the region, it appears the Prince may be seeking to draw inspiration from Queen Victoria, who used her influence in 1843 to help suffering Christians in the Middle East.[13] On the visit the Prince clarified statements he made concerning being a 'defender of the faiths.' He said, "At the same time as being Defender of the Faith, you can also be protector of other faiths."[14]

If Britain's future kings or queens break the ancient covenant with God – originally made by King Ethelbert of Kent (560-616), reconfirmed by King Alfred (849-899), re-established in 1534 and solidified in 1558 with Queen Elizabeth I, then what will be the Divine reply? Christ is the Head of His Church and the British Constitution points to the monarch as the Supreme Governor of the Church of England, submitting to the true Head, Jesus Christ (Ephesians 5:23).

Today, with almost two full decades to pass before the five hundred anniversary of the establishment of that religious covenant, which the nation made with God, we may also be laying the foundations for the removal of the political covenant made between the Head of State and God Almighty.

Beginning with the Coronation Oath Act 1689, kings or queens of England have been required to covenant with God, by swearing an Oath in His presence, "To maintain the Laws of God the true profession of the Gospel and the Protestant Reformed Religion established by law." As kings or queens in Britain reign, but do not rule, they make this Oath on behalf of the people of Britain, who invest their political capital into Parliament. As the monarch no longer has a political or executive role, he or she cannot pass legislation, vote or veto the will of Parliament. Thus it is Parliament who must live up to this Oath or dismiss it.

Several decades ago, David E. Gardner, author of the 1980s three volume *Trumpet Sounds for Britain* spoke with Lord Denning, when he was Master of the Rolls (the second most senior judge in England and Wales). David Gardner asked if the monarch's Coronation Oath was being ignored. "Yes, it is," replied Lord Denning. David continued, "Is it being ignored or set aside by Prime Ministers?" "Yes, it is," said Lord Denning. "Is it being ignored, set aside or being swept under the carpet by Parliament?" Lord Denning thought carefully and replied, "Yes, it is. The answer to all your questions is yes, unfortunately." Feeling saddened, David asked, "Does what is embodied and was undertaken in that Oath count for anything now?" "Very little," said Lord Denning with regret.[15]

The Constitution, with the Coronation Oath expresses that the monarch derives all authority from God, and invests it in Parliament, for the express will of maintaining a Christian nation, under God's guidance and protection. As Parliament began to ignore this Oath from the 1960s onwards, the wall of protection around Britain, and the blessing upon the nation also withdrew.

Nevertheless the personal devotion of Queen Elizabeth II may well stand for much in the heavenly realms, because as Head of

State, the line of authority in a biblical understanding is very important. However, if the next monarch, whomever that may be, tears-up or waters-down the covenant our Heads of State have made with God, the future may be bleaker.

The Bible provides exhortations and warnings: 'I exhort first of all that supplications, prayers, intercessions, and giving of thanks be made for all men, for kings and all who are in authority, that we may lead a quiet and peaceable life in all godliness and reverence. For this is good and acceptable in the sight of God our Saviour, who desires all men to be saved and to come to the knowledge of the truth. For there is one God and one Mediator between God and men, the Man Christ Jesus (1 Timothy 2:1-5).

If Christianity is being undermined in the political and religious spheres of Britain, there are some who want to hold firm. By 1999, some leaders in the Church of England desired to openly challenge unbelieving vicars in new tribunals, and the headlines of 'The vicars who don't believe in God,' referring to 'godless vicars' and 'atheist priests,' cited up to seven hundred vicars from several denominations with profound doubts.[16]

In the first few years of the twenty-first century it was reported that one-third of Church of England vicars did not believe in the bodily resurrection of Jesus Christ, regardless of the fact that Paul said that the faith is futile, if Christ was not raised from the dead (1 Corinthians 15:15). In response by 2005, the Church of England was still seeking trials for heresy,[17] but by 2014, the word 'sin' and the need to 'repent' was removed from some ceremonies. One senior member of the General Synod said, "This is more like a benediction from the Good Fairy than any church service. The trouble is that large parts of the Church of England don't believe in hell, sin or repentance. They think you can just hold hands and smile and we will all go to heaven. That is certainly not what Jesus thought. There is so much left out that one wonders why do it at all? If you exclude original sin and repentance there is very little substance left. It doesn't just dumb the service down – it eviscerates it. It destroys the significance of the rite by watering down the concept of sin and repentance."[18]

There is something profoundly dishonest, hypocritical and exploitative for unbelieving vicars or bishops to continue to lead churches, preach and teach people who do believe, whilst in their hearts, the leaders do not. The apostasy is here!

Has Britain smashed its national and religious covenant with God? Can Britain learn from Hosea? The Lord said, "Can he break a covenant and still be delivered?…Since he despised the oath by breaking the covenant and in fact gave his hand and still did all these things." Therefore thus says the Lord God, "As I live, surely My oath which he despised and My covenant which he broke, I will recompense on his own head" (Ezekiel 17:15, 18-19). "Set the trumpet to your mouth! He shall come like an eagle against the house of the Lord, because they have transgressed My covenant and rebelled against My law. Israel will cry to Me, 'My God, we know You!' Israel has rejected the good; the enemy will pursue him" (Hosea 8:1-3).

During the Cold War, some believed God would allow Britain to experience a military defeat or invasion, to provide it with an understanding of how far it has fallen. But instead, many have witnessed that God simply withdrew and 'gave them over to their own stubborn hearts' (Psalm 81:12), and to a 'debased mind' (Romans 1:28). We have reaped what we have sown (Galatians 6:7). 'They sow the wind and reap the whirlwind' (Hosea 8:7).

Some believe we have made elements of our society a living hell, but we have also perfected throughout society, the ability to hide sin and dysfunction, behind obscure statistical data on abuse of power and authority. It appears as if we have built a fire-wall around our hearts and minds, to convince us that everything is fine. Journalist Adam Curtis gave this analysis: 'Wherever you look there are lying politicians, crooked bankers, corrupt police officers, cheating journalists and double-dealing media barons, sinister children's entertainers, rotten and greedy energy companies and out-of-control security services. And what makes the suspicion worse is that practically no-one ever gets prosecuted for the scandals. Certainly nobody at the top.'[19]

Adam Curtis believes we never allow ourselves to see the big picture. 'Every month or so there is a new scandal – mass snooping by the NSA, allegations of price-fixing by giant energy companies, major banks corruptly rigging interest rates, giant modern bureaucracies...ripping off the taxpayer, children's entertainers from the past charged with sexual abuse. But these stories never seem to add up to a bigger picture. They are isolated events. And our reaction is always the same – shock and horror, and then it all subsides and we are ready to be shocked and horrified when the next scandal comes along. It's like a ritualised dance – or the surprised.'[20]

Scripture provides some hard insights into human nature:

'All have turned away, all have become corrupt; there is no one who does good, not even one' (Psalm 14:3).

'The way of peace they do not know; there is no justice in their paths. They have turned them into crooked roads; no one who walks along them will know peace' (Isaiah 59:8).

Western nations were once able to project power overseas without any fears at home, by contrast now we no longer have control over our own borders, let alone rogue states and terrorist organisations abroad. Britain's Home Office recently announced it has lost track of almost 175,000 illegal immigrants,[21] and there are as many as 860,000 in the country, which costs the taxpayer £3.7 billion a year.[22] In 2013, there was an estimated twenty million illegal immigrants in the U.S.,[23] and by 2014 the southern U.S. border was overrun in parts, with more than 300,000 people entering illegally.[24] How many terrorists have hid amongst these poor people desperately seeking a better life?

A report by the National Audit office found that 'Britain spends up to £1 billion a year dealing with foreign criminals,' and one in six foreign criminals living in the U.K. have disappeared.[25]

Britain, American and several European nations have suffered many attacks from nationals with foreign beliefs and convictions, and some people have tried to blame God for allowing it to happen. "Where was God?" is the cry from unbelievers. Ann Graham Lotz, daughter of the evangelist Billy Graham was asked why God allowed 9/11 and she replied, "I believe God is deeply saddened by this, just as we are, but for years we've been telling God to get out of our schools, to get out of our government and to get out of our lives, and being the Gentleman He is, I believe He has calmly backed out. How can we expect God to give us His blessing and His protection if we demand He leave us alone?"[26]

Instead of trying to blame God for the troubles in our nations, Shakespeare says, "Men at some time are masters of their own fates: The fault, dear Brutus, is not in our stars, but in ourselves."[27] Paul declares: 'Do not be deceived, God is not mocked; for whatever a man sows, that he will also reap' (Galatians 6:7). A.W. Tozer said, "Since the fall of man, the earth has been a disaster area and everyone lives with a critical emergency.'[28]

Britain, the United States and other nations with a Christian heritage have two choices. We can repent and invite Christ to transform us into His image and return our hedge of protection, as other generations have, or we can choose the alternative by our inaction. The second option is to close the door on God and allow ourselves to create a living hell behind them. Our hedge of protection is broken, and it is our sin which has smashed it and caused misery for so many. C.S. Lewis said, "I willingly believe that the damned are, in one sense, successful rebels to the end; that the doors of hell are locked on the inside."[29]

Chapter Thirty-One

Christianity and Safeguarding Liberty

Lord Denning (1899-1999), the most celebrated English judge of the twentieth century, believed that Christianity was essential to safeguard democracy and the impartial rule of law. He said that "without religion there can be no morality and without morality there can be no law."[1] According to Lord Denning, only eternal, unchanging values, grounded in faith in the unchanging Christian God, can last and protect the liberties of free people. "The spirit of truth and justice is not something you can see. It is not temporal but eternal. How does man know what is truth or justice? It is not the product of his intellect, but of his spirit." In another address, Lord Denning linked the Christian concept of justice, to the eternal realm of God and Christ, "Surely we ought to go back two thousand years and say, 'What doth it profit a man if he gain the whole world and lose his own soul?' "[2]

Lord Denning pointed out that as soon as a nation begins to undermine and remove the foundational Christian beliefs from society, and instead presents all beliefs as equal, you do not create equality, but rather undermine your own foundations for justice. He explained, "Religion [meaning Christianity for Lord Denning] concerns the spirit in man, whereby he is able to recognise what is truth and what is justice: whereas law is only the application, however imperfectly, of truth and justice in our everyday affairs. If religion perishes in the land, truth and justice will also." Justice in English law was, according to Denning, "The application of the injunction to 'Love thy neighbour' to social institutions." Yet, when the foundations of society are removed, laws and liberty are no longer protected by multigenerational Christian beliefs, but become subject to the whims and political interests of changing governments. This is why Lord Denning in a speech entitled, 'What Life Has Taught Me' said, "The most important thing that life has taught me is to believe in God."[3]

Lord Denning witnessed what happened to Nazi Germany and Russia, as they rejected their Christian heritage, and law became a mercurial instrument for the state to abuse, harass and limit rights and freedoms In his lifetime he found that democracy can restrain unjust rulers and keep them accountable, but it can also be manipulated and undermined, to give a mandate to dictators and maniacs. In the last German multi-party elections of 1933 before the war, 17,277,180 Germans voted for the Nazi party. What followed was the Reichstag Fire Decree and then the Enabling Act, which gave Hitler plenary powers; civil liberties were abolished and the election created a de facto legal dictatorship. After annexing Austria in March 1938, a month later, on 10 April, Germany held its final elections to the Reichstag during Nazi rule, which was the last chance Germany had for a referendum to approve Nazi policies. Turnout was 99.5%, with 98.9% or 44,451,092 million people approving Nazi plans. Less than 1% of the population voted against or spoiled the forms. [4]

The experience in Germany proves that democracy and liberty can be abolished by the ballot box, but it can also be diminished in Britain and America, through fickle policies. Winston Churchill, understanding the problem of human government said with tongue-in-cheek, "Democracy is the worse form of government, except for all those others that have been tried."

It could be asked, can governments who have rejected the Christian moral foundations and belief in hard work, honesty, thrift and economic prudence, which made the West strong, be trusted to put the long-term interests of the public at the fore? The following quote, often accredited to Alexander Tytler (1747-1813), sums up the fear that democracy can lead to government overspending, creating huge debts, in order for today's voter to enjoy the highlife, at the future peril of the nation and its descendants: 'A democracy is always temporary in nature; it simply cannot exist as a permanent form of government. A democracy will continue to exist up until the time that voters discover that they can vote themselves generous gifts from the public treasury. From that moment on, the majority always votes for the candidates who promise the most benefits from the public treasury, with the result that every democracy will finally collapse due to loose fiscal policy, which is always followed by a dictatorship. The average age of the world's greatest civilisations from the beginning of history has been about two hundred years. During those two hundred years, these nations always progressed through the following sequence: From bondage to spiritual faith; from spiritual faith to great courage; from courage to liberty; from liberty to abundance; from abundance to complacency; from complacency to apathy; from apathy to dependence; from dependence back into bondage.'[5]

In Britain, Old Testament styled bishops once kept government accountable and restrained the abuse of power by drawing it back to Christian moral values. This heritage is still reflected in the practice of British judges wearing robes, as a reminder of the religious origins of the office. Government accountability was recognised as needful, as Britain acknowledged human sinfulness based upon the Bible. As society accepted that 'all have sinned,' it resulted in the acceptance that no one body of government should have excessive power. Thus the executive, legislative and judicial functions of government are undertaken by different entities. In other words, those who make laws must be different from those who enforce and interpret them.

The legislative and judicial authorities evolved to monitor government, to make sure it conformed to the law, and the Christian spirit behind the law. These checks and balances provide protections from an all-powerful state. Of course, abuse of power can be judicial, as well as political. Judges must interpret the law, with commonsense, fairly and rationally.

In 2012, the U.K. High Court ruled that Bideford Town Council had acted unlawfully by allowing prayers to be said during meetings, regardless that the practice in England dates back to the days of Queen Elizabeth I, who ruled from 1558 to 1603.[3] Some in the government perceived this as a case of a judge overturning historical precedent, overreaching power and limiting freedoms. 'The controversial judgment has been regarded by many as an example of the marginalisation of Christianity, as well as a test case that has applied to councils in England and Wales since 10 February,' reported the BBC. 'The government argues that it was not the intention or will of Parliament for this act from 40 years ago to be used to prohibit prayers.'

"The High Court judgment has far wider significance than just the municipal agenda of Bideford Town Council," explained the Communities Secretary Eric Pickles, as he fast-tracked a new law to give back powers to councils to pray, as part of the drive for transparency and accountability.[7] He added, "By effectively reversing that illiberal ruling, we are striking a blow for localism over central interference, for freedom to worship over intolerant secularism, for Parliamentary sovereignty over judicial activism, and for long-standing British liberties over modern-day political correctness." He added that the Bideford council case should be "a wake-up call...for too long, the public sector has been used to marginalise and attack faith in public life, undermining the very foundations of the British nation."[8]

For centuries in Britain, judges and politicians believed that they worked under the cloud of God's witness. This conviction led to a belief that people 'may get away with it now,' but ultimately, God will hold all to account. But today, without a clear sense of accountability to God, those with power can exercise it for their own ends and some have enforced their own limited worldview of liberal secular humanism. Edmund Burke articulated that accountability to God and liberty are conjoined, "If all dominion of man over man is the effect of Divine disposition, it is bound by the eternal laws of Him who gave it."

Many now feel it is fair to say that Western governments for several decades have behaved in the most undemocratic way. Christian values have been thrust aside, to adopt liberal secular humanism as the default position, which has been reflected in legislation, legal judgments, in school teaching and in the media. When did these governments seek an open mandate to bulldoze the traditional moral foundations of the West, to accept liberal secular humanism, which in itself is an unrecognised faith commitment? This seismic shift in policy has led to state sector employees being targeted, disciplined, suspended or dismissed for following traditional Christian practices, once encouraged by the state, such as praying for the sick, wearing a cross or even for merely mentioning the name of Jesus Christ.

Whilst Christians have been harassed at work for following the traditions of the hospital matron, who once opened the wards with prayer, in modern Britain, turban-clad Buddhist healers were awarded hundreds of thousands of pounds to 'channel healing energy' to correct 'energy flow imbalances,' in what some called The National Health Service (NHS) Voodoo spiritual healing.[9]

From top level government to city councils, Christians have experienced hostilities on many fronts, for continuing British religious traditions. In the U.K., police forces have arrested preachers and evangelists, under a new law which made "insulting words or behaviour" a criminal offence. What happened to freedom of speech and open religious debate? Article 10 of the 1998 Human Rights Act states: 'Everyone has the right to freedom of expression. This right shall include freedom to hold opinions and to receive and impart information and ideas without interference by public authority and regardless of frontiers.' However, in practice evangelists are being intimidated by authorities to make them feel they are not welcome to share their faith in public. Rights and tolerance must be a two-way street. You cannot demand tolerance and rights for one set of views, whilst being intolerant and excluding Christian views.

A report by the Equality and Human Rights Commission found that 'employees and students' have 'encountered hostile and unwelcoming environments,' because of their faith. It found employers and service suppliers are confused about the laws protecting religion and belief in the country.[10] The BBC added: 'Religious employees feel under pressure to keep their beliefs and faith symbols hidden at work.'[11]

For over a thousand years, Britain was a theocratic state, in the sense that English and later Scottish laws were intended to reflect the revealed will of God in Scripture. The law therefore acknowledged and sought to represent Christian teaching in all areas of the lives of Britons, from supporting the traditional family, honouring God, protecting worship, to caring for the poor etc. The freedom which Britain gained in 1689 and America declared in 1776, are founded upon a Christian faith commitment – that government is subject to customary law of the land, which is also subject to a higher law, and all are accountable to Him. Freedom is a gift from God, which has to be protected and no man, or government, can strip another of it.

John Locke expressed it this way: 'Ultimately, all obligation leads back to God and we are bound to show ourselves obedient to the authority of His will, because both our being and our work depends of His will.' Life and liberty are a gift from God, Britain believed, so to respect our own rights we must respect others. Paul preached, "He is not far from each one of us; for in Him we live and move and have our being" (Acts 17:27-28).

Liberty emerged in Britain and the U.S. due to the theological understanding that every individual has innate dignity, and must choose between the right and wrong, as revealed by God in Scripture. It was the confidence our forefathers had in an absolute set of rules – God's right and wrong, which enabled democracy to emerge. For without a final revelation of rights, given by God to mankind, man is tempted to find how his rights, can override others. China is still ruled by a government which believes it knows better than the people what is good for them. The vacuum of faith in China in the 1940s led to a system of elite arbitrary rulers, with a misguided ideology, seizing power and reducing the common person to dust. Alexis de Tocqueville said, "Despotism may govern without faith, but liberty cannot."[12]

Democracy and the rule of law emerged in Britain because a coherent belief system enabled citizens to believe that objective truth exists and is revealed in Christian teaching. This led to the conviction that the rights and concerns of all should be heard and taken into account. This is why under the law, the rights of an uneducated poor person, must be regarded as equal to the superrich. This belief never made an impact in China, nor in many other nations The foundational Christian conviction that all are or equal worth, regardless of wealth or status has been a safeguard against the arbitrary abuse of power. Christianity strengthened this conviction, that the individual must have a say in how they are ruled, based upon a set of non-negotiable God given values. Christian belief therefore became an anchor for government, to keep it from sailing away into waters of ever-changing values and the popular re-labelling of right and wrong.

Many states in the world claim to be democratic, but without the liberty for people to express their opinions and to circulate details about government without repression, their liberty is undermined and limited. To be free, people need the information which enables them to know who or what, they are voting for. Nevertheless, even this is being undermined in the West. Policy is presently ignoring the traditions of society and the democratic will of the people, in favour of reflecting the agenda of the elite, enacted without the consent of those whom it affects.

When the coalition government in Britain decided to follow other nations in 2012 and planned to redefine marriage, it chose to reject centuries of British law and tradition, two thousand years of Christian teaching and it ignored Jesus' definition of marriage, which is the lifelong union between one man and one woman for life (Mark 10:7-9). To get its way the government decided to disregard the democratic process on such a polemical and transformational issue. Archbishop Nichols, the leader of the Catholic Church in England and Wales, said of the gay marriage plans, "There was no announcement in any party manifesto, no Green Paper, no statement in the Queen's Speech. And yet here we are on the verge of primary legislation... from a democratic point-of-view, it's a shambles. George Orwell would be proud of that manoeuvre, I think the process is shambolic." He went on to add that public opinion and the will of the people were, "7-1 against same-sex marriage."[13] The government went on to redefine marriage and disregarded the process of democracy. Britain was changed by the elite that refused to listen or reflect the convictions of the majority of its citizens.

In a representative democracy, the law which affects all should only be implemented, updated or reversed by the mechanism that involves consent. Concessions to the EU over borders and law, handing over many areas of sovereignty to obscure and seemingly unaccountable Eurocrats, surrendering to legal apartheid, ignoring the rise of Sharia law, the sale of unlabeled halal meat (prayed over in Islamic tradition and distressingly slaughtered) have all been allowed without consent. Government exists to serve the will of the people, not the other way around.

Today Britain has over eighty-five functioning Sharia courts, with Sharia patrols enforcing strict Islamic law on some streets. Legal apartheid is not a warning for the future – it is taking place now and is largely unchallenged. One exception is Baroness Cox, who has tried to introduce an equality bill to protect Muslim women, saying in Parliament, "The growth of Sharia Courts and Councils in the U.K. is cause for deep concern. They inherently promote gender discrimination, inflicting suffering on women which would make our Suffragettes turn in their graves; and they threaten liberal democracy's fundamental principle of One Law For All."[14]

In many European nations there is a deeply worrying trend emerging of Western-born Muslims being coerced into submitting to and participating in Sharia Courts, or having to suffer the consequences of being treated as an infidel (filthy unbeliever), in closed-knit Muslim communities. Baroness Cox has warned that the rights of girls and women are being restricted by Sharia Courts: 'The protection of children is one of the essential principles of civilised society,' writes Baroness Cox, 'yet the duty to safeguard the vulnerable seems in danger of being undermined out of sensitivity towards some minorities…

'This disturbing trend has been highlighted this week by revelations that, during an undercover investigation, two imams from Islamic centres, one based in Peterborough, the other in East London, expressed their willingness to marry an under-age Muslim girl – aged just 12 – to a man in his 20s under the aegis of Sharia law…this most recent case demonstrates once again how women's and girls' rights are subverted under Sharia…it's a disturbing picture in a country in which equality for all is meant to be a guiding principle of the justice system.

'That great ideal stretches back centuries to the Magna Carta, requiring that everyone should be treated equally under the law, regardless of their wealth or status. In recent years, however, the concept of judicial equality has come under severe pressure, due to the increasing official acceptance of Islamic Sharia law. No longer do we have a single legal code in our society. Instead, alongside our own law, there is now effectively a parallel quasi-legal system operating within some Muslim communities…

'Sharia law, imported from theocracies like Afghanistan and Saudi Arabia, first began to be used here in a strictly limited form, dealing mainly with narrow issues like Islamic financial contracts. But as the Muslim population has grown and the pervasive creed of multiculturalism has become ever more powerful, so Sharia law has rapidly grown in influence within some communities…the courts, which also claim to cover matters such as marriage, divorce, domestic violence and child custody, take place in private and do not publish their judgments...No society can function effectively with a parallel quasi-legal system, with some people having, in practice, drastically diminished legal rights because of their religion and their gender...this situation also leads to open discrimination against women. In so many ways, Sharia law treats women as second-class citizens, whether it be in inheritance rights or divorce...according to Sharia law, for instance, a woman's word counts for only half the value of that of a man. Polygamy is also tolerated, with men allowed to take multiple wives. This attitude to women has devastating consequences for many women appearing before the Islamic courts.'[15]

In an age which has rejected the core Christian foundations for liberty, the free and fair debates of the past, giving a fair tolerant hearing to the opinions of others, have also been shut-down in the name of political correctness. We have created a society where certain beliefs, most notably some Islamic convictions, cannot be challenged because of the threat of a backlash or violence by a minority. Is this right, especially when we consider how Islamic traditions have shaped societies in the Middle East? Of course, the Christian belief of treating others as you wish to be treated, remains central to such conversations; all Christians are compelled by Christ's teaching to show grace and respect.

Britain's tradition of free speech and being able to challenge the thoughts and ideas of others, whilst respecting the individual, has protected us from the rise of various forms of hate-filled extremism. By permitting free speech, restricted practices have been tested in the court of public opinion. No-where enshrines this liberty as well as Speakers' Corner in London, where the 1872 Parks Regulation Act gave permission for people to meet and speak out on any issue, without fear of arrest. Nevertheless, whilst Christianity has come under intense attack and scrutiny in Britain since the 1950s, and every possible angle of attack has manifested, other faiths with troubling traditions have been granted special protection. A candidate in the South East European elections, incensed at the double standards, wanted to test Britain's commitment to free speech and according to the BBC was arrested by up to seven officers, for publicly reading the words of Prime Minister Winston Churchill on Islam.[16]

Winston Churchill was an eyewitness of Britain's war against the Madhi's government in Sudan in the late 1899, founded upon Sharia law, which reintroduced slavery into the nation. Churchill in his account of *The River War* wrote: 'The fact that in

Mohammedan law every woman must belong to some man as his absolute property – either as a child, a wife, or a concubine – must delay the final extinction of slavery until the faith of Islam has ceased to be a great power among men. Thousands become the brave and loyal soldiers of the faith: all know how to die but the influence of the religion paralyses the social development of those who follow it. No stronger retrograde force exists in the world. Far from being moribund, Mohammedanism is a militant and proselytising faith.'[17]

In 1807 and 1833, British Christians succeeded in making the slave trade and slavery illegal. Meanwhile, the practice of slavery continued in the Islamic world far into the twentieth century. Under pressure by Britain in 1936, Saudi Arabia signed a decree ending the importation of new slaves into the country, and Article 4 of the Universal Declaration of Human Rights, was designed to address, in part, traditional slavery in the Middle East: 'No one shall be held in slavery or servitude; slavery and the slave trade shall be prohibited in all their forms.' The abolition of slavery in Saudi Arabia and Yemen finally took place in 1962 and by 1964, the Islamic world officially supported ending traditional slavery.[18]

However, new forms of slavery include bonded labour, forced marriages, human trafficking with prostitution, as its main source, is growing worldwide. Also, traditional slavery has re-emerged. The leader of the Islamist group Boko Haram, which kidnapped hundreds of girls from a school in Nigeria said, "By Allah, I will sell them in the marketplace,"[19] and in Iraq and Syria in 2014, the United Nations found that British-born Muslim women were running open slave markets, and thousands of non-Muslims have been sold into sexual slavery in their Islamic State.[20] These Islamic extremist groups tell Muslims in the West that they have betrayed the heart of Islam by conforming to Western values, which include giving women equal rights, and they need to return to the true faith which spread, by Jihad, from Saudi Arabia to occupy the Middle East in less than a century.

In history, Britain fought against Islamic extremist governments such as the Mahdi's Empire, built on slavery in Sudan (1881-99). The famed Christian General Gordon (1833-1885) was martyred by Islamists in his campaign to end the ongoing Arab slave trade on the Nile, but today British Muslim citizens have gone to the Middle East to enslave and behead. The masked Islamic State militant known as 'Jihadi John' was not raised in poverty in the deserts of a militant area of the Middle East like the Mahdi, instead this middle class man walked the streets of London, and studied computer programming at university, with the kind of people he would later brutally behead with his knife.[21]

Jihadi John, contrary to the convictions of many Muslims, believed he was fulfilling the will of Allah, as described in the Koran: 'When you encounter the unbelievers on the battlefield, strike off their heads until you have crushed them completely' (Koran, Surat 47:4). The most important biography of the founder of Islam, which is praised by Muslim scholars for its accuracy, describes this event: 'The Jews were made to come down and Allah's Messenger imprisoned them. Then the prophet went out into the marketplace of Medina (it is still its marketplace today), and he had trenches dug in it. He sent for the Jewish men and had them beheaded in those trenches. They were brought out to him in batches. They numbered 800 to 900 boys and men.'[22]

Radical Muslim extremists believe they are fulfilling the will of Allah and following in the footsteps of the founder of Islam. They have brought their message to the West with the visas and citizenship they received from politically correct governments. Now some of these radicals are flying from the West to kill others in the name of their religion. A report by the United Nations found 'more than 25,000 foreign fighters have travelled to join militant groups such as al-Qaeda and Islamic State.'[23]

Why have so many Western governments allowed such voices to go unchecked up until 9/11, whilst ignoring or harassing Christians who raised the warning? It must be remembered that most Muslims who came to Britain were moderates and desired to escape extremism and Sharia law. However, governments in the West buried their heads in the sand as Islamists came to radicalise moderate Muslims, in a deliberate action to introduce an angry, aggressive Islamist agenda. They brought with them a 'crusader victim mentality,' dragging up complaints from wars which began over a thousand years ago, and tried to make Western-born Muslims feel that they too are the victims of these ancient, and once forgotten wars.

Somali-born British journalist and Muslim Rageh Omaar said, "In the West the crusades are events in the distant past, which have little bearing on our everyday lives, but in the Middle East it's very different. Take the town of Ma'arrat Al-Numan (Syria); for many locals the crusader massacre that took place here over nine hundred years ago, may as well have happened yesterday...the people I met in Ma'arrat now see all Western involvement in the Middle East through the prism of what happened here...I may not believe the West is waging a new crusade, but millions of Muslims do...in the Muslim world we have too much history, we see everything that involves the West and the West's involvement in the Muslim world as a crusade; whether it's to do with democracy today or oil, or in liberating the Holy Land for Christ a thousand years ago. It's why Osama Bin Laden and other leaders of al-Qaeda keep referring to their fight being with the crusaders today. Because for them, the West's involvement in the Muslim world is a re-enactment of the crusaders and don't under estimate the power of that appeal...in the West the crusades are a chapter of Christian history that has little impact upon our lives today, but what few people realise is that today's Islamist suicide bombers believe they are still fighting crusaders."[24]

Western nations, following Christian teaching have a history of forgive and forget; that's why European nations are now in a union with Germany, the nation that devastated Europe twice in the twentieth century. Forgiving wrongs of other generations frees future generations from paying the price for their ancestors' sins. The crusades were a disaster for Jews, Christians and Muslims. The only permanent victim of the crusades was the Byzantine Christian Kingdom in Turkey, which never recovered from the Western siege of 1204, leading to its ultimate collapse, occupation and takeover by Muslim forces in 1453.

In 2006, Bishop Michael Nazir-Ali, from Pakistan, whose father converted from Islam to Christianity, warned that some Muslims have developed a "dual psychology" of "victimhood and domination," because of radical Islamist preachers, who ignore non-Muslim victims of war. He said, "Their complaint often boils down to the position that it is always right to intervene when Muslims are victims, as in Bosnia or Kosovo, and always wrong when the Muslims are the oppressors or terrorists, as with the Taliban or in Iraq." He explained this mentality flourished because Britain allowed radical Muslim preachers to enter the nation, unchallenged. Extremism in Muslim communities is rising because, "The two main causes of the present situation are fundamentalist imams and material on the internet."[25]

Western governments ignored these radical Muslims, as these extremists spread their vision to have all Muslim communities modelled on the extreme Islam of Saudi Arabia or Iran, or worse, depending on their Shia or Sunni Islamic traditions. Their views went unchallenged because political correctness targeted people who raised questions and labelled them as 'racist, intolerant or bigoted.' By restricting freedom of speech in the West, governments have sown the seeds of Islamic discord and terror, at home and abroad.

In 2015, Egyptian President Abdel Fattah al-Sisi warned that

Muslims are in danger of being trapped within a 'mindset' which is tearing apart the world. He said, "The thinking that we hold most sacred causes the entire umma [the Islamic world] to be a source of anxiety, danger, killing and destruction for the rest of the world...this umma is being torn...by our own hands."[26]

If a few leaders in the Muslim world are prepared to address these problems, why is the West avoiding them, by limiting free speech? One reporter said of the U.K.'s restrictions on speech, "In today's Britain, pastors, street evangelists, and political activists all risk being hauled into police stations and either being arrested or warned for speaking out against Islam, immigration or homosexuality. Evangelical Pastor James McConnell was questioned by Belfast police for a possible 'hate crime' after a controversial sermon...McConnell said he went to the police station voluntarily, and he also apologised. But should he have had to?" George Igler, with the Discourse Institute said, "He was expressing a view about a particular religion. You can't have freedom of religion without the freedom to have religious views about particular religions."[27]

The Western world now only has an illusion of free speech. Policies implemented with inclusion in mind, have led in practice to the exclusion of Christians and their traditional British beliefs. Tolerance should be a two-way street, but instead, tolerance of post-Christian values has led to intolerance of Christian values. Britain's most senior judge, Lord Neuberger, the President of the Supreme Court has warned that freedom of expression is being limited in Britain, as once common held opinions are now deemed "unacceptable." He said, "As has been said on more than one occasion, freedom only to speak inoffensively is a freedom not worth having...the more that arguments and views are shut out as unacceptable, the less diverse we risk becoming in terms of outlook, and the less diverse we become in terms of outlook, the more we risk not valuing diversity and the more we therefore risk losing diversity in practice."[28]

Britain's most senior female judge, Lady Hale, the Deputy President of the Supreme Court, said in a speech that the U.K. is now "less respectful" towards people with traditional Christian views than other countries, despite its long Christian history. During a speech at the prestigious Yale Law School she argued that Christians with traditional beliefs should be given the protection of "reasonable accommodation" in law. Citing several cases in which EU anti-discrimination law has been used to silence and punish Christians for holding beliefs, which were once accepted by most in society. She commented, "It is not difficult to see why the Christians feel that their religious beliefs are not being sufficiently respected." She asked, "Would it not be a great deal simpler if we required the providers of employment goods and services to make reasonable accommodation for the religious beliefs of others?"[29]

The future of Britain, America and the West is now in the balance; either we will re-embrace the faith and values of our forefathers, or we will continue down a path of making another round of endless seemingly little concessions, until we find ourselves miles away from the Christian values and principles of liberty, which enabled religious freedom, democracy and the rule of law to emerge. Britain has freedom of speech and liberty of belief because it is a Christian nation and without confidence in this tradition, these cherished freedoms will be lost to an empty sacrifice to political correctness.

Christians and their beliefs which are the bedrock of Western civilisation are increasingly becoming targets of the intolerance of the 'tolerant.' Government Cabinet Member Michael Gove wrote: 'To call yourself a Christian in contemporary Britain is to invite pity, condescension or cool dismissal. In a culture that prizes sophistication, non-judgmentalism, irony and detachment, it is to declare yourself intolerant, naive, superstitious and backward. The contrast between the Christianity I see our culture belittle nightly and the Christianity I see our country benefit from daily, could not be greater...the reality of Christian mission in today's churches is a story of thousands of quiet kindnesses. In many of our most disadvantaged communities it is the churches that provide warmth, food, friendship and support for individuals who have fallen on the worst of times. The homeless, those in the grip of alcoholism or drug addiction, individuals with undiagnosed mental health problems and those overwhelmed by multiple crises are helped, in innumerable ways, by Christians. Churches provide debt counselling, marriage guidance, childcare, English language lessons, after-school clubs, food banks, emergency accommodation and, sometimes most importantly of all, someone to listen.'[30]

Canon J. John said, "Western civilisation is unquestionably Christian. It is a slight embarrassment to the adherents of atheism or agnosticism that the very values that they uphold are Christian. To say that is not, of course, to deny that the roots of Christian ethics lie in the Jewish faith or to ignore the fact that some of our values are affirmed by other faiths. Yet much that is prized in Western culture – the right to free speech, the value of every individual, the recognition of love as the highest virtue, the commitment to charity and many other values – all come from the Christian faith. True, Christians have not always lived up to these values, but many have and their expression of the faith has shaped the world that we are happy to live in...There is a naive view that all human beings are fundamentally nice people and that any external morality is utterly unnecessary. Recent events have demonstrated that there are very different codes and belief systems in operation and some of them are really not very nice at all."[31]

Does all religious expression and belief lead to public welfare? Not in Britain or elsewhere. By allowing radical Islamists to enter Europe in the cause of absolute tolerance of all things, Western governments laid the foundations for the rise of a new form of anti-Semitism. In 2015, a report found that anti-Semitic attacks the year before doubled in Britain and are on the rise throughout Europe. Britain's Home Secretary Theresa May said, "I never thought I would see the day when members of the Jewish community in the United Kingdom would say they were fearful of remaining here."[32] In the same year an Islamist massacre took place in France, which targeted satirists and Jews.

Journalist Rod Liddle pondered what accounts for the rise in attacks against Jews? He wrote: 'I think the giveaway, though, is some of the graffiti which accompanies these attacks: Allahu Akbar! Jihad! Stuff like that. It's obvious...there is a strain of anti-Semitism running through Islam, and a mistrust or even loathing of Jews is firmly rooted within both our Muslim communities and in Muslim countries from Turkey to the Indonesian archipelago. This does not mean for a moment that all Muslims are anti-Semites, and nor of course should that conclusion be drawn.'[33]

One respected moderate British Muslim journalist wrote on the subject: 'It pains me to have to admit this but anti-Semitism isn't just tolerated in some sections of the British Muslim community; it's routine and commonplace. Any Muslims reading this article – if they are honest with themselves – will know instantly what I am referring to. It's our dirty little secret. You could call it the banality of Muslim anti-Semitism. I can't keep count of the number of Muslims I have come across – from close friends and relatives to perfect strangers – for whom weird and wacky anti-Semitic conspiracy theories are the default explanation for a range of national and international events...we're not all anti-Semites. But, as a community, we do have a 'Jewish problem.' There is no point pretending otherwise.'[34]

Chapter Thirty-Two

Apostasy and Conversion

Christians in Britain, Europe and the United States now live in a pluralized society of multiple beliefs and unbelief. If the coming Christian awakening which leads towards the end times (Joel 2:28-32), does not see the vast majority of secular individuals and immigrant citizens, plus their descendants converted to faith in Jesus Christ, then the age of Christian nations and the renewal of their covenants with God may be finished.

In many ways, history tells us that even the 'Christian nations' of the past have been undermined by unbelief and disobedience, and in that sense, were not truly 'Christian.' William Wilberforce wrote a book about real Christianity by contrast to the nominal faith in his age.[1] If such circumstances prevail, as in times past, we will be returning to the times of the apostles, where Christianity was a minority religion, amongst a sea of religions and unbelief.

What surprised me in the book of *Confessions* by St Augustine is that he experienced the same difficulties of being a Christian in a culture which was similar in its hostility to Christianity as today. There were many diverse faiths, sceptics, cynics, doubters, discouragers, apostates and a strong culture which pulled on him, "seeking unreal happiness." Many tried to undermine the authority of Scripture and challenged how he believed in it. He confessed, "We lived seduced and seducing, deceived and deceiving, in divers lusts; openly, by sciences which they call liberal; secretly, with a false-named religion; here proud, there superstitious, everywhere vain. Here hunting after the emptiness of popular praise...for what am I to myself without Thee, but a guide to mine own downfall?"

Now that our Christian nations have become pluralized, they can either experience a great Holy Spirit inspired revival and the masses will find Jesus Christ, or the multi-faith pluralization and secularisation will deepen, towards the age of the antichrist. The challenge for Christianity can be viewed as an end to the Christian era, or a new opportunity for evangelism and revival awakening. If a great majority of Western immigrant families are converted in a Christian awakening, it may not necessarily lead to a peaceful transition from one faith to another. The vast majority of Muslim nations have made it illegal for Muslims to convert to another faith, and the view that any Muslim who changes his or her faith should be punished has been imported into the West.

Twenty-three majority Islamic nations have laws which make apostasy a crime. Punishments range from possible execution, a prison term, to being 'culturally shamed' and rejected by society. State punishment for apostasy in Islamic nations is a violation of universal human rights, and revokes individual freedom of faith and conscience – but it continues worldwide almost unchallenged and mostly unreported by the West. In Sudan, the law states: 'Whoever is guilty of apostasy is invited to repent over a period to be determined by the tribunal. If he persists in his apostasy and was not recently converted to Islam, he will be put to death.'[2] Meriam Ibrahim is the most famous Sudanese woman who was sentenced to death for apostasy from Islam in May 2014. She escaped the country in July after an international outcry, having been forced to give birth in chains.[3]

When I was in the Middle East, the local Christians explained what it is like living in a Muslim nation. One said to me, "When you call the police because you have been robbed, the first question you are asked is, 'Are you a Muslim?' And when I reply, 'No,' the police treat me as the criminal and I must pay the Muslim thief for making an accusation against him." In Malaysia, which presents itself as a modern metropolitan nation, I was told by Christians they never share the gospel with Muslims because they will be arrested. Article 11 of Malaysia's Constitution grants theoretical freedom of religion, but in practice many Malaysian states enforce Islamic laws. Laws in the Malaysian states of Kelantan and Terengganu make apostasy in Islam a crime punishable with death, while laws in Perak, Malacca, Sabah, and Pahang declare apostasy by Muslims as a crime punishable with jail terms.

This may all seem a long way from the West, but immigrant communities come from this tradition, and some bring it with them. Pakistan is notorious for treating Christian citizens as second-class and under Article 295-C of its penal code, Pakistani Muslims who feel their religious feelings have been hurt, directly or indirectly for any reason by another Pakistani citizen, can accuse them of blasphemy and open a criminal case against them. Many Muslims abhor this intolerance, but are fearful for standing up for non-Muslims because they can be labelled as an enemy.

Islamabad based think-tank, the Center for Research and

Security Studies explains there has been a surge in accusations of insulting Islam, resulting in non-Muslims languishing 'for years in jail without trial because lawyers are too afraid to defend them.'[4] In any dispute, a Muslim can accuse a non-Muslim of blasphemy to help their case because, 'Blasphemy carries the death penalty in Pakistan' and many of 'the accused are often lynched.'[5] One Pakistani journalist explained how two young girls 'were tortured by a mob of religious fanatics because their Christian mother was accused of blasphemy.'[6] A few weeks later it was reported that: 'A Christian couple in Pakistan have been beaten to death by an angry crowd.'[7]

With more than a million people with Pakistani heritage living in the U.K., what happens if only 0.1 percent bring this aspect of their culture with them? Dr Michael Nazir-Ali, a Christian born in Pakistan has warned of the rising number of attacks against converts from Islam, now taking place in Britain. One research project found up to three thousand converts from Islam to Christianity have suffered persecution. Nissar Hussein, speaking to Channel 4's Dispatches, which investigated violence and intimidation of former Muslims, explains that he was forced to move home after more than a decade of almost daily abuse and violence from local Muslims in Bradford. He had his property smashed and the words, 'Christian dog' put on his front gate. "They told me categorically had I been in an Islamic country, i.e. Pakistan, the Middle East, that they would actually be the first to chop off my head," he said.[8]

Patrick Sookhdeo, director of the Barnabas Fund, which studies persecution said, "I think the situation is worsening in the U.K. because we are moving towards parallel communities – I don't like to use the word 'ghettoisation.' Muslims feel abandoning their religion is like a betrayal."[9] Nazir-Ali said of Muslim leaders, "It's not for me to put words into their mouths, but I would look to them to uphold basic civil liberties, including the right for people to believe what they wish to believe and even to change their beliefs if they wish to do so."[10]

In Britain, converts from Islam have already been hospitalised and the police have ignored cases, because of fear of upsetting these communities. The first publicised safe-house for converts from Islam was established in Britain in 2014 and it is thought several thousands of former Muslims are at risk.[11] Due to the nature of the problem, statistics are hard to find, but I have met a former Muslim who was hospitalised for his conversion and the police said, "There is not enough evidence to investigate the incident." When this man spoke with some young Muslims and explained his conversion they said, "You deserve to die," and spat on him, calling him an "infidel." Someone has to ask, who radicalised these apparently secular young British Muslims and taught them to embrace hate? The answer is found in radical foreign Muslim preachers, entering the West as sheep on paper, and importing the extremist teaching of wolves, alongside 'the crusader victim' mentality into moderate Muslim communities. They bring with them systemic anti-Semitism and align the Koran with the hostile foreign policies of Middle Eastern Muslim nations. Powers to exclude hate preachers came in decades too late.[12]

On 9 October 2012, Malala Yousafzai was shot by the Taliban in Pakistan for campaigning for girls to be allowed an education. In the West she is hailed as a hero, becoming the youngest person to be awarded the Nobel Peace Prize. Meanwhile, in her birth nation of Pakistan, she is regarded by many as an enemy to Islam, because in the view of many Pakistani Muslims, Islam dictates women can only be daughters, wives and mothers, and they do not need a formal education for that.[13] Education officials in Pakistan have banned Malala's book from 40,000 schools because it "does not show enough respect for Islam," and complained that the book mentioned how non-Muslim minorities are attacked in Pakistan.[14] Seventy percent of all females in Pakistan cannot read or write, and according to the UN, forty-five percent of all women in the Arab world are illiterate.[15]

How is hatred spreading from one generation to the next? The BBC interviewed one head Pakistani teacher, who cites Osama Bin Laden as one of his heroes and teaches this to his students. He is responsible for training five thousand young people each year. He said, "We share the same objectives as the Taliban, but we don't offer military training. We work on minds. The Taliban are more hands-on. We teach about the principles of Jihad. It's up to students if they want to get military training after they leave here. We don't discourage them." One of his students, who is just one of eighteen new imams sent out to preach this message, said to the BBC, "The Taliban ran Afghanistan very well. They created a just society that was the envy of the world. We all have the same aim – to create a society in which there is no corruption. We want justice for everyone. The only way to achieve that is through Sharia law and an Islamic state."[16] What happens when naive young men like this come to the West and preach to Western-born moderate Muslims? Radicalisation!

The BBC's religious affairs correspondent, Caroline Wyatt, in 2014 wrote: 'Across much of the globe, at the start of the 21st century, religion is once again a matter of life and death – quite literally in Iraq and Syria, while elsewhere, admitting or defending your faith can land you in jail...of the 196 nations surveyed, between 2012 and 2014, one report concluded that religious freedom was compromised in 116, where religious minorities experienced persecution, violence and systematic discrimination.' Why she asked, is it 'that violence or intolerance in the name of religion is staging such a dramatic comeback in much of the Middle East, Asia and parts of Africa?...The religion editor of the *Times* Literary Supplement, Rupert Shortt, in his book *Christianophobia*, points to the politicisation of Islam, and the growing conservatism of some of the faithful that have made it progressively harder for Christians and Muslims to live side by side in many countries including Nigeria, Iraq, Syria and Egypt.'[17]

If Islam wants to be known as a religion that stands for justice and peaceful coexistence, its imams must begin to act to protect the rights of non-Muslims in Muslim lands. Intolerance and aggression against non-Muslims and of Sunnis against Shiites is rising exponentially in the Middle East, and spreading to the nations. If these views are spreading in Muslim nations, what happens when traditional Islamic views are imported into Britain, Europe and America? Are Western Muslims being encouraged to integrate by their leaders or to segregate? Do they learn a respect for the rule of law or Sharia law? Is democracy being embraced or undermined? Are there freedoms of speech and religious liberty, or restrictions?

One study found some Muslim children have been withdrawn from music lessons in the U.K. because they are considered 'un-Islamic.' The Muslim Council of Britain admitted music lessons were likely to be unacceptable to around ten percent of the Muslim population.[18] One report found that up to eight thousand Muslim girls have disappeared from schools in one city alone in England, because of fears that a Western education will undermine the influence of Islam in their lives.[19] Tragically these views are similar to those of Boko Haram, the Islamic terrorist group that kidnapped over two hundred school girls in Nigeria and has killed thousands in terror attacks. Boko Haram means 'Western education is forbidden,' but the real name of Boko Haram is 'People Committed to the Prophet's Teachings for Propagation and Jihad.' They believe they are fully embracing the teaching of the Koran, whilst they think secular Muslims have ignored or compromised its teaching.

It is certainly true that many Western Muslims find the views of Islamist groups repugnant, but what happens when immigrant populations live in segregation and don't have any way to 'buy into' Western beliefs about liberty, because they don't have the ability to communicate with people outside of their community? Official figures found there are almost 800,000 people living in England and Wales with little or no English, with more than half not working.[20] Journalist Leo McKinstry said, "Real integration is impossible when ethnic groups are encouraged to cling to customs, practices, even languages from their homeland... Female emancipation has been set back by misogyny imported from the developing world, as reflected by honour killings, forced marriages and female genital mutilation. There are estimated to be 66,000 cases of such torture in Britain yet not a single prosecution has been mounted. In the name of liberal tolerance, vicious intolerance is flourishing in our midst, repressing free speech and promoting dangerous extremism.'[21]

We may be praying for a Christian awakening, but Leonard Ravenhill reminds us that Pentecost led to the intolerant putting preachers in prison. It gave the disciples empowerment and banishment. It led to favour with God and hatred by men. Pentecost led to miracles and obstacles. Paul and Wesley saw revival and riots.[22] Christians pray for peace, not all faiths do.

U.S. Governor Piyush Bobby Jindal, whose parents came from Punjab, a region in India where Sikhs and Muslims experienced conflict, explained that if Islam is a religion committed to peace, its leaders must move beyond the rhetoric in interviews and make that commitment clear to all who attend their mosques. He argued that if Islam is going to modernise peacefully, its leaders must destroy the cult of suicide bombers, speak out against Jihadists and undermine the terrorist views about destroying democracy to build an Islamic state based upon Sharia law. "Here is my challenge to Muslim leaders," he said, "because Islam has a problem. Now I hope and believe that the vast majority of Muslims don't agree with the actions taken by these radical, terrorist, murdering thugs. But here is what Muslim leaders need to do. It's not enough to condemn acts of violence. They've got to condemn the individuals. They need to clearly say these are not martyrs. They are not going to enjoy a reward in the afterlife. We shouldn't be glorifying them. Instead, they should be saying very clearly these fools are going straight to hell."[23]

It has been argued that the duel philosophy of some Islamic leaders of claiming rights in the West, whilst ignoring the denial of rights to non-Muslims in Islamic nations must end. Why have Muslim leaders in the Middle East been quiet about the mass expulsion of non-Muslims from the region? If Osama Bin Laden was not a Muslim, why do polls show many Muslims respect him, and why did the U.S. do everything possible to assure Muslims that he was buried at sea according to Muslim tradition?[24] If he was not a Muslim, why assure all he was?[25] The contradiction is self-evident. If terrorists like Osama Bin Laden are acting contrary to Islam, they must be denounced by Muslim leaders, and all their material must be destroyed. Those who call these terrorists martyrs or Islamic heroes must be called to account.

Several undercover investigations have highlighted how books and DVDs which contain teaching similar to Osama Bin Laden's are easily available in some Western mosques. Views expressed include advocating violent Jihad against infidels and predicting that an army of Muslims will arise against the non-Muslims in England.[26] One leader speaking on marriage with girls before puberty, said, "The prophet Muhammad practically outlined the rules regarding marriage prior to puberty. With his practice, he clarified what is permissible; and that is why we shouldn't have any issues about an older man marrying a younger woman, which is looked down upon by this society today. But we know that Prophet Mohammed practised it, it wasn't abuse or exploitation, it was marriage."[27]

Whilst being secretly filmed, another shared how Muslims can use rights given to them in a democracy to eventually overthrow it, "They will fight in the cause of Allah. I encourage all of you...to begin to cultivate ourselves for the time that is fast approaching, where the tables are going to turn and the Muslims are going to be in the position of being uppermost in strength."[28] One leader said, "You are in a situation in which you have to live like a state within a state, until you take over."[29]

Meanwhile, a minority of Muslims have urged others to boycott democracy, to wait for the time when they have supremacy and can enforced Sharia law on all. In the last general election, in Grangetown, Cardiff, which is a predominantly Muslim neighbourhood of the Welsh capital, a series of posters were placed around the area. They stated: 'Democracy is a system whereby man violates the right of Allah,' and they urged Muslims to boycott the election.[30]

The problems inside Islamic communities in the West are more than cultural, because they are found in a variety of cultures where Islam is practiced worldwide. In the U.K., on the subject of all women being covered, one preacher said, "By the age of ten, it becomes an obligation on us to force her to wear hijab and if she doesn't wear hijab, we hit her."[31] In 'moderate' Malaysia, the same teaching is prominent. In Kuala Lumpur, the police were called to investigate an incident of 'molestation' because a Korean band was videoed on stage embracing their teenage female fans. The incident triggered a nationwide debate about all girls needing to wear the hijab and their need to be isolated; whilst the teenagers in question were urged to report to their local police station to give account for possible violations of Sharia law.[32] In Britain, one Muslim leader was filmed undercover praising the Sharia police in Saudi Arabia, as reports of unofficial U.K. Sharia police increase. He said, "They send the police and they say, 'Well, if you don't come for prayer and close your shop, we will arrest you. But if you don't, then we have to bring the punishment on you, you will be killed.' "[33]

Moderate and peaceful Muslims have spoken of their dismay at the radicalisation of some Muslims within their own communities, including more extreme views that all women should wear a veil, burqua or chador. The Arabic word hijab can be translated into the word veil. The Koran does not mention the hijab, burqua or chador, but imams who demand women should be covered call upon two verses from the Koran. 'And say that the believing women that they should lower their gaze and guard their modesty that they should not display their beauty' (Sura 24 (An-Nur), ayat 30-31, Koran), and, 'O Prophet! Tell thy wives and thy daughters and the women of the believers to draw their cloaks close round them. That will be better, so that they may be recognised and not harassed' (Sura 33 (Al-Ahzab), ayah 59, Koran).

Why do more Muslim women in the West feel the need to wear the hijab, burqua or chador? In Iran, women are punished for not covering their hair. In article 638 of the Islamic Penal Code it states: 'Women, who appear in public places and roads without wearing an Islamic hijab, shall be sentenced to ten days to two months' imprisonment or a fine of fifty thousand to five hundred Rials.' Previous to the 1978–79 Iranian Islamic Revolution, black full body chadors were reserved for women to wear at funerals and during periods of mourning, now they are forced into them daily. Brave Muslim women campaigners have said forcing them to wear these items makes women "effectively to disappear from a young age," it, "strips them of their individuality" and "alienates women under the guise of religious freedom."

The Geneva Summit for Human Rights and Democracy gave Iranian-born Masih Alinejad its women's rights award for "giving a voice to the voiceless, and stirring the conscience of humanity to support the struggle of Iranian women, for basic human rights, freedom and equality." She founded a Facebook campaign which encourages Iranian women to experience freedom and has attracted over 800,000 likes. Masih explained, "From seven-year-old schoolgirls to 70-year-old grandmothers, women in Iran are all forced to wear the hijab."[34] On the page women are free to comment on what it feels like to be forced into oppressive black clothing by government. One said, "As I was driving, I realised that my headscarf slipped off and the wind blew through my hair. That is when it dawned on me that this headscarf had so much taken away my simple liberty as a woman. Being a woman is not a crime and I simply want to be myself."[35]

In many predominantly Muslim nations, devout Islamists rule over moderate Muslims and non-Muslims alike, by adopting policies which use fear, intimidation and the power of the state to force their will on all. In these nations, moderate Muslims feel unable to argue against this, as the Islamists cite verses from the Koran and examples from the life of the founder of Islam to justify their actions.

In Malaysia the Pan-Malaysian Islamic Party plans to implement harsher Islamic laws in the province of Kelantan. These laws restrict most rights and prescribe punishments such as 'public beatings, stoning, amputation and public execution.'[36] The journalist Aisyah Tajuddin made a light hearted video about the issue and the response included death and rape threats, with people saying, "Those who insult the laws of Allah, their blood is halal for killing." One terrified journalist urged the police to investigate those who threatened violence, saying, "I am positively terrified that these crazy, rape-frenzied people are actually the majority in my country." The police then arrested her and investigated her for blasphemy. The police reminded all that the country's top policeman has warned that any criticism of Islamic policies will not be tolerated, saying, "Be careful about speaking about something. Don't speak words that will invite [us] to take action. Dare to speak, dare to face the consequences."[37]

Whilst Western values are undermined in the West in the cause of unrequited tolerance, Christians worldwide are suffering from profound rising persecution. According to the International Society for Human Rights, Christians today are now the victims of eighty percent of all acts of religious discrimination.[38] While Muslims are free to practice their religion peacefully in the West, Christians, Jews and others are not free in predominantly Muslim nations. Pope Francis and Patriarch Bartholomew issued a joint statement in 2014, to express their dismay at the expulsions and persecution of Christians in the Middle East. They declared, "We cannot resign ourselves to a Middle East without Christians, who have professed the name of Jesus there for 2,000 years...many of our brothers and sisters are being persecuted and have been forced violently from their homes."[39] Journalist Louis Raphael Sako wrote: 'This exodus and its causes, largely ignored in the West, constitute a growing crisis with both humanitarian and security implications. In most of these countries, Islamist extremists see Christians as an obstacle to their plans.'[40]

Whilst Western leaders are often politically correct, side stepping serious issues, trying not to offend Muslim minorities, Christians in the Middle East are experiencing the hot, sharp-end of a very real persecution – so real, that they feel the need to flee, abandoning their two thousand years of heritage.

The future of the West has also never been as uncertain as it is today, with such diverse views and beliefs having profound influence, and spreading. If Western Muslims choose to stand up against hate speech and the restriction of rights, full integration may be possible, with democracy and the rule of law flourishing; but if moderate Muslims remain silent, then Islam in the West may follow the path of Turkey and become more radical and influential. One poll of Muslim opinion in Britain found positive trends that the majority feel loyal to Britain and its laws. It also revealed trends of growing extremism. Only 49% of British Muslims polled felt they could agree with this statement: 'Muslim clerics who preach that violence against the West can be justified are out of touch with mainstream opinion.' 27% agreed they had some 'sympathy for the motives' behind the 2015 terror attacks in Paris. 8% agreed that: 'I know Muslims who feel strongly sympathetic towards people fighting for IS and al-Qaeda.'[41]

Despondency in Islamic nations and radicalisation has also had an unexpected effect. Today, more Muslims than ever are becoming Christians worldwide. One Islamic leader spoke on Al-Jazeera about the decline of Islam in Africa, and other regions, saying, "Every year, six million Muslims convert to Christianity."[42] Many Muslims report having dreams and visions of Jesus.[43]

One former Iranian revolutionary and Islamic terrorist has made it his mission to share how faith in Jesus transformed him and can do the same for all. Daniel Shayesteh said, "I had been told for thirty-two years that Christianity was the worst religion in the world. From childhood I had always been taught that Islam is the winner, Islam is the best, without any deeper logic about it. Islam must dominate the world and to ensure that, we must call people to follow Islam. If they do not listen, we must threaten and attack them through terrorism. That was my mindset. That is what all radical Muslims in the world think, and that's why they are practicing terrorism ..Many times I cried, 'Allah, I want to kill Christians, I want to kill Jews.' We planned a lot of things, evil things for the Christian world, cruel things for the Jewish world. It is by the grace of God that I am here."[44]

Daniel Shayesteh explained that Islamists encourage hatred in Muslims, feed-off this anger and then manipulate it for their causes. The result of this sequence is a generation of seething, angry young Muslims, who feel at war with everything, including Muslims from other traditions. "Many people in Islamic countries, especially young Muslims, are exhausted and overwhelmed," he said. "They are tired. They want to take shelter in a peaceful belief. But if you do not have peace with God, you will not be able to have peace with others, no matter how much you would love to. So, with Christianity, there is an open door for us to touch the hearts of millions of Muslims all over the world."[45]

Christians who work sharing their faith with Muslims tell us that the best Christian witness is one filled with love and shared in deep peace. Hostile arguments feed into the agenda of Islamists and their hate preachers, but Christian compassion, grace and love, with understanding, opens the door for Him who walks in the sandals of the gospel of peace. Whilst truth forces us to understand the reality of life in the Muslim world, the Christian guiding principle is this: 'Walk in love' (Ephesians 5:1).

Chapter Thirty-Three

Christian Heritage in Peril

The Rev. Duncan Campbell witnessed the beginning of the apostasy of the Church in Britain, Europe and America, quoting Isaiah, saying, "To the law and to the testimony: if they speak not according to this word, it is because there is no light in them" (Isaiah 8:20).

When faced with Christian apostasy, the Baptist preacher C.H. Spurgeon (1834-1892) declared, "It is time that somebody should spring his rattle and call attention to the way in which God is being robbed of His glory, and man of his hope. It now becomes a serious question how far those who abide by the faith, once delivered to the saints, should fraternise with those who have turned aside to another gospel. Christian love has its claims and divisions are to be shunned as grievous evils; but how far are we justified in being in confederacy with those who are departing from the truth? It is a difficult question to answer so as to keep the balance of the duties...numbers of easy-minded people wink at error, so long as it is committed by a clever man and a good-natured brother, who has so many fine points about him. Let each believer judge for himself; but, for our part, we have put on a few fresh bolts to our door, and we have given orders to keep the chain up; for, under colour of begging the friendship of the servant, there are those about who aim at robbing the Master."

Leonard Ravenhill also gave a warning of how the apostate church and the living Church of Christ began to co-exist side by side, just as Jesus taught it would. The Lord said, "The Kingdom of Heaven is like a man who sowed good seed in his field; but while men slept, his enemy came and sowed tares among the wheat and went his way...the servants said to him, 'Do you want us then to go and gather them up?' But he said, 'No, lest while you gather up the tares you also uproot the wheat with them' " (Matthew 13:24-25, 28-29).

Ravenhill asked churches to examine their hearts and witness. He suggested there are many types of churches that do not honour God. There are those with stern ritualism, dry formalism, leaky liberalism or stark sensationalism, and others filled with incense or with nonsense. He warns that too many Sunday morning religious rituals add up to the tragically misnamed thing we call 'worship.'[1]

Does our moral and spiritual compass point towards God's will and the revelation in His Word, or are they magnetised towards the pull of the world? What about the Great Commission? Have we forgotten the whole of history is centred on the death and resurrection of Jesus Christ? Have we forgotten that an innocent Man was crucified for the sins of the world? That Man was like no other, He was God, invading His creation in disguise.

Are we living for the completion of Jesus' final command, or have we been distracted with temporal pleasure? Did God give us life and invest so much in us, so we could build our own little kingdoms or spiritual empires? Are we here to consume, or to be consumed with Him? Are we sold out to the world, or possessed by the Person of the Holy Spirit? Do we live for His Kingdom to come and for His will to be done?

The Bible reveals a good God of justice, a God who warns, exhorts and encourages. The God of Holy Scripture tells us plainly what will happen if we obey or disobey. The ultimate will of God is to express His love to all, by forgiving all who choose to put their faith in Jesus' death and resurrection, and revealing His good, pleasing and perfect plan for their lives (Romans 10:9-13, 12:1-2).

God finds no pleasure in judgment, nor in punishing people for their sins of omission or commission, but He is just and justice demands action. ' "For I have no pleasure in the death of one who dies," says the Lord God, "therefore turn and live!" ' (Ezekiel 18:32). It is not God's will for any to perish (2 Peter 3:9), but many will reject God's narrow way and choose an eternity without Him. Jesus said, "Enter by the narrow gate; for wide is the gate and broad is the way that leads to destruction, and there are many who go in by it. Because narrow is the gate and difficult is the way which leads to life, and there are few who find it" (Matthew 7:13-14).

What does this mean for the future of Britain? Constitutionally, historically, institutionally and culturally Britain is a Christian nation. But do all agree? In 2014, fifty leading scientists, writers and academics signed a joint public statement objecting to the characterisation of Britain as a Christian country.[2] The response to this statement for many was a sense of shock and horror, that just fifty of Britain's elite believed they had the right to try to re-write history and re-define a nation, out of which 33.2 million people voluntarily identified themselves as Christian in the last census!

In Britain, journalist Harry Cole declared: 'The irony that it was

Easter, top and tailed by two bank holidays where their entire 'non-Christian country' shuts down for 96 hours in celebration of the resurrection of Christ was lost on these modern day Doubting Thomases. No doubt they will resurrect their arguments when Christmas arrives...leaving aside the fact that 59% of the U.K. population self-defines as Christians, we need only look at our institutions and state structure to see how bizarre this row has been. England has an Established Church. English bishops sit in our Parliament. A glance around the rim of our £1 coin will show you that our Head of State has another far more interesting title – Defender of the Faith. The Left weren't so snooty about the Archbishop of Canterbury, our state-declared spiritual leader, when he was defending foodbanks...we have a Constitutional framework, legal system and legislature that is built around Judeo-Christian values. Almost every single bank holiday we have in this country is to mark some sort of Christian festival. Tens of thousands of children are educated every day in church-supported schools, and what is the first word of the national anthem again? [God] Some of Cameron's fiercest critics over the weekend have also been amongst the loudest supporters for the NHS. They might not want to self-declare as Christians any more, but the ethos at the heart of the system is one of Christian compassion. Perhaps they should remind themselves of Andy Burnham's favourite Nye Bevan quote: 'The NHS is a little piece of Christianity.' I say all this as a lapsed agnostic, open to the idea of a disestablished church and booting the bishops out of the Lords. But to deny we are a Christian country is progressive revisionism of the highest order. Some people do not like the fact that we are a Christian country – but they should say so, rather than pretend otherwise. Attempting to rewrite history and ignore our heritage, as well as our current governing structure, is at best delusional. At worst it shows metropolitan liberal society attempting to cleanse the parts of Britain it finds distasteful.'[3]

The effective influence of Christianity upon Britain has shaped a nation, where Christian tradition and belief are everywhere. Yet, without any doubt, there has been a sharp decline of Christianity in Britain and the result is self-evident. In the major censuses of 2001 and 2011, in England and Wales, respondents provided information regarding their religious beliefs. In 2001, seventy-two percent said they were Christian, a decade later only fifty-nine percent declared an allegiance. During the same period followers of Islam jumped from 3 percent to 5, whilst the number of Hindus at 1.5 percent and Sikhs, Jews and Buddhist remained similar, at about one percent. Nevertheless, the religious question was voluntary and over four million citizens did not provide any details – how many were Christians that no longer felt they could trust government with their religious convictions?

If Christian values are being eroded, at least the Constitutional and cultural nature of Britain is still alive. The Queen retains the title Head of State and Supreme Governor of the Church of England and is the Defender of the Faith. Those who say Britain is not Christian, have chosen to snub history, disregard heritage and the Constitution, the titles of the monarch and the tens of millions who identified themselves as Christian in the census.

The Defender of the Faith, Queen Elizabeth II, is also the Constitutional monarch of fifteen of the fifty-three member states in the Commonwealth of Nations. Elizabeth II is the Queen of Britain, Canada, Australia, New Zealand, Jamaica, Barbados, the Bahamas, Grenada, Papua New Guinea, Solomon Islands, Tuvalu, Saint Lucia, Saint Vincent and the Grenadines, Belize, Antigua and Barbuda, and Saint Kitts and Nevis. However, the Queen's religious role differs in each nation. In all realms except one, the Queen is sovereign, "By the Grace of God," a phrase which forms a part of her official title within these states.

In Canada, the United Kingdom and New Zealand, the Queen is the "Defender of the Faith," as part of the royal title, and the sovereign is anointed as such. However only in Britain does the Queen actively partake a role in the Church. As Supreme Governor of the Church of England, she officially appoints bishops and archbishops, on the advice of the prime minister, who considers the names selected by a Church Commission. Afterwards they act as her Lords Spiritual, the twenty-six bishops in the House of Lords. In Scotland, the Queen swears an Oath to uphold and protect the Church of Scotland, and sends a Lord High Commissioner as her representative to meetings of the Church's General Assembly, when she is not personally in attendance.

In the future, when Queen Elizabeth II is no longer reigning, the change will inevitably trigger Constitutional debate and reform in many nations, and the historic links will probably be broken. Presently, the official titles of Queen Elizabeth in many nations include an expression of faith in God. In Canada: 'Elizabeth the Second, by the Grace of God, of the United Kingdom, Canada and Her other Realms and Territories Queen, Head of the Commonwealth, Defender of the Faith.' In Australia: 'Elizabeth the Second, by the Grace of God, Queen of Australia and Her other Realms and Territories, Head of the Commonwealth.' In New Zealand: 'Elizabeth the Second, by the Grace of God,

Queen of New Zealand and Her Other Realms and Territories, Head of the Commonwealth, Defender of the Faith.' Her Majesty the Queen is also recognised as Head of the Commonwealth in India, Ghana, Cyprus, Tanzania, Uganda, Kenya, Zambia, Malawi, Singapore, Botswana, Guyana, Nauru, Gambia, Sierra Leone, Bangladesh, Sri Lanka, Malta, Trinidad and Tobago, Seychelles, Dominica, Kiribati, Vanuatu, Maldives, Namibia, Mauritius, South Africa, Fiji, Pakistan, Cameroon and Mozambique, together with the Federation of Malaysia, Lesotho, Swaziland, Tonga, Samoa and Brunei.

True Christianity can never be tied to a monarch and yet, the Bible points to the importance of national covenants made with God. If these covenants are broken, there will continue to be a further separation between the Christian nations that made these covenants, and the God who blessed them in their obedience. In Britain's history it seems that the nation has been blessed or troubled, depending on its faithfulness to its covenant with God. Britain's historic covenant with God is transparent in the law of the land, and it is not the only nation that has made a covenant with God.

Chapter Thirty-Four

We want it Now!

In Britain and the United States there is a growing consensus among Christians that something has drastically gone wrong in our nations. When the elite tear down another ancient Christian foundation it is celebrated as a new milestone towards equality, but at the same time, the general population sense that our nations are becoming darker and less free.

We have removed the ancient landmarks of our forefathers, ignored the covenants they made with God, and rejected the values which God loves and cherishes. According to Scripture, God will bless a people or nation that serves His will and purposes. 'Good and upright is the Lord...the humble He guides in justice and the humble He teaches His way. All the paths of the Lord are mercy and truth, to such as keep His covenant and His testimonies...He himself shall dwell in prosperity and his descendants shall inherit the earth. The secret of the Lord is with those who fear Him and He will show them His covenant' (Psalm 25:9-14).

The Bible indicates that when a nation serves the Lord it will find justice, liberty, protection and prosperity, but when it strays, God will give His people many warnings to awaken them out of slumber and sleep, to bring them back to repentance, so He can save them from the disasters they are making. 'Knowing the time, that now it is high time to awake out of sleep' (Romans 13:11); 'Therefore He says: "Awake, you who sleep, arise from the dead and Christ will give you light" ' (Ephesians 5:14).

We are also warned that the more God blesses us, the more we tend to trust in our own strength, might and confidence, until God allows the rug to be pulled out from under our feet. God said, "I spoke to you in your prosperity, but you said, 'I will not hear.' This has been your manner from your youth, that you did not obey My voice. The wind shall eat up all your rulers and your lovers shall go into captivity; surely then you will be ashamed and humiliated for all your wickedness" (Jeremiah 22:21-22).

We learn from biblical history that one of God's judgments on nations who refuse to repent, is a failure of leadership and the 'captivity' of strength – the wealth which provides power. For the past five centuries, many Western nations have had dynamic economies, shaping the world, enabling the West to project power all over the planet. Britain was able to dismantle the global slave trade network because it had the world's largest navy and an economy which sustained it. Since 1815, some suggest earlier, the English speaking Protestant nations have been the world's pre-eminent powers, being able to defend liberty on multiple fronts, all over the globe. From 1815 to 1914, Britain dominated the world and continued shaping it into the Second World War. From 1943 till 1990 the United States was one of the world's two superpowers, and from 1991 to 2003, America was the world's only superpower.

There have been some terrible failures of foreign policy and yet, why has Britain and the United States been able to project power worldwide, by defeating dictators, restraining tyrants and fighting for liberty? The answer is the economy, grounded in our religious convictions based on the Bible, which led to us cherishing liberty and the rule of law. A prosperous economy pays for our defence and encourages the spread of liberty worldwide.

Britain's economic might from 1700-1929 and the United States from 1941-2003, enabled both nations to protect their liberties, by taking the fight to their enemies. As Scripture states: 'Your descendants shall possess the gate of their enemies' (Genesis 22:17). But has this ability now been fundamentally undermined?

Scripture states God 'has pleasure in the prosperity of His servant' (Psalm 35:27), and the prosperity of the English speaking peoples has no parallel in history; but what happens if we are no longer His servants and do not serve His purposes in the world?

The Bible says a sign of God's blessing is lending to the nations and the sign of Divine displeasure is debt (Deuteronomy 28:13-15, Proverbs 22:7). God said, "The alien who is among you shall rise higher and higher above you, and you shall come down lower and lower. He shall lend to you, but you shall not lend to him; he shall be the head, and you shall be the tail. Moreover, all these curses shall come upon you and pursue and overtake you, until you are destroyed, because you did not obey the voice of the Lord your God, to keep His commandments and His laws which He commanded you" (Deuteronomy 28:43-45). It seems this Scripture is already being fulfilled in our nations.

The following financial information may seem unspiritual or bleak, and yet behind the facts is a growing picture of the decline of the West, which is spiritual in nature. Secularisation and consumerism offers no other vision for life, apart from buying and spending, for the sake of it, and this lack of vision has led to a huge financial cloud smothering the West. When all people live for is to consume, borrowing to fund unaffordable lifestyles, the possible hopeful future is sacrificed for today's unfunded extravagant spending. When secularisation and consumerism rule, the national vision of playing a positive role in the world is constantly undermined by greed, deficits, debt and selfishness. Like the Emperor Nero, the West fiddles as Rome burns.

The West's most recent financial crisis in 2007/8 all started with greed, dishonesty and reckless lending. Everybody wanted more – bigger houses, more expensive cars and it became easier to borrow money, as cheap Chinese money flooded into the West. With more demand for homes, prices soared, and loans became bigger and people borrowed more based on their perceived value of their homes.

In the past, the local bank manager would check if people could afford to repay their loans before paying out. But the banks now made billions selling these mortgages onto investment banks, and the investment banks made greater profits selling shares in the mortgages, which they called 'mortgage backed securities,' and hungry investors wanted more. However, the problem was that all the safe and manageable lending was exhausted in the West, so to continue the cycle of selling more debt, or another set of, 'I Owe You' promises, the banks began lending to people who could never afford to repay, and when they sold these debts onto others, they labelled them as excellent, safe, or 'Triple A.'

All these bad debts were sold onto others so quickly that the lenders did not fear, because they became someone else's problem. Journalist Matt Frei said, "Lots of people on Wall Street knew they were toxic. In the privacy of their own offices they called it 'toxic waste,' but they didn't let on. Instead, they tied it up in shiny rapping giving their packages a fancy label 'collateralized debt obligations' and then they passed the parcel and no-one bothered to unwrap them."[1]

Meanwhile, political parties found it harder to get elected, so they began offering voters benefits for choosing them, which they could not afford. They began spending on the nation's credit card and someone else could worry about paying for it later! With so much cheap cash floating around, governments, business and individuals borrowed record amounts and went on a spending spree. "The proportion to debt and income is enormous," said BBC economics editor Robert Peston.[2]

As cheap credit flowed, billions were made which encouraged the regulators to look the other way, when they saw cracks in the 'perfect system' which had 'abolished' boom and bust. In 2002 the financial expert Robert Prechter warned, "Confidence is the only thing holding up this giant house of cards."[3] In Autumn 2006, it was becoming clear that 'Subprime Lending,' which means risky loans to people on low incomes, were turning bad very quickly. Loans marked 'Triple A,' the highest possible rating, began defaulting and nobody knew any longer which were junk loans or safe, so banks stopped lending and went broke.

On 9 October 2007, America's Dow Jones Industrial Average hit an all-time high closing at 14,164.43. Then the financial crisis hit, and by 5 March 2009 it had fallen more than fifty percent to 6,594.44.[4] Tens of millions of people worldwide lost their jobs and homes, and international companies came to bankruptcy. By the end of 2008, Robert Peston said, "If you add together corporate debt, business debt and government debt, and compare it to the national income of the U.S., or the U.K. you get three hundred percent. That's a lot of debt to clear."[5]

Banks had lent more money than their savers deposited and when debts were called, they had nothing. So they went to governments and told them that without emergency loans (paid for by the taxpayer – a bailout) they would close tomorrow. Then all the cash machines and bank accounts in the West would cease to work. Banks became what we now say, 'Too big to fail,' and a choice was presented – go back to bartering with chickens in the new Middle Ages, or pay up. As 2009 emerged, four trillion dollars had been poured into banks by governments worldwide and it rose and rose.[6] With banks no longer lending, huge multinational companies came close to bankruptcy and the taxpayer gave them a bailout.

This economic disaster enabled the privatisation of profit for the top one percent and the nationalisation of debt, failure and loss for the ninety-nine. These bailouts proved to be the biggest welfare cheque in history and when they were paid, company bosses gave themselves bonuses from the bailout.

"So in 2007 and 2008, vast numbers of loans to poor Americans went bad, U.S. house prices plummeted and banks all over the world incurred losses, sometimes devastating losses," explains Robert Peston. "The initial economic effect was a slump in consumer spending, as millions of poor Americans saw the value of their loans drop below the value of their debts, many lost their homes and vast numbers lost their jobs. The important point is that poor people have no cushion of savings to eat into when their incomes fall, so when they become poorer, they spend much less; and when millions of them spend much less – a recession is more-or-less inevitable."[7]

The recession led to lower taxes coming into governments, growing deficits, debts and higher bills on interest payments, and larger benefits bills. The response of governments was to create stimulus packages, which meant heavy government borrowing and spending, to stop the world's economy spiralling downward out of control, into another Great Depression. Thus the recovery was sponsored by massive government debts and spending.

"Now a lot of people would say you're just putting off the pain for a later date," said the financial expert Victor Mallet, "and indeed we are. What we're doing, is those governments are taking on debt to do that, and its our children and grandchildren who, presumably will have to repay that debt, in order to finance our little rescue today, which might not work, and might only put a day of reckoning off for another couple of years."[8]

Smaller nations like Greece, Ireland and Iceland had borrowed heavily during the boom years with low interest rates, which they could no longer afford to repay. The Eurozone Crisis was triggered and ten central and eastern European nations sought bailouts from their richer neighbours. With huge cuts to the public sector, which hurt the poor the most, unemployment rose to 27 percent in Greece and Spain.

A few developing nations entered the crisis with a surplus, but Britain already had half a trillion pounds of debt[9] and the United States had over twelve trillion dollars of debt![10] To maintain lifestyles that were unaffordable governments borrowed like never before in peace time, as public expenditure continued for years to exceed revenue. By 2009, the International Monetary Fund summarised the costs so far of the crisis was almost $12 trillion.[11] By 2014, the U.S. government estimated it had cost Americans alone $22 trillion.[12] Perhaps this helps us learn the Bible lesson to never to put our 'hope in wealth, which is so uncertain,' but to put our 'hope in God, who richly provides us with everything for our enjoyment" (1 Timothy 6:17). But today the West seems to put its confidence in anything but God!

This financial disaster also put Britain's and America's military spending in jeopardy, which limits our ability to defend ourselves and help bring order to the world. Today, the West is borrowing money to project power overseas, meanwhile foreign jets and submarines are breaching our defences and we can't always stop them.[13] Britain's scrapped Nimrod maritime surveillance aircraft, has led to the country being unable to see potential enemies around British waters, which is disastrous for an island nation. Meanwhile, the U.S. is borrowing at a calamitous rate to pay for a world order that it cannot afford, and if this order, established in 1945 changes, it will affect all.

Whilst plenty of money is being spent on vanity projects, tainted and unaccountable climate change fancies and special interest government spending, the money needed to defend the order and peace of the world has been slashed. General Sir Richard Shirreff, until recently the second in command in Nato's military structure said, "What we have seen in the last two decades is a form of physical and moral disarmament...we're in a very dangerous place."[14] Former Deputy Chief of the U.S. Air Force, Lt. Gen David Deptula, believes America no longer has enough combat aircraft, saying, "We have a geriatric air force."[15]

Whilst nations with no commitment to democracy, the rule of law, liberty and religious freedom are expanding their military capabilities, the West is being forced to down-size because we have wasted our prosperity and spent tomorrow's wealth. Compared to twenty years ago, Britain now has half the number of cruisers, destroyers and frigates. In addition, Britain's army may soon be the smallest it's been for two hundred and fifty years, if overall troop levels fall to just 50,000 soldiers. A report by the International Institute for Strategic Studies concludes that from 2010-2015, the up to 9 percent decrease in Britain's military defence budget 'has led to a 20 percent to 30 percent reduction in conventional capability.'

Today's recognised system of international law and order is being challenged worldwide, and the West is doing little to defend them. The West, led by the United States has embraced a declinist worldview, retreating from the world, and fearful of confronting evil abroad. American power, made globally stronger with its allies, is indispensable to world peace and to maintain stability, and yet this is now in profound decline.

The West may be weary of intervening abroad and confused by failed foreign policies, but retreating from caring for others overseas and refusing to act to protect global stability, has led to Islamists advancing, and struggles for power elsewhere. In fact, more people have been killed, exiled and made refugees during the years of disengagement from 2008-2015, then between the war years of 2001-2007. Iraqis, Syrians, Ukrainians and citizens of the South China Sea coastal nations are paying a high price for the West's withdrawal from defending international law.

One of the great problems is that the money is no longer available to properly defend the world order. Britain and America have developed combat aircraft which are so sophisticated, that they are too expensive to purchase in the numbers needed. Britain has two aircraft carriers, yet it cannot afford to buy the planes designed for them, and the carriers will not be fully operational till 2020.[16] Britain intended to obtain 14 production F-35B aircraft; the first order was slashed to just 4.[17]

America, with a huge economy, is in a far stronger position, but the same problem of overpriced aircraft persists. In 2014, the United States acquired fewer new planes in any year since 1915, whilst for the first time Russia outstripped the U.S. in fighter deliveries. When new equipment is too expensive, obsolete aircraft are maintained. America presently has a fleet of bombers which are 38 years old and fighters that average 24 years in age. Pierre Sprey, chief designer on the F-16 fighter said, "Basically we've ruined American air power."[18]

When I visited China and spoke with the kind people, it became clear that the Chinese communist government has been stirring up national pride and is creating a sense of 'enemies abroad.' To avoid questions of its own legitimacy, the regime promotes hostility towards its Asian neighbours and the United States, to take Chinese minds off its appalling abuse of human rights.

Whilst the West has to cut its defence budgets or sink into debt, China has eight aircraft carrier projects on the drawing board. Meanwhile, China has initiated 'Island Factories,' as it literally builds islands in the seas by its neighbours, to claim the region.[19] While America's Navy has 71 commissioned submarines, the Chinese has 77 principal combatant ships, 61 submarines, 55 large amphibious ships and 85 missile-equipped ships.[20]

Since 2008, the power-vacuum the United States created under a new administration has been filled by Islamists in the Middle East and North Africa, China in the seas of Asia and Russia in Eastern Europe. The world has not felt this unstable since the fall of the Soviet Union.

Our debts mean that the West may no longer be able to underpin the future peace of the world, as our nations spend tomorrow's prosperity and leave a bleak future. Ahead are decades of cuts, austerity and huge debt repayments or financial meltdown into bankruptcy. Let us not forget the biblical sign of God's blessing is lending, the sign of Divine displeasure is debt (Deuteronomy 28:13-15, Proverbs 22:7).

Britain safeguarded relative world peace from 1815 to 1914, and the U.S. from 1945 onwards, but now instability worldwide is growing. What is God saying to the West? "I spoke to you in your prosperity, but you said, 'I will not hear' " (Jeremiah 22:21).

Chapter Thirty-Five

Crisis, what Crisis?

The Great Recession beginning in 2007 led to national deficits rising, leading to Western nations borrowing extensively to pay their bills, which led to Herculean debts and interest payments. According to expert analysis, the crisis left the U.S. sixteen percent poorer than it would have been if previous growth trends were sustained and Europe seventeen percent poorer. Inequality between rich and poor grew, and a survey by the U.S. Federal Reserve showed the incomes of America's poorest twenty percent, fell eight percent between 2010 and 2013. Whilst the incomes of the richest ten percent rose ten percent.[1] Robert Peston said, "There is perhaps something slightly odd about an economic system in a democracy which channels the spoils only to the richest."[2]

The West is continuing to raise mountains of debt. By 2018, the U.S. national debt is expected to rise from $17 trillion to $23 trillion.[3] By 2022, it is estimated the U.S. could spend $1 trillion a year on interest alone, with a minimum of $700 billion.[4] In 2014, Britain's debt was £1.4 trillion.[5] By 2017-18, interest payments of £71.3 billion on Britain's national debt will eclipse the combined budget for schools and police.[6] Meanwhile, we presently have some of the lowest interest rates in history; what will happen when interest rates rise to the normal average of 3-6 percent?

How large is the mammoth debt? Let's view the numbers again:
One thousand = 1 x 1,000.
One million   = 1,000 x 1,000.
One billion   = 1,000 x 1,000,000.
One trillion   = 1,000 x 1,000,000,000.[7]

We also hear about the importance of our debt to GDP (Gross Domestic Product) ratio, reaching higher levels each year. Our GDP is the total market values of goods and services produced by workers and capital within the nation, during the given period. If our debt to GDP ratio reaches 102 percent, it means for every £1 or $1 we have earned, the government owes £/$1.02 to someone, which we have yet to earn and must pay interest on.

All this debt means that the bitter hangover of the last financial crash will be a dark cloud over our nations for decades – as long as everything goes well and our economies grow. The bigger the debts of a nation, the harder it becomes for them to be repaid, as interest payments alone creates another mountain. This is the equivalent of maxing out our credit cards and getting another set, to pay off the interest on the first set of credit cards. It took Britain sixty-one years to pay off its debt from fighting and recovering from World War Two,[8] which eventually grew to an enormous debt to GDP ratio.[9] Britain's interest payments reached thirteen percent of government spending in 1960/1.[10]

No expert can accurately predict when Britain or America will clear its debts. Britain is aiming to balance the budget and slay the deficit by 2019, but the Institute for Fiscal Studies states massive cuts will be needed to do this, and Britain has often been years behind deficit reduction plans.[11] Consequently, if plans are delayed by five years, by 2024 Britain may receive in taxes all it needs to pay its bills, and then it must continue to pay the interest, as it attempts to begin to eat into the debt itself. This means the debt mountain will grow for potentially almost a decade. Afterwards, Britain will still have to pay its huge interest bill, as it begins to try to break into the mountain of debt – little by little.[12] A very optimistic prediction is for Britain to clear its debt by 2044.[13] Some believe the debt burden is so great, a more realistic goal is 2088.[14]

The tragedy in the United States is the rising mountain of debt is being ignored by many in power and the question remains, how long can policy makers defer dealing with the problem? The United States is creating the biggest debt mountain in history, with earth's largest debt repayments, and failure to act will lead to doubling-up trouble for future generations.

In simple terms, a deficit means spending more than you have earned and Britain and the U.S. have been running a fiscal deficit for at least the last fourteen years, long before the financial crisis.[15] If the aspirational goal of balancing Britain's books by 2019 is achieved, the nation will still have run a deficit, creating huge debts, for eighteen consecutive years in a row.[16]

In the U.S. in 2013, interest payments on the national debt totalled $223 billion, or 6.23 percent of all federal outlays.[17] But when all government debts are piled together to find gross treasury costs, the U.S. paid out an estimated $421 billion in interest.[18] China is America's largest overseas creditor, holding more than $1.1 trillion in U.S. treasuries.[19]

The debt burden in the U.S. is growing fast and by 2018, interest costs on federal debt is estimated to increase by 80 percent to $741 billion, leading to almost 16 percent of the federal budget on interest payments alone.[20] Nobody is sure if or how America can pay back this giant debt. Financial expert Ronald Cooke said, "This raises an interesting question. If there is no attempt to control the amount of debt on America's balance sheet, at what point does America become a bad credit risk? And what would happen next?"[21]

When we examine fiscal history, we find that Britain's debt is a manageable nightmare,[22] but if present trends persist, America's debt could lead to financial catastrophes for the world, because, "When America sneezes the world economy catches a cold, but when America gets pneumonia, the world has a heart attack."

Politicians have hinted at the debt burden, but they do not want to create a panic because consumer 'confidence' is essential for a growing economy.[23] With short-sighted elections focussing on 'today's problems,' the leaders of today will be long retired when the full implications of the debt burden begin to mount. Did British politicians in 1945 think it would help their careers to tell voters that there was almost a decade of rationing and austerity ahead? Who could have predicted that debts built up from 1939, would grow throughout the 1950s and would only be finally paid off in 2006! But that's exactly what happened and who could have predicted it?[24]

Huge debts and a deficit are a moral and spiritual problem, as well as an economic problem. There is a reason why the words deceit, deficit and debt are akin. An economic deficit is merely a reflection of the spiritual and moral deficit of a nation, which should be bolstered by Christians. Money is essential for survival and yet in Jesus' words, "Life is more than food and the body more than clothes" (Luke 12:23). We are warned to keep our hearts pure, but have any of us heeded God's warning? Have churches preached eternal values or a desire for wealth?

'But godliness with contentment is great gain. For we brought nothing into the world, and we can take nothing out of it...those who want to get rich fall into temptation and a trap and into many foolish and harmful desires that plunge people into ruin and destruction. For the love of money is a root of all kinds of evil. Some people, eager for money, have wandered from the faith and pierced themselves with many griefs' (1 Timothy 6:6-10).

The West has a love of money and it tends to suffer from 'confidence bias' or the 'overconfidence effect,' which leads politicians to believe in their 'illusion of control,' saying, "It will all work out fine," regardless of hard facts. Overconfidence has been called the most "pervasive and potentially catastrophic" of all the cognitive biases to which human beings fall victim, leading to several stock market crashes, etc.[25]

Is the future as secure? Financial experts state that if there is another financial shock, no-one knows if we have enough money to save the banking system again, and fund another decade of substantial deficits. Some believe the new 'House of Cards,' which enables America's debt ceiling to rise and rise, could lead to collapse, and loss of confidence worldwide – with a new global depression following. Others believe the world's second largest economy – China is also built on sinking sand, and may trigger a global recession.

On my visit to China, in a number of provinces, what shook me was the way field after field were being transformed into high rise homes and cities. Driving through a brand new empty city, which few Chinese people can afford to live in, raises many questions. Who is losing money on these 'Ghost City' investments and how long is it sustainable?

When the West stopped buying Chinese goods on mass in 2008, the government of China pumped in a $680 billion stimulus package, to build and build. That kind of money bought a lot of jobs and kept China growing, but at what cost? The analyst Charlene Chu describes the Chinese credit binge, "Most people are aware we've had a credit boom in China but they don't know the scale. At the beginning of all of this in 2008, the Chinese banking sector was roughly $10 trillion in size. Right now it's in the order of $24 to $25 trillion. That incremental increase of $14 to $15 trillion is the equivalent of the entire size of the U.S. commercial banking sector, which took more than a century to build. So that means China will have replicated the entire U.S. system in the span of half a decade."[26]

Perhaps the future is safer than we expect, as some financial experts have pointed out that 'Chinese Exceptionalism,' has succeeded so far. Chinese Exceptionalism means that somehow normal rules have not applied to China and has kept China growing for decades without a crash, and China is supplying a 'soft landing' to normal borrowing and growth. Others suggest that lending can only go on for so long and the 1997 Asian Financial Crisis is a small road-map to the future of China.

Nevertheless, regardless of what else could happen, we are still trying to deal with Western debts, deficits and cuts. Due to the substantial debts of Western nations, governments have responded by quantitative easing, which is a clever name for 'electronically' printing money. Quantitative easing does not create new money, it just devalues the money we have. Just imagine the whole economy is a pie which costs £1 and using quantitative easing, the government electronically creates 10p –

this does not make the pie any bigger, it just means the pie now cost £1.10. That's why real inflation, the cost of the things we all need, rose five+ percent each year from 2009 to 2011 in Britain, dropping to three percent for a few years, whilst pay remained stagnant or rose by a smaller percentage. U.K. inflation fell in 2014 because of the falling oil price due to overproduction and price wars in supermarkets, fused together with low interest rates and government interference with the real value of the currency.

Quantitative easing is another tool for undisclosed taxation used by the government, because it inevitably leads to inflation, as the money you earn purchases less and less, just as your savings, produce less interest and the currency is devalued. Using quantitative easing, governments spend their 'new money' on assets, like government bonds or lend to banks, so they can keep paying bonuses. When currencies are manipulated, medium incomes stagnate and the Christian inspired link of the Protestant Work Ethic, between honest effort and reward is undermined, as the 99% are punished, in favour of the 1%.[27]

If money is printed in large amounts, such as in Zimbabwe in 2008-9, hyperinflation is the result, which led to inflation of 79.6 billion percent in November 2008! Zimbabwe's currency became worthless, as I found whilst I was in Africa in July of the same year. For this reason, developed nations limit quantitative easing to lower percentages, which enables them to obscure the slow devaluation of their currencies, as inflation makes the cost of living more severe, especially for the poorest. Reporter Richard Bilton said, "In the past six years (2008-2014), the cost of basics – bills, food and clothes has risen twenty-eight percent, but average earnings by only 9 percent...for the first time the majority of people in poverty are from working households.[28] The Child Poverty Act 2010, defines poverty in Britain as 'household income below sixty percent of median income.'

Steve Forbes, chairman and editor-in-chief of Forbes Media, said, "Money measures wealth; it is not wealth itself. It is a claim on products and services that people have created. That's why counterfeiting is illegal; it's thievery. But when government does this, it's called quantitative easing, or stimulus."[29]

What the West has lived through since 2008 is the greatest exchange of wealth taken from the middle and lower classes for a century, sending living standards on a downward spiral.[30] This exchange of wealth will continue for decades, as the average person's taxes will increasingly find its way to the top one percent who benefit from debt repayments.

For the first time in seventy years, people now accept the next generation will have lower standards of living than their parents. According to the Institute for Fiscal Studies, the average hourly wage for all employees in 2015 is 4.7 percent lower than in 2008, once inflation is taken into account.[31] Meanwhile, Oxfam found that the share of the world's wealth owned by the richest one percent has increased from 44 percent in 2009 to 48 percent in 2014. If present trends persist the wealthiest 1 percent will own more than 50 percent of the world's wealth by 2016.[32]

The debt burden on Western nations is so high, that no one can predict when they will be paid off, and some are warning of the danger of 'perpetual debt repayments,' which cost far more than the initial loan. The concept of 'perpetual debt repayments' may seem ridiculous, but in 2014, it was revealed that the British government has paid a total of £1.26 billion in interest on debts dating back to World War One, which were still valid.[33] These debts are mostly held by retailers that accept 'perpetual' interest, and allow the loans to be paid off when government wants, and the benefits of the interest is passed from one generation to another.[34] Some government debts still being held are from the eighteenth century![35] In 2014, the British government decided to pay off debts from Neville Chamberlain's 'perpetual' war bonds from 1932, to get better rates today.

With Christian beliefs being diminished in society, so too are the values which made the West strong – hard work, thrift, honesty and delayed gratification. As we wanted everything 'now,' we are today passing debt to our children, instead of wealth. National debt is the consumption today of wealth that has yet been earned. For several decades we have been borrowing from our children's future wealth, to pay for today's party. When money is borrowed from future generations, the wealth which is meant to fund their education, healthcare, infrastructure etc., will have to be spent on interest and capital re-payments. This means future generations will have to pay for our consumption, because we continuously ran over-budget, accepting two decades of deficit.

The moral and spiritual problem of spending our children's wealth today must be addressed. The Lord taught wealth can be a substantial distraction from our eternal concerns. Jesus Christ said, "The worries of this life and the deceitfulness of wealth choke the word, making it unfruitful" (Matthew 13:22). The Lord also reminds us that our attitudes toward money will also reveal our true heart attitude towards God. Jesus said, "Do not store up for yourselves treasures on earth, where moths and vermin destroy, and where thieves break in and steal. But store up for yourselves treasures in heaven...for where your treasure is, there your heart will be also" (Matthew 6:19-21).

In Matthew 24-25, Jesus tells us what the world will look like as it heads into the end times. The Lord said, "You will hear of wars and rumours of wars. See that you are not troubled; for all these things must come to pass, but the end is not yet. For nation will rise against nation and kingdom against kingdom. And there will be famines, pestilences, and earthquakes in various places. All these are the beginning of sorrows" (Matthew 24:6-8).

In the full teaching we learn it will be a time of multiple religious claims, intolerance towards followers of Jesus and international upheavals etc. Nonetheless, aspects of normal life will continue. Jesus said, "As the days of Noah, so also will the coming of the Son of Man be. For as in the days before the flood, they were eating and drinking, marrying and giving in marriage, until the day that Noah entered the ark" (Matthew 24:37-38).

We are told not to try to pinpoint the time because "of that day and hour no one knows" (Matthew 24:36); instead we are told to be ready, to prepare ourselves – to live for eternity! Jesus said, "Who then is a faithful and wise servant...? Blessed is that servant whom his master, when he comes, will find so doing" (Matthew 24:45-47). Christ warns us never to waste our lives on worldliness and abuse His grace (Matthew 24:48-51).

In the Parable of the Ten Virgins, Christ tells us to get ready, to do what we can, as led by His Spirit, and not wait until it is too late (Matthew 25:1-13). In the Parable of the Talents the Lord tells us to stake all in His eternal Kingdom (Matthew 25:14-30). The Bible predicts a coming season, when mankind will rebel against God to such a degree that it will return to the manifestations of the Noah and Babel generations. The Christian response will be to live pure and holy lives, in an impure and unholy age, and to redeem those who respond to Christ's call.

Chapter Thirty-Six

Being Honest about our Need

If churches and Christians are God's ambassadors on earth (2 Corinthians 5:20), then it follows that Christ's representatives must share a great deal of responsibility for failing to recognise and effectively deal with the spiritual and moral deficit in our nations. 'For the time has come for judgment to begin at the house of God' (1 Peter 4:17). This does not mean that believers must be at the forefront of economics, politics or anything else, which may help, but that Christians should be establishing a spiritual foundation in Christ, which will enable the Holy Spirit to be poured out, leading to the reviving of our nations (Psalm 85:6). When men and women are truly born again, their moral compasses are re-set, and the Spirit of God in them will give them more joy when they forget self and give, rather than by becoming empty debt-ridden consumers.

Our national problems are spiritual problems, and correcting spiritual problems is the responsibility of God's representatives on earth. If the blind have been leading the blind, where have been those who claim to see? (Luke 6:39).

We must pray for those in power, but government is not the reason for the decline of Christianity in Britain or America. They may have facilitated the transformation away from Christian values to a secular void, but government is not, nor ever has been the answer to our moral and spiritual problems. For 'the natural man does not receive the things of the Spirit of God, for they are foolishness to him; nor can he know them, because they are spiritually discerned' (1 Corinthians 2:14-15).

Every reversal of Christian traditions and observance in Britain or America is a failure of prayer. Every battle lost in our nations is a sign that the Church has failed to walk in and exercise the authority that Christ has given to His people. 'To the intent that now the manifold wisdom of God might be made known by the Church to the principalities and powers in the heavenly places, according to the eternal purpose which He accomplished in Christ Jesus our Lord' (Ephesians 3:10-11).

God is not weak, He is Almighty, but the release of His power is dependent upon His Church paying the full price, in humility, repentance, prayer and by meeting all the conditions He sets to be a faithful witness to Him. Our battle today is not against human beings. The Church of Jesus Christ is not called into a war of words with whoever is a perceived threat to challenge Christian values. Our battle is according to Paul 'not against flesh and blood.' We are not battling against opinions, surveys, or public opinion, but against evil spiritual powers, which seek to have dominion over God's people and the nations.

There is a structure of demonic power which seeks to influence events on earth, and Paul tells us what that structure is: 'For we do not wrestle against flesh and blood, but against principalities, against powers, against the rulers of the darkness of this age, against spiritual hosts of wickedness in the heavenly places' (Ephesians 6:12).

In the Bible we find a principle that dark powers in the heavenly places can only plunder if they first bind the defenders of light. It is the Church who is called to bind the strong man and plunder, but since the 1960s, it is the Church which has often been bound and plundered. Jesus said, "If a house is divided against itself, that house cannot stand...no one can enter a strong man's house and plunder his goods, unless he first binds the strong man. And then he will plunder his house' (Mark 3:25-27).

The Church in Britain and America, through sin, complacency and by being lukewarm have given the keys of many strongholds over to demonic strong men, who have been ruling and reigning, causing havoc in the nations. This lesson is illustrated by the testimony of R.B. Watchman in his book *The Holy Spirit in a Man*, concerning how the Lord led him into spiritual warfare: 'As a Christian, I was aware that Christians dedicate buildings and areas of land over to the Lord, often anointing them with oil, but only through my experiences was I beginning to be taught by the Holy Spirit the difference between holy consecrated land and demonic strongholds over buildings, villages, towns and cities (Ephesians 6:12). I learnt that defiled structures and buildings could be cleansed and territorial spirits over areas can be commanded to leave. All of this is clear in the Bible, but until the Holy Spirit makes it real, you just don't see it. Babylon was 'a habitation of demons' (Revelation 18:2), and Daniel saw two demonic strongholds called the 'Prince of Persia and Greece' (Daniel 10:13, 20).

'Before Israel entered the Promised Land they were told that there were high places where demons were worshipped and they had to be cleansed (Deuteronomy 12:2-4), or there would be a curse on the land and people (Jeremiah 3:1-9)...I was not aware of this at the time, but my trips around Britain over the subsequent two decades would concentrate on claiming and cleansing the land from demonic bondage, in preparation for a future move of the Holy Spirit. In past revivals and awakenings, it has become clear that moves of God have been restricted by unseen geographical boundaries in the spiritual realm, and these must be removed, *but* only as the Holy Spirit leads.'[1]

As I was writing this chapter, the Holy Spirit spoke to a prophet I know and told him to return to two churches he served in, one and two decades previously. I was invited with a small team to join. Both churches were once lively centres of the community, with exuberant praise and the gifts of the Spirit flowed; and yet, these churches were behind the veneer, half-hearted, cold and distant from God. The outward vestiges of religion were evident and they called them 'on-fire,' but few took any of the prophecies or warnings they received seriously.

The Lord sent prophets and servants of God to speak to these churches, and miracles, words of knowledge and other powerful manifestations proved these servants were trustworthy Christians, sold out to God. But when these same people gave prophecies of repentance and restoration, confirmed by other servants of the Lord, they were ignored and taken for granted. The gifts of the Spirit flowed, but they were treated as if they meant nothing. Did God speak or not? Was He directing them or not? After the leaders refused to heed what the Holy Spirit was warning them, there was a noticeable parting of the waves, and people wondered why the prophets moved on, and no others came. When the prophets become silent in churches and begin to leave, it is a sure sign that God is grieved and is about to exit the church, leaving the disobedient to their empty religious rituals (Amos 5:21-23, 3 John 1:9-11).

As we walked to the buildings where these churches were once held, this prophet reminded us of the prophecies and God's plan to bless and expand His work in these churches. But as God's people refused to heed His voice, the light was extinguished and the churches closed. One of the buildings is now used for secular purposes, another is boarded up. The prophet was visibly moved as he reminded us of God's goodness, and His plan to use these churches to reach the lost. But the people did not hear and God allowed the work to close because it lost its saltiness. Jesus said, "You are the salt of the earth; but if the salt loses its flavour, how shall it be seasoned? It is then good for nothing but to be thrown out and trampled underfoot by men" (Matthew 5:13).

Between the years 1980 to 2005, 8,356 churches closed in Britain, whilst the population grew from 56.3 Million to 60.2

Million.[2] The Methodist Church suffered a drop of 43% in attendance, with Presbyterians shrinking by 31.2%, and the Church of England suffered a fall of 14%.[3] In the United States, 4,000 churches close each year, and there is one third fewer churches in the U.S. than sixty years ago.[4]

God is still at work and new churches are being established, but not enough to cancel out the losses. Some may ask, "Why is God allowing this to happen?" The answer can be found in the words of Jesus Christ, as He encouraged and warned the seven churches in the book of Revelation. The Lord told John, "The seven *lampstands* which you saw are the seven *churches*" (Revelation 1:20), and Jesus said, "I have this against you, that you have left your first love…repent and do the first works, or else I will come to you quickly and remove your *lampstand* from its place – unless you repent" (Revelation 2:4-5). Each lampstand was a real church!

God permitted both Israel and Judah to be exiled because they were no longer salt or light amongst the nations. As the Lord Jesus Christ told His churches in His letters in Revelation, He still closes churches for the same reason. We are His witnesses and ambassadors (2 Corinthians 5:20), and in many ways, churches are God's embassies on earth – showing the way to receive free citizenship of heaven, through repentance and faith in Jesus' death and resurrection (Philippians 3:20). But if we are failing to offer any hope, fulfil our commission or be a good witness, Jesus said this is the result, "It is then good for nothing but to be thrown out and trampled underfoot by men" (Matthew 5:13).

Many wonder how the decline of the West has happened so quickly, and the reason, according to Scripture, must always be placed at the feet of God's people. We are the ones who have been given authority by Christ; we are people who have been given revelation through Scripture and by the Spirit to understand the true nature of the conflict. Some may say the situation is not that bad and use the argument of the Laodiceans, "We are rich" (Revelation 3:17). A couple of days ago in a broadcast from a U.S. mega church, all its members were encouraged to stand up and chant, "It is God's will for me to prosper." Certainly those who have can help those who are in need, but is not our first and greatest need to be conformed to the image of Christ? (Romans 8:29). Paul lamented, 'For all seek their own, not the things which are of Christ Jesus' (Philippians 2:21).

Paul taught this is God's will for His people: 'I beseech you therefore, brethren, by the mercies of God, that you present your bodies a living sacrifice, holy, acceptable to God, which is your reasonable service. And do not be conformed to this world, but be transformed by the renewing of your mind, that you may prove what is that good and acceptable and perfect will of God' (Romans 12:1-2). C.S. Lewis warned, "Prosperity knits a man to the world. He feels that he is finding his place in it, while really it is finding its place in him."[5] Jesus said, "Take heed and beware of covetousness, for one's life does not consist in the abundance of things he possesses" (Luke 12:15).

Chapter Thirty-Seven

Hope for a Christian Awakening

In the second half of the twentieth century there were many prophecies concerning a new great awakening sweeping the world, in fulfilment of the prophecy of Joel and Peter's prophetic confirmation (Acts 2:17-21). These include Smith Wigglesworth's 1947 revival prophecy, Tommy Hicks' 1961 worldwide prophecy, to Jean Darnall's 1967 revival vision, and many others.

Some preachers have taught it is impossible for another revival or spiritual awakening to transform our nations, because the end time prophecies in Scripture concern apostasy. It is true that the great apostasy is taking place and will get worse, yet it is very sad when people use one-sided teaching to prop-up their own unbelief, cynicism and doubt of an Almighty God who can do all things! G. K. Chesterton said, "Christianity has died many times and risen again; for it has a God who knows the way out of the grave." From the very beginning of the Church age, God told His Church that His outpouring of the Holy Spirit, which began at Pentecost, will continue until the height of the end times, when the sun will be turned to darkness and the moon to blood. This will take place when the sixth seal is opened (Revelation 6:12).

Take heed to the prophecy of Joel, "And it shall come to pass afterward that I will pour out My Spirit on all flesh; your sons and your daughters shall prophesy, your old men shall dream dreams, your young men shall see visions. And also on My menservants and on My maidservants I will pour out My Spirit in those days. And I will show wonders in the heavens and in the earth: blood and fire and pillars of smoke. The sun shall be turned into darkness and the moon into blood, before the coming of the great and awesome day of the Lord. And it shall come to pass that whoever calls on the name of the Lord shall be saved" (Joel 2:28-32).

The promises from Scripture for the outpouring of the Holy Spirit which were claimed by Jonathan Edwards, the Wesleys, George Whitefield, Evan Roberts and Duncan Campbell are still waiting to be claimed today! God has not changed or updated Holy Scripture or His promises since their days! The Bible is clear: the Holy Spirit will continue to be poured out, as long as we meet the conditions, until the very end times!

What are these conditions? Joel's prophecy started with: "And it shall come to pass afterward?" After what, we may ask? God says, ' "Turn to Me with all your heart, with fasting, with weeping and with mourning." So rend your heart and not your garments; return to the Lord your God. For He is gracious and merciful, slow to anger and of great kindness; and He relents from doing harm. Who knows if He will turn and relent and leave a blessing behind Him?...Call a sacred assembly; gather the people, let the priests, who minister to the Lord, weep between the porch and the altar. Let them say, "Spare Your people, O Lord and do not give Your heritage to reproach, that the nations should rule over them. Why should they say among the peoples, 'Where is their God?' " ' (Joel 2:12-14,17).

Having attended special prayer meetings and days of prayer, I believe that organised days of prayer are important, yet there is always the danger of these events becoming overwhelmed with celebrity preachers and popular bands. Such meetings have formal times for prayer, but true heartfelt intercession and repentance are difficult to achieve when so many come, with varying agendas and different walks with God. This can also be true of networking Christians, who spend so much time talking and networking with others, that very little is prayed.

When we become highly successful at organising things, there is always the danger that we plan God out of the equation, and trusting in ourselves, fulfil this Scripture: ' "Woe to the rebellious children," says the Lord, "who take counsel, but not of Me and who devise plans, but not of My Spirit" ' (Isaiah 30:1). Professor L.E. Maxwell gave this lesson, "Unless the Church senses her Divine resources unseen, untapped, unlimited, she is tempted to resort to any means, fair, fleshly, or foul, to command attention. We need to remember that heresy of method can be as deadly as heresy of message."

What British and American history seems to reveal is that God often burdens one or two, or a few people, who are called to meet together and push through in intercession, until God rends the heavens in power. This happened with Evan Roberts who was broken-hearted over 'religious' Wales, whilst many fellow Christians perceived no problem. The same happened with a group of elders on the Isle of Lewis in Scotland, before Duncan Campbell preached and revival began. The same took place when the Wesleys and Whitefield met for prayer at their holy club in London. When I walked down Fetter's Lane, there is a small plaque on the new building recalling the exact spot where the fire of God fell upon a few, before it fell upon a nation.

It is evident that God has started to light little fires around Britain, America and elsewhere, but it is concerning that the enemy is striking hard and fast to shut them down. I recall a church which held an all-night prayer meeting on Friday. It was very hard-going but many felt we had to press through and claim the promises God was offering to us, through prophetic words. For about eight months we met every Friday night till at least midnight, to seek God's face and cry out for revival. People in the church were inspired and the Sunday evening prayer meetings grew from a few to a great crowd. We all cried out to God and sought Him with such passion, as we responded to the prophetic guidance God gave us. Many of us were tired at playing church and re-running old meetings, without God's power present.

Some in the church were deeply troubled about the promise of a coming revival and one man was so fearful, that he spent a whole week with the elders, who finally encouraged him that it was a good thing to witness a Christian awakening! However, it was noticeable that this one person had drained much of the energy and vision from the leadership, and some did not turn up for the late night prayer meetings any more. In the Sunday meetings one said, "Now we've all got to calm down and pray one by one." Within a month the vision was dead and I marvel how one person, played a role in killing the prophecies and prayers of a whole church. Later he became a leader!

Jesus said, "The Kingdom of Heaven is like a man who sowed good seed in his field; but while men slept, his enemy came and sowed tares among the wheat and went his way. But when the grain had sprouted and produced a crop, then the tares also appeared. So the servants of the owner came and said to him, 'Sir, did you not sow good seed in your field? How then does it have tares?' He said to them, 'An enemy has done this' " (Matthew 13:24-28).

I am reminded of another incident. One elder was burdened by the Holy Spirit to start meeting with other leaders, to repent for the sins of God's people, humble themselves and pray. It was noted that the conditions of 2 Chronicles 7:14 are: humbling ourselves, praying, seeking God's face and turning from wicked ways, which will result in the forgiveness of sins and the healing of the land. Nevertheless, it is observed that in many meetings Christians tend to quote 2 Chronicles 7:14, but rarely do we actually get around to meeting the conditions! Consequently, a few Christian leaders began to meet to fulfil these conditions. Soon word got out among Christian leaders in the area of what was happening, and one minister arrived saying, "I've heard you're meeting to pray for revival. I want to join, but I'm not coming to talk; we must pray or not meet at all."

At the first meeting this minister attended, he poured out his heart to God in Holy Spirit led prayer and repentance. For weeks there were times of very sincere repentance, intercession and seeking God in humility. As the weeks progressed more leaders from the area began joining and it was soon being hailed as a great achievement for Christian unity. More pastors, vicars and elders began meeting, and as these new participants were senior in the area, they began to command a stronger influence.

Now the minister who had poured out his heart to God in his first meeting, returned with greater passion and cried out for God to move, and expressed his burden for the lukewarm, sinful and half-heartedness of the Church. Suddenly one of the senior ministers said, "Oh no! You can't take that burden on you," and began to lecture the weeping minister on why there is no real problem, because of all that is being achieved.

The elders who founded the meetings, as led by the Holy Spirit, were now junior members and looked at each other in disbelief! Over the following months, humility, prayer, repentance and intercession all ceased, as the new leaders 'organised' the meetings. "Let's learn this new song," one said, and another, "I've invited an outreach worker to tell us about his work."

In this example, the enemy used a few unmoved leaders to torpedo the times of intercession, which the Holy Spirit began with a few broken-hearted believers. Jesus said to them, "An enemy has done this" (Matthew 13:28). What lessons can we learn? Perhaps the lesson is that we must stop organising, networking and talking, and start weeping and repenting. If God joins people together, great, but beware the tare, who comes with a mission to kill, steal and destroy (John 10:10). John said, "They went out from us, but they were not of us; for if they had been of us, they would have continued with us" (1 John 2:19).

Throughout history there is a lesson that God has drawn aside to himself men and women who are one hundred percent committed to seek Him, whilst many others continue to play at Christianity. Dr Martyn Lloyd-Jones once spoke on this Scripture: 'Moses took his tent and pitched it outside the camp, far from the camp, and called t the tabernacle of meeting. And it came to pass that everyone who sought the Lord went out to the tabernacle of meeting which was outside the camp' (Exodus 33:7-8). The picture he drew was this: There is a large body of people, called 'God's people,' but Moses cannot meet with God amongst them. They are worldly, rebellious and half-hearted. He has to go into the silence and meet with God alone, and others followed.

Dr Martyn Lloyd-Jones said, "In the noise and bustle of the camp, Moses and Joshua couldn't have the quiet and the peace to wait upon God. This demanded some special effort...and so Moses and those who felt this burden to plead with God, would go out of the camp, and there plead with God.

"There have been examples of this throughout the centuries. You get this in the life of individuals. You are familiar of the story of the life of Martin Luther. This man knew of this thing, of being drawn aside. Here was this great Roman Church, with fifteen centuries of tradition, and yet, this one man feels the state of the burden of the whole Church and he passed through this process of drawing aside, a kind of separation – it's inevitable.

"Some things cannot be done in the midst of the camp and revival has always led to a separating of certain choice souls, who felt the burden of the situation and always felt this absolute necessity of withdraw, as it were, from the middle of the camp, in order that they may intercede truly before God. And so you have found it with many others since. The most striking and well known example of all, of this thing, is with the Great Evangelical Awakening. That wasn't a series of organised evangelistic campaigns you know, it was God breaking in upon churches and people. But what was the precursor?"

Dr Martyn Lloyd-Jones explained that the Wesleys, with George Whitefield and others "began to feel dissatisfied at the whole state of the Church. They had been brought up religiously, most of them, some of them were the sons of parsons, clergymen and they were moral men, good men – religious men. But they became dissatisfied. They were destined to become ministers and they were trained, but they thought, 'This is not enough.' The times were so evil, the state of the Church was so deplorable and the state of the morals of the nation beyond description.

"These young men felt they should take some special step so they formed, what they called the Holy Club, and they met together in this club, every week, to read the Scriptures together and to pray together; to seek the face of God and to find what He would have them do...They were students and they were zealous students, but they felt over and above all the studies and lectures and tutoring, and everything they received, that they must take a further step and they did this voluntarily. They went out of their way to do it.

"Like Moses, they took their tabernacle out of the camp. They segregated themselves because they realised that the only men who were of value in such a situation, were the men who felt the burden. They wouldn't admit anyone who came in out of curiosity, or to enjoy himself. He had to testify that he was concerned, deeply concerned. This is history! It was the Holy Club which was used of God in bringing that great and mighty awakening and revival.

"You've read of Jonathan Edwards going out of his house into the woods to be alone with God and there he would pray. The same is true of David Brainerd and others. This is something which I say is invariable. Now I don't want to press this too hard, but I am pressing a principle. I am not saying, that of necessity you have to leave a denomination immediately, but I am saying that in a kind of spiritual way, you have to draw apart from it, if the bulk of the people in that denomination are uncertain of their faith and are not spiritually minded, and don't believe in prayer. You may have to act without them and you may have to do something in your own homes or houses, anywhere you like, in order that you respond to this movement of the Spirit of God within you.

"Moses was responding to the dealing of the Spirit with him...our real danger at the present time is to be content with what we are doing and to be so pleased with ourselves, and with the measure of success that is happening, that we feel nothing else is desired. To me the most appalling thing about the Christian Church today is our self-satisfaction. Some of us boast in our orthodoxy, some of us boast in our activities, our business – something happening in the church every night – marvellous, wonderful! Collections good, everything seems to be aright and they say, 'What are you disturbed about? Why are you weeping, crying and talking about revival?' "[1]

Could it be possible that part of the Church has become a people without a vision and is thus perishing? (Proverbs 29:18). Why do some denominations seem so lost and uncertain of what the Church exists for? Have we forgotten that our few decades on earth will define our eternal lives where a trillion times a trillion years, will be as nothing? Have we forgotten we are entrusted with treasures in earthen vessels? Have we considered that the Master has entrusted us with a little temporal time, power and money, to see if we can be trusted with true eternal riches? (Luke 16:10-11).

The Rev. Duncan Campbell, used by God in the Lewis Awakening, warned that evil forces in the 1960s and 70s were beginning to overturn every known Christian principle and they were taking the field. Then he gave hope saying, "But if God shows His hand, if God takes the field, mountains will flow before Him – mountains of indifference, mountains of materialism, and mountains of humanism will flow before His presence, and nations; not just individuals, but nations shall be made to tremble!...We have seen communities, parishes, districts in the grip of God, in a matter of hours when God came down...It is true we have seen man's best endeavour, in the field of evangelism, leaving the community untouched. We have seen crowded churches, we have seen many professions of faith, we have seen hundreds and thousands responding to what you speak of, as the altar call. But I want to say this and say it without contradiction, that you can have all that, without God!

"You can have all that on human levels without God...this is the difference between evangelism and revival, and that's why I say our only hope is not in crusades – thank God for all that is being done in evangelism, missions and crusades, through the effort of evangelists and ministers, bringing one here and one there to a saving knowledge of Jesus – but our supreme need and the only answer to the problem that confronts the Christian Church today is a visitation from God.

"God is a covenant keeping God and must be true to His engagements, and God to vindicate His own honour will listen to the prayers (of those who meet His conditions). Oh that God may find a people ready to fulfil and comply with the governing principles, relative to spiritual quickening (of 2 Chronicles 7:14 and Joel 2:12-17)...God is the God of revival, but we are the human agents through which revival is possible."[2]

Other Books by the Author

- *Holy Spirit Power: Knowing the Voice, Guidance and Person of the Holy Spirit*
- *Heaven: A Journey to Paradise and the Heavenly City*
- *How Christianity Made the Modern World*
- *The Exodus Evidence In Pictures – The Bible's Exodus:* 100+ colour photos
- *The Ark of the Covenant – Investigating the Ten Leading Claims:* 80+ colour photos
- *Jesus Today, Daily Devotional: 100 Days with Jesus Christ*
- *Samuel Rees Howells: A Life of Intercession* by Richard Maton, with Paul and Mathew Backholer

Sources and Notes

Chapter One: How Britain Became a Christian Nation
1. Historians can find no mention of Joseph of Arimathea until the thirteenth century, in the copy of *Life of Mary Magdalene* attributed to Rabanus Maurus.
2. Significance of the Lullingstone Roman Villa by English Heritage, english-heritage.org.uk, 4 August 2014.
3. How God made the English, a chosen people? With Diarmaid MacCulloch, BBC, 17 March 2012.
4. Ibid.
5. *Ecclesiastical History of the English People* by Bede, c.731.
6. How the Celts Saved Britain, A New Civilisation, with Dan Snow, BBC, October 2010.
7. The Bible: A History by Ann Widdecombe, Channel 4, 7 February 2010.
8. Some have pointed to Saint Lucius, as the first Christian King of the Britons from the second century. As a legendary man, he is first mentioned in the sixth century version of the *Liber Pontificalis*. If he did exist, his legacy was short; there is not enough evidence.
9. The coronation oath, last made on 2 June 1953 by Queen Elizabeth II.

Chapter Two: A Nation Covenanted To God
1. *Commentaries on the Gallic War* by Julius Caesar, Book V, 49 BC.
2. Lindow Man, mid-first century AD, Cheshire, England, The British Museum.
3. *The History of the English Speaking Peoples,* Volume 1, by Winston Churchill, Chapter IV, Henry II, Cassel and co, 1956.
4. In 1497, the pennant of the Cross of St George was flown by explorer John Cabot when he sailed to Newfoundland, and later by Sir Francis Drake and Sir Walter Raleigh. By the late eighteenth century, royal banners, naval ensigns and military flags gave way to the concept of a national flag, with this cross at its centre.
5. Coronation ceremony, 2 June 1953, royal.gov.uk, 4 July 2014.
6. British Prime Minister David Cameron said, "We are a Christian country and we should not be afraid to say so...I believe we should be more confident about our status as a Christian country, more ambitious about expanding the role of faith-based organisations, and frankly, more evangelical about a faith that compels us to get out there and make a difference to people's lives." The Prime Minister's King James Bible speech by David Cameron, Oxford, 16 December 2011, and, My Faith in the Church of England, speech by David Cameron, 4 July 2014. Deputy British Prime Minister Nick Clegg said, "I'm not a man of faith, but I think it's stating the obvious that we are a country underpinned, informed, infused by Christian values, Christian heritage, Christian history, Christian culture and Christian values. That is something that is obvious about our identity as a nation. We are also a very tolerant nation. In fact one of the great Christian values is tolerance and respect for other people, people of other faiths, other views. So I think our Christian heritage sits very comfortably alongside our plurality and our tolerance." U.K. non-Christians claims absurd, senior Tories say, BBC.co.uk, 23 April 2014.
7. Archbishop's speech on the Criminal Justice and Immigration Bill, 5 March 2008.
8. From the Constitution to the calendar: Britain is a Christian country, *Telegraph*, 22 April 2014.
9. How can the law of a Constitutionally Christian country refuse protection to religious belief? By Gerald Warner, *Telegraph*, 1 May 2010.
10. Coronation broadcast, 2 June 1953, royal.gov.uk, 4 July 2014.
11. Coronation ceremony on 2 June 1953, royal.gov.uk, 4 July 2014.
12. Ecclesiastes 5:5, Psalm 55:20, 89:34, Proverbs 20:25, Isaiah 33:8, Jeremiah 11:10, 33:21, Ezekiel 17:18, 44:7, Malachi 2:10-12, Mark 14:24.
13. Debate in the House of Lords, *Hansard*, 5 March 2008.
14. Queen Elizabeth I, addressing Parliament in her 'farewell' golden speech, 30 November 1601.
15. Queen Ann was the last monarch to veto legislation in the Scottish Militia Bill of 1708, and Queen Victoria in 1892, was the last to veto a ministerial appointment.
16. How God made the English, a chosen people? by Diarmaid MacCulloch, BBC, 17 March 2012.
17. Archbishop's blog on a Christian country, archbishopofcanterbury.org, 24 April 2014.
18 The Attorney General, Dominic Grieve, Telegraph.co.uk, 22 April 2014.
19. Ibid.
20. Churchgoing in the U.K., Tearfund. Research carried out between 8 February and 5 March 2006. Since then large numbers of practicing Christians from Europe have moved to live in Britain, so the statistics remain viable, if not a littler underestimated now.
21. The Attorney General, Dominic Grieve, Telegraph.co.uk, 22 April 2014.
22. U.K. non-Christians claims absurd, senior Tories say, BBC.co.uk, 23 April 2014.
23. The British monarch, the Queen and the U.K., the National Anthem, royal.gov.uk, 8 August 2014.
24. Ibid.
25. The British monarch, the Queen and the Church, royal.gov.uk, 8 August 2014.

26. Farooq Murad, of the Muslim Council of Great Britain said, "No one can deny that Britain remains largely a Christian country, with deep historical and structural links with the Established Church. The 2011 census indicates that more than sixty percent of the English self-identify as Christian. We respect that." Lord Indarjit Singh, of the Network of Sikh Organisations said, "Christianity is the religion of the majority. It is not the greatest sin to say this. What is of greater concern is the letter in response, which says we are not a religious country." Anil Bhanot of the Hindu Council U.K., said he was 'grateful' for Christianity's inclusive attitude Source: Britain is a Christian country – and we respect that: Hindu, Muslim and Sikh leaders back the PM after militant atheists tell him to keep quiet on religion by Jason Groves and Louise Eccles, *Daily Mail*, 22 April 2014; and David Cameron risks alienation public figures claim, BBC, 21 April 2014.
27. U.K. Church Statistics 2: 2010-2020 by Peter Brierley, Brierley Consultancy.
28. Eight arguments about whether the U.K. is a Christian country by Jon Kelly, BBC News magazine, 23 April 2014.
29. Ibid.
30. How God made the English, a chosen people? by Diarmaid MacCulloch BBC, 17 March 2012.
31. Inside a church for Born Again Christians: Speaking to God in a Manchester multiplex by Charlotte Philby, *Independent*, 26 July 2014.

Chapter Three: Celtic Christianity
1. Religions, Christianity in Britain, BBC.co.uk/religion, 2 July 2014.
2. Christianity, A History, Dark Ages, by Dr Robert Bedford, Channel 4, 2009.
3. *Adversus Judaeos* by Tertullian, Part 7:4, c.AD 200.
4. *Demonstratio Evangelica* by Eusebius, Book 3, chapter 5, AD 311.
5. Significance of the Lullingstone Roman Villa by English Heritage, english-heritage.org.uk, 4 August 2014.
6. The British state mustn't let go of the Church by Michael Portillo, *Telegraph*, 16 January 2009.
7. The 'Lead Tank' from Icklingham, British Museum, 4 August 2014.
8. Silver plaque and Gold Disc from Water Newton, British Museum, 4 August 2014.
9. Cup from the Water Newton treasure, British Museum, 4 August 2014.
10. *De Synodis or De fide Orientalium* by the Bishop of Poitiers, point 11, AD 358.
11. Collected Works of John Chrysostom, Nicene and Post-Nicene Fathers, London, 1889.
12. *De Excidio et Conquestu Britanniae* by Gildas the Wise, AD 540.
13. Historians can find no mention of Joseph of Arimathea until the thirteenth century, in the copy of *Life of Mary Magdalene* attributed to Rabanus Maurus.

Chapter Four: Darkness and Light
1. How God made the English, a white and Christian people? by Diarmaid MacCulloch BBC, 31 March 2012.
2. Ibid.
3. Ibid.
4. Ibid.
5. Christianity, A History, Dark Ages by Dr Robert Bedford, Channel 4, 2009.
6. *The Confession of St. Patrick*, translated from the Latin by Ludwig Bieler, c.AD 440.
7. Ibid.
8. Ibid.
9. Ibid.
10. Ibid.
11. How the Celts Saved Britain, A New Civilisation, with Dan Snow, BBC, October 2010.
12. Patricius: The True Story of St. Patrick by David Kithcart, CBN.com.
13. *The Confession of St. Patrick*, translated from the Latin by Ludwig Bieler, c.AD 440.
14. Saints and Sinners: Britain's Millennium of Monasteries with Dr Janina Ramirez, BBC, 23 February 2015.
15. *The Confession of St. Patrick*, translated from the Latin by Ludwig Bieler, c.AD 440.
16. Ibid.
17. Christianity, A History, Rome, with Michael Portillo, Channel 4, 2009.
18. The British state mustn't let go of the Church by Michael Portillo, *Telegraph*, 16 January 2009.
19. *The Confession of St. Patrick*, translated from the Latin by Ludwig Bieler, c.AD 440.
20. Ibid.

Chapter Five: The Celtic Golden Age
1. How the Celts Saved Britain, A New Civilisation, with Dan Snow, BBC, October 2010.
2. How the Celts Saved Britain, Salvation, with Dan Snow, BBC, October 2010.
3. Ibid.
4. Christianity, A History, Dark Ages by Dr Robert Bedford, Channel 4, 2009.
5. *Ecclesiastical History of the English People* by Bede, Book III, 731, chapter 2.
6. How the Celts Saved Britain, Salvation, with Dan Snow, BBC, October 2010.
7. Ibid.
8. Ibid.
9. Treasures of the Anglo-Saxons by Dr Janina Ramirez, BBC, 10 August 2010.

10. How the Celts Saved Britain, A New Civilisation, with Dan Snow, BBC, October 2010.
11. Ibid.
12. Christianity, A History, Dark Ages, by Dr Robert Bedford, Channel 4, 2009.

Chapter Six: Power and Pain
1. Christianity, A History, Rome, with Michael Portillo, Channel 4, 2009.
2. North Yorkshire, Archaeology, Constantine the Great, by James Gerrard, BBC.co.uk, 27 September 2005.
3. Christianity, A History, Rome, with Michael Portillo, Channel 4, 2009.
4. Ibid.
5. Ibid.
6. Ibid.
7. Ibid.
8. *Codex Theodosianus* XVI 1.2. by Emperor Theodosius I, AD 439.
9. Ibid.
10. Christianity, A History, Rome, with Michael Portillo, Channel 4, 2009.
11. Ibid.
12. Ibid.

Chapter Seven: Celtic or Catholic
1. How the Celts Saved Britain, Salvation, with Dan Snow, BBC, October 2010.
2. Silver and gold buckle decorated with a fish from Crundale Down, Kent, Anglo-Saxon, mid-seventh century, British Museum.
3. Treasures of the Anglo-Saxons by Dr Janina Ramirez, BBC, 10 August 2010.
4. Christianity, A History, Dark Ages, with Dr Robert Bedford, Channel 4, 2009.
5. Ibid.
6. Ibid.
7. *Ecclesiastical History of the English Nation*, Book III, by Bede, 731, Chapter XXV.
8. Ibid.
9. Ibid.
10. Ibid.
11. How the Celts Saved Britain, Salvation, with Dan Snow, BBC, October 2010.
12. *An Introduction to Anglo-Saxon England* by Peter Hunter Blair, Cambridge University Press, 1977, p.129.
13. How the Celts Saved Britain, Salvation, with Dan Snow, BBC, October 2010.
14. Treasures of the Anglo-Saxons by Dr Janina Ramirez, BBC, 10 August 2010.
15. The Chapel is assumed to be that of 'Ythanceaster' mentioned by Bede, book III, chapter XXII.
16. Saints and Sinners: Britain's Millennium of Monasteries, with Dr Janina Ramirez, BBC, 23 February 2015.
17. How God made the English, a chosen people? by Diarmaid MacCulloch, BBC, 17 March 2012.
18. Ibid.
19. Christianity, A History, Dark Ages by Dr Robert Bedford, Channel 4, 2009.
20. Ibid.

Chapter Eight: Alfred the Great
1. How God made the English, a chosen people? by Diarmaid MacCulloch, BBC, 17 March 2012.
2. The anonymous account of the *Translation of St Cuthbert*, 1104. Later reprinted in *The Biographical Writings and Letters of Venerable Bede*, translated from the Latin by J. A. Giles; James Bohn, London, 1845, pp.181-218.
3. Ibid.
4. Ibid.
5. *The History of the English Speaking Peoples*, Volume 1, by Winston Churchill, Chapter IV, Henry II, Cassel and co, 1956.
6. Ibid.
7. How God made the English, a chosen people? by Diarmaid MacCulloch, BBC, 17 March 2012.
8. Treasures of the Anglo-Saxons by Dr Janina Ramirez, BBC, 10 August 2010.
9. King Alfred to Bishop Wærferth, preface to *Pastoral Care* by Pope Gregory, AD 590.
10. Ibid.
11. Ibid.
12. Ibid.
13. Christianity, A History, Dark Ages by Dr Robert Bedford, Channel 4, 2009.
14. How God made the English, a chosen people? by Diarmaid MacCulloch, BBC, 17 March 2012.

Chapter Nine: The Three Hundred Year Prophecy
1. *Macbeth* by William Shakespeare, Act 3, Scene VI, c.1606.
2. St. Ælred, Abbott of Rievaulx, in Yorkshire, England, relates this account, c.1160.
3. *Vita Beati Edwardi Regis et Confessoris*, manuscript Selden 55, Bodleian Library, Oxford, c.1100.
4. *The English and the Normans: Ethnic Hostility, Assimilation, and Identity 1066-1220* by Hugh M. Thomas, Oxford University Press, 2003, p.56.

Chapter Ten: Medieval Life
1. The Magna Carta, Article 1, 1215.
2. David Starkey's Magna Carta by Dr David Starkey, BBC, 26 January 2015.
3. Ibid.
4. Britain's bloodiest dynasty with Dan Jones, Channel 5, 4 December 2014.
5. Ibid.
6. Ibid.
7. The chronicler provides us with details of the Provisions of Oxford of 1258, rather than a formal document.
8. Britain's bloodiest dynasty with Dan Jones, Channel 5, 4 December 2014.
9. Medieval Realms, The Church, The British Library, 7 October 2014.
10. *Daily Life in the Middle Ages* by Paul B. Newman, MacFarland and Co, 2001, p.184.
11. How God made the English, a white and Christian people? by Diarmaid MacCulloch, BBC, 31 March 2012.
12. Ibid.
13. Saints and Sinners: Britain's Millennium of Monasteries with Dr Janina Ramirez, BBC, 27 February 2015.
14. Ibid.
15. Ibid.

Chapter Eleven: New Testament Christianity
1. Christianity, A History, Reformation, with Ann Widdecombe, Channel 4, 2009.
2. Ibid.
3. Ibid.
4. Ibid.
5. Queen Elizabeth's response to a Parliamentary delegation on her potential marriage to Philip of Spain, 1559.
6. Queen Elizabeth I, rebuke to her pro-Catholic bishops, 1559.
7. Ibid.
8. Articles VI, XX, XXIII, XXVI and XXXIV are regularly cited.
9. Queen Elizabeth I, addressing Parliament, 1583.
10. How God made the English, a tolerant people? by Diarmaid MacCulloch, BBC, 24 March 2012.
11. Queen Elizabeth I, addressing Parliament in her 'farewell' golden speech, 30 November 1601.
12. Gunpowder 5/11. The Greatest Terror Plot, BBC, 22 October 2014.
13. Ibid.
14. Ibid.
15. Ibid.
16. Ibid.
17. Ibid.
18. Saints and Sinners: Britain's Millennium of Monasteries with Dr Janina Ramirez, BBC, 5 March 2015.

Chapter Twelve: Empowering Parliament
1. The King James Bible, the book that changed the world by Lord Melvyn Bragg, BBC, March 2011.
2. Ibid.
3. Cromwell's letter to Charles Fleetwood, 1652.
4. *Leviathan, or the Matter, Form and Power of a Commonwealth, Ecclesiastical and Civil,* Chapter XLVII, 1651.
5. A Jewell of Democracy by Tristram Hunt, the *Guardian*, 26 October 2007.
6. Ibid.
7. The Prime Minister's King James Bible Speech by David Cameron, Oxford, 16 December 2011.

Chapter Thirteen: The Glorious Revolution
1. *History of the English Speaking Peoples* by Winston Churchill, Orion Publishing Co, 1956, 2002.
2. Empire of the Seas, part 1, by Dan Snow, BBC, March 2012.
3. Citizenship, Bill of Rights, 1639, The U.K. National Archives.
4. The Coronation Oath, Library of the House of Commons, compiled by Lucinda Maer and Oonagh Gay, 27 August 2008.
5. Ibid.
6. Archbishop's speech on the Criminal Justice and Immigration Bill, 5 March 2008.
7. How God made the English a tolerant people? by Diarmaid MacCulloch, BBC, 24 March 2012.
8. John Churchill, First Duke of Marlborough: Part One (1650-1700), BBC.co.uk, 2011.
9. Letter in support of William of Orange, with sympathies made known in person to Sidney Godolphin, by John Churchill, November 1688.
10. *The Fifteen Decisive Battles of the World* by Edward Shepherd Creasy, Harper and Brothers, 1851, Chapter 11.
11. *Marlborough: His Life and Times*, Book One by Winston Churchill, George. G. Harrap and Co, 1934, p.15.

Chapter Fourteen: Liberty, Justice and Education
1. Christianity isn't dying, it's being eradicated by Cristina Odone, *Telegraph*, 1 March 2011.
2. Speech by David Lloyd George on John Wesley, to raise funds for Wesley's Tomb in London, 29 July 1922.
3. *George Whitefield: The Awakener* by Albert D. Belden, Rockliff, Foreword,1953.

Chapter Fifteen: Christianity, Commerce and Civilisation
1. Some smaller exceptions: Irish uprising (1848), Crimean War (1853-56), The Anglo-Zulu War (1879), Indian rebellion (1857), Sudan Campaign 1896-1899, the Boer Wars in South Africa (1881, 1899-1902).
2. David Livingstone's speech to students at Cambridge University, 4 December 1857.
3. Queen Victoria's speech, Parliament, 27 August 1839.
4. Ibid. 26 January 1841.
5. Ibid. 22 June 1841.
6. Ibid. 2 February 1843.
7. Ibid. 1 February 1849.
8. Ibid. 31 January 1850.
9. Ibid. 6 February 1872.
10. Queen Victoria's Journal entry, Windsor Castle, Tuesday, 14 October 1851.
11. Ibid. Tuesday, 18 November 1851.
12. Queen Victoria's Journal entry, Buckingham Palace, Thursday, 13 July 1854.
13. Queen Victoria's Journal entry, Osborne House: Friday, 4 August 1854.
14. Queen Victoria's Journal entry, Buckingham Palace, Saturday, 13 February 1858.
15. Queen Victoria's Journal entry, Osborne House, Sunday, 28 July 1872.
16. Queen Victoria's Journal entry, Dunrobin, Monday, 9 September 1872.
17. Queen Victoria's Journal entry, Osborne House, Saturday, 18 April 1874.
18. Queen Victoria's Journal entry, Buckingham Palace, Tuesday, 2 July 1861.
19. How God made the English, a white and Christian people? by Diarmaid MacCulloch, BBC, 31 March 2012.
20. Niall Ferguson – Empire: How Britain Made the Modern World - The Mission, Channel 4, October 2009.
21. Slavery, The Royal Navy website, royalnavy.mod.uk, 2008.
22. *Economic Growth and the Ending of the Transatlantic Slave Trade* by Professor David Eltis, Oxford University Press, 1987.
23. Our Duty in India Speech by Winston Churchill, Royal Albert Hall, London, 18 March 1931.

Chapter Sixteen: The Faith of Queen Victoria
1. Queen Victoria's Journal entry, Tunbridge Wells, Sunday, 14 September 1834.
2. Queen Victoria's Journal entry, St Leonard's, Sunday, 11 January 1835.
3. Queen Victoria's Journal entry, Ramsgate (Albion House), Sunday, 6 December 1835.
4. Queen Victoria's Journal entry, Ramsgate (West Cliff), Sunday, 9 October 1836.
5. Queen Victoria's Journal entry, Buckingham Palace, Tuesday, 15 December 1840.
6. Queen Victoria's Journal entry, Windsor Castle, Sunday, 31 December 1843.
7. Ibid. Tuesday, 31 December 1844.
8. Ibid. Thursday, 1 January 1846.
9. Ibid. Friday, 25 December 1846.
10. Ibid. 6 February 1847.
11. Queen Victoria's Journal entry, Buckingham Palace, Sunday, 23 February 1851.
12. Queen Victoria's Journal entry, Glasgow, Sunday, 8 October 1854.
13. Question originally published in the *Court News* and personal response to John Townsend.
14. Queen Victoria's Journal entry, Buckingham Palace, Saturday, 23 June 1855.
15. Queen Victoria's Journal entry, Windsor Castle, Wednesday, 9 November 1859.
16. Ibid. Thursday, 5 June 1862.
17. Queen Victoria's Journal entry, Coburg (Rosenau), Saturday, 29 August 1863.
18. Queen Victoria's Journal entry, Balmoral Castle, Monday, 28 September 1868.
19. Queen Victoria's Journal entry, Windsor Castle, Saturday, 23 December 1871.
20. Queen Victoria's Journal entry, Sandringham House, Monday, 1 January 1872.
21. Queen Victoria's Journal entry, Osborne House, Friday, 1 January 1875.
22. Queen Victoria's Journal entry, Windsor Castle, Wednesday, 20 December 1876.
23. Queen Victoria's Journal entry, Osborne House, Sunday, 1 April 1877.
24. Queen Victoria's Journal entry, Balmoral Castle, Sunday, 9 June 1878.
25. Queen Victoria's Journal entry, Osborne House, Saturday, 1 January 1881.
26. Ibid. Wednesday, 1 January 1890.
27. Queen Victoria's Journal entry, Windsor Castle, Sunday, 20 June 1897.
28. Queen Victoria's Journal entry, Osborne House, Tuesday, 31 July 1900.

Chapter Seventeen: Fighting for Liberty
1. Graphic World War One etchings discovered a century after French ban by Tom Rowley, the *Telegraph*, 27 July 2014.

2. *SGM, the Word at War* by Bethan Collingridge, sgmlifewords.com, 14 January 2014.
3. Ibid.
4. Ibid.
5. Ibid.
6. *The World Crisis 1911-1918* by Winston Churchill. His memoirs of World War I. Free Press, 1931, pp.46-47.
7. Ten of the greatest classic British Army victories by Richard Holmes, *Daily Mail*, 23 January 2010.
8. World War One: Beyond the Trenches. The famine of Mount Lebanon, BBC News, November 2014.
9. *The Last Word On The Middle East* by Derek Prince, Chosen Books, 1982, pp.47-48.
10. The untold story: The role of Christian Zionists in the establishment of modern day Israel by Rabbi Jamie Cowen, Leadership University, 13 July 2002.
11. National debt to GDP, 1919 - 127%, by 1933 - 179%.
12. National debt to GDP reached 225% in 1945!

Chapter Eighteen: Divine Intervention
1. King George VI calls for a National Day of Prayer, Sunday, 26 May 1940.
2. The *Daily Sketch*, 27 May 1940.
3. C.B. Mortlock, the *Daily Telegraph*, 8 June 1940.
4. We Shall Fight on the Beaches Speech by Winston Churchill, 4 June 1940.
5. *The Private Diary of Winston Churchill*, 10 May 1940.
6. *The Hitler Book: The Secret Dossier Prepared for Stalin* edited by Henrik Eberle, Matthias Uhl, John Murray, 2005, p.68.
7. The German Threat to Britain in World War Two by Dan Cruickshank, BBC, 21 June 2011.
8. War of the Unknown Warriors, Speech by Winston Churchill, BBC radio, 14 July 1940.

Chapter Nineteen: The Battle of Britain
1. *Rees Howells Intercessor* by Norman Grubb, Lutterworth Press, 1952.
2. Strangest story of the war, the testimony of Mr Fowler and Mrs Evans, the *News Chronicle*, 1942.
3. Vicar interprets the vision in the sky, the *Christian Herald*, 1943.
4. Angel seen, testimony by Mr D.L. Philips, *South London Newspaper*, 8 September 1944.
5. *Miracles & Angels* by Dr E. K. Victor Pearce by Eagle Publishing, 2007.
6. The Churchill Centre, Winston Churchill looking back in 1950, winstonchurchill.org.
7. The Atlantic Charter broadcast by Winston Churchill, 24 August 1941.
8. Onward, Christian Soldiers, words written by Sabine Baring-Gould, 1865. The music was composed by Arthur Sullivan in 1871. Read 2 Timothy 2:3.
9. *The Looting of Asia* by Chalmers Johnson, London book review, volume 25, 2003, p.3.

Chapter Twenty: Turning the Tide
1. Comments made by Winston Churchill in Wales, 31 October 1942, reprinted in *Finest Hour*, The International Churchill Society, number 69, 1990.
2. Victory at El-Alamein, G.W. Price, *Daily Mail*, 14 November 1942.
3. World War Two, Battle of the Kasserine Pass, 14 February 1943, History.com.
4. *Alanbrooke War Diaries 1939–1945* by Field Marshal Lord Alanbrooke, Phoenix Press, 2001.
5. Message from His Majesty King George VI, inscribed at the beginning of a small volume of the New Testament given to all serving British Forces in World War II, 15 September 1939.
6. Operation Tiger: D-Day's Disastrous Rehearsal, npr.org, 28 April 2012.
7. The D-Day Connection, christchurchportsdown.org, 10 September 2014.
8. Speech by General Dwight Eisenhower, 4 June 1952, reported in *Time* magazine, 16 June 1952.
9. Ibid.
10. A personal message from Montgomery to 21 Army Group, 6 June 1944.
11. Canon Llewellyn Hughes, sermon on the eve of D-Day, 5 June 1944.
12. Broadcast by King George VI, on D-Day, 6 June 1944.
13. Orders to the Soldiers, Sailors and Airmen of the Allied Expeditionary Force by General Eisenhower, 6 June 1944.
14. The D-Day Landings, BBC history, 8 September 2014.
15. Landing at Normandy: The 5 Beaches of D-Day by Jesse Greenspan, History.com, 6 June 2014.
16. D-Day, the *Times of London*, 11 September 1944.
17. Comments by Field Marshal Bernard Montgomery, after the triumphant Allied sweep through France, 1944.
18. End of the War in Europe by Winston Churchill, House of Commons speech and broadcast, 8 May 1945.
19. War and the Abbey 1939-1945, westminster-abbey.org, 10 September 2014.
20. On War Memorials, Winston Churchill to the Archbishop of Canterbury, June 1945.
21. The Miracle of D-Day by General Sir Frederick E. Morgan, *Daily Telegraph*, 1947.
22. Prime Minister Stanley Baldwin, on The Responsibility of Empire, BBC Radio, April 1937.
23. *Britain and Palestine in Prophecy* by James Mcwhirter, Methuen & co, 1937, p.83.
24. Why Churchill Lost in 1945 by Dr Paul Addison, BBC.co.uk, 17 February 2011.
25. Speech by Winston Churchill on Party Principles, at the Conservative Party Conference, Blackpool, 5 October 1946. Clement Attlee won the 1950 election, but it was close and trouble led to

another election in 1951. Despite Churchill's age, Labour still spent the next thirteen years in the political wilderness.

Chapter Twenty-One: Democracy and Social Justice
1. Inauguration Sermon: The Archbishop of York, 1 December 2005.

Chapter Twenty-Two: Christianity, Devotion and Dedication
1. C.S. Lewis' broadcast talks on BBC Radio, 1941-44, published as *Mere Christianity*, Geoffrey Bles, 1952.
2. Religions, Pentecostalism, BBC.co.uk, 12 August 2014.
3. *An Introduction to Pentecostalism: Global Charismatic Christianity* by Allan Anderson Cambridge, CUP, 2004, p.95.
4. I'm not surprised evangelicals are on the rise by Ed West, the *Telegraph*, 14 December 2009.
5. 2011 British Census.
6. Churchgoing in the U.K., Tearfund, April 2007.
7. In an era of feeble bishops, Elizabeth the Christian Queen has helped keep the faith alive by Damian Thompson, the *Telegraph*, 3 June 2012.
8. More than any monarch, Queen Elizabeth II understands the spiritual element of her coronation oath by Francis Phillips, *Catholic Herald*, 7 February 2012.
9. Ibid.
10. The Royal Collection Trust, The Sovereign's Orb, 12 August 2014.
11. The Royal Collection Trust, The Sovereign's Sceptre with Dove, 12 August 2014.
12. The Queen's 2011 Christmas message was recorded on 9 December and broadcast on Christmas Day.

Chapter Twenty-Three: The Great Storm of Change
1. *The Lewis Awakening 1949-1953* by Duncan Campbell, The Faith Mission, Edinburgh, Scotland, 1954, p.31. Principles that govern spiritual awakenings, a sermon by Duncan Campbell, The Faith Mission.
2. Why I hate the sixties, the decade that was too good to be true, BBC, 2004.
3. Ibid.
4. Ibid.
5. Women suffer poor self-esteem due to airbrushing in advertising, the *Telegraph*, 27 November 2009.
6. Why I hate the sixties, the decade that was too good to be true, BBC, 2004.
7. *The Four Loves* by C.S. Lewis, Geoffrey Bles, 1960.
8. Single-parent Britain: One in five children lives with just mum or dad by Steve Doughty, 29 December 2011.
9. Why I hate the sixties, the decade that was too good to be true, BBC, 2004.
10. Ibid.
11. We paid the price for free love by Virginia Ironside, *Daily Mail*, 18 January 2011.
12. An Overview of Sexual Offending in England and Wales, the Ministry of Justice, Office for National Statistics, January 2013.
13. The research, conducted by academics at the University of Bristol's School for Policy Studies and the University of Central Lancashire. 4 in 10 teenage girls coerced into sex acts by Heather Saw, *Independent*, 12 February 2015.

Chapter Twenty-Four: A Bitter Price to Pay
1. One in four young people first view porn at age 12 or under, BBC.co.uk, 10 April 2014.
2. Abortions stats by Steven Ertelt, LifeNews.com, 8 October 2012.
3. 27 percent of all human deaths in England and Wales are due to abortion by Dr Peter Saunders, Christian Medical Blog, 22 October 2012.
4. Why I hate the sixties, the decade that was too good to be true, BBC, 2004.
5. Mother releases image of baby born at 24 weeks in a bid to challenge U.K. abortion laws, metro.co.uk, 13 September 2014.
6. NHS England and Wales, 2012. In this year, 185,122 abortions were carried out in England and Wales. 3,702 were performed between twenty and twenty-four weeks and 160 after. In the forty-eight years since legalisation the number of late-term abortions have changed, but averaged out, we find up to 120,000 late-term abortions. Abortion 24 week limit: Q&A, the *Telegraph*, 2 October 2012.
7. Abortion should not be used as a contraceptive, says Lord Steel, father of 1967 act that legalised the practice. 36 percent of abortions are to those who have already had one, by Daniel Martin, *Daily Mail*, 19 June 2013.
8. Ibid.
9. Why I hate the sixties, the decade that was too good to be true, BBC, 2004.
10. An enquiry led by Mr. Hugh Griffiths, Q.C found that poor design and construction led to the partial collapsed of Ronan Point, the twenty-two storey tower block in Newham, East London on 16 May 1968.
11. *Celebration of Discipline: The Path to Spiritual Growth* by Richard J. Foster, HarperCollins, SanFrancisco, 1998, p.80.

12. Child poverty statistics and facts, barnardos.org.uk, 23 September 2014.
13. The loss of childhood survey, Netmums.com, 5 March 2013.
14. Why I hate the sixties, the decade that was too good to be true, BBC, 2004.
15. Aids: Origin of pandemic was 1920s Kinshasa by James Gallagher, BBC.co.uk, 3 October 2014.
16. Ibid.
17. Global cost of HIV treatment and prevention could reach $35 billion by 2031 by Carole Leach-Lemens, Aidsmap.com, 10 November 2009.
18. Sexual Exposure How at Risk Are You? wishmedical.com.
19. Ibid.
20. Calculators.lloydspharmacy com/SexDegrees.
21. Sexually transmitted infections (STIs), the World Health Organisation, November 2013.
22. Children orphaned by HIV and AIDS, avert.org.
23. The Fire of God, a sermon by Duncan Campbell, Faith Mission, 1961.
24. Teachers told: sex at 13 is normal part of growing up by Graeme Paton, the *Telegraph*, 4 November 2014.
25. Is England a nation on anti-depressants? by Mark Easton, BBC.co.uk, 3 August 2013. This statistic includes England, Scotland, Wales and Northern Ireland.
26. In the 1960s/70s, many of the most popular bands were raided and arrested for possessing and using drugs. The police involved now acknowledge they lost the war and taking illegal drugs is now accepted by many in society. Portillo's State Secrets with Michael Portillo, episode 3, celebrity and scandal, BBC, 25 March 2015
27. British drugs survey 2014: drug use is rising in the U.K. – but we're not addicted by Jim Mann, the *Guardian*, 5 October 2014.
28. Charities estimate thirty to fifty percent of people with a mental health problem have co-existing illicit drug and alcohol problems.

Chapter Twenty-Five: An Outcry Heard in Heaven
1. Office for National Statistics, Crime in England and Wales, year ending March 2014, crimesurvey.co.uk, 17 July 2014. Approximately 85,000 women are raped on average in England and Wales every year and over 400,000 women are sexually assaulted each year. Rapecrisis.org.uk/Statistics2.php.
2. The Relationship Foundation, cost of family breakdown, 2010-11.
3. Free sex: Who pays? by Guy Brandon, jubilee-centre.org, January 2012.
4. *The Screwtape Letters* by C S. Lewis, Geoffrey Bles, 1941, p.3.
5. *God in the Dock, Answers to Questions on Christianity* by C.S. Lewis, Eerdmans, 1970.
6. Ibid.
7. Normalizing Sexual Violence. Young Women Account for Harassment and Abuse by Heather R. Hlavka, Marquette University, USA, 28 February 2014.
8. Hidden in Plain Sight: A Statistical Analysis of Violence against Children by Unicef, September 2014.
9. Peeping Tom by Michael Powells, released in 1960, contains the first female nude scene in a mainstream post war English language feature film. There was nudity before, but this was mainstream and widely available.
10. The 1967 films Ulysses and I'll Never Forget are probably the first films to use the F word.
11. Game of Thrones is the most popular series in HBO's history criticized by Actor Stephen Dillane and the Washington Post's Anna Holmes, November 2014.
12. The Wolf of Wall Street in 2013 contains 569 F words, Swearnet: The Movie in 2014, counts 935.
13. 36 Companies Have $1,000 Million-Plus Ad Budgets by Christina Austin, Business Insider, 11 November 2012.
14. Has TV changed Bhutan? BBC, 17 June 2004.
15. U.K. has 250,000 paedophiles, says police study by Adam Lusher, the *Telegraph*, 31 December 2000.
16. Paedophilia is natural and normal for males by Andrew Gilligan, the *Telegraph*, 5 July 2014.
17. Ibid.
18. *Pornified: How Pornography is Damaging our Lives, our Relationships and our Families* by Pamela Paul, Owl Books, 2005, p.253.
19. The pornification of American culture by Ed Stetzer, *Christianity Today*, 27 July 2011.
20. British culture increasingly pornified by Diana Abbott, BBC.co.uk, 22 January 2013.
21. Ibid.
22. Ibid.
23. Ibid.
24. The pornification of Britain's high streets by Zoe Williams, the *Guardian*, 16 July 2013.
25. Ibid.
26. Parents Television Council report. Are Women On TV Being Sexually Exploited? Female TV Characters Are Sexual Targets, says New Study by Lynn Elber, Huffingtonpost.com, 7 October 2013.
27. Charlotte Church attacks 'sexist' music industry, BBC.co.uk, 15 October 2013.
28. Ibid.
29. Ibid.
30. Did a director push too far? The Stars of Blue is the Warmest Colour interview on 9 January 2013,

NewYorker.com, 24 October 2013.
31. Trainspotting romp put Kelly Macdonald off nude scenes, speaking to Canada radio, Dailyrecord.co.uk, 24 September 2012.
32. Ewan's wife 'mad' to feel jealous over Trainspotting sex, the *Scotsman*, 21 October 2014.
33. Models reveal why they need a union by Denis Campbell, the *Observer*, 16 December 2007.
34. Ibid.
35. Child sex exploitation social norm in Greater Manchester, BBC.co.uk, 30 October 2014.
36. Rochdale Grooming Case Is Tip Of Iceberg, Sky News, 12 June 2012.
37. Ibid.
38. The Rochdale sex ring shows the horrific consequences of Britain's Islamophobia witch-hunt by Melanie Phillips, *Daily Mail*, 9 May 2012.
39. Ibid.
40. Ibid.
41. The Sexual Revolution and its Victims by Anthony Esolen, *Crisis* Magazine, 8 October 2012.
42. My generation created the sexual revolution – and it has been wrecking the lives of women ever since by Bel Mooney, *Daily Mail*, 2 December 2009.
43. Ibid.
44. Pornography addiction worry for tenth of 12 to 13-year-olds by Patrick Howse, BBC.co.uk, 31 March 2015.
45. Ibid.
46. Lord Chief Justice, evidence by Lord Thomas to MPs, 27 January 2015. Lord Thomas of Cwymgiedd said internet porn "played a real part" in the actions of Jamie Reynolds, 23, who murdered 17-year-old Georgia Williams in a copycat pornographic photoshoot.
47. Ibid.

Chapter Twenty-Six: Spiritual, but Not Religious
1. Statement by the Episcopalian Bishop James Pike, the *Christian Century*, 21 December 1960.
2. Comments by Bishop James Pike, *Redbook* magazine, August 1961.
3. Statement by the Archbishop of Canterbury Michael Ramsey, *Daily Mail*, 2 October 1961.
4. The Fire of God, a sermon by Duncan Campbell, Faith Mission, 1961.
5. Comments by Dr. Van Buren, author of *The Secular Meaning of the Gospel: Based on an Analysis of Its Language*, Macmillan, 1963.
6. Why I hate the sixties, the decade that was too good to be true, BBC, 2004.
7. C.S Lewis' final interview by Sherwood Eliot Wirt, Cambridge, England, 7 May 1963.
8. Must our Image of God Go? by C.S. Lewis, the *Observer*, 24 March 1963.
9. C.S Lewis' final interview by Sherwood Eliot Wirt, Cambridge, England, 7 May 1963.
10. Archbishop Robert Runcie, London Weekend Television interview, 18 April 1982.
11. One of the largest demonstrations was in St Nicholas' Parish Church, Liverpool, 11 March 1982.
12. *Fern-Seed and Elephants: Modern Theology and Biblical Criticism* by C.S. Lewis, Cambridge, 11 May 1959.
13. Ibid.
14. Profile: The one true Bishop of Durham: Dr David Jenkins, the *Independent*, 5 February 1994.
15. Ibid.
16. David Jenkins' comment was that the resurrection "is real. That's the point. All I said was 'literally physical.' I was very careful in the use of language. After all, a conjuring trick with bones proves only that somebody's very clever at a conjuring trick with bones." Profile: The one true Bishop of Durham: Dr David Jenkins, the *Independent*, 5 February 1994.
17. The British state mustn't let go of the Church by Michael Portillo, the *Telegraph*, 16 January 2009.
18. Letters to the *Times*, including the wrath of God, 11 July 1984.
19. Where Rowan Williams meets Dostoevsky by A.N. Wilson, the *Telegraph*, 27 September 2008.
20. C.S Lewis' final interview by Sherwood Eliot Wirt, Cambridge, England, 7 May 1963.
21. Christianity, A History, Reformation, with Ann Widdecombe, Channel 4, 2009.
22. How God made the English, a white and Christian people? by Diarmaid MacCulloch, BBC, 31 March 2012.
23. Fern Britton meets John Simpson, BBC, 2 December 2013.
24. Is Theology Poetry? A speech by C.S. Lewis, to the Oxford Socratic Club, Oxford, 1945.
25. *Memoirs of the Life, Exile and Conversations of the Emperor Napoleon*, volume two, by Emmanuel-Auguste-Dieudonné comte de Las Cases, Redfield, 1857, p.256.
26. *The Character of Jesus Charles* by Edward Jefferson, Grosset and Dunlap, 1908, p.64.
27. *Explore the Book* by J. Sidlow Baxter, Zondervan 1966, p.308.

Chapter Twenty-Seven: Tearing Down the Altar to One God
1. 1945-1965, New Australia, New South Wales exhibition, Immigration Heritage Centre, 15 August 2013.
2. *The History of the English Speaking Peoples*, Volume 1, by Winston Churchill, chapter IV, Henry II, Cassel and co, 1956.
3. Church attendance has been propped up by immigrants, says study by Ruth Gledhill, the *Guardian*, 3 June 2014.
4. Out of 40,000 people the study found that 3,666 were unemployed and 1,870 were on national

assistance, or benefits.
5. Speech by Winston Churchill on Party Principles, at the Conservative Party Conference, Blackpool, 5 October 1946.
6. Archives expose Churchill's true thoughts on immigrants by David Ward, the *Guardian*, 6 August 2007.
7. What Churchill said about Britain's immigrants by David Smith, the O*bserver*, 5 August 2007.
8. *Inside Right a Study of Conservatism* by Ian Gilmour, Hutchinson, 1977, p.134.
9. Foreign-born population National Statistics Online, 24 October 2006.
10. Migration and Social Cohesion in the U.K. by Mary J. Hickman, Nicola Mai, Helen Crowley, Palgrave Macmillan, 2012, p.24
11. History of Islam in the U.K., BBC, 7 September 2009.
12. British religion in numbers, Islam, brin.ac.uk/figures.
13. One in ten babies in England is a Muslim: by Emily Davies, *Daily Mail*, 10 January 2014.
14. Christianity declining 50pc faster than thought – as one in 10 under-25s is a Muslim by John Bingham, Religious Affairs Editor, the *Telegraph*, 16 May 2013.
15. 1925: 0.0228 percent of 44 million people equals 10,032 people. The 34,900 percent increase took place between 1925-2015.
16. Number of U.S. mosques up 74% since 2000 by Cathy Lynn Grossman, *USA Today*, 29 February 2012.
17. Will Britain one day be Muslim? by Ruth Dudley Edwards, *Daily Mail*, 5 May 2007.
18. Muslim population rising 10 times faster than rest of society, the *Times*, 30 January 2009.
19. Ibid.
20. Muslim pupil numbers in England and Wales double since 2001, BBC.co.uk, 12 February 2015.
21. Muslim Europe: the demographic timebomb transforming our continent by Adrian Michaels, the *Telegraph*, 8 August 2009.
22. Black majority churches and Islam are Britain's religious future, Christiantoday.com, 10 Feburary 2015.
23. Turkey rallies over murder of woman who 'resisted rape' by Selin Girit, BBC.co.uk, 15 Feburary 2015.
24. Pope Francis' visit: Turkey's Christians face tense times by Mark Lowen, BBC.co.uk, 27 November 2014.
25. Ibid.
26. Ibid.
27. Ibid.
28. Ibid.
29. Turkey President Erdogan: Women are not equal to men, BBC.co.uk, 24 November 2014.
30. The Saudi women taking small steps for change by Sue Lloyd-Roberts, BBC Newsnight, 28 March 2011.
31. Ibid.
32. CIA World fact book, Lebanon, 7 October 2014.
33. Speech by Amine Gemaye, the former president of Lebanon, Boston College, U.S., 25 March 2015.
34. Kill the Christians, This World with Jane Corbin, BBC, 15 April 2015.
35. The British child brides: Muslim mosque leaders agree to marry girl of 12 by Ryan Kisiel, *Daily Mail*, 10 September 2012.
36. Ibid.
37. David Cameron: forced marriage is little more than slavery, the *Telegraph*, 10 October 2011.
38. Number of Muslims in prison doubles in a decade by Nigel Morris, *Independent*, 15 October 2014.
39. Top-security U.K. prison where terror fanatics serve life sentences is al-Qaeda recruiting centre by Nick Dorman, Sean Rayment, *Mirror*, 29 March 2014.
40. Paris attacks: Prisons provide fertile ground for Islamists by Henri Astier, Paris, BBC.co.uk, 5 February 2015.
41. Ibid.
42. The Future of the Global Muslim Population, Pew Research, 27 January 2011.
43. Demographics, Religion and the Future of Europe by Philip Jenkins, A Journal of World Affairs, vol. 50, no. 3, Orbis, 2006, p.533.
44. Ignore our Christian values and the nation will drift apart by Michael Nazir-Ali, the *Telegraph*, 5 April 2009.
45. Extremism flourished as U.K. lost Christianity by Michael Nazir-Ali, Bishop of Rochester, the *Sunday Telegraph*, 6 January 2008.
46. Islamic Ghettos by Communities Secretary Hazel Blears, 3 April 2008.
47. Why are only Muslims allowed to visit Mecca, Saudi Arabia? islam.about.com, 23 October 2014.
48. Ibid.
49. Iran, marking 1979 Revolution, predicts Islamic awakening will spread by Patrick Goodenough, CNSnews.com, 11 February 2013.
50. Ibid.
51. Iraq's fleeing Christians rebuild shattered lives by Leela Jacinto, France24, 14 August 2014.
52. Exodus: Christians of the Arab world flee their biblical homeland by Robert Fisk, *Independent*, 24 September 1997.

53. Center for Inquiry defends freedom of expression at the U.N. Human Rights Council, 17 September 2008.
54. Ibid.
55. Pakistanis in U.K. fuelling corruption, says law chief: Attorney General warns politicians to wake up to the threat posed by minority communities by Gerri Peev, *Daily Mail*, 23 November 2013.
56. Ibid.
57. Ibid.
58. Minister apologises for Pakistani corruption remarks by Edward Malnick, the *Telegraph*, 23 November 2013.
59. Tower Hamlets election fraud, mayor Lutfur Rahman removed from office, BBC.co.uk, 23 April 2015.
60. Labour peer Lord Ahmed suspended after 'Jewish claims,' BBC.co.uk, 14 March 2013.
61. Baroness Warsi quits as Foreign Office Minister over Gaza, BBC.co.uk, 5 August 2015.
62. After Paris, the battle for British Islam, Panorama, BBC, 12 January 2015.
63. Ibid.
64. Ibid.
65. Ibid.
66. Ibid.
67. Muslim pupil numbers in England and Wales double since 2001, BBC.co.uk, 12 February 2015.
68. After Paris, the battle for British Islam, Panorama, BBC, 12 January 2015.

Chapter Twenty-Eight: Society and Shared Values
1. Radicalisation is political and religious failure, BBC, 22 August 2014.
2. Ibid.
3. Britain seeks assistance of moderate Imams, the *Hindu Times*, England, 25 August 2014.
4. Britain will face costs of Islamic extremism for many years, says Cressida Dick, the *Telegraph*, 22 June 2014.
5. Profile: Abu Hamza, BBC, 9 May 2014.
6. Abu Hamza: from Egypt to a U.S. prison, via Finsbury Park mosque by Josh Halliday, the *Guardian*, 20 May 2014.
7. Wahhabism by Dr Taj Hargey, *Daily Mail*, 23 November 2010.
8. Why I, as a Muslim, am launching a campaign to ban the burka in Britain by Dr Taj Hargey, *Daily Mail*, 17 July 2014.
9. The fight against intolerance by Eric Pickles MP, the *Telegraph*, 5 September 2014.
10. Nicolas Sarkozy joins David Cameron and Angela Merkel's view that multiculturalism has failed, *Daily Mail*, 11 February 2011.
11. Merkel says German multicultural society has failed, BBC, 17 October 2010.
12. TWR U.K., speaks with Bishop Michael Nazir-Ali about his book *Triple Jeopardy for the West*. 13 September 2014.
13. How God made the English, a white and Christian people? by Diarmaid MacCulloch, BBC, 31 March 2012.
14. The end of Christianity in the Middle East could mean the demise of Arab secularism by William Dalrymple, the *Guardian*, 23 July 2014.
15. The Christian exodus, the disastrous campaign to rid the Middle East of Christianity by Reza Aslan, *Foreign Affairs Publication*, September/October 2014, Volume 5, Number 93.
16. Study: U.S. is an oligarchy, not a democracy, BBC.co.uk, 17 April 2014.
17. The U.S. Federal Election Commission, 31 March 2013.
18. Testing theories of American politics, elites, interest groups and average citizens by Martin Gilens and Benjamin Page, Princeton University, 9 April 2014.
19. An idiots Guide to Politics, BBC, 11 February 2015.
20. 101 days to General Election: Here are 101 promises broken by Con/Dem Coalition government by Jack Blanchard, *Mirror*, 25 January 2015.
21. David Cameron speaking to Sky News political editor Adam Boulton, Sky News, 3 May 2010.
22. An idiots Guide to Politics, BBC, 11 February 2015.
23. Ibid.
24. The strange truth about how and why we vote by Brian Wheeler, BBC.co.uk, 1 December 2014.
25. How the Nixon-Kennedy Debate Changed the World by Kayla Webley, *Time* magazine, 23 September 2010.
26. The strange truth about how and why we vote by Brian Wheeler, BBC.co.uk, 1 December 2014.
27. Ibid.
28. Professor Roger Trigg's address at the Equality, Freedom and Religion, Church in the Public Square Conference, Belfast, 9 October 2014.
29. Faith schools damaged by British values curriculum by Javier Espinoza, the *Telegraph*, 12 March 2015.
30. Why I'm proud to be a Christian by Michael Gove, *The Spectator* magazine, 4 April 2015.

Chapter Twenty-Nine: Limitations on Liberty
1. Revisiting the Treaty of Lisbon, The Irish Society for Christian Civilisation, 2 September 2009.
2. *Harold Berman On Law*, Eliade Encyclopaedia of Religion 1987, p. 463.

3. Summary of Professor Julian Rivers thoughts, Religion and Law, Theos, 2012.
4. Section 57 of the Offences against the Person Act 1861.
5. The Men with Many Wives, Channel 4, 24 September 2014.
6. Ibid.
7. Ibid.
8. The Men with Many Wives: the British Muslims who practise polygamy by Rachel Stewart, the *Telegraph*, 24 September 2014.
9. David Cameron's welfare speech, at Bluewater, Kent, 25 June 2012.
10. First time buyers, life begins at 40 by Kunal Dutta, *Independent*, 20 November 2011.
11. David Cameron's welfare speech, at Bluewater, Kent, 25 June 2012.
12. The welfare state we're in by Matt Chorley, *Daily Mail*, 17 April 2014.
13. Just how big is Britain's debt mountain? by Mehreen Khan, the *Telegraph*, 24 September 2014.
14. Ibid.
15. Can we afford the welfare state? by Nicholas Timmins, the *Independent*, 24 September 1995.
16. Shame of Britain's Muslim schools by Tazeen Ahmad, *Daily Mail*, 13 February 2011.
17. British Muslims must confront the truth of the Trojan Horse schools by Douglas Murray, the *Spectator*, 24 July 2014.

Chapter Thirty: Rejecting God's Protection
1. Sharia law – What did the Archbishop actually say? Rowanwilliams.Archbishopof canterbury.org, 8 February 2008.
2. Multiculturalism has brought us honour killings and Sharia law, says Archbishop, by Matthew Holehouse, the *Telegraph*, 24 August 2014.
3. *Mere Christianity* by C.S. Lewis, Geoffrey Bles, 1952, chapter seven.
4. Prince Charles to be known as Defender of Faith by Andrew Pierce, the *Telegraph*, 13 November 2008.
5. Koran should be read at Prince Charles' coronation says top bishop: Critics attack proposal and accuse Church of England of losing confidence in its own traditions by Steve Doughty, *Daily Mail*, 29 November 2014.
6. Douglas Murray and Lord Harries, the Today programme, BBC radio 4, 28 November 2014.
7. Ibid.
8. Koran should be read at Prince Charles' coronation says top bishop: Critics attack proposal and accuse Church of England of losing confidence in its own traditions by Steve Doughty, Daily Mail, 29 November 2014.
9. Turkey was the only nation where Islam, democracy and the rule of law were thought to flourish, but in the past fifteen years, it has become more Islamic in character and nature, with new restrictions for all.
10. Queen and the Church of England, royal.gov.uk, 24 September 2014.
11. Prince Charles and religion: a very special faith by Tom Rowley, the *Telegraph*, 10 November 2013.
12. The Sunday Hour with Diane Louise Jordan speaking with Prince Charles, BBC Radio 2, 8 February 2015.
13. Queen Victoria's Speech, Parliament, 2 February 1843. The Queen said, "In concert with her allies, Her Majesty has succeeded in obtaining for the Christian population of Syria the establishment of a system of administration which they were entitled to expect from the engagements of the Sultan, and from the good faith of this country."
14. The Sunday Hour with Diane Louise Jordan speaking with Prince Charles, BBC Radio 2, 8 February 2015.
15. Conversation between David E. Gardner and Lord Denning, May 1976. *The Trumpet Sounds for Britain, Volume 3*, Jesus is Alive Ministries, 1985, p.60.
16. The vicars who don't believe in God, BBC, 13 July 1999.
17. 10 things that could land your vicar in trouble, BBC, 17 February 2005.
18. Welby casts out sin from christenings by Jonathan Petre, *Daily Mail*, 4 January 2014.
19. Adam Curtis' BBC blog, suspicious minds, BBC.co.uk, 2 April 2014.
20. Adam Curtis' BBC blog, BBC.co.uk, 5 December 2013.
21. Complacent Home Office loses 175,000 illegal immigrants by Ian Drury, *Daily Mail*, 4 September 2014.
22. Illegal immigrants cost taxpayer more than £4,000 a head each year by David Barret, the *Telegraph*, 31 October 2013.
23. Nearly 20 million illegal immigrants in U.S., former Border Patrol agents say by Stephen Dinan, *Washington Times*, 9 September 2013.
24. The town where immigrants hits a human wall by Jennifer Medina, *New York Times*, 3 July 2014.
25. One in six foreign criminals living in the U.K. have disappeared, ITV News, 22 October 2014.
26. Ann Graham Lotz on CBS's Early Show, with Jane Clayson, 13 September 2001.
27. *The Tragedy of Julius Caesar* by William Shakespeare, Act 1 Scene 2, c.1599.
28. *That Incredible Christian* by A.W.Tozer, Tyndale House, 1977, p.104.
29. *The Problem of Pain* by C.S Lewis, Geoffrey Bles, 1946, p.130.

Chapter Thirty-One: Christianity and Safeguarding Liberty
1. *The Right Standards of Conduct by Lord Denning*, Law Society's Gazette, 1957, 609.
2. What Life Has Taught Me, speech by The Hon. Mr Justice Denning on file at the Hampshire Record Office.
3. Ibid.
4. Official statistics for the elections during Nazi rule.
5. *This is the Hard Core of Freedom* by Elmer T. Peterson, 9 December 1951, *Daily Oklahoman*, p.12. Alexander Fraser Tytler may not be correctly credited.
6. High Court ruling against Bideford Town Council based on an interpretation of Section 111 of the Local Government Act 1972, rather than on equality or human rights grounds.
7. Eric Pickles gives councils back the freedom to pray, Department for Communities and Local Government. Making local councils more transparent and accountable to local people and local government, gov.uk., 17 February 2012.
8. Councils win prayer rights as Localism Act powers fast tracked, BBC, 18 February 2012.
9. Voodoo row as the Lottery gives £200k to spiritual healers available on NHS by Jonathan Petre, *Daily Mail*, 20 July 2011.
10. Largest ever consultation reveals widespread confusion over laws protecting religion or belief, the Equality and Human Rights Commission, 11 March 2015.
11. Religious employees 'under pressure' to hide faith, BBC.co.uk, 12 March 2015.
12. *Democracy in America* by Alexis de Tocqueville, Bantum Classics, 2002, p.357.
13. Archbishop of Westminster attacks gay marriage plan, BBC.co.uk, 25 December 2012.
14. Baroness Caroline Cox, Arbitration and Mediation Services (Equality) Bill, 11 June 2014.
15. From a distinguished peer fighting to protect women...Sharia marriages for girls of 12 and the religious courts subverting British law by Baroness Cox, *Daily Mail*, 14 September 2012.
16. Euro candidate arrested, BBC.co.uk, 28 April 2014.
17. *The River War Volume II* by Winston Churchill, London: Longmans, Green & Co, 1899, pp.248-250.
18. Slavery in History, freetheslaves.net, 9 October 2014.
19. Nigeria's abducted schoolgirls: We'll sell them as slaves, pledges Boko Haram terror leader by Catrina Stewart, the *Independent*, 6 May 2014.
20. Iraq Slave Markets Sell Women for $10 to Attract Isis Recruits by Fiona Keating, the *Times*, 4 October 2014.
21. IS militant 'Jihadi John' named as Mohammed Emwazi from London, BBC.co.uk, 26 February 2015. He is thought to have been pictured in the videos of the beheadings of U.S. journalist Steven Sotloff, British aid worker David Haines, British taxi driver Alan Henning, and American aid worker Abdul-Rahman Kassig, also known as Peter.
22. *History of al-Tabari*, the English translation of *The History of the Prophets and Kings* by the Muslim historian Ibn Jarir al-Tabari, c.AD 915, Vol. 8, p.35.
23. UN says 25,000 foreign fighters joined Islamist militants, BBC.co.uk, 2 April 2015.
24. Christianity, A History, Crusade, with Rageh Omaar, Channel 4, February 2009.
25. Bishop of Rochester Criticises Muslim 'Victim Mentality,' Christiantoday.com, from interview in *Sunday Times*, 6 November 2006.
26. Egyptian President Abdel Fattah al-Sisi, speaking before Al-Azhar and the Awqaf Ministry in Egypt, 1 January 2015.
27. Britain's Lost Freedoms: We're Living in a Madhouse by Dale Hurd, CBN News, 18 July 2014.
28. People cannot debate traditional issues because of liberal censoriousness, says Lord Neuberger by John Bingham, and Christopher Hope, the *Telegraph*, 13 March 2014.
29. Christian beliefs should be accommodated under law – top judge by John Bingham, the *Telegraph*, 20 March 2014.
30. Why I'm proud to be a Christian by Michael Gove, the *Spectator*, 4 April 2015.
31. The Persecution of Christians by Revd Canon J.John, philotrust.com, 2 September 2014.
32. U.K. must do more to 'wipe out' anti-Semitism – Theresa May, BBC.co.uk, 19 January 2015.
33. Who's responsible for these anti-Semitic attacks? Give me one guess by Rod Liddle, the *Spectator*, 16 August 2014.
34. The sorry truth is that the virus of anti-Semitism has infected the British Muslim community by Mehdi Hasan, Newstateman.com, 21 March 2013.

Chapter Thirty-Two: Apostasy and Conversion
1. *A Practical View of the Prevailing Religious System of Professed Christians in the Higher and Middle Classes in this Country, Contrasted with Real* Christianity by William Wilberforce, Robert Dapper, 1797.
2. Article 126.2 of the Penal Code of Sudan, 1991.
3. Sudanese woman spared death sentence for apostasy by Mart Tran, the *Guardian*, 24 July 2014.
4. I was tortured by the men who sentenced my Christian mother to death for blasphemy by Aoun Sahi and Simon Tomlinson, *Daily Mail*, 23 October 2014.
5. Ibid.
6. Ibid.
7. Pakistan mob kills Christian couple over blasphemy, BBC.co.uk, 4 November 2014.
8. Unholy War – Investigation of the violence and intimidation facing Muslims who convert to

Christianity in Britain, Dispatches, 17 September 2007.
9. Bishop Nazir-Ali Warns of Attacks on Muslim-Christian Converts, ChristianToday.com, 17 September 2007.
10. Ibid.
11. Christians offer safe houses to Muslim converts by Nicholas Hellen, the *Sunday Times*, 25 May 2014.
12. Hate preachers' must prove they renounce extremism or face U.K. ban by Deborah Summers and Alan Travis, the *Guardian*, 28 October 2008. And: The sorry truth is that the virus of anti-Semitism has infected the British Muslim community by Mehdi Hasan, Newstateman.com, 21 March 2013.
13. Malala, hailed around the world, controversial at home by Philip Reeves, Npr.org, 10 December 2013.
14. Malala Yousafzai's book banned in Pakistani private schools, the *Guardian*, 10 November 2013.
15. Muslim girls struggle for education by Safa Faisal, BBC Arabic Service, 24 September 2003.
16. The school that says Osama Bin Laden was a hero by Mobeen Azhar, BBC World Service, 12 November 2014.
17. Growing religious persecution a threat to everyone by Caroline Wyatt, 14 November 2014.
18. Muslim pupils taken out of music lessons because Islam forbids playing an instrument by Laura Clark, *Daily Mail*, 2 July 2010.
19. The mystery of the missing Muslim girls by Fran Abrams, the *Independent*, 15 February 1996.
20. The 800,000 people living in Britain with little or no English by John Bingham, the *Telegraph*, 24 October 2014.
21. A multicultural hell hole that we never voted for by Leo McKinstry, *Daily Express*, 18 November 2013.
22. *Sodom Had No Bible* by Leonard Ravenhill, Bethany Press, 1979, p.85.
23. U.S. Governor Bobby Jindal speaking with David Brody, blogs.cbn.com, 27 January 2015.
24. 'BBC security correspondent Frank Gardner says that, to many in the West, Bin Laden became the embodiment of global terrorism, but to others he was a hero, a devout Muslim who fought two world superpowers in the name of jihad.' Osama Bin Laden, al-Qaeda leader, BBC.co.uk, 2 May 2011.
25. 'Bin Laden was buried at sea after a Muslim funeral on board an aircraft carrier, Pentagon officials said...the body was buried at sea to conform with Islamic practice of a burial within 24 hours.' Osama Bin Laden, al-Qaeda leader, BBC.co.uk, 2 May 2011.
26. Revealed: preachers' messages of hate by Jamie Doward, the *Observer*, 7 January 2007.
27. Dr Bilal Philips on marriage with girls before puberty. U.K. TV uncovers Islamic supremacist by Yaakov Lappin, Ynetnews, 16 January 2007.
28. Undercover Mosques, Channel 4, 15 January 2007.
29. Comments by Dr. Mian. British Muslims get their soapbox by Brendan Bernhard, the *New York Sun*, 19 January 2007.
30. General Election 2015: Posters seen in Cardiff tell Muslims not to vote by Zachary Davies Boren, the *Independent*, 18 April 2015.
31. Comments by Al Jibali. Undercover Mosques, Channel 4, 15 January 2007.
32. Why did teenage hugs touch off a debate in Malaysia? BBC.co.uk, 15 January 2015.
33. Comments by Dr. Mian. Undercover Mosques, Channel 4, 15 January 2007.
34. Iranian woman wins rights award for hijab campaign by Saeed Kamali Dehghan, the *Guardian*, 24 February 2015.
35. Comment on facebook.com/StealthyFreedom, 25 February 2015.
36. The perils of speaking out against Islamic law in Malaysia by Tse Yin Lee, BBC.co.uk, 29 March 2015.
37. Ibid.
38. Douglas Alexander: The government is stepping back from the issue of religious freedom by Douglas Alexander, the *Telegraph*, 20 December 2014.
39. Pope Francis and Patriarch Bartholomew I in Constantinople, Istanbul, Turkey, 30 November 2014.
40. We will all lose if Christians flee the Middle East by Louis Raphael Sako, the *Telegraph*, 13 December 2013.
41. The poll, carried out by ComRes between 26 January and 20 February 2015, surveyed one thousand British Muslims. Most British Muslims oppose Muhammad cartoons reprisals, BBC.co.uk, 25 February 2015.
42. Sheikh Ahmad Al Katani speaking on Al-Jazeera, 12 December 2012. He said, "In every hour, 667 Muslims convert to Christianity. Everyday, 16,000 Muslims convert to Christianity. Every year, 6 million Muslims convert to Christianity."
43. *A Wind in the House of Islam* by David Garisson, Wigtake Resources LLC, 2014.
44. Islamic terrorist lays down jihad for Jesus Christ by Stacy Long, *Charisma* News, 4 April 2015.
45. Ibid.

Chapter Thirty-Three: Christian Heritage in Peril
1. *Sodom Had No Bible* by Leonard Ravenhill, Bethany Press, 1979, p.96.
2. David Cameron fosters division by calling Britain a Christian country, *Daily Mail*, 20 April 2014.
3. The U.K. is a Christian country, whether the Left like it or not by Harry Cole, the *Spectator*, 22 April 2014.

Chapter Thirty-Four: We want it Now!
1. Rotten roots of the crunch by Matt Frei, BBC, 20 October 2008.
2. Peston's Global Assessment by Robert Peston, BBC, 20 October 2008.
3. *Conquer the Crash* by Robert Prechter, John Wiley & Sons, 2002.
4. Stock Market Crash of 2008 by Kimberly Amadeo, About.com, 19 July 2014.
5. Peston's Global Assessment by Robert Peston, BBC, 20 October 2008.
6. Ibid.
7. Is inequality the enemy of growth? By Robert Peston, BBC, 6 October 2014.
8. Comments by Victor Mallet, from the *Financial Times*, Meltdown, CBC, 2009.
9. Britain's debt at end of 2008, ukpublicspending.co.uk/uk_national_debt.
10. U.S. debt at the end of 2008, usgovernmentdebt.us/spending_chart.
11. IMF cost of crisis by Edmund Conway, the *Telegraph*, 8 August 2009.
12. Financial Crisis Losses, GAO, U.S. Government Accountability Office, 14 February 2014.
13. Philip Hammond, the Foreign Secretary said in 2014 there has been "extremely aggressive probing" of British airspace by Russian aircraft and their submarines have been breaching European sea defences. Britain forced to ask Nato to track Russian submarine in Scottish waters by Ben Farmer, the *Telegraph*, 9 December 2014.
14. Is the West losing its edge on defence? by Newsnight diplomatic and defence editor, Mark Urban, BBC, 14 April 2015.
15. Ibid.
16. An aircraft carrier without planes is the perfect metaphor for Britain's diminished global status by Iain Martin, the *Telegraph*, 4 July 2014.
17. HMS Queen Elizabeth: The sensitive aircraft carrier issue by Newsnight diplomatic and defence editor, Mark Urban, BBC.co.uk, 14 April 2015.
18. Is the West losing its edge on defence? by Newsnight diplomatic and defence editor, Mark Urban, BBC.co.uk, 14 April 2015.
19. China's island factories by Rupert Wingfield-Hayes, BBC.co.uk, 9 September 2014.
20. Experts: U.S. overlooking its biggest threat, China, CBN News, 14 April 2015.

Chapter Thirty-Five: Crisis, what Crisis?
1. Is inequality the enemy of growth? by Robert Peston, BBC, 6 October 2014.
2. Ibid.
3. How bad are U.S. debt levels? BBC.co.uk, 17 October 2013.
4. National debt interest payments dwarf other government spending by Danielle Kurtzleben, USnews.com, 19 November 2012.
5. Just how big is Britain's debt mountain? by Mehreen Khan, the *Telegraph*, 24 September 2014.
6. Budget 2013. Interest payments on national debt to eclipse combined budget for schools and police by James Kirkup, the *Telegraph*, 20 March 2013.
7. Understanding one trillion, BBC, 1 February 2010.
8. The U.K. treasury sent £42.4 million to the U.S. and £9.98 million to Canada, 29 December 2006.
9. In the 1950s, national debt increased to over 230% of GDP.
10. U.K. annual debt repayments, 1960-1961.
11. Osborne's timetable for eliminating U.K.'s structural deficit by Rowena Mason, the *Guardian*, 10 February 2014. Also, Public borrowing rises, BBC, 21 October 2014, and, U.K. economic growth to fall, BBC, 20 October 2014.
12. David Cameron tells porkies about Britain's national debt by Fraser Nelson, the *Spectator*, 23 January 2013.
13. Twenty years to clear this size of debt is very optimistic – see the next point. Nobody can predict what will happen because the variables are extreme. Britain faces 20 years of crippling debt by Julia White, *Express*, 28 January 2009.
14. Financial experts struggle when making long-term predictions and many tend to avoid forecasting about a world economy, no-one can imagine. Who could have predicted the rise of China? But if British debt is £1.6 trillion by 2024 and it pays off £50 billion from this debt each year, without factoring in interest repayments, it would take Britain thirty-two years to clear them by 2056. However, if Britain paid off £25 billion a year instead, without factoring in interest repayments, it would take sixty-four years, by 2088. Quantitative easing, leading to inflation may make it quicker and easier to pay off debts, and if the economy surges and expands greatly, debt repayment will shrink by percentage of GDP. An optimistic view is possible, but baby boom retirement and care costs, plus additional benefit costs, recessions and unpredicted wars could overwhelm the situation.
15. Britain and the U.S. last balanced their books and had a surplus in 2001.
16. U.K. Budget Deficit history 2001-2015. ukpublicspending.co.uk/budget_ukgs.php.
17. 5 facts about the national debt: What you should know by Drew Desilver, Pewresearch.org, 9 October 2013.
18. Ibid.
19. Ibid.
20. If the federal budget is (as proposed) $4.7 trillion. Will America ever pay off its debt? by Ronald Cooke, Financialsense.com, 4 May 2013.
21. Ibid.
22. The National Debt in Perspective by Robert Neild, Royal Economics Society, 18 October 2014.

23. Why consumer confidence impacts your debt and equity investments by Phalguni Soni, marketrealist.com, 20 April 2014.
24. The U.K. treasury sent £42.4 million to the U.S. and £9.98 million to Canada, 29 December 2006.
25. *The Psychology of Judgment and Decision Making* by Scott Plous, Mcgraw-Hill, 1993.
26. Will China shake the world again? by Robert Peston, BBC, 17 February 2014.
27. What is quantitative easing? BBC, 7 March 2013.
28. Workers on the Breadline, Panorama, BBC, 6 October 2014. Sources: Centre for Research in Social Policy, Loughborough University, Joseph Rowntree Foundation.
29. Money is not wealth by Steve Forbes, *Forbes* Magazine, 20 October 2014.
30. *Money: How the Destruction of the Dollar Threatens the Global Economy* by Steve Forbes, McGraw-Hill Professional, 1 June 2014.
31. Men's pay has fallen more than women's in real terms, BBC.co.uk, 30 January 2015.
32. Richest 1% to own more than rest of world, Oxfam says, BBC.co.uk, 19 January 2015.
33. Government to retire some of its WW1 debt, BBC.co.uk, 31 October 2014.
34. U.K. government finally repays World War One bonds by Ben Wright and Denise Roland, the *Telegraph*, 31 October 2014.
35. Government to retire some of its WW1 debt, BBC.co.uk, 31 October 2014.

Chapter Thirty-Six: Being Honest about our Need
1. *The Holy Spirit in a Man* by R.B. Watchman, ByFaith Media, 2015, p.103.
2. Is the number of Churches in decline? Source: Religious trends 5, Brieley, 2005, Tables 12.12.1, whychurch.org.uk.
3. Ibid. Tables 12.11.
4. Why we are losing so many churches in the United States? by Jack Wellman, patheos.com, 26 October 2013.
5. The *Screwtape Letters* by C.S. Lewis, Macmillan, 1976, pp. 130-131.

Chapter Thirty-Seven: Hope for a Christian Awakening
1. Revival and Renewal by Dr Martyn Lloyd-Jones, c.1964.
2. Principles that govern spiritual awakenings, a sermon by Duncan Campbell, The Faith Mission c.1962.

ByFaith Media Books

Revival Fires and Awakenings – Thirty-Six Visitations of the Holy Spirit by Mathew Backholer.

Reformation to Revival, 500 Years of God's Glory: Sixty Revivals, Awakenings and Heaven-Sent Visitations of the Holy Spirit by Mathew Backholer

How to Plan, Prepare and Successfully Complete Your Short-Term Mission by Mathew Backholer.

Revival Fire – 150 Years of Revivals by Mathew Backholer documents twelve revivals from ten countries.

Discipleship for Everyday Living by Mathew Backholer. A dynamic biblical book for Christian growth.

Global Revival, Worldwide Outpourings, Forty-Three Visitations of the Holy Spirit by Mathew Backholer.

Understanding Revival and Addressing the Issues it Provokes by Mathew Backholer.

Extreme Faith – On Fire Christianity by Mathew Backholer. Powerful foundations for faith in Christ!

Revival Answers: True and False Revivals by Mathew Backholer. What is genuine and false revival?

Short-Term Missions, A Christian Guide to STMs, *For Leaders, Pastors, Students…* by Mathew Backholer.

Budget Travel, A Guide to Travelling on a Shoestring Explore the World, A Discount Overseas Adventure Trip: Gap Year, Backpacking by Mathew Backholer

Prophecy Now, Prophetic Words and Divine Revelations, For You, the Church and the Nations by Michael Backholer.

Samuel Rees Howells: A Life of Intercession by Richard Maton. Learn how intercession and prayer changed history.

Samuel, Son and Successor of Rees Howells by Richard

Maton. Discover the full biography of Samuel Rees Howells.

The Holy Spirit in a Man by R.B. Watchman. An autobiography.

Tares and Weeds in your Church: Trouble & Deception in God's House by R.B. Watchman.

How Christianity Made the Modern World by Paul Backholer.

Holy Spirit Power: Knowing the Voice, Guidance and Person of the Holy Spirit by Paul Backholer.

Heaven: A Journey to Paradise and the Heavenly City by Paul Backholer.

The Exodus Evidence In Pictures – The Bible's Exodus by Paul Backholer. 100+ colour photos.

The Ark of the Covenant – Investigating the Ten Leading Claims by Paul Backholer. 80+ colour photos.

Jesus Today, Daily Devotional: 100 Days with Jesus Christ by Paul Backholer.

Britain, A Christian Country by Paul Backholer.

Celtic Christianity and the First Christian Kings in Britain by Paul Backholer.

The Baptism of Fire, Personal Revival and the Anointing for Supernatural Living by Paul Backholer.

Glimpses of Glory, Revelations in the Realms of God by Paul Backholer

Lost Treasures of the Bible by Paul Backholer.

The End Times: A Journey Through the Last Days. The Book of Revelation… by Paul Backholer.

Debt Time Bomb! Debt Mountains: The Financial Crisis and its Toxic Legacy by Paul Backholer. Ebook.

ByFaith Media DVDs

Great Christian Revivals on 1 DVD. Filmed on location across Britain, the stories of the Welsh Revival (1904-1905), the Hebridean Revival (1949-1952) and the Evangelical Revival (1739-1791), are told in this 72-minute documentary.

Israel in Egypt – The Exodus Mystery on 1 DVD is the very best of the eight episode TV series *ByFaith – In Search of the Exodus.* See the exodus evidence! 110+ minutes.

ByFaith – Quest for the Ark of the Covenant on 1 DVD. Experience an adventure and investigate the mystery of the lost Ark of the Covenant! Explore Ethiopia's rock churches; find the Egyptian Pharaoh who entered Solomon's Temple and search for the Queen of Sheba's Palace. Four episodes. 100+ minutes.

ByFaith – World Mission on 1 DVD. Pack your backpack and join two young adventurers as they travel through 14 nations on their global short-term mission (STM). An 85-minute adventure; filmed over three years.

ByFaith – In Search of the Exodus on 2 DVDs. The Quest to find the evidence for Joseph and Israel in Egypt, the Red Sea and Mount Sinai in eight TV episodes. 200+ minutes.

Visit **www.ByFaith.org** to watch the trailers for these DVDs and for more information.

www.ByFaithDVDs.co.uk

Notes

Notes

Notes

www.ingramcontent.com/pod-product-compliance
Lightning Source LLC
Chambersburg PA
CBHW060654100426
42734CB00047B/1643